GENDER AND SOCIA

Gender Studies in Wales
Astudiaethau Rhywedd yng Nghymru

Series Editors
Jane Aaron, University of Glamorgan
Brec'hed Piette, University of Bangor
Sian Rhiannon Williams, University of Wales Institute Cardiff

Series Advisory Board
Deirdre Beddoe, Emeritus Professor
Mihangel Morgan, Aberystwyth University
Teresa Rees, Cardiff University

The aim of this series is to fill a current gap in knowledge. As a number of historians, sociologists and literary critics have for some time been pointing out, there is a dearth of published research on the characteristics and effects of gender difference in Wales, both as it affected lives in the past and as it continues to shape present-day experience. Socially constructed concepts of masculine and feminine difference influence every aspect of individuals' lives; experiences in employment, in education, in culture and politics, as well as in personal relationships, are all shaped by them. Ethnic identities are also gendered; a country's history affects its concepts of gender difference so that what is seen as appropriately 'masculine' or 'feminine' varies within different cultures. What is needed in the Welsh context is more detailed research on the ways in which gender difference has operated and continues to operate within Welsh societies. Accordingly, this interdisciplinary and bilingual series of volumes on Gender Studies in Wales, authored by academics who are leaders in their particular fields of study, is designed to explore the diverse aspects of male and female identities in Wales, past and present. The series is bilingual, in the sense that some of its intended volumes will be in Welsh and some in English.

GENDER AND SOCIAL JUSTICE IN WALES

Edited by

Nickie Charles and Charlotte Aull Davies

CARDIFF
UNIVERSITY OF WALES PRESS
2010

www.uwp.co.uk

British Library Cataloguing-in-Publication Data
A catalogue record for this book is available from the British Library.

ISBN 978-0-7083-2268-0
e-ISBN 978-0-7083-2269-7

Printed in Wales by Dinefwr Press, Llandybïe

Contents

Contents

III. CONCLUSION

Tables and Figures

Tables

Figures

Glossary

ACCAC	Awdurdod Cymwysterau, Cwricwlwm ac Asesu Cymru / Qualifications, Curriculum and Assessment Authority for Wales. In 2006, ACCAC merged with the Welsh Assembly Government's Department for Education Lifelong Learning and Skills (DELLS).
AM	Assembly Member (elected member of the National Assembly for Wales)
BAWSO	Black Association of Women Step Out. Voluntary organization, affiliated to Welsh Women's Aid, providing specialist services to black and minority ethnic women and children.
Chwarae Teg	An organization helping women to enhance their employment prospects.
CRE	Commission for Racial Equality
Cymdeithas Tai Hafan (or Tai Hafan)	A housing association set up specifically to provide move-on accommodation for women and children leaving refuges.
EHRC	Equality and Human Rights Commission
EOC	Equal Opportunities Commission
EOC (Wales)	Welsh regional office of Equal Opportunities Commission
Estyn	Her Majesty's Inspectorate for Education and Training in Wales
IDVA	Independent Domestic Violence Adviser
LGB	Lesbian, Gay, Bisexual

LGBT	Lesbian, Gay, Bisexual, Transsexual
MARAC	Multi-Agency Risk Assessment Conference
Merched y Wawr	National, voluntary women's organization in Wales, similar to the *Women's Institute* but its activities are conducted through the medium of Welsh.
MEWN Cymru	Minority Ethnic Women's Network Wales
NAW	National Assembly for Wales
Plaid Cymru	The Party of Wales. Aims to attain full national status for Wales within the EU.
SARC	Sexual Abuse Referral Centres
Stonewall Cymru	Lesbian, gay, bisexual charity in Wales
SDVC	Specialist domestic violence court
Twf	'Transmission within families'. A programme to promote the use of Welsh in families.
TGWU	Transport and General Workers' Union
UNISON Wales/Cymru	Trade union for public sector workers in Wales
VSPC	Voluntary Sector Partnership Council
WAG	Welsh Assembly Government
WAW	Wales Assembly of Women
WI	Women's Institute. Voluntary organization for women in the UK.
WWA	Welsh Women's Aid
WRVS	Organization providing voluntary services to help older people.
WWNC	Wales Women's National Coalition

Notes on Contributors

Wendy Ball is a senior research officer in the Centre for Children and Young People's Health and Well-Being in the School of Human and Health Sciences, Swansea University. Wendy was a research fellow at the Centre for Research in Ethnic Relations, University of Warwick, for several years before moving on to lectureships in sociology at various universities. In 2002 Wendy joined Swansea University as a postgraduate research student in sociology and she was awarded her Ph.D. in 2007. This research explored childcare policy and service delivery in Wales following devolution and involved ethnographic fieldwork with families with young children in Swansea. This research is to be published in the Politics and Society in Wales series for University of Wales Press. Wendy is currently conducting research into the demand for children's services in a Welsh local authority with reference to issues of parenting support.

Sandra Betts is a lecturer in sociology at Bangor University. Her research interests and publications include the family in Wales, civil society in Wales, the impact of devolution on women's groups in Wales, inclusive and participatory governance and devolution.

Vanessa Burholt is professor of Gerontology and director of the Centre for Innovative Ageing at Swansea University. She is a social gerontologist with fifteen years' experience of conducting research with older people. She has been involved in longitudinal projects (for example, the twenty-year Bangor Longitudinal Study of Ageing) and projects that span European and international locations. These include Families and Migration: Older People from South Asia and a six-country European Study of Adult Well Being. More recently she has directed a participatory project with Age Concern Gwynedd a

Môn (Rural North Wales Initiative for the Development of Support for Older People – RuralWIDe) in which older people were trained as researchers. Her areas of expertise include intergenerational relationships; support and social relationships; rurality; attachment to place, housing and migration of older people (including ethnic minority elders) and she has published widely on these topics. Vanessa holds a public appointment as the research member on the National Partnership Forum for Older People in Wales.

Paul Chaney is senior lecturer at Cardiff University School of Social Sciences. His publications include: *Equal Opportunities and Human Rights: The First Decade of Devolution* (Manchester: EHRC, 2009); *Women, Politics and Constitutional Change* (co-edited with Fiona MacKay and Laura McAllister); and *New Governance: New Democracy?* (co-edited with Tom Hall and Andrew Pithouse, Cardiff: University of Wales Press, 2001). He is convenor of Cardiff University's M.Sc. degree scheme in Equality and Diversity and co-editor of the journal *Contemporary Wales* and the book series *Politics and Society* (University of Wales Press).

Nickie Charles is professor and director of the Centre for the Study of Women and Gender at the University of Warwick. She has recently completed an ESRC-funded project on gender and political processes in the context of devolution which she carried out with Charlotte Davies and Stephanie Jones. She has published widely on many aspects of gender including feminist social movements, the gendered division of paid and unpaid work and the refuge movement. Her most recent book is *Families in Transition* (with Charlotte Aull Davies and Chris Harris, Bristol: The Policy Press, 2008). Other books include *Gender in Modern Britain* (Oxford: Oxford University Press, 2002); *Feminism, the State and Social Policy* (London: Macmillan, 2000), *Gender Divisions and Social Change* (Hemel Hempstead: Harvester Wheatsheaf, 1993); and (with Marion Kerr) *Women, Food and Families* (Manchester: Manchester University Press, 1988).

Charlotte Aull Davies is honorary research fellow at Swansea University. She was co-investigator on the recently completed ESRC project Gender and Political Processes in the Context of Devolution. Recent publications include *Reflexive Ethnography* (London: Routledge, 2008); and 'Language and nationalism', in *Understanding Contemporary Wales* (edited by Hugh Mackay, University of Wales Press, 2010).

Susan Hutson has recently retired as professor of Sociology at the University of Glamorgan. She has looked at housing, homelessness and policy issues in Wales over the last two decades. Many of her publications have been concerned with youth homelessness.

Stephanie Jones is coordinator of the Older People and Ageing Network (OPAN) Cymru and academic consultant for International College Wales Swansea. She was co-investigator on the recently completed ESRC project Gender and Political Processes in the Context of Devolution. She has researched and published in the areas of disability, community, political representation, and gender.

Alison Parken has a Ph.D. in mainstreaming equality theory, policy and practice. She has been the lecturer for core modules of the M.Sc. in Equality and Diversity at Cardiff University since 2003, where she is currently engaged in researching the knowledge economy from a gender perspective. A former director of Stonewall Cymru, she provides research and policy analysis for statutory and voluntary organizations in Wales, primarily in relation to equality in employment, economic and community regeneration. Recent publications include an account of action research on a multi-strand basis, towards creating an intersectional mainstreaming model for the Welsh Assembly Government, which is published in the journal *Policy and Politics*.

Sue Sanders worked in education for thirty-eight years. She taught in primary and secondary schools and was senior advisory teacher for mathematics for the City of Birmingham before moving to the university sector in Wales. She was dean of the Faculty of Education and Health Studies at the University of Swansea and the last head of its Department of Education. As well as her policy work for mathematics and research interests in education Sue has been involved with the advancement of women in education and issues of equality and gender since her early career.

Tamsin Stirling is an independent housing consultant carrying out work for central and local government, housing providers and voluntary organizations. She has twenty years' experience of the housing sector in Wales working as a consultant, policy officer, research assistant and housing officer. She works as an associate with the Housing

Associations' Charitable Trust and HouseMark and is editor of *Welsh Housing Quarterly* (*www.whq.org.uk*) which is published by Cardiff University. She is involved with a number of housing organizations in a voluntary capacity, including Llamau and Bron Afon Community Housing.

1

Setting the Scene: Devolution, Gender Politics and Social Justice

NICKIE CHARLES

In 1997 a Labour government was elected in the UK committed to constitutional reform which included the devolution of government to Scotland, Wales and Northern Ireland. It was also committed to improving the political representation of women. In Wales an assembly was proposed with powers to develop and implement policy in a number of key areas including education and training, health, housing, social services and local government. The first elections to the National Assembly for Wales were held in 1999 and an unprecedented number of women representatives were returned constituting 40 per cent of AMs (Assembly members). In 2003 this proportion increased to 50 per cent which was hailed as a 'world record' for a legislative body (Watt, 2003). In this chapter we explore how it was that this gender balance was achieved in Wales, how the gender balance in the Assembly compares with the proportion of women representatives at other levels of government, and how it relates to the politics of the feminist movement and other gender-based organizations in Wales. We briefly describe the powers of the National Assembly and discuss how gender and social justice can be conceptualized, developing a theoretical framework for the more empirically focused chapters which follow.

Achieving a gender balance

There are four important elements to the achievement of gender balance in political representation in the National Assembly: the involvement of 'strategic women' in the devolution campaign;

feminist organizing during the 'Yes campaign'; the input of women's organizations into the constitutional blueprint for the National Assembly; and the activities of women and feminists within the political parties. A comprehensive account of these different elements can be found in Chaney, Mackay and McAllister (2007). Here we draw on this account to show how it was that a gender balance in political representatives was achieved in the National Assembly and how a commitment to equality of opportunity was written into its constitution.

Strategic women and the devolution campaign

The Campaign for a Welsh Assembly was launched in 1987, eight years after the failed referendum in 1979, but it was not until the early 1990s that women began to mobilize within it to ensure that gender equality was taken seriously. Their lobbying bore fruit and, in 1994, when the Campaign for a Welsh Assembly became the Parliament for Wales Campaign, it produced a declaration which committed it to ensuring a gender balance in elected political representatives in any future legislative assembly and addressed the question of how this could be achieved. Feminists active within the campaign argued that parties should be legally required to select an equal number of women and men candidates. In the event this did not happen but the campaign explicitly recognized that devolution would provide a unique opportunity to improve the political representation of women within Wales (Chaney et al., 2007: 38).

Although the Welsh Labour Party, Plaid Cymru and the Parliament for Wales Campaign actively supported devolution, it was not until 1996, when the referendum was announced, that they began to work together in a campaigning organization called Yes for Wales. The 1997 general election and the victory of New Labour galvanized the campaign and, at the same time, women's visibility within it was raised; it made a commitment to the principle of gender balance which was immediately visible in the gender composition of speakers on all public platforms. In 1997 'Women Say Yes' was launched which 'involved strategic women who were also leading members of the overall campaign, such as Val Feld' (Chaney et al., 2007: 42). Many of the women involved were subsequently elected as AMs. Women Say Yes was able to raise 'the profile of gender equality within the context of the overall "Wales Says Yes" devolution campaign' (Chaney et al.,

2007: 43) due to the 'key role . . . played by "strategic women"' (ibid.: 44). It also initiated a campaign to make sure that 'equality [was] at the heart of the Assembly's activities' (National Library of Wales, 1997, cited in Chaney et al., 2007: 45, n. 23).

The debates about devolution, and pressure from organizations such as Cymdeithas yr Iaith, provided the opportunity to ensure that 'traditional social justice concerns' were linked with concerns about gender and other equalities (Chaney et al., 2007: 49). Because of the weakness of the women's movement within Wales, however, it was 'strategic women' who were instrumental in ensuring that issues of gender parity in representation and gender equality were central to these debates. Such women were also instrumental in establishing the women's organizations and networks which would later influence the devolution settlement. Thus, Val Feld, in her capacity as director of the Equal Opportunities Commission (EOC) in Wales, was involved in the creation of Chwarae Teg, MEWN Cymru and, in 1997, the Wales Women's National Coalition. Helen Mary Jones, in her capacity as a senior manager within the EOC Wales and a Plaid Cymru activist, was also involved in this 'network building'. According to Chaney, Mackay and McAllister, this was significant because it meant 'that there was an organized and credible women's coalition in place in time to back the strategic women's demands in the intensive period of institutional design in 1997–8' (Chaney et al., 2007: 51). Thus, 'Strategic women with women's movement credentials, many with personal networks rooted in earlier phases of the women's movement mobilization, adopted a mainly insider and elite strategy, but also worked to remobilize and re-energize the women's sector' (ibid.: 51–2). Strategic women, when working within state bureaucracies, either as political representatives or in other capacities, and attempting to pursue a feminist agenda, are often referred to as femocrats (see chapter 4).

Equal opportunities

These strategic women and women's organizations were instrumental in ensuring that gender equality was enshrined in the legal framework of the National Assembly. Thus in June 1997, Ron Davies, the secretary of state for Wales, met representatives of what was then the Wales Women's Coalition and the EOC Wales to discuss how equal opportunities would be made integral to all the activities of the devolved Assembly. He was presented with a draft equality clause that could be

3

included in a future Government of Wales Bill (Chaney et al., 2007: 54). This was an idea that originated from within the Welsh Labour Party at their conference in 1996 and was enshrined in their policy document, *Preparing for a New Wales* (WLP, 1996). It eventually led to clause 120 of the Government of Wales Act 1998 which places an 'absolute duty' on the National Assembly to operate according to the 'principle that there should be equality of opportunity for all people' (Government of Wales Act 1998, section 120).[1] The equality duty is unique within the UK in so far as it creates a legal requirement on government to promote equality of opportunity. And evidence suggests that its inclusion in the legislative framework of the National Assembly was due to feminist women organizing within and without political parties and, in particular, to the efforts of Val Feld (Chaney et al., 2007; Chaney and Fevre, 2002; Dobrowolsky, 2002). Feminist activists, equality campaigners and women's organizations were also influential in deciding how the National Assembly should operate, through their involvement in the National Assembly Advisory Group. This group eventually recommended, among other things, family-friendly working hours, appropriate use of language, gender-neutral titles, a standing equal opportunities committee, which would be concerned with gender, race and disability, and working practices that would be different from those at Westminster (Chaney et al., 2007). The standing committee on equal opportunities was necessary in order to meet the requirements of the equality duty.

Political representation

Within the political parties women activists were also instrumental in ensuring that greater numbers of women were elected to the National Assembly than was the case for Westminster or local government. It was the Welsh Labour Party and Plaid Cymru which took specific measures to ensure a gender balance of political representatives rather than this requirement being written into the constitutional settlement as had been suggested. The Labour Party committed itself to a gender balance in the devolved legislature in the early 1990s; this led to the policy of twinning constituencies, a measure which was also adopted in Scotland, and meant that, for each pair of constituencies, a woman and man were selected as candidates. Plaid Cymru also introduced positive measures by putting women candidates at the top of the regional lists. It should be noted that a system of proportional representation was adopted for elections to the National Assembly. There are sixty AMs, forty of whom are elected on a first-past-the-post system in the UK parliamentary constituencies, while the other twenty are elected using regional lists from which four representatives are elected in the five European Parliament regions. Twinning was possible only for the first Assembly elections, although the UK Labour Party has now adopted a policy of all-women shortlists to be used (usually) where an incumbent steps down. Plaid Cymru, however, has recently abandoned the policy of putting women at the top of the regional lists although if a man heads the list a woman has to be in second place. For the first National Assembly elections these measures resulted in 40 per cent of AMs being women and, in 2003, this proportion increased to 50 per cent. The proportion of women AMs during the second Assembly rose to 52 per cent because of a by-election but, after the 2007 elections, went down to 46.7 per cent. Nevertheless, this marks the National Assembly as differently gendered from other levels of government in Wales and demonstrates a level of political representation which is much more representative of the gender balance of the population. In terms of inclusivity of other marginalized groups, however, it was not until the 2007 elections that a minority ethnic Plaid Cymru AM (male) was elected on the South Wales East regional list.

The distinctiveness of the gendering of the National Assembly is evident if we look at the gender composition of local government in Wales. After the 2004 local government elections, 21.8 per cent of councillors were women and three out of twenty-two council leaders were women. The proportion of councillors rose to 24.8 per cent following the 2008 elections but the number of women leaders went down to one. These averages hide considerable variation between local authorities; a few have a third or more women councillors (Vale of Glamorgan 38.3 per cent; Cardiff 36.0 per cent; Torfaen 34.1 per cent) while others have fewer than a tenth (Merthyr Tydfil 6.3 per cent; Ynys Môn 5.0 per cent). Indeed, the *average percentage* of women councillors across the twenty-two local authority areas is 23.7 per cent. Although this compares unfavourably with the gender balance that has been achieved by the National Assembly, it is slightly better than the UK Parliament, where the big breakthrough for women in the 1997 general election still meant that women MPs were only 18.2 per cent of the total. This rose to 19.8 per cent in the 2005 general election. Of the forty-one Welsh MPs, eight (19.5 per cent) are women; seven of these are Labour (three of whom were elected as a result of all-women shortlists in Bridgend, Llanelli and Swansea East), and one is a Liberal Democrat (Chaney et al., 2007: 71).

Bringing about change

It is clear from the discussion so far that a commitment to a gender balance in terms of political representatives in the National Assembly was an important part of the devolution campaign and that this commitment came about because of the activities of feminists and women activists within the campaign and within the political parties. Similarly, the equality duty owes its existence, inter alia, to the activism of women with a history of participation in the women's movement. There was an assumption on the part of these women that a gender balance in political representation, or an improvement in women's descriptive representation, would mean that women's issues would be pursued within the National Assembly and that this would have an impact on policy development and implementation, thereby improving the lives of women in Wales (Chaney et al., 2007). Thus descriptive representation would be translated into substantive representation. There is considerable debate in the literature about how and whether this happens (see, for example, Mackay, 2004 and 2008; Phillips, 1998; Childs and Krook, 2006) and it is one of the questions addressed in the chapters that follow. Here we wish to reflect on the changes in the political and discursive opportunity structure that were brought about by the creation of the National Assembly and how this both led to a differently gendered political opportunity structure and facilitated the involvement of social movement organizations in the formal political process.

Political and discursive opportunity structures

In understanding how social movements, such as the women's movement, influence policy development and implementation we need to take a step back and consider how they engage with political processes and, in particular, with different levels of the state. It is generally agreed that social movements bring about social change in two ways: through engaging with the state to bring about policy change and through creating new meanings and understandings of the world; that is, they operate at both a political and a cultural level (Roseneil, 1995; Eyerman and Jamison, 1991; Melucci, 1989). Their ability to bring about change, however, depends on the nature of the political and discursive opportunity structures with which they engage and within which they construct meanings and contest power (Ferree, 2003; Charles, 2004; Ball and Charles, 2006). The political opportunity structure is generally understood as being constituted by the state and other political institutions such as political parties; in other words, it is the political context within which social movements have to operate. This concept has been criticized for being over-structural and not taking sufficient account of the cultural dimensions of social movements and there have been several attempts to incorporate the cultural dimension of social movement activity into an understanding of how social movements bring about social change. Thus it has been argued that social movements change meanings, that is, they reframe and redefine issues so that they are understood differently. In turn, this may lead to a shift in dominant definitions and a cultural change which can 'create a climate both inside and outside political institutions which is conducive to policy change' (Ball and Charles, 2006: 174). An example of reframing is provided by the way in which second-wave feminism defined domestic violence in terms of male power over women rather than as a problem of individual male pathology or family-based violence (Charles, 2000).

The idea of framing has, however, also been criticized for failing to attend to issues of power and it has been argued that the concept of a discursive opportunity structure, which conceptualizes discourses and frames of meaning as being rooted in 'key political institutions', is needed to understand the struggle over meanings in which social movements and the state are engaged (Naples, 2002: 244; Ferree, 2003). Furthermore, the political opportunity structure is characterized by 'systemic inequalities of gender, race, class, and sexuality' (Whittier, 2002: 295) and dominant discourses reinforce existing power relations and social inequalities (Naples, 2002). Thus social movements, as well as being constrained by these structures of power and meaning, can and do challenge and transform or modify them. In the process, however, they may themselves be transformed, particularly if incorporation into political institutions involves a process of compromise and reframing of issues. Incorporation may also involve some feminist framings becoming dominant while others are marginalized (Ferree, 2003; Charles, 2004). Thus,

> Feminist social movements, in developing discourses and meanings that
> have cultural resonance and are likely to be effective in influencing
> policy, may move away from a gendered discourse which places women
> at the centre to a non-gender-specific discourse that is compatible with
> liberal individualism and renders women – particularly working-class
> and ethnic minority women – invisible. (Charles, 2004: 301)

Examples of this can be seen in the way that feminist framings of
childcare have shifted from one of women's rights and gender difference to one which defines it in terms of children's rights, equal
opportunities and economic efficiency (Ball and Charles, 2006). This
is explored in Wendy Ball's chapter in this volume. Similarly, domestic
violence had, since the 1970s, been defined as a housing issue and as
relating to gendered power relations. Now, however, it is defined
primarily as a criminal justice issue. This reframing has implications
for the autonomous women's movement. Thus, while domestic
violence was defined as a housing issue, women's refuge groups and
Welsh Women's Aid were 'able to retain their autonomy' and 'operate
as feminist, collective, non-hierarchical organizations' (Charles, 2004:
302). Now, however, domestic abuse has been redefined as a criminal
justice issue and, because of the way women's refuge groups and
Welsh Women's Aid are funded, they have lost much of their
autonomy and have, by and large, adopted a more hierarchical form
of organization (Charles, 2000 and 2004; Ball and Charles, 2006). The
way issues are framed, therefore, and the embedding of this framing
in policy development, has implications both for the autonomy of
feminist-based organizations and for the distribution of resources.
These issues are explored in Nickie Charles and Stephanie Jones's
chapter in this volume.

A changed opportunity structure

If we now return to devolution and the involvement of the women's
movement and key feminist actors in the devolution process we can
see that the election of New Labour in 1997 brought about a significant change in the political and discursive opportunity structure. Its
policies had been influenced by feminists active within the party
during its time out of office as had its attitude towards the political
representation of women (Lovenduski, 1996; Perrigo, 1996). Similarly,
feminist involvement in Plaid Cymru had shifted its policies in the
direction of gender equality and a commitment to ensuring a gender

balance in the National Assembly. The Liberal Democrats and the Conservatives had not taken any significant measures to increase women's representation. Outwith the political parties feminist activism and the influence of organizations committed to the equalities agenda had a major impact on the constitutional settlement and on the workings of the new political institution. The commitment to both devolution and a higher political representation of women on the part of New Labour, therefore, created an opportunity for feminist activists and women's organizations to influence both the shape of the new institution and its gendering which, in turn, created a differently gendered political opportunity structure with which social movement and other civil society organizations could engage. This engagement is the subject of several of the chapters in this volume and its development during the first Assembly is explicitly addressed by Sandra Betts in chapter 3.

Alongside this the political rhetoric in Wales, particularly during the devolution campaign, emphasized inclusivity and the importance of redistributive social justice. Inclusivity had originally been advanced as a coded reference to proportional representation. However, it was broadened out to 'signal a general concern with equality of opportunity and pluralism' (Chaney et al., 2007: 57) and created a discursive opportunity structure which was favourable to demands for gender equality and a gender balance of political representatives. It is also associated with consensual politics, cross-party working and the inclusion of marginalized groups. The idea of inclusivity, meaning that 'the Assembly would reach out to all sections of Welsh society, healing old rifts, and bringing disengaged and marginalized groups into the policy-making arena', marked the devolution campaign. And the policy machinery with which to ensure that this happened was linked to the Assembly's commitment to equality of opportunity which was enshrined as an 'absolute duty' in its constitution (Day, 2006: 647; Chaney and Fevre, 2002).

The involvement of strategic women in the devolution campaign and pressure for change within the major political parties in Wales, together with an engagement with the processes leading to a constitutional settlement and the creation of a new political institution, were critical in bringing about a differently gendered political and discursive opportunity structure in Wales. This was because the devolution project itself created a new political terrain within which women's movement activists could engage and contribute to the creation of a political institution and culture which gave a high priority to gender equality both symbolically and in terms of political practice. The powers of the National Assembly are, however, limited and, as we shall see in the chapters that follow, this circumscribes its ability to transform ideals into reality (see particularly chapters 5 and 9).

The 1998 Government of Wales Act essentially transferred the executive functions of the secretary of state for Wales to an elected body. This meant that the National Assembly had very restricted powers compared to the power to enact new legislation that was given to the Scottish Parliament. Its powers were limited to the enactment of secondary legislation primarily in the areas of agriculture; culture; education and training; the environment; health; sport; economic development; local government and housing; social services; transport; and the Welsh language. These limited powers have been the cause of much dissatisfaction and, in 2006, a new Government of Wales Act substantially revised the devolution settlement and has the potential to give the National Assembly much more extensive powers. The 2006 Act, while not placing the National Assembly on the same level as the Scottish Parliament, nevertheless provides a mechanism to achieve the same type of constitution with primary law-making powers after a referendum. In the meantime, the Act creates an intermediate period during which some primary law-making powers in specified areas may be transferred to the National Assembly. This transfer of law-making powers will allow the National Assembly 'to modify – i.e. amend, repeal or extend – the provisions of Acts of Parliament in their application to Wales, or to make new provision' (Wales Office 2005, section 3.16). The mechanism put in place to establish the areas in which this legislative activity will be valid is a new type of 'Orders in Council', referred to as Legislative Competence Orders. Each Legislative Competence Order must be developed by the National Assembly and presented to Parliament for the approval of both Houses before the National Assembly can enact measures in the area that it covers: the efficacy of this mechanism has not yet been tested. In relation to issues of equality and social justice, however, the 2006 Government of Wales Act retains the 'absolute duty' and, as we shall see, social justice is claimed to be of central importance to the Welsh Assembly Government. Equal opportunities and social justice, therefore, continue to be both symbolically and institutionally integral to the workings of the National Assembly.

The National Assembly and social justice

According to a Welsh Assembly Government policy adviser, social justice is at the heart of policy development (Drakeford, 2007). Certainly in 2003, once the Labour Party had a won a majority in the Assembly, the first minister established the post of minister for social justice and regeneration and, prior to this, reclaimed for Welsh Labour the class-based politics that had marked the post-war Labour government and the consensus over the welfare state. He did this by the use of a brilliant trope, claiming that 'clear red water' separated Welsh Labour from its UK counterpart and that communities were the bedrock of creating a new, more inclusive society. Communities were "the raw material, the social heritage out of which Welsh devolution has been created – and in which we can now make our own social policy in Wales, for Wales" based on a "Welsh version of the so-called post-war consensus"' (Morgan, 2002, cited in Mooney and Williams, 2006: 616). Furthermore, achieving social justice was defined in terms of a politics of redistribution which would ameliorate inequalities based on class. The rhetoric was very much that of social democracy and the main inequalities to be tackled were structural. This reflected the political culture of Wales and its 'genuinely long-term commitment to left of centre redistributive politics, stretching for more than 150 years, from 19th century Liberalism through 20th century Labourism and on to the present day' (Drakeford, 2006: 172). The commitment to equality of opportunity is also reminiscent of the aspirations surrounding the establishment of the post-war welfare state and, particularly, the development of education policies during and after the Second World War (Addison, 1977; Fraser, 2002; Lowe, 1998). At that time equality of opportunity was seen in class terms. Since then, however, so-called new social movements have drawn attention to other bases of inequality, such as gender, and inequalities are now understood as plural and cross-cutting, they are not only inequalities of class but inequalities based on gender, sexuality, race, age, disability, religion and language (this is discussed in relation to sexuality by Parken and to language by Davies in this volume).

A commitment to equality is, therefore, central to Welsh Assembly Government (WAG) policy making. In a recent lecture, the then first minister argued that, 'Inequality is the most insidious form of injustice because it prevents individuals from achieving their full potential' (Morgan, 2006). And it has been suggested that equality of outcome is now driving WAG policy-making rather than the more usual equality of opportunity (Drakeford, 2007). Greater equality is regarded as a social good for various reasons.

> More equal societies enjoy greater economic success . . . More equal societies enjoy better health . . . More equal societies enjoy lower levels of crime . . . and, even more importantly, are marked by lower levels of fear of crime. There is a sense of individual validation and social solidarity that greater equality brings. Moreover, the sum of freedom in a more equal society will always be greater than in unequal societies, where freedom is unfairly divided. (Drakeford, 2007: 176)

This commitment to tackling inequalities and the political rhetoric which accompanies it is distinctive to Wales. It is also reflected in, amongst other things, a commitment to universal rather than means-tested provision. Although social security is not devolved, which limits the ability of the Welsh Assembly Government to counter the targeting of benefits on 'the poor' or other social groups, the measures it has been able to introduce, such as free prescriptions, free swimming and free breakfasts in primary schools, have been available to all not just to 'the poor' (Drakeford, 2007). This has important social justice implications because, in contrast to benefits which are means tested, universally available benefits avoid stigmatizing those who receive them. The commitment to tackling inequalities is also reflected in the refusal to resort to private finance initiatives within the health service and to shape education policy in a way that avoids the creation of city academies (Drakeford, 2007; see chapter 7 in this volume for a discussion of gender inequalities and education since devolution). Furthermore, as we have already mentioned, there is a commitment to engaging civil society actors in the creation of policy; this means that participation is seen as central to policy development as well as to social justice: 'If social justice is rooted in a commitment to the equal worth of every individual, then the need to draw on the talents of all our citizens applies as much to government itself as to any other aspect of life' (Drakeford, 2007: 174). There is, therefore, a political commitment to social justice and to greater equality, which is evident in the discourses mobilized by political representatives and Welsh Assembly Government advisers, and there is a related set of institutional processes and procedures as well as policy initiatives. The political and discursive opportunity structure is one that is open to claims framed in terms of equality and/or social justice. It is not altogether clear, however, how these terms are defined and how they relate to each other. It is, therefore, important to consider the definitions of social justice and equality that underpin policy and practice, the links between them and the extent to which they are understood in terms of gender.

Theorizing social justice

There is considerable debate about the meaning of equality, how it relates to sameness and difference, how equality and social justice are linked and how ideas of social justice relate to a politics of both redistribution and/or recognition. Until the emergence of 'new' social movements in the 1960s and 1970s, social justice had been understood in terms of redistribution, usually a redistribution of income, wealth or, in Marxist terms, the means of production (Fraser and Honneth, 2003) and, as we have seen, it is a class-based politics of redistribution that is apparent in Rhodri Morgan's policy statements. However, social movements, such as second-wave feminism, as well as advancing claims for redistribution, such as equal pay, also advanced claims for recognition, such as an end to discrimination against lesbian mothers in custody cases and an end to violence against women. Arguably it is these claims that have led to the institutionalization of the cross-party Standing Equal Opportunities Committee (see chapters 2 and 6 for further discussion). If this is the case then there is an institutional basis within the National Assembly for both redistribution and recognition – which are argued by Nancy Fraser to be two dimensions of social justice. More recently Fraser has argued that social justice has a third dimension which is that of representation (see also Lister, 2007a). Indeed, she has coined the phrase, 'no redistribution or recognition without representation' (Fraser, 2007: 23). Here we focus on the arguments made for an understanding of social justice which incorporates redistribution, recognition and representation and the ways in which gender has to be taken into account in order that social justice might be achieved. We look first at Nancy Fraser's argument that redistribution and recognition are fundamental to any conception of social justice but that they emerge from different philosophical and political traditions.

Fraser argues that redistributive claims have their origins in the liberal philosophical tradition while recognition relates to 'Hegelian philosophy . . . [and] . . . the phenomenology of consciousness' (Fraser and Honneth, 2003: 10). These conceptions of social justice are difficult to reconcile because the Hegelian argument that individuality and subjectivity become possible only within already existing social relations is at odds with the liberal contention that the solitary individual of the social contract is prior to rather than constituted by social relations. Furthermore, the politics of redistribution and recognition are often associated with different forms of political action. Thus the politics of redistribution is associated with labour movements and a politics of class, while the politics of recognition is associated with so-called new social movements – such as the women's liberation movement, the sexual liberation movement, black consciousness movements, disability rights movements, movements for national liberation or self-determination (which, in the context of the UK, have taken the form of campaigns for devolution) – and a politics of identity (Lister, 2007b). Moreover, the politics of recognition is ideal-typically associated with relations of domination and oppression rather than relations of economic class exploitation; such domination has been conceptualized as 'cultural imperialism' in order to make explicit the devaluing and 'othering' processes which result in the denial of equal status to oppressed groups (Young, 1990). Despite these different provenances, however, redistribution and recognition are key dimensions of social justice. Furthermore, they can be brought 'within the purview of a single integrated normative framework' (Fraser and Honneth, 2003: 37) by means of parity of participation which 'requires social arrangements that permit all (adult) members of society to interact with one another as peers'. In order for this to be achieved, material resources must be distributed in such a way 'as to ensure participants' independence and "voice"' and 'institutionalized patterns of cultural value [must] express equal respect for all participants and ensure equal opportunity for achieving social esteem' (ibid.: 36).

In making the distinction between a politics of redistribution and a politics of recognition Fraser follows Weber in distinguishing between the class and status orders of society. In her formulation, claims for redistribution relate to the economic structure of society and its class order, that is, economic inequalities, while claims for recognition relate to the status order of society and involve inequalities of esteem (Fraser and Honneth, 2003). This distinction underlines the significance of universal as opposed to means-tested benefits – the former ensure parity of esteem which is important to the politics of recognition while, although means-tested benefits may ensure some redistribution, they are associated with inequalities of esteem. Both dimensions of social justice are important. In Fraser's contrasting ideal-types, however, claims for redistribution relate to the economy while claims for recognition relate to culture and the legal system (Fraser, 2007: 17). This, however, is a 'false antithesis' and in reality the two types of claims are deeply interwoven, with each having implications for the other.

Fraser's argument about the need to develop a concept of social justice that includes both redistribution and recognition is based on the emergence of 'new' social movements advancing recognition claims. In her more recent writings, however, she argues for the need to develop the concept further so that it includes representation. This argument arises from processes of globalization and the patterns of inequality and injustice that are no longer, if they ever were, confined within the boundaries of the nation-state. It also arises from global social movements which confront transnational structures of power, whether these be economic or political. These global processes result in the 'decentering [of] the national frame that previously delimited most struggles for justice, whether focused on status or class' (Fraser and Honneth, 2003: 91) and mean that it is no longer axiomatic that it is the nation-state which provides the arena for claims making. Furthermore it problematizes both who is included as part of the political community and the boundaries of that community.

Fraser suggests that there are two questions which need to be addressed: 'Do the boundaries of the political community wrongly exclude some who are actually entitled to representation? Do the community's decision rules accord equal voice in public deliberations and fair representation in public decision-making to all members?' (Fraser, 2007: 21). This latter question relates to debates about political representation and the importance of a politics of presence; in relation to gender it highlights the importance of remedying the under-representation of women in legislative assemblies and at other levels of the political system (Phillips, 1998). The question about the boundaries of the political community, however, relates to how the political community is defined and whether such definitions wrongly exclude some who should be included: Fraser calls this misframing (Fraser, 2007). There are also struggles around framing, that is, defining the appropriate institutional framework within which justice claims should be made. Such a framework, or frame, may relate to the nation-state, but it may also be subnational or supranational (Lister, 2007: 118). This is particularly relevant when we are considering inclusion in the context of devolution and in a political and ideological context where inclusivity is highly valued.

Not everyone agrees that this third dimension of social justice – representation – is separable from the other two. Ruth Lister, for example, argues that representation or voice is an aspect of the politics of recognition rather than an analytically distinct dimension of social justice claims. 'Recognition claims are about how people are represented (for instance, in the media and in political debate) and how they are treated. They are also about representation in the political sense of 'voice' or having a say: recognition that one's views count' (Lister, 2007: 116). This position, however, while recognizing the importance of political representation, fails to take on board the significance of frame setting or defining the boundaries of political inclusion and exclusion which can lead to misrepresentation and the denial of voice (Fraser, 2007). The significance of how the boundaries of political communities are defined is not new.

> The nation was never as naturalized as it normally appears in retrospect and the dismantling of institutionalized obstacles to the participation of some people on a par with others has been a recurrent feature of past struggles. The question of who is included and who excluded from the circle of those entitled to make justice claims on one another, and the meta question of the procedures which structure such public processes of frame setting and misframing, have been the stuff of political argument from the start of the modern era. (Lara and Fine, 2007: 44)

This question is particularly pertinent in the context of devolution which, in some senses, can be seen as the outcome of struggles for a reframing of the political community within the boundaries of the nation-state. This, however, is an '*affirmative* politics of framing' as it accepts that 'state-territoriality is the proper basis for considering the "who" of social justice' (Fraser, 2007: 24). There is also a transformative politics of framing which challenges the state-territorial principle, arguing that many of the causes of social injustice and inequality are situated beyond the territorially based nation-state and cannot therefore be challenged by claims which are territorially bounded (Fraser, 2007).

Emerging from these debates and particularly from Fraser's contributions, there are three dimensions of social justice which need to be considered. These are distribution, recognition and representation, all of which are analytically separable but empirically deeply enmeshed with each other. In this analysis the influence of Weber's sociology is clear with his separation of the economic, the cultural and the political; social justice claims cross all three domains as does the actual experience of daily life where injustice and inequality affect individuals and communities.

As we have already suggested, the redistribution and recognition dimensions of social justice take institutional form within the National Assembly, and it is clear that the representation dimension also informs the National Assembly's structure and the policies it develops. However, it seems that the machinery of government separates the recognition and redistribution dimensions of social justice in so far as equalities and human rights are institutionally distinct from social justice. There are two divisions within the Assembly, the Equalities and Human Rights Division and the Social Justice and Local Government/Regeneration Division. This separation has also been noted in the Scottish Parliament where it has been linked to a conception of equality which relates primarily to recognition and the elimination of different forms of 'discrimination, victimisation or exploitation' experienced by specific social groups, and a conception of social justice which relates to 'economic or income inequalities' (SCVO, 2008). This distinction can also be found within the Welsh Assembly Government and the Assembly civil service and, indeed, the social justice policy agenda seems to be driven primarily by the need to remedy economic and income-based inequalities. It is, therefore, a redistributive policy agenda and rhetoric that defines social justice within the Welsh Assembly Government. However, the centrality of the equality duty in the Assembly, and the requirement that all policies are checked for their implications in terms of equalities and human rights as part of the 'equalities' agenda, means that the policy machinery also incorporates a recognition-based conception of social justice. The incorporation of these two different definitions of social justice, one being named as social justice and the other as equalities and human rights, could be argued to reflect the influence of different social movements on political processes and policy development. And their coexistence, rather than integration, suggests that they remain discursively as well as institutionally distinct. The implications of this for social justice for women in Wales are explored in the chapters that follow.

The structure of the book

The new gender balance of political representatives at the level of the National Assembly, together with an institutional framework which reflects the importance of equalities and social justice, has the potential to create new opportunities for the development of social policies which address gender and other social inequalities. This institutional framework, however, has to be set against the limited powers of the National Assembly and the constraints of policy frameworks which, in many instances, are controlled by Westminster. The contributors to this volume investigate different substantive areas in order to assess how policies are affecting gender inequalities and whether they are having an impact on social justice for women in Wales. Each chapter focuses on a particular aspect of social policy, exploring the way it has developed since devolution and the extent to which considerations of gender and social justice for women are central to this development.

The first part of the book explores the mechanisms established by the National Assembly to increase political participation which, as we have seen, is an important dimension of social justice. Chapters 2 and 3 explore different aspects of participation and the institutional mechanisms which support equalities and social justice. Chapter 2 focuses on gender mainstreaming and chapter 3 on the participation of civil society organizations in the processes of government.

Chapter 2 sets out the institutional framework underpinning the Welsh Assembly Government's commitment to gender equality and provides a critical assessment of progress towards gender mainstreaming in the first decade since devolution. In it, Paul Chaney outlines the institutional mechanisms that were put in place to ensure that the commitment to mainstreaming was translated into practice, arguing that devolution provided a political opportunity structure that was open to interventions from women's movements and that 'strategic' women were crucial in taking forward the equalities agenda. The commitment to equality of opportunity took institutional form in the cross-party Standing Committee on Equality of Opportunity, the establishment of the Equality and Human Rights division in the Welsh Assembly Government civil service and the various partnership and consultative arrangements that have been set up with, for example, the voluntary sector, public services, Stonewall Cymru and the Wales Women's National Coalition. Chaney argues, however, that despite these developments and the 'absolute duty', progress towards gender mainstreaming and mainstreaming of equalities more generally has been beset by difficulties. He highlights the gap between rhetoric and reality, suggesting that one of the factors contributing to this gap is 'institutional resistance' on the part of the 'government bureaucracy', something which it was difficult to do anything about at least in the early years of the National Assembly. He also notes that very early on in the life of the Equalities Committee the idea of gender mainstreaming was subsumed under a commitment to a generic notion of mainstreaming equalities and that this courts the danger of gender sliding down the equalities agenda. His analysis shows that, although gender has become less visible over the ten-year period, a commitment to gender equality is beginning to be more firmly embedded in many of the institutional mechanisms of the Assembly. He argues that this has been achieved both by means of an 'expert bureaucratic approach' involving legal and institutional measures and through a commitment to the participation of marginalized groups and their involvement with government. This involvement is something that is taken up in several of the chapters. Despite these developments, however, Chaney argues that the impact of gender mainstreaming has, as yet, been minimal in terms of policy outcomes and that gender equality has become less visible. He is careful to say, however, that this does not mean that it is afforded a lower priority, although, in the 2006 Mainstreaming Strategy, there is no reference to gender budgeting despite the recommendations of the Mainstreaming Review.

In chapter 3, Sandra Betts explores the relationship between the voluntary sector and the National Assembly, focusing on women's organizations in civil society. Her analysis is based on research that was carried out during the first term exploring the extent to which devolution has resulted in 'a more inclusive and participatory democracy'. The voluntary sector has been identified by New Labour and by the Welsh Assembly Government as key to increasing participation. This chapter explores how the Wales Women's National Coalition, the gender consultative policy network, operates and the extent to which women's organizations participate in the processes of government.[2] Betts mobilizes the concept of social capital to explain the differences in levels of participation between women's organizations; those that are embedded in social networks that connect them with the National Assembly – and previously with the Welsh Office – report far more effective participation than those that are not. Women's organizations are classified as promotional, political and social/service and it is those which fall into the first category that have more involvement in policymaking and political structures. Moreover, her findings show that devolved government has not been associated with an increase in participation of grass-roots members of women's organizations; indeed, many felt that they had no influence over decision making at Assembly level. Neither were they aware of their organization's involvement with the Wales Women's National Coalition. This suggests the need for 'more open and flexible opportunity structures' in order to facilitate inclusiveness and participation of marginalized groups and the chapter concludes with a discussion of recent developments which are aimed precisely at extending participation. These findings suggest that reliance on umbrella organizations, such as the Wales Women's National Coalition, to increase participation and widen democracy may not be sufficient to engage those who are not already engaged in the political process. Such a top-down approach has limited success in encouraging the generation of social capital within civil society and more recent attempts, which take a 'bottom-up' approach, may be more successful. What this chapter shows is that some women's organizations are extremely well-connected and their participation in the process of government has been effectively institutionalized but, for the majority, this is not the case and, despite the best efforts of the Welsh Assembly Government, their participation remains low.

The second part of the book explores various different policy areas in order to evaluate progress towards equality and social justice for women since devolution. Chapter 4 focuses on childcare policy. Wendy Ball shows that the process of consultation and development of childcare policy was characterized by some organizations – several of which were social movement organizations – being incorporated into the political opportunity structure, rather in the way outlined by Sandra Betts, while others who mobilized a different discourse remained marginalized. Those organizations whose voices had been heard and whose views were incorporated into policy are those that already had connections with government and were mobilizing a discourse of equality based on economic considerations, while those that were marginalized were those which mobilized a discourse based on difference. This discourse, Ball argues, represented a different framing of the issue which resonated neither with the dominant feminist discourse about childcare being a means of enabling mothers to participate in the workforce and providing equal opportunities for women, nor the children's rights discourse which sees childcare as of benefit to children. Instead, it challenges domestic divisions of labour and the gendering of care work, demanding that this be recognized as a valid and valuable form of work rather than as something which detracts from the achievement of gender equality (see Fraser, 1997). Ball situates this analysis in the context of the views of parents and policymakers at local and national level, showing that there is a disjunction between these two levels in the value attached to care. She argues that there is a lack of understanding at national level of the interconnections of gender, care and paid work and that it has been assumed that all women will benefit from an expanded provision of childcare. This contrasts with views at local level which recognize the desire of many women to prioritize caring over paid work but which are not framed in terms of gender equality. Current childcare policy, she argues, ignores the need to recognize the value of the care work that women do and contributes to the cultural devaluing of such work. This has implications in terms of social justice as claims for the cultural recognition of unpaid care, on the one hand, and a redistribution of resources, on the other, are constructed as mutually exclusive. This chapter, together with chapter 3, points to the difficulties of a top-down approach to policy implementation and the need to ensure that the views and values of those at local level are incorporated into policy development.

Chapter 5 investigates the development of the all-Wales domestic abuse strategy, comparing it with developments at UK and local level. Here the limits placed on the National Assembly's ability to develop policy are highlighted and the significance of the ways in which issues are framed is brought out. Domestic violence is defined in policy terms as a criminal justice issue and criminal justice is not a devolved area. This means that the ability of the National Assembly to develop policy on domestic violence is circumscribed. This notwithstanding, a Welsh strategy has been developed as have strategies at local level. The authors argue that, while there have been significant improvements in the ways in which women experiencing or threatened with domestic violence are treated within the criminal justice system, there are some worrying developments which relate to the emergence of a discourse of gender neutrality. This is something that is also noted in chapter 4. The emergence of this discourse is linked to the involvement of criminal justice agencies in the development of the all-Wales and local strategies and is apparent in the definitions of domestic violence that have been adopted which no longer refer to its gendered nature. At the same time there is pressure for service providers to adopt gender-neutral practice which, in effect means that women's refuges or refuges for black and minority-ethnic women should open their doors to men and/or women of any ethnicity. This is justified in terms of equality. The chapter explores the implications of these developments in terms of the cultural recognition of the nature of domestic violence and of the distribution of resources within the domestic abuse sector, arguing that although there has been a marked improvement in provision of support for women as 'victims' within the criminal justice system, this goes hand in hand with a shift away from the recognition that domestic violence is gendered. Furthemore, although strategic women at the level of the National Assembly and organizations such as Welsh Women's Aid were influential in drafting the all-Wales strategy, the absence of strategic women at local level is associated with a denial of the gendered dimensions of domestic violence.

In chapter 6 Alison Parken explores how policy on sexual orientation in Wales has developed since devolution. Her main argument, which echoes that of Wendy Ball, is that sexual orientation policy has developed within the policy frames of gender mainstreaming and sexual orientation policy and that both policy areas have been marked by a decoupling of gender and sexuality. Within the sexual orientation policy framework, discrimination on grounds of gender has been divorced from discrimination on grounds of sexual orientation, resulting in a failure to recognize discrimination against lesbian women and gay men on the grounds of sexuality when it is gendered behaviour that is at issue. Furthermore, gender mainstreaming is based on an assumption of heterosexuality which remains implicit; this results in measures to advance gender equality being inappropriate for lesbians and gay men and a failure to question the 'heterosexual gender contract' which structures the gender divisions of labour and inequalities which are seen as in need of transformation. She argues that sexual orientation policy is gender blind and that gender mainstreaming is sexuality blind; this means that neither policy adequately addresses the situation of the lesbian, gay, bisexual, transsexual (LGBT) communities despite the creation by the National Assembly of the policy consultative network Stonewall Cymru. In practice, however, particularly in relation to anti-bullying policy and practice within the education sector, the intersectionality of sexuality and gender are recognized. Education policy is a devolved area, unlike domestic violence and, as we see in the following chapter, developments in Wales have taken a different direction from those in England. This chapter makes a strong argument for recognizing the intersectionality of different equalities strands and argues that in Wales, because of the incorporation of LGBT organizations into the political opportunity structure and the high profile given to sexual orientation as one of the equalities strands, there is a real possibility of developing policies which recognize the intersectionality of sexuality and gender.

In chapter 7 Sue Sanders explores the ways in which education has developed since devolution. She explores the gender composition of the education workforce, the impact of strategic women on education policy and the visibility of gender as an issue, and the way that, despite a commitment to equality, gender is visible in policy only as a concern with boys' so-called under achievement and the shortage of male teachers. This chapter looks at the prospects for changing the gender balance amongst teachers where it is still the case that men are over-represented as head teachers and women are over-represented in the lower ranks of the schools' workforce. Sanders argues that there is now a critical mass of women who would be able to take on headships and that this provides grounds for optimism about future developments. However, in comparison with England, progress towards gender equality within the teaching workforce has been disappointing in view of the fact that at national level strategic women have been so much in evidence. Indeed, there is a marked contrast between national and local level such that while the two key education positions – minister for education and lifelong learning and chief inspector of schools – were held by women, at local government level the management of schools is in the hands of men. This echoes the findings of chapter 5 on domestic violence and is something that we take up in the concluding chapter. Sanders also notes that there is no information in the public domain about the gender composition of school governing bodies and that this is possibly an area where gendered views about head teachers prevail. She concludes by suggesting that education policy, while pursuing equality of opportunity and social justice, is relatively silent on the question of gender inequalities, and that it is through increasing the proportion of women at management levels and on governing bodies that the situation for women could be improved. She also raises the issue of gender neutral language and the unavailability of a gender breakdown of some crucial statistics. The question of gender neutrality is a central concern of chapter 5 and is also noted in chapter 4, and it is something that we return to in the concluding chapter.

Chapter 8 explores the ways in which housing and homelessness policy has developed since devolution, arguing that, as with education, policies have taken a different trajectory from those in England. This chapter is based on interviews with a number of senior women in the field of housing and homelessness which were undertaken expressly for this volume. It provides an overview of the development of housing policy, particularly the widening of the priority categories which resulted in an increase in the numbers of statutorily homeless. Services for the homeless have also expanded and this expansion has been aided by the introduction of Supporting People funding; this, of course, is also relevant to the funding of women's refuges and is addressed in chapter 5. The voluntary sector is identified as being of particular importance to the implementation of homelessness policy and the National Assembly was seen by the women interviewed as having taken a very positive stance; a strategic woman was identified by many as having been central to this. However, despite these positive developments, the situation of women and children has deteriorated since devolution both in terms of access to housing and in terms of feminist groups, such as refuge groups, providing services for women who are homeless. These groups have had their ability to 'shout for women' curtailed by mainstreaming which has reduced their ability to 'be radical'. This is another example of more radical feminist voices being marginalized by the incorporation of feminist issues framed in a particular way into the government agenda; a process also highlighted in chapters 4 and 5. Furthermore, there appears to be no consideration of women as a significant category in policy and legislation – it is, rather, people in other categories, such as 'drug and alcohol', 'learning difficulties', 'elderly', who are seen as having particular needs – and the use of gender-neutral language only serves to reinforce women's invisibility.

Chapter 9 takes a slightly different approach, reporting on a large-scale study into the material resources of older women in Wales and the extent of poverty. This is an area where the National Assembly has limited powers as social security is not a devolved area. However, there has been considerable effort put into ensuring increased uptake of benefits amongst older people and a strategy for older people in Wales has been developed. This chapter shows how access to material resources amongst older people is shaped by gender, with women generally being worse off than men and more vulnerable to poverty. Women are also more reliant than are men on state pensions and the decline in the value of the basic pension is, therefore, particularly problematic for them. The strategy for older people aimed to 'tackle poverty and social exclusion' amongst older people; however, there seems to be a lack of commitment to implementing this at local level and Vanessa Burholt is not optimistic about the possibility of the Welsh Assembly Government's being able either to tackle poverty amongst older people or to reduce gender inequalities. This sombre assessment of WAG policy does not augur well for older women in Wales who, as in other parts of the UK, far outnumber men, especially in the 'old old' categories.

The focus of chapter 10 is Welsh language policy, how this has developed both prior to and subsequent upon devolution, women's centrality to the transmission of language and culture and the relationship between the Welsh language and other equality strands. Language is one of the seven equality strands that are discussed in the National Assembly's Mainstreaming Strategy, although it is not mentioned in the newly introduced, generic equalities impact assessment tool which is supposed to ensure that all the equalities strands are considered in policy development (see chapter 2). Charlotte Davies points out that women have always been heavily involved in language campaigns in Wales and in local campaigns for such things as Welsh-medium schools. Since devolution the National Assembly has developed its Welsh-language policy which now aims to create a bilingual nation. This is to be achieved in various ways and, Davies argues, women are key to many of them, particularly the goals of increasing the number of families who have Welsh as their main language, increasing the number of children receiving education through the medium of Welsh and supporting communities where Welsh is the first language of the majority of residents. Women's responsibility for childcare and their centrality to informal networks within communities mean that they are likely to be crucial to these aspects of Welsh language policy. Davies also explores the conflicts that have arisen between the rights of Welsh speakers and other equality streams such as race and gender. This relationship has improved but the status of the Welsh language in relation to the other equality strands still seems to be problematic.

Together these chapters provide an insight into the involvement and influence of women in different policy areas, the extent to which policy development is gender sensitive, and the ways in which the National Assembly's commitment to gender equality and social justice is affecting the lives of women in Wales. We return to these issues in the final chapter of the book.

Notes

[1] This 'absolute duty' is now enshrined in section 70 of the Government of Wales Act 2006.
[2] The Wales Women's National Coalition closed at the end of June 2010 due to the loss of WAG funding.

References

Addison, P. (1977). *The Road to 1945*, London: Quartet Books.
Ball, W. and N. Charles (2006). 'Feminist social movements and policy change: Devolution, childcare and domestic violence policies in Wales', *Women's Studies International Forum*, 29, 172–83.
Chaney, P. and R. Fevre (2002). *An Absolute Duty: The Equality Policies of the Government of the National Assembly for Wales*, Cardiff: Institute of Welsh Affairs.
——, F. Mackay and L. McAllister (2007). *Women, Politics and Constitutional Change: The First Years of the National Assembly for Wales*, Cardiff: University of Wales Press.
Charles, N. (2000). *Feminism, the State and Social Policy*, Basingstoke: Palgrave Macmillan.
—— (2004). 'Feminist politics and devolution: a preliminary analysis', *Social Politics*, 11, 2, 297–311.
Childs, S. and M. L. Krook (2006). 'Should feminism give up on critical mass? A contingent yes', *Politics and Gender*, 2, 4, 522–30.
Day, G. (2006). 'Chasing the dragon? Devolution and the ambiguities of civil society in Wales', *Critical Social Policy*, 26, 3, 642–55.
Dobrowolsky, A. (2002). 'Crossing boundaries: exploring and mapping women's constitutional interventions in England, Scotland, and Northern Ireland', *Social Politics*, 9, 293–340.
Drakeford, M. (2007). 'Social justice in a devolved Wales', *Benefits*, 15, 2, 171–8.
Eyerman, R. and A. Jamison (1991). *Social Movements: A Cognitive Approach*, Cambridge: Polity Press.
Ferree, M. M. (2003). 'Resonance and radicalism: feminist framing of abortion in the United States and Germany', *American Journal of Sociology*, 109, 304–44.
Fraser, D. (2002). *The Evolution of the British Welfare State*, 3rd edn, Basingstoke: Palgrave Macmillan.

Fraser, N. (1995). 'From redistribution to recognition? Critical reflections on the "postsocialist condition"', *New Left Review*, 212, 68–93.

—— (1997). 'After the family wage: a postindustrial thought experiment', in N. Fraser, *Justice Interruptus: Critical Reflections on the "Postsocialist" Condition*, London and New York: Routledge.

—— (2007). 'Re-framing justice in a globalizing world', in T. Lovell (ed.), *(Mis)recognition, Social Inequality and Social Justice*, Routledge: London and New York: pp. 17–35.

—— and A. Honneth (2003). *Redistribution or Recognition? A Political-Philosophical Exchange*, London: Verso.

Lara, M. P. and R. Fine (2007). 'Justice and the public sphere: the dynamics of Nancy Fraser's critical theory', in Lovell (ed.), *(Mis)recognition, Social Inequality and Social Justice*, pp. 36–48.

Lister, R. (2007a). 'Social justice: meaning and politics', *Benefits*, 15, 2, 113–25.

—— (2007b). '(Mis)recognition, social inequality and social justice: a critical social policy persepctive', in Lovell (ed.), *(Mis)recognition, Social Inequality and Social Justice*, pp. 157–76.

Lowe, R. (1998). *The Welfare State in Britain since 1945*, 2nd edn, Basingstoke: Palgrave Macmillan.

Lovenduski, J. (1996). *Women and European Politics: Contemporary Feminism and Public Policy*, Brighton: Wheatsheaf Books.

Mackay, F. (2004). 'Gender and political representation in the UK: the state of the discipline', *British Journal of Politics and International Relations*, 6, 1, 99–120.

—— (2008). '"Thick" conceptions of substantive representation: women, gender and political institutions', in *Representation*, 44, 2, 125–38.

Melucci, A. (1989). *Nomads of the Present: Social Movements and Individual Needs in Contemporary Society*, London: Hutchinson Radius.

Mooney, G. and C. Williams (2006). 'Forging new "ways of life"? Social policy and nation building in devolved Scotland and Wales', *Critical Social Policy*, 26, 3, 608–29.

Morgan, R. (2002). Speech to the University of Wales Swansea, National Centre for Public Policy, Third Anniversary Lecture, 11 December.

—— (2006). 'Twenty-first century socialism: a Welsh recipe', Swansea, *www.compassonline.org.uk/news_comments.asp?r.=338*, 1 December.

Naples, N. A. (2002). 'Materialist feminist discourse analysis and social movement research: mapping the changing context for "community control"', in D. S. Meyer, N. Whittier and B. Robnett (eds), *Social Movements: Identity, Culture, and the State*, Oxford: Oxford University Press.

National Library of Wales (1997). Quotations from: *Women Say Yes* (1997), Whitland Rally publicity flyer, National Library of Wales Archive and

Manuscript Collection, Aberystwyth, 'Yes For Wales Referendum Campaign Records', Box 6/G12/1/4.

Perrigo, S. (1996). 'Women and change in the Labour Party 1979–1995, in J. Lovenduski and P. Norris (eds), *Women in Politics*, Oxford: Oxford University Press.

Phillips, A. (1998). 'Democracy and representation: or, Why should it matter who our representatives are?', in A. Phillips (ed.), *Feminism and Politics*, Oxford: Oxford University Press.

Roseneil, S. (1995). *Disarming Patriarchy: Feminism and Political Action at Greenham*, Milton Keynes: Open University Press.

SCVO (Scottish Council for Voluntary Organisations) (2008). 'Social justice – unpacking the equalities dimension', SCVO Briefing June 2003, *http://www.scvo.org.uk/Equalities/resource_base/mainstreaming/sj_and_equalities.htm*, accessed 1 November 2008.

Wales Office (2005). *Better Governance for Wales*, London: Stationery Office.

Watt, N. (2003). 'Equality: women win half Welsh seats', *Guardian*, 3 May.

Welsh Labour Party (WLP) (1996). *Preparing for a New Wales,* Cardiff: Welsh Labour Party.

Whittier, N. (2002). 'Meaning and structure in social movements', in D. S. Meyer, N. Whittier and B. Robnett (eds), *Social Movements: Identity, Culture and the State*, New York: Oxford University Press.

Young, I. M. (1990). *Justice and the Politics of Difference*, Princeton, NJ: Princeton University Press.

I

GENDER, POLITICAL REPRESENTATION
AND SOCIAL JUSTICE

2

Delivery or Déjà Vu? Gender Mainstreaming and Public Policy in Post-devolution Wales

PAUL CHANEY

Public policymaking during the period of administrative devolution under the Welsh Office (1964–99) did little to address prevailing patterns and processes of gender inequality and sex discrimination. In part this stemmed from the ministry's limited policy capacity. As one account concludes, it was 'a department tightly constrained by the British constitutional framework, engaged for the most part in the humdrum business of implementing policies decided elsewhere' (Rawlings, 1998: 466). Another factor was that the majority of government employees in the Welsh Office had not received training on equality matters (WAG, 2001). Yet it also reflected an absence of political will. For example, in 1996 William Hague, then secretary of state, refused to meet the equal opportunities commissioner for Wales, stating: 'there is nothing to talk about' (Chaney et al., 2007: 156).

In response, in the 1990s feminist activists seized the political opportunity structures associated with the pro-devolution campaign in order to lobby for a reprioritization of equality matters and for the institutional design of the National Assembly for Wales to incorporate mechanisms to promote gender – and other modes of equality – in public policymaking. Early evidence of discontinuity with past practices came within days of the National Assembly's assumption of its policy- and law-making powers. In July 1999 the minister with responsibility for equalities announced 'the executive, will need to take equality of opportunity factors into account in every policy decision. This mainstreaming approach is fundamental' (NAW, 1999).

This chapter will critically assess whether, a decade on, the Welsh Assembly Government's aim of gender mainstreaming is being realized. Accordingly, attention is focused on the legal and institutional factors that have shaped the development of mainstreaming in devolved policymaking. Examples of Assembly government policy, the views of policy actors and evaluation reports are then used critically to assess progress. In making this assessment a range of key questions will be addressed including: to what extent has the Welsh government's espousal of mainstreaming translated into policy outcomes? Has the incorporation of gender as a mainstream issue resulted in a decrease in its visibility? Has gender equality slipped down the policy agenda? Is there evidence of institutional resistance to gender mainstreaming within the Assembly government bureaucracy? Has the Assembly government's approach followed the 'expert-bureaucratic' or the 'participative-democratic' route to gender mainstreaming? Before we address these issues, we first outline the concept of gender mainstreaming.

Gender mainstreaming

Feminists working on international economic aid programmes in the 1970s began developing what subsequently emerged as the gender mainstreaming concept. As a new social and political priority, it came to wider prominence at the United Nations (UN) Third World Conference on Women in Nairobi, Kenya, in 1985, a time when it was also developing in the domestic policies of several European countries, such as the Netherlands, Sweden and Norway (Pollack and Hafner-Burton, 2000). Continued focus was placed upon mainstreaming at the 1995 UN World Conference on Women held in Beijing and it has subsequently developed into an internationally recognized approach to delivering gender equality outcomes in a broad range of organizational contexts. Whilst the initial focus was on gender equality, in some contexts the mainstreaming concept has subsequently been applied to a range of equality dimensions such as disability, language and ethnicity. There are competing definitions of the mainstreaming concept. The UN defines it as a

> strategy for making women's as well as men's concerns and experiences an integral dimension of the design, implementation, monitoring and evaluation of policies and programmes in all political, economic and societal spheres so that women and men benefit equally and inequality is

not perpetuated. The ultimate goal is to achieve gender equality. (UN, 1995: 2)

In contrast, the Council of Europe offers a more policy-oriented definition:

> Gender mainstreaming is the (re)organization, improvement, development and evaluation of policy processes, so that a gender equality perspective is incorporated in all policies at all levels and at all stages, by the actors normally involved in policy-making. Gender mainstreaming cannot replace specific policies, which aim to redress situations resulting from gender inequality. Specific gender equality policies and gender mainstreaming are dual and complementary strategies and must go hand in hand to reach the goal of gender equality. (CoE, 2004)

Mainstreaming has been characterized as 'a new approach to equality policy making and practice' (EOC, 2003: 2). It aims to build equality considerations into policymaking from the outset and is based upon a series of policy tools that includes: gender disaggregated statistics; gender impact assessments; equality indicators; monitoring, evaluating, auditing techniques; gender balance in decision making; and gender budgeting. According to Rees (1998) mainstreaming is underpinned by three principles: treating the individual as a whole person (by 'visioning' a person's different needs); democracy; and equity and justice.

A full discussion of mainstreaming theory is beyond the present purposes. Indeed, a review of the literature shows it to be a contested concept. Moreover, recent academic analysis has criticized the mainstreaming concept on a number of grounds. For example, Beveridge and Nott (2002: 299) question 'whether mainstreaming can address the patriarchal nature of laws and legal systems and the essentializing tendencies of law, and whether mainstreaming can effectively tackle market driven inequality'. Elsewhere, Walby (2005: 322) also highlights a range of issues including: 'whether the *vision* of gender equality can be distinguished from the strategy to get there'; the relationship between gender equality and other inequalities (for example, around faith, ethnicity, language etc.); the need to rethink the concept and practice of democracy to include gender equality; and the relationship between mainstreaming and human rights discourse.

Notwithstanding such practical and conceptual issues, in the wake of the Treaty of Amsterdam (1997), gender mainstreaming has been adopted by the European Union as the foundation of its gender policy (see also chapter 6). More broadly, its widespread adoption by governments around the world can be seen as a significant development in practical and normative aspects of public policy-making. In 2005 a UN survey revealed that 165 member states reported some form of 'national machinery' for mainstreaming by government (IANWGE, 2005: 61) thereby lending credence to the idea that it is 'one of the most rapidly adopted social justice-oriented initiatives endorsed by the international community' (Chaney and Rees, 2004: 104).

Devolution: an enabling context?

Over recent decades, constitutional reform of unitary states associated with the international development of multi-level governance and the trend towards (quasi-)federalism (Bulmer et al., 2002; Bache, 2005) has provided political opportunity structures for women's movements to mobilize and press for the incorporation of gender equality mechanisms in the institutional design of new legislatures (Beckwith, 2003). In many instances this has underpinned the rise of 'state feminism' (McBride, 1995) – or the development of 'government structures that are formally charged with furthering women's status and rights' (Stetson and Mazur, 1995: 1). The Welsh experience is no exception to this trend. In response to the male domination of Welsh politics and the exclusive practices of the Welsh Office, 'strategic' women activists in concert with elements of the women's movement used the opportunities presented by the post-1987 devolution campaign in Wales to lobby for the inclusion of equality mechanisms in the institutional 'blueprint' of the National Assembly for Wales (see Chaney, 2007). These ultimately found their way into the devolution statute, the Government of Wales Act (1998). Of foremost importance is the principal equality clause in the act. It is an example of a 'fourth generation' equality duty (see Fredman, 2000) and is unique amongst the devolution statutes (see Chaney, 2004) for it requires government to take a proactive stance and promote equality for all people and in respect of all Welsh Assembly Government functions. Further aspects of state feminism arising from the earlier actions of strategic women include the legislature's cross-party Standing Committee on Equality of Opportunity and associated reporting mechanisms to measure progress in relation to the developing equalities agenda. The latter include the requirement in the National Assembly's standing orders for the government to 'submit an annual report to the Assembly on arrangements [to promote equality] and their effectiveness'. The combination of the Assembly's equality duty and associated instruments of state feminism together with the election of women as 40 per cent of Assembly Members in 1999 (rising to 50 per cent in 2003, and subsequently 47 per cent in 2007) can be seen to provide an 'enabling context' (Mackay and Bilton, 2000: 109) for gender mainstreaming.

As noted, the reprioritization of gender equality became apparent in July 1999, at the first meeting of the Assembly's cross-party Equality Committee when the equalities minister set out the aim of a new approach to policymaking through the application of mainstreaming. A significant aspect of this declaration is the explicit broadening out from *gender* mainstreaming to mainstreaming *equalities*, as reflected in the following definition of mainstreaming adopted by the Welsh government:

> the integration of respect for diversity and equality of opportunity principles, strategies and practices into the every day work of [government . . .] and other public bodies. It means that equality issues should be included from the outset as an integral part of the policy-making and service delivery process and the achievement of equality should inform all aspects of the work of every individual within an organization. The success of mainstreaming should be measured by evaluating whether inequalities have been reduced. (NAW, 2004: 6)

According to Rees, the new mainstreaming approach represented a 'test-bed for initiatives in gender equality' (Rees, 2002: 62). Yet, in order for it to succeed, the government strategy paper acknowledged that there was a need to ensure that a 'proper framework [wa]s in place to support the delivery of the Assembly's duty on equal opportunities' (NAW, 1999). We now turn to consider aspects of the ensuing reform of government administrative practices and procedures designed to provide such a framework.

Institutional prerequisites for mainstreaming in government

The civil service transferred from the Welsh Office to the National Assembly in 1999 represented a powerful continuity with the earlier approach to public administration – as noted, one that had little to say on the topic of equalities. Accordingly, it possessed none of the institutional prerequisites or 'building blocks' necessary for the application of gender mainstreaming (Mackay and Bilton, 2000). These are broad in scope and include: awareness raising, training, expertise, appropriate staffing, reporting mechanisms, incentives to 'build ownership' of the promotion of equality and the securing of adequate resources. New institutionalist theory suggests that the initial absence of these building blocks presents a major obstacle to realizing the goal of mainstreaming. Hall (1986: 19) offers a conceptual explanation for this; he states: 'the organization of policy making affects the degree of power that any one set of actors has over policy outcomes . . . organizational factors affect both the degree of pressure an actor can bring to bear on policy and the likely direction of that pressure'. In short, when applied to the case of the National Assembly, this perspective suggests that, on its own, political will is insufficient to achieve equality outcomes; rather, it needs to be accompanied by effective institutional mechanisms. The following examples illustrate the way in which, during the past decade, measures have been taken to increase the National Assembly and Welsh government's capacities to mainstream equality in public policy.

Prominent examples of new institutional arrangements are the dedicated Equality and Human Rights Division in the Assembly Government civil service[1] (an administrative department with no parallel in the former Welsh Office) and, as noted, the cross-party Standing Committee on Equality of Opportunity. These have been accompanied by mandatory reporting mechanisms to measure progress in relation to the developing equalities agenda. The involvement of experts drawn from outside the civil service has fostered another dimension integral to a mainstreaming approach, namely, raising awareness of equality issues. This has been achieved through inter-agency and cross-party working as evidenced by the Assembly government's successive Close the Pay Gap campaigns to promote equal pay for women and men in respect of work of equal value. In terms of resources, although difficult to quantify (for equality has not generally been listed as a discrete heading in Assembly government budget data), it is clear that, when compared to the 'zero base' of administration under the Welsh Office, there has been a significant increase in the capital sum and staffing levels allocated to the promotion of equality in areas such as policymaking, training and consultation. Elected devolution has also resulted in initiatives – such as a new *Code of Practice for Ministerial Appointments to Public Bodies* (NAW, 2002) – designed to put in place a more diverse workforce in order to underpin the commitment to mainstreaming. A further reform has seen the introduction of compulsory equality training for all Assembly staff.

There has also been progress in developing structures and mechanisms to transfer equality policies at Assembly level to other areas of economic and political life. Key examples are set out in the 'Inclusive exercise of functions' section in part 2 of the Government of Wales Act (2006),[2] notably the Partnership Council (72), Local Government Scheme (73) and the Voluntary Sector Scheme (74). Each of these statutory partnership arrangements with the Welsh government is used for lobbying and consultation, as well as the development of policy and service delivery. For example, the Voluntary Sector Scheme is a binding agreement that sets out how the Assembly government will work with voluntary organizations. Section 2.7 of the scheme notes the need for compliance with the Welsh government's statutory equality duty and states that its 'goal is the creation of a civil society which . . . [is based on] equality of opportunity' (NAW, 2000a). Linked to the scheme is the Voluntary Sector Partnership Council (VSPC), a collection of over twenty policy networks organized around policy areas or social groups, including a network focussed on 'gender' (see also chapter 3). In addition to a range of consultative structures associated with the VSPC, representatives of each network have the right to biannual meetings with government ministers (see Chaney and Fevre, 2001). In respect of Welsh government funding of voluntary organizations the Voluntary Sector Scheme requires the VSPC to determine 'how funding streams can be used to promote equal opportunities by grant beneficiaries' (WAG, 2008c: 8). The latest annual report on the scheme details how the VSPC is a nexus between government and third-sector organizations for policy relating to equalities and mainstreaming (see WAG, 2008c: 12).

Similarly, the Partnership Agreement for Public Services in Wales, an accord between government and public sector bodies, cites equalities as one of its core themes and highlights 'the need for further work to reflect legislative policy changes. The [Partnership Council] stakeholders are committed to developing good practice in partnership with the equality community' (WAG, 2007: 7). In like manner, the Local Government Partnership Scheme asserts that 'Assembly Government will seek to empower local authorities so that they can . . . promote the aim of equality in the local democratic process, access to effective services and employment' (WAG, 2004, section.1.2.4). As well as these statutory partnerships with government, ministerial remit letters, statutory codes of practice and Wales-only legislation provide further key policy transfer mechanisms in relation to the promotion of equalities (Chaney, 2006).

Despite the progress made in developing some of the institutional prerequisites for mainstreaming equality into the work of government, three successive reviews of the Welsh Assembly Government's approach to equalities and mainstreaming have highlighted a number of significant shortcomings and areas for improvement. We now turn to consider these and the government's response. We conclude with an assessment of the current position and future prospects for gender mainstreaming by the Welsh government.

The government's response to the mainstreaming review

The beginning of the Assembly's second term saw the commencement of a systematic, cross-party review into 'how equality can be mainstreamed into the work of the National Assembly and the Welsh Assembly Government' (NAW, 2004: 5). The mainstreaming review was organized around four key themes: strategy and leadership; people; practical action, levers, guidance and advice; and monitoring and evaluation. It is significant that a systematic review of mainstreaming in government took place at such an early stage in the development of the National Assembly. Within an international perspective such a comprehensive review of mainstreaming in government has few precedents.

The review's conclusions in respect of 'strategy and leadership' were an indictment of the equalities minister[3] and senior policy officials. Using stark language, it concluded that: 'currently the Assembly does not have an overall equality strategy, and in our view there is no doubt that this is hampering the Assembly's efforts in relation to mainstreaming equality'. It continued, 'there is a lot of positive activity going on but with little strategic direction ... there [is] a high level of variation across the organization' (NAW, 2004: 31–2). A review of government policies bears this out. A key failing has been the absence of a systematic and robust process of setting equality targets and subsequent monitoring of whether policy goals have been met. Figure 2.1. details rare examples of where gender equality outcomes can be linked to government policies; these are by far the exception rather than the rule.

Careers advice

The public sector careers advice service Careers Wales has developed policies to challenge gender perceptions of career choice.* In 2007, the Welsh state education inspectorate produced a policy evaluation report that concluded: 'there are examples of good practice in each of the Careers Wales companies ... commitment at chief executive and senior management level to setting challenging targets and putting robust monitoring and reporting processes in place to take forward equality and diversity, including gender stereotyping' (Estyn, 2007: 5).

Public appointments

Between 1 April 2006 and 31 March 2007, 180 appointments and reappointments were made to bodies regulated by the Office of the Commissioner for Public Appointments (OCPA) in Wales. Statistics show that the diversity of those appointed is improving, and better reflecting the make-up of the population of Wales. In 2006–7, the percentage of females appointed was 48% (WAG, 2008: 18).**

Education

In 2001 the Welsh state schools curriculum authority ACCAC produced guidance on the opportunities in the school curriculum to teach and learn about issues of equality and diversity relating to disability, gender and race. In 2005, the state education inspectorate produced a policy evaluation report that concluded: 'many schools have reviewed the content of textbooks and purchased new books that have less cultural and gender bias ... Most schools address discrimination and stereotyping in schemes of work ... This is generally done well and is reflected in the increased understanding and awareness that pupils have of these issues' (Estyn, 2005: 27).***

Economic development

Equality of opportunity was one of the cross-cutting themes of the multi-billion-pound European Structural Fund economic aid programmes between 2000–2006. The policy document that set out the targets of the programme stated: 'gender is a major cause of inequality of opportunity in the West Wales and the Valleys region and

* Estyn (2007). A Report on the Careers Services in Wales: Good Practice in how Careers Wales Companies Challenge Gender Stereotyping, Cardiff: Estyn.
** WAG (2008). The Eighth Annual Equality Report: 2006--2007, Cardiff: WAG, p.18.
*** Estyn (2005). *Equal opportunities and Diversity in Schools in Wales*, Survey on the implementation of ACCAC guidance on the promotion of equal opportunities and diversity (2001), Cardiff: Estyn.

that the labour market is characterized by horizontal, vertical and contractual segregation. A key to addressing this issue is to pursue gender mainstreaming in projects'.**** A 2006 evaluation report gave the following assessment of policy outcomes:

Objective 1 target 30% of start up Small Medium Sized Enterprises (SMEs) assisted to be owned by women. Some indication of progress in this area can be obtained from wider labour market data. For the Objective 1 region in 1999/2000 32.7% of the self-employed were female; this had risen to 34.4% in 2003/04. As a comparator, the all-Wales measure had a larger increase from 32.3% in 1999/2000 to 36% in 2003/04.

Objective 1 target 50% of higher level training places to be taken up by women. Enrolments in Higher Education Institutions (HEIs) in Wales (undergraduates and postgraduates) in 1998/99 included 51,890 women (52.8%), which in 2002/03 had risen to 65,576 women (56.1%). This represents an increase of 26.4% of women across Wales.

Objective 1 target to increase female participation rates in the labour market to 70%. The Economic Activity Rate of the Working Age Population of women in the Objective 1 area in 1999/2000 was 67.1%; in 2004/05 this had risen to 71.1% (ECOTEC, 2006).

**** Wales Economic Funding Office (1999) Single Programme Document: Objective One Economic Development Aid for West Wales and the Valleys, Cardiff: WEFO.

Figure 2.1 Examples of gender equality policy outcomes

In response, the review made a range of recommendations. In order to address the variability between government departments it asserted that Assembly government ministers should ensure that equality is mainstreamed in all the policy areas for which they are responsible. It also signalled the need for an ongoing programme of equality training that moved beyond the initial equality awareness instruction given to all Assembly government staff. In addition, it called for improvements in order to address existing shortcomings in the Assembly civil service's capacity to offer advice and guidance – both to internal Assembly government civil service divisions and to external public bodies. Importantly, it highlighted the need for the future use of gender needs assessments and gender budgeting to assess the level of equity in financial allocations.

In many respects the mainstreaming review's conclusions confirmed the findings of an earlier report into the impact of the National Assembly's statutory equality duty commissioned in 2002 by the three statutory equality commissions (Chaney and Fevre, 2002). This found that, between 1999 and 2002, the new duty had led directly to a reprioritization of equality in the process of government such that equality of opportunity was beginning to be addressed systematically at an all-Wales level of government for the first time. Yet, as with the subsequent mainstreaming review, it also highlighted a number of key failings in the post-devolution equality agenda. These included the fact that the National Assembly's policy committees were generally failing to oversee the mainstreaming of equality into their respective policy making areas. Moreover, it was found that the majority of policies exhibited a 'declaratory' approach to equalities – meaning that they espoused the need for change but were often vague on the means to achieve reform. Crucially, the 2002 report found that in the bulk of cases policies lacked specific and measurable equality targets linked to a prescribed time frame. Compounding this problem was the fact that policies generally failed to specify the individuals or organizations responsible for implementing equality reforms. In addition, the report's analysis showed that financial and human resource implications were frequently ignored or not addressed in a comprehensive manner (Chaney and Fevre, 2002: 78).

In response to the mainstreaming review, Cabinet approved the Welsh Assembly Government's new mainstreaming strategy on 8 May 2006 (WAG, 2006). According to the government, the strategy 'will ensure equality and diversity considerations are integral to the development of all its policies and strategies enabling it to meet and exceed its statutory duties' (WAG, 2006: 5). In September 2006, seven years on from her initial strategy paper on mainstreaming equalities, business minister Jane Hutt AM's introductory comments to the National Assembly's Equality Committee on the government's mainstreaming strategy provide an insight into the government's view of the progress made to date. She stated:

> when we consider how we change hearts and minds, it is about how we can enable the integration of the thinking, the planning and the policy making with mainstreaming equality, so that it is integrated into the everyday work of the civil service, and then, hopefully, the whole Welsh public service. That is beginning to emerge, *although it obviously has to be tested in terms of delivery.* (NAW, 2006a: 26, emphasis added).

Opposition parties' comments reflect evident frustration at the limited rate of progress. For example, Helen Mary Jones AM (Plaid Cymru) said: 'the Minister will understand if there is a slight sense of déjà vu for some of us present, because it has taken us a long time to get to this position'. She continued, 'to get this agenda sorted out, and I am sure that the Minister would agree, we really must have a political commitment to give it a priority'.[4]

In 2007 the new equalities minister Brian Gibbons AM (Welsh Labour) reaffirmed that the political commitment was in place to deliver the strategy:

> it is not in doubt that equality is firmly part of the strategic thinking of the Welsh Assembly Government, and is clearly at the heart of our policy-making process. The challenge for every Cabinet Minister and their departments is to show how the actions undertaken have made a difference to the lives of individuals across our diverse communities.[5]

Institutional resistance to mainstreaming within the government bureaucracy is a factor that needs to be considered when looking for an explanation of the slow progress made towards mainstreaming up until 2006. This refers to some overt but mostly covert ways in which organizational elites operate to subvert reforms that conflict with their traditional norms, interests and values. As such they are notoriously hard to research, particularly in closed organizational contexts such as government bureaucracies (cf. Dierickx, 2003). Indeed, frustration with one official's response to proposed equality reforms led an opposition AM to speak of 'the way that cultures within organizations can unconsciously protect themselves against change . . . and this has got "unconscious resistance" written through it like a stick of Brighton rock'.[6]

The government's 2006 mainstreaming strategy was linked to an independent externally commissioned equality audit of Assembly government policies, strategies and programmes (NAW, 2007). A 'stocktaking' exercise, its purpose was to provide information on the extent to which equality and diversity were embedded in policymaking. As with the two previous reviews, the audit highlighted a number of key shortcomings including that: 'delivering equality as a fundamental theme throughout policy implementation was not always articulated within policy documents'. Reflecting earlier concerns over a 'declaratory' approach to equalities, the equality audit stated that policy documents: 'did not always directly refer to how they would – or direct others to – fulfil and go beyond their legislative obligations in order to eliminate discrimination, promoting equality of opportunity and good relations'. Moreover, the audit underlined the fact that, in the government's policies, 'direct reference to explicit measures for monitoring diversity strands was rarely evident'. Importantly, the study found that, 'the understanding of the purpose and systematic processes of [equalities] impact assessment appeared to be limited' (NAW, 2007: 63–5).

Opposition AMs debating the latest annual report on the government's approach to equalities emphasized these findings. For example, David Melding AM (Welsh Conservatives) observed:

> it is about time, given that the single equality scheme is about to be produced, for us to get this right in having a really rigorous approach. That will do an enormous amount for the equalities agenda. We must recognize the importance of measuring the difference that government action makes . . . rather than simply measuring what it does.[7]

In addition, Eleanor Burnham AM (Welsh Liberal Democrat) highlighted another key problem relating to the dearth of equalities data: 'there is still an inadequate evidence base, and that needs to be rectified before we can quantify the effects of policies to promote equality'.[8]

In response to these critical views, the Welsh government's mainstreaming strategy sets out the difference mainstreaming is intended to make to policy development. It states that:

> We will develop, pilot and disseminate tools that take a generic approach to equality and diversity, standardized across [ministerial] portfolio areas. We will develop a tool kit which guides work cross-strand and thematically. We have already developed a number of successful tools that better enable us to consider some equality and diversity dimensions in our work. (WAG, 2006: 7)

A key aspect of the strategy is the introduction of Single Equality Action Plans.[9] According to the government, these 'will provide clarity over [government] departments' equality priorities. This will enable those developing policy to focus on the equality outcomes that are of the greatest significance to the respective department' (NAW, 2007: 3). The latter is a potentially significant development, one that is restated in the latest government annual report on its equalities policies. This asserts: 'in the Action Plans departments have been asked to identify key objectives within their Operational Plans *along with their outcomes across all equality strands*' (WAG, 2007a: 15, emphasis added). If fully implemented, the provision of such equality indicators or benchmarks will go a long way to facilitating effective evaluation of the impact of government equalities policies 'on the ground' in terms of whether they have succeeded or failed.

The mainstreaming strategy has also placed greater focus upon the development of mainstreaming tools – notably, through a commitment to the development of a generic 'cross strand' equality impact assessment tool (that is, one capable of simultaneously assessing the equality implications of policy in relation to more than one equality 'strand'). This policy tool emerged in 2008 and is set out in the document *Inclusive Policymaking Toolkit* (WAG, 2008). It is aimed at assisting in all areas of policymaking and sets out a fixed impact assessment procedure for officials to follow (see figure 2.2). The toolkit advises officials:

> if the evidence suggests that there is actual or potential differential impact, or opportunities to promote equality, a Full Impact Assessment is required to identify all the implications of the policy on each of the equality groups. It will also assist you to identify what actions can be taken to remove or minimize negative effects and to avoid illegal discrimination. (WAG, 2008a: 4)

Whilst such developments may reflect a technical or 'expert bureaucratic approach'[10] to gender mainstreaming (Donaghy, 2004) there is also evidence of a commitment to the participatory dimension of mainstreaming. The 2006 mainstreaming strategy states:

> The Assembly has a statutory duty formally to consult with individuals and organizations and engage them in discussing, shaping and delivering policy. To complete this process we must consider the impact of a policy in the widest possible terms and engage with all those who could be affected, including under-represented groups. We have a process in place that provides our policy makers with guidance on best practice in consultation, and further work in train where this needs to be developed. This process should be reviewed to ensure it is fit for purpose in the new context and is proactive in generating policy to promote equality. (WAG, 2006: 10)

In relation to securing equality in decision making (a key precondition of mainstreaming), November 2006 saw the launch of the government's Diversity Delivery Plan (WAG, 2007b). This set targets for the percentage of women, minority ethnic and disabled staff in the senior civil service. Whilst the numbers of Welsh speakers, disabled people

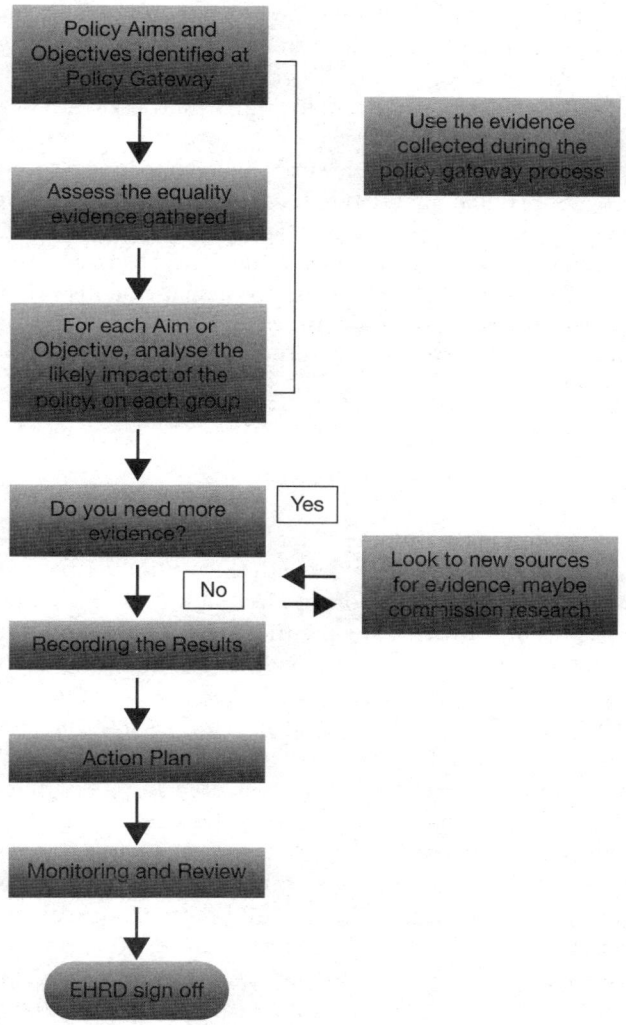

Figure 2.2 The Welsh Assembly Government's equality impact assessment procedure*

Source: WAG, 2008.

* Key to terms/ abbreviations: 'Policy Gateway' = the Assembly government's policy development tool for officials; 'EHRD' = Equality and Human Rights Division of the Assembly government.

and those from an ethnic minority background remain disappointingly low, there is evidence of some progress towards gender balance. Data show that the number of women holding the most senior grades within the Assembly government increased from a total of 25.6 per cent in January 2000 to 35 per cent by March 2007 (WAG, 2007b: 5)

Overall, the government's response to the mainstreaming review can be viewed as potentially noteworthy in a number of respects. Not least, it has resulted in official recognition of existing failings. Moreover, through the publication of the strategy (and associated documents) it has begun to set out measures to embed mainstreaming tools into the policy process in a more systematic manner than seen hitherto. We now turn to consider the significance and implications of these developments in relation to future policymaking practices and equalities outcomes.

Discussion

The evidence of the first decade of the National Assembly shows that there are significant discontinuities with the previous era of administrative devolution. The promotion of equalities by government in Wales has been prioritized for the first time. This is an important shift in the political framing of equalities and it echoes aspects of the post-devolution experience in Scotland (see Breitenbach, 2006; Breitenbach and Gallighan, 2006). These changes have, in part, been symbolic in nature and concerned with signalling a break with the past, none more so than the announcement in July 1999 that mainstreaming would inform all policymaking. Subsequent developments have included new institutional mechanisms such as the Equality and Human Rights Division in the government and the state sponsoring of equalities policy networks. Significantly, the structures of devolved governance such as the formal statutory partnership arrangements between government and the voluntary, public and private sectors – as well as ministerial remit letters, statutory codes of practice and Wales-only legislation – provide a further key mechanism whereby equalities policies at the Assembly level can be transferred to other areas of economic and political life. A further notable aspect of the difference that devolution has made has been the new discursive practices around equalities in politics and policymaking. Whilst it is important not to overstate these developments it is also necessary not to overlook their worth – for, as noted, prior to 1999 there was generally an absence of political will, institutional practices and expertise to promote equalities in Welsh public policy.

However, a key question is the extent to which the Welsh government's espousal of mainstreaming has been translated into policy outcomes. No less than three formal reviews into the promotion of equality in public policy during the period 1999–2006 have concluded that, in terms of policy outcomes, the impact of the mainstreaming agenda has been limited. There are few policies from this period that could be highlighted as examples of best practice in mainstreaming. A number of factors can be offered to explain this, not least the reality that mainstreaming is a challenging and bold concept that aims to secure a radical and transformative approach to policymaking. There are few international examples of *established* legislatures that offer an effective template for the application of mainstreaming in government. Against this background, the Welsh government chose to adopt mainstreaming from the outset of the National Assembly in 1999 – yet, at the same time as embracing this ambitious concept, a considerable amount of AMs' and officials' energy and effort was absorbed in the institutional development of the National Assembly (not least in trying to make sense of the legislature's often opaque powers as well as making the cumbersome notion of a 'body corporate' that characterized the 1998 devolution statute a workable reality). As noted, a further brake on progress was presented by the National Assembly's inheritance of the organizational culture of the Welsh Office civil service. This brought with it attendant issues of institutional resistance to the implementation of the mainstreaming agenda.

Overall, devolution has provided government with new structures of governance – as well as policy- and law-making powers, to secure the transfer of equalities policies from a government level to society and the economy in general. However, the evidence to date suggests that these opportunities have not been exploited to the fullest extent. Given the protracted period applying to these shortcomings, a further related concern is the adequacy of the scrutiny offered by opposition parties, backbench AMs and external organizations with an interest in equalities – as well as the robustness of public sector inspection regimes in respect of the government's statutory duty to 'have due regard to the principle that there should be equality of opportunity for all people'.

Against the background of a broadening of the British and European legal framework around equalities witnessed over the past decade it is also salient to ask whether there has been a comparative decrease in the visibility of gender equality. There is evidence to support this. Not least because from the outset the Welsh government has applied a *generic* approach to *equalities* mainstreaming – rather than a specific focus on *gender* mainstreaming. It is also pertinent to note here that, in the early years of the Assembly, prioritizing gender (and race and disability) was formalized in the legislature's procedural law or standing orders. These stated that 'the [Equality] Committee shall also have *particular regard* to the need for the Assembly to avoid discrimination against any person on grounds of race, sex or disability' (NAW, 2000b, standing order 14.1, emphasis added). Over time both the Welsh government and the legislature's cross-party Equality Committee have broadened the focus of their equalities work (as typified by policy work in relation to a range of social groups including gypsy travellers; migrant workers; asylum seekers; faith groups; and lesbian, gay and bisexual people). Furthermore, in terms of the institutional arrangements around the representation of equalities interests, there has been the same broadening of focus – as exemplified by Stonewall Cymru and the Welsh Language Board joining the three statutory equality commissions as permanent advisors to the Equality Committee during the second Assembly. Overall, the picture has been one of increasing competition as other equalities groups and organizations have jostled to make their policy demands on government.

The resulting decline in the visibility of gender does not necessarily reflect a downgrading of gender equality as a policy priority. Rather, it can also be viewed in the context of the growing attention to intersectionality in both feminist politics and contemporary equalities practices (cf. Yuval-Davis, 2006); a shift that is acknowledged in the Welsh government's mainstreaming strategy: 'every project, programme, policy or strategy must begin with a clear understanding of its impact in respect of equality and diversity across all the [equality] dimensions' (WAG, 2006: 2). A positive interpretation of this development is that it may allow a move away from potentially reductive and essentialist tendencies in equalities practice that project gender as an homogenous social category. Instead, it could facilitate a more nuanced approach that relates to multiple and simultaneous identities shaped not only by gender but cross-cut by characteristics such as faith, language, economic status and sexual orientation. This point was acknowledged by the equalities minister when, reflecting on the government's mainstreaming strategy, he said: 'no-one fits into designated boxes, and a single equality scheme will better allow us to address that'.[11]

Weighed against such developments, how can the Welsh government's record in relation to mainstreaming gender and other dimensions of equality be summarized? In general, the period 1999–2006 can be characterized as one of 'institutional decoupling' (Chaney, 2006) – or the means by which an organization manages a disjuncture between formal rules, informal practices and actual activities – such that it espouses one thing but generally practices another (Meyer and Rowan, 1991; Dahlström, 2004). Linked to this there has been an emphasis on bureaucratic processes associated with government equalities initiatives rather than the results that they achieve. This is a point repeatedly emphasized by observers of the developing equalities agenda – as typified by the comments of Helen Mary Jones AM (Plaid Cymru) who observed: 'we still have a long way to go before we will be focusing sufficiently on outcomes – the actual difference that the policy action has made to the people that the actions are aiming to help and support'.[12]

Given the mixed progress that has been made to date, what can be said of the future prospects for mainstreaming? Here, the government's 2006 mainstreaming strategy is a potentially significant development; one that may offer the means to deliver the original 1999 commitment to mainstreaming. Frustratingly, the hiatus in the process of government around the period of the May 2007 elections to the National Assembly, the subsequent necessity to implement the wide-ranging provisions of the Government of Wales Act (2006), the extended inter-party negotiations over forming a coalition government in 2007 – together with a protracted timetable for the implementation of some of the measures set out in the mainstreaming strategy – all combine to preclude this account from offering a full evidence-based assessment of the effectiveness of the devolved government's revised post-2006 approach to mainstreaming. However, what is detectable is evidence of a more joined-up and systematic approach to mainstreaming equalities than seen hitherto. Notably, through the development of mainstreaming tools – including new equality impact assessment procedures and improved equalities data gathering designed to inform both policymaking and policy evaluation. There is also emerging, albeit limited, evidence that these measures are beginning to shape the way that new policy documents address gender equality concerns.[13]

Notwithstanding these factors, there remain a number of causes for concern. For example, despite the recommendations of the main-streaming review, there is an absence of any reference to gender budgeting in the mainstreaming strategy.[14] In addition, although the strategy articulates its aims in relation to seven equality 'strands' (WAG, 2006: 3) the new generic equalities impact assessment tool is based upon six strands – for it omits language (see WAG, 2008b).[15] However, an overriding concern relates to the legislative and policy scrutiny capacity of an undersized sixty-member National Assembly (see, for example, Navarro and Lambert, 2007). This has particular relevance to the mainstreaming agenda and has international reso-nance. As Beveridge and Nott observe, accountability and scrutiny issues are pivotal to success: 'lack of ownership ha[s] served to make it easy for governments to embrace the mainstreaming concept and to adopt policy initiatives in its name'. (2002: 299) The formalisation of a quasi-parliamentary mode of devolution in 2006–7 finally gives *de jure* 'ownership' of the mainstreaming agenda to the Welsh govern-ment.[16] Under the provisions of the Government of Wales Act (2006) responsibility for meeting the statutory duty to promote equality in all devolved policy- and law-making lies with Welsh government minis-ters. Thus, it is argued, a key factor in the future success or failure of mainstreaming will be the role of opposition parties and external bodies (including, potentially, the Equality and Human Rights Commission)[17] in holding the government to account in relation to its statutory equality duty and delivery of its mainstreaming strategy. This scrutiny role should be made easier by the strategy's promise to deliver 'a clear equality and diversity baseline and monitor[ing] targets. . . [in order to] evaluate how effective policy is in achieving its aims' (WAG, 2006: 19). Furthermore, scrutiny of the effectiveness of the government's mainstreaming strategy will also be facilitated by section 77 of the 2006 devolution statute, clause 2 of which states that: 'after each financial year the Welsh Ministers must publish a report containing . . . an assessment of how effective those arrangements were in promoting equality of opportunity, and must lay a copy of the report before the Assembly'. Thus, in addition to the government's competence and commitment, the extent to which opposition parties and external organizations draw upon on the aforementioned legal and policy developments to provide effective scrutiny will be a key factor in determining whether it is déjà vu or delivery time for main-streaming in public policy.

Notes

[1] Hitherto known as the Equality Policy Unit and the Strategic Equality and Diversity Unit.

[2] These replace similar clauses in the Government of Wales Act (1998), e.g. sections 114, 115 and 120.

[3] Edwina Hart AM.

[4] The Record of Proceedings, Tuesday, 6 November 2007.

[5] Ibid.

[6] Helen Mary Jones AM, Proceedings of the Assembly Equality Committee, 30 January 2002, S4C2 TV.

[7] The Record of Proceedings, Tuesday, 6 November 2007.

[8] Ibid.

[9] From April 2008

[10] Donaghy (2004: 51). 'The expert-bureaucratic model relies heavily on a 'gender' expert(s) being located within the bureaucracy, such as a women's unit, and has been popular in countries such as Australia (both at federal and state levels), New Zealand and Canada. The participative-democratic model is the more recently developed (and tends to be the model which is most likely to incorporate multiple equality areas). It relies primarily on the participation of civic and community groups through a consultation process.'

[11] The Record of Proceedings, Tuesday, 6 November 2007.

[12] Ibid.

[13] See, for example, Environment Strategy for Wales (2006): 'Reducing greenhouse gas emissions / Pollution – specifically any future actions to reduce emissions – Relevant to race, gender and disability equality strands due to differing emission patterns, for example as a result of different patterns of car ownership' (p. 67); and the Social Services Strategy for Wales, "Fulfilled Lives, Supportive Communities' (2007): 'It is important that the principles of quality, responsiveness and equality will become core features of social care in Wales. In tailoring services to the needs of individuals and their carers, social services need to take account of religious, cultural, and ethnic needs as well as age, gender and sexual orientation' (p.20). For a further discussion see Chaney (2008).

[14] NAW (2004: 64) 'Recommendation 20: We recommend that the Assembly Government pilots gender budgeting in a policy area to assess the level of equity in financial allocations, with a view to expanding its use across the Assembly.' The Welsh government's Annual Equality Report (2007) notes: 'the Finance Department is providing support to policy colleagues on gender budgeting. These are the tools and processes designed to facilitate a gender analysis in the formulation of budgets and the allocation of resources. This will enable understanding of the differential impact of spending on the two genders' (WAG, 2007: 18).

[15] WAG (2008). *Inclusive Policy Making: Full Impact Assessment*, Cardiff: WAG. See especially the pro forma for policy officials on p. 7. There are no incidences of the word 'language' or 'Welsh' in the document.

[16] In legal terms, under s.120 of the Government of Wales Act (1998) the Welsh statutory duty to have due regard to equalities applied to the National Assembly as a whole up until May 2007. Subsequently, the Government of Wales Act (2006) separated the executive and legislative branches and placed the duty on Welsh ministers (see s.77).

[17] The Equality Act (2006) that sets out the powers and functioning of the EHRC gives the commission enforcement powers over the Welsh government in relation to adherence to the GB-wide race, gender and disability acts but not S.77 of the Government of Wales Act (2006) that requires Welsh ministers to 'make appropriate arrangements with a view to securing that their functions are exercized with due regard to the principle that there should be equality of opportunity for all people'. Time will determine the extent to which the EHRC scrutinizes the Welsh government's actions in relation to s.77.

References

Bache, I. and M. Flinders (eds) (2005). *Multi-level Governance*, Oxford: Oxford University Press.

Beckwith, K. (2003). 'The gendering ways of states: women's representation and state reconfiguration in France, Great Britain and the United States', in L. Banaszak, K. Beckwith and D. Rucht (eds), *Women's Movements Facing the Reconfigured State*, Cambridge: Cambridge University Press, pp. 169–203.

Beveridge, F. and S. Nott (2002). 'Mainstreaming: a case for optimism and cynicism', *Feminist Legal Studies*, 10, 299–311.

Breitenbach, E. (2006). *The Scottish Executive and Equality*, paper presented to the ESRC public policy, equality and diversity in the context of devolution seminar, School of Education, Edinburgh University.

—— and Y. Galligan (2006). 'Measuring gender equality: reflecting on experiences and challenges in the UK and Ireland', *Policy and Politics*, 34, 4, 597–614.

Bulmer, S., B. Martin, C. Christopher and P. Hogwood (2002). *British Devolution and European Policy-making: Transforming Britain into Multi-level Governance*, Basingstoke: Palgrave Macmillan.

Chaney, P. (2004). 'The post-devolution equality agenda: the case of Welsh assembly's statutory duty to promote equality of opportunity', *Policy and Politics*, 32, 1, 37–52.

—— (2006). *The Devolved Context: Matrix of Welsh Public Policy and Law – Advice and Guidance to Public Service Providers: Promoting Multi-*

Strand Equality in the Welsh legislative Context and Beyond – An Interim Report to the Project Group of the Commission for Equality and Human Rights Cross–Strand Modelling Project, Cardiff: CEHR Transition Group.

—— (2007). 'Strategic women, elite advocacy and insider strategies: the women's movement and constitutional reform in Wales', *Research in Social Movements, Conflicts and Change*, 27, 123–55.

—— (2008). 'Devolved governance and the substantive representation of women: the second term of the National Assembly for Wales, 2003–2007', *Parliamentary Affairs*, 61, 2, 272–90.

—— and R. Fevre (2001). 'Inclusive governance and "minority" groups: the role of the third sector in Wales', *Voluntas — International Journal of Third Sector Research*, 12, 2, 131–56.

—— and R. Fevre (2002). *The Equality Policies of the Government of the National Assembly for Wales and their Implementation*, Cardiff: Institute of Welsh Affairs.

—— and T. Rees (2004). 'The Northern Ireland section 75 equality duty: an international perspective', in E. McLaughlin and N. Faris (eds), *Northern Ireland Office – The Section 75 Equality Duty – An Operational Review*, vol. 2, Belfast: Northern Ireland Office, pp. 1–51.

——, F. Mackay and L. McAllister (2007). *Women, Politics and Constitutional Change*, Cardiff: University of Wales Press.

Council of Europe (CoE) (2004). *http://www.coe.int/T/E/Human_Rights/Equality/02._Gender_mainstreaming*

Dierickx, G. (2003). 'Senior civil servants and bureaucratic change in Belgium', *Governance*, 16, 3, 321–48.

Donaghy, T. B. (2004). 'Applications of mainstreaming in Australia and Northern Ireland', *International Political Science Review*, 25, 4, 393–410.

ECOTEC (2006). Cross-cutting Themed Research Project (Objectives 1 and 3), Final Report, C3008/April 2006, Cardiff: ECOTEC.

Equal Opportunities Commission (EOC) (2003). *Mainstreaming: Everything you wanted to know about mainstreaming but were afraid to ask*, Manchester: EOC.

Estyn (2005). *Equal Opportunities and Diversity in Schools in Wales*, Cardiff: Estyn.

—— (2007). *A Report on the Careers Service in Wales*, Cardiff: Estyn.

Fredman, S. (2000). 'Equality: A new generation?', *Industrial Law Journal*, 30, 145–16.

Hall, P. A. (1986). *Governing the Economy: The Politics of State Intervention in Britain and France,* Cambridge: Polity Press.

Inter-Agency Network on Women and Gender Equality (IANWGE) (2005). *Summary of the Online Discussions Held in Preparation for the 10 Year Review and Appraisal of the Implementation of the Platform for*

Action in the 49th Session of the Commission on the Status of Women, New York: United Nations.

McBride, D. (1995). *Comparative State Feminism*, New York: Sage.

Mackay, F. and K. Bilton (2000). *Learning from Experience: Lessons in Mainstreaming Equal Opportunities*, Edinburgh: University of Edinburgh, the Governance of Scotland Forum.

National Assembly for Wales (NAW) (1999). *The Approach to Equal Opportunities*, paper presented to the Assembly Equality Committee, July 1999, Cardiff: NAW.

—— (2000a). *Voluntary Sector Scheme*, Cardiff: NAW.

—— (2000b). Standing Orders, Cardiff: NAW.

—— (2001). *Equality Training and Awareness Strategy for Assembly Staff* (October 2001), Cardiff: NAW.

—— (2002). *The National Assembly For Wales, Code of Practice for Ministerial Appointments To Public Bodies,* Cardiff: NAW.

—— (2004). *Mainstreaming Review*, Cardiff: NAW.

—— (2006a). *Transcript of Proceedings, the National Assembly for Wales Committee on Equality of Opportunity*, 27 September, Cardiff: NAW.

—— (2006b). *Mainstreaming Equality into the Work of the Welsh Assembly Government*, WAG paper presented to the National Assembly Equality of Opportunity Committee, February 28, Cardiff: NAW.

—— (2007). *Policy Review Project Report*, papers of the National Assembly Equality of Opportunity Committee, February 28, Cardiff: NAW.

Navarro, M. and D. Lambert (2007). 'Some effects of the Government of Wales Act 2006: the Welsh journey from administrative decentralization passing through executive devolution to quasilegislative devolution in less than eight years', *Contemporary Wales*, 20, 13–30.

Pollack, M. A. and E. Hafner-Burton (2000). 'Mainstreaming gender in the European Union', *Journal of European Public Policy*, 7, 3, 432–56.

Rawlings, R. (1998). 'The new model Wales', *Journal of Law and Society*, 25, 4, 461–509.

Rees, T. (1998). *Mainstreaming Equality in the European Union*, London: Routledge.

—— (2002). 'The politics of mainstreaming gender equality', in E. Breitenbach, A. Brown, F. Mackay and J. Webb (eds), *The Changing Politics of Gender Equality in Britain*, Basingstoke: Palgrave, pp. 84–97.

Stetson, D. M. and A. G. Mazur (1995). 'Introduction', in D. M. Stetson and A. G. Mazur (eds), *Comparative State Feminism*, Thousand Oaks: Sage, pp. 1–23.

United Nations (UN) (1995) *Global Platform for Action – Beijing*, New York: UN.

—— (2001). *United Nations Administrative Committee on Coordination, Interagency Meeting on Women and Gender Equality Report*, workshop on approaches and methodologies for gender mainstreaming, 27 February – 2 March, New York: UN.

Walby, S. (2005). 'Gender mainstreaming: productive tensions between theory and practice', *International Feminist Journal of Politics*, 7, 4, 321–43.

Welsh Assembly Government (WAG) (2001). *Equality Training and Awareness Strategy for Assembly Staff*, Cardiff: WAG.

—— (2004). *Local Government Partnership Scheme*, Cardiff: WAG.

—— (2006). *Mainstreaming Equality in the Work of the National Assembly*, paper presented to the National Assembly Equality of Opportunity Committee, 27 September, Cardiff: NAW.

—— (2007). *Equality Report on Staffing 2006–07*, Cardiff: WAG.

—— (2007). *Welsh Assembly Government's Race, Disability and Gender Summary Progress Report 2006–2007*, Cardiff: WAG.

—— (2007a). *Partnership and Managing Change: A Partnership Agreement for Public Services in Wales*, Cardiff: WAG.

—— (2008a). *Inclusive Policymaking Toolkit*, Cardiff: WAG.

—— (2008b). *Inclusive Policy Making: Full Impact Assessment*, Cardiff: WAG.

—— (2008c). *Voluntary Sector Scheme Annual Report 2006–07*, Cardiff: WAG.

Yuval-Davis, N. (2006). 'Intersectionality and feminist politics', *European Journal of Women's Studies*, 13, 3, 193–209.

3

Gender and Political Representation: Views from the Grass Roots

SANDRA BETTS

The nature and extent of citizens' participation in politics has been a major topic of debate in recent decades (Parry et al., 1992, Verba et al., 1978, 1995). Participation lies at the very heart of conceptualizations of democracy (Pateman, 1970; Dahl, 1989) such that 'where few take part in decisions there is little democracy' (Verba and Nie, 1972: 1). According to this argument the trend of public disengagement with politics witnessed in Europe and North America over recent decades serves to undermine democracy. Devolution in the United Kingdom is a prominent example of recent reforms aimed at countering this trend and re-engaging citizens in politics in order to create a more inclusive and participatory democracy (Welsh Office, 1997: 13).

At the heart of the movement to modernize government is the idea that government is both more effective and more legitimate if more people get involved in making decisions, particularly the decisions that affect them personally. This is the rationale for innovations in governance that create new opportunities for the organizations of civil society, for example, voluntary organizations, to participate in decision making. The devolution programme places emphasis not only on revising the structures but also on the process of governance, notably in relation to policymaking. 'Inclusiveness' is a keystone of the new approach (Cabinet Office, 1999: 4, para.7). This is seen in terms of 'ensuring that policy makers take as full account as possible of the impact the policy will have on different groups – families, businesses, ethnic minorities, older people, the disabled, women – who are affected by the policy' (Cabinet Office, 1999: ch. 8, para. 8.1, unpaginated). In Wales the promise was that 'the National Assembly will be able to develop . . . [a] partnership; the Government will encourage it to harness the special contribution which voluntary organizations can make in a wide range of policy areas' (Welsh Office, 1998: 19). This plan also stated that 'greater participation by women is essential to the health of our democracy' and concluded that 'by establishing the National Assembly the government is moving the process of decision-making closer to the citizen' (Welsh Office, 1997: 15, paras 3.1–3.2 and 24, para. 4.7; NAAG, 1998: 26, para. 4). Such inclusive language was used to argue that increasing citizen activism and securing greater involvement of civil society groups in government not only strengthened democracy but also had the potential to deliver more effective governance (Paterson and Wyn Jones, 1999: 183)

In Wales the voluntary sector is at the heart of National Assembly policy to promote participation. The 1998 Government of Wales Act required the National Assembly to show how in the exercise of its functions it would promote the interests of relevant voluntary organizations. Consequently, a new and singular statutory partnership between national Welsh government and the voluntary sector is enshrined in the constitutional reform together with a unique legal duty requiring that government promote equality of opportunity for all people in the exercise of its functions. The Voluntary Sector Scheme, adopted by the National Assembly in July 2000, sets out commitments to designate a named minister to have specific responsibility for the interests of the voluntary sector, while expecting every part of the National Assembly – Cabinet, committees and officials – to promote the interests of the voluntary sector in its work and decision making. The scheme underpins the work of the Voluntary Sector Partnership Council (VSPC) which provides an interface between the voluntary sector and elected politicians. It comprises National Assembly Members, the WCVA (Wales Council for Voluntary Action) and representatives of the twenty-one voluntary sector networks in Wales. These interest-based consultative policy networks have been created to reflect the breadth of voluntary activity in Wales. They are predominantly comprised of voluntary organizations that represent the interests of previously marginalized groups (see Chaney et al., 2001; Chaney et al., 2007). One such network is the Wales Women's National Coalition (WWNC) – the 'gender strand' of the Voluntary Sector Partnership Council. Founded in 1997, WWNC is a partnership of national women's voluntary organizations in Wales and organizations consisting mainly of women. It is the gender equality policy network seeking to promote the best interests of women in Wales and to promote the participation of women in decision making at all levels. Funded from 2001 to 2010 by the Welsh Assembly Government, the coalition's terms of reference state that this umbrella body aims to be 'a forum through which the National Assembly for Wales can consult women'. It was described by the minister who chaired the Equality Committee in 2001 as 'our arm in the community . . . we can use them as our sounding board and vice versa. So what we'd like is a bottom up process so people can say these are the genuine equality issues.'

WWNC has a broad and diverse membership ranging from what might be termed 'single issue' groups such as Women in Agriculture, to what are effectively distinct women's networks in their own right, such as the Wales Assembly of Women. Whilst this diversity may be viewed as a strength it may also present problems. The WWNC 2001 Memorandum of Association stated:

> The Coalition membership represents a wide range of women in Wales from all walks of life. The membership itself has a wealth of expertise which will be utilized, and we will endeavour to extend the Coalition membership further and target groups where we are under represented or lack expertise. (WWNC, 2001)

Membership has expanded from just over twenty affiliated organizations in 2005 to thirty-three organizations in 2008 and WWNC remains the key consultative umbrella organization representing women's views to policymakers in Wales. However, its journey has not been without problems, as will be discussed and evidenced later in this chapter, and a 'rebranding' of WWNC has recently taken place together with a rethink of some of its aims and activities. For WWNC the early years of devolution have been a journey of discovery and a learning curve. New levels of participation in governance have presented a series of ongoing challenges and issues for women's groups and organizations. WWNC has been pivotal in this and remains crucial to current and future attempts to reach out and encourage the political participation of women in Wales.

The promise of devolution is one of greater public participation and involvement in policy- and decision-making. As Day et al. note,

> the notion of 'inclusivity' has been pervasive in both political rhetoric and the emerging new political culture of Wales. Part of the inclusiveness has been a determined effort by the National Assembly to work more

closely with the voluntary sector in Wales in an attempt realistically to engage with civil society. (Day et al., 2006: 3)

Whether these promises are fulfilled and whether devolution does in fact make government more effective and legitimate depends on the way the new innovations work out in practice. For example, it depends on exactly how the organizations of civil society are able to access and use the new opportunities to ensure that they are able to pursue the interests of their constituencies and involve the people they represent in decision making. It also depends on the degree to which the policies produced by the new structures meet the needs and wants of those whom these organizations seek to represent.

Such concerns about improving (in political or economic terms) the position of marginalized groups and developing a partnership with civil society are central to recent debates about social capital (Portes, 1995, 1998; Baron et al., 2000). These debates direct our focus to the social networks and norms that underpin civil society and collective action more generally (Portes, 1998). Putnam (2001) focuses on the ability of civil society to generate social capital – the idea that our social networks can engender norms, trust and reciprocity, elements that can act as the social glue that makes society cohesive, encourage a civic culture and combat a lack of engagement in the political process. Strong social capital is viewed as the bedrock of civil society and is, therefore, something that policymakers are keen to encourage. But the crucial question is whether social capital can be 'encouraged' in a 'top-down' manner? Whether statutory duties and new mechanisms can in fact widen participation in the political process? Social capital theory suggests that the success of the attempts to bring marginalized groups into decision making rests on the existence of particular social ties between the ordinary members of these groups and the people acting as their representatives, and between the latter and policymakers. (Woolcock, 1998; Putnam, 1993). Drawing upon the findings of a major research project, the remainder of this chapter will consider the extent to which the National Assembly's new measures and mechanisms were successful in widening the participation of women – a previously marginalized group – in the decision-making process in the early years of devolution.[1]

One aim of the research reported here was to investigate the nature and extent of women's participation in the work of devolved government. We wished to assess the quantity and quality of women's participation in decision-making within the new structures. The

National Assembly had issued an invitation to women and to other previously marginalized groups to be included and to participate in governance. To what extent had the invitation been received and accepted? A number of interviews with managers of women's NGOs (non-governmental organizations) were undertaken, and an extensive survey of grass-roots members of women's groups and organizations was carried out in 2002–3. The main focus here is on the survey results. See Chaney et al. (2007) for discussion of the views of managers and officers of NGOs.

Women's organizations

A range of women's organizations formed the basis of this study.[2] Most were indigenous Welsh organizations, although some were Welsh federations of GB or UK bodies. The groups ranged from small campaigning bodies with under 150 members (for example, Women in Agriculture), to traditional long-established, mass-membership women's organizations (such as the Women's Institute). Some, such as Welsh Women's Aid (WWA) and Women's Royal Voluntary Service (WRVS) were not membership organizations but service providers. Most were located in the voluntary sector, the exceptions being trade associations (Royal College of Nursing) and women trade unionists (from UNISON Wales/Cymru and TGWU). The majority were organizations that belonged to the Wales Women's National Coalition (WWNC), the National Assembly-sponsored umbrella body/policy network. Almost two thousand questionnaires were distributed to members of these organizations. The response rate was just over 43 per cent (total of 843 completed questionnaires). The question-naire was wide ranging, concerned to investigate issues of organizational membership, involvement and participation, networks, trust and norms as well as issues relating to devolution and the impact of the National Assembly. It is this latter theme that will be the main focus here.

Belonging to an organization

Women participate in organizations for a wide variety of reasons and with differing motivations. Among the most frequently cited reasons were social reasons (to meet and socialize with others), mentioned by

62 per cent of respondents; to make a difference to a social issue, mentioned by 57 per cent; and to provide a service to others, mentioned by 37 per cent. Influencing politicians and promoting the rights of women were not majority responses for the group as a whole. However, a breakdown of the responses to the question of participation by individual organization revealed some interesting differences. Table 3.1 highlights the top three or four reasons given by respondents in each of the organizations studied.

Table 3.1: Reasons for membership and participation in women's organizations[3]

Wales Assembly of Women	Promote rights of women	80.4%
	Help and be of service	71.4%
	Duty as citizen	71.4%
Chwarae Teg	Promote rights of women	73.0%
	Help and be of service	70.3%
	Duty as citizen	54.1%
Welsh Women's Aid	Promote rights of women	79.5%
	Help and be of service	72.7%
	Duty as citizen	50.0%
Unions	Help and be of service	74.5%
	Duty as citizen	55.9%
	Promote rights of women	38.9%
Agriculture	Duty as a citizen	57.1%
	Influence politicians	47.6%
	Help and be of service	47.6%
Nurses	Help and be of service	50.0%
	Duty as a citizen	20.0%
	Make me a better person	20.0%
	Influence politicians	17.5%
Merched y Wawr	Duty as a citizen	78.1%
	Social reasons	75.6%
	Help and be of service	63.3%
Women's Institute	Duty as a citizen	66.7%
	Social reasons	66.2%
	Help and be of service	64.4%
WRVS	Help and be of service	91.2%
	Duty as citizen	82.4%
	Make me a better person	52.0%

It is clear that issues of helping and being of service to others are central to most women's motives in being part of an organization. So too is the idea of fulfilling one's duty as a citizen. These reasons feature frequently in the responses of women from all organizations. However, focus on other reasons cited and on the rank order of reasons begins to reveal some significant differences between organizations. Members of Wales Assembly of Women, Chwarae Teg and Welsh Women's Aid are clearly motivated by the desire to promote the rights of women. These are promotional, campaigning organizations with a clear brief to advance the cause of women within Welsh society. Members of Merched y Wawr, the Women's Institute (WI) and the WRVS are strongly motivated by social and service reasons. Members of the remaining groups are not so easily classified and to some extent bridge the other two categories. Women trade union members see themselves as providing help and service to others, but also show a concern with promoting the rights of women. Members of Women in Agriculture and the Royal College of Nursing are also motivated by reasons of help and service to others but this is linked to influencing politicians.

The data suggest a possible classification of women's organizations into 'promotional', 'political' and 'social/service' oriented organizations. Members of all groups see themselves as belonging to their organization for reasons of help, service and duty, but members of Wales Assembly of Women, Chwarae Teg and Welsh Women's Aid are also motivated by the cause of promoting women's rights. These are 'promotional' organizations. Members of Women in Agriculture, trade unions and the Royal College of Nursing link notions of duty and service to both promotional and political activity. These are politically oriented organizations. Members of Merched y Wawr, the WI and the WRVS are strongly motivated by duty as citizens but emphasize social and service reasons as underlying their membership. These three organizational groupings – promotional, political and social/service – were used as a framework for investigating members' responses to the impact of devolution and to their participation/inclusion in political processes.

Devolution making a difference? Views from the grass roots

The members of the organizations surveyed were active, civic-minded, involved women. Most invested considerable time and energy in their organization. They were committed members even to the extent of taking the time to complete and return our lengthy questionnaire. If devolution was making a difference on the ground – at grass-roots level – we might expect to see evidence of it amongst these women. However, the overall response of women to the question 'has the National Assembly made a difference to your organization?' showed that only 13.5 per cent of women felt that the Assembly had made a difference; 43.1 per cent said no and 43.4 per cent did not know if it had made a difference. At one level this may seem to be a rather depressing picture, but a more detailed analysis of responses by organizational category revealed substantial variations between groups.

Among members of the promotional groups attitudes towards devolution and to the National Assembly were highly favourable. Well over half the members of Chwarae Teg and nearly one-third of members of Wales Assembly of Women and of Welsh Women's Aid were of the opinion that the National Assembly had made a difference to their organization. By contrast almost half of the members of Merched y Wawr, WI and WRVS (social/service organizations) said that the National Assembly had made no difference to their organization and of the remainder the vast majority did not know if the National Assembly was having any impact.

Similar results were apparent with respect to questions about their organization's working relationship with the National Assembly and about lobbying the Assembly. Members of 'promotional' groups and members of 'political' groups claimed a much stronger relationship with the National Assembly than members of social/service organizations. More than three-quarters (78.4 per cent) of Chwarae Teg members claimed a strong or good working relationship with the National Assembly, as did 48.3 per cent of members of Wales Assembly of Women and 46.5 per cent of Welsh Women's Aid members. By contrast such relations were claimed to exist by only 24.5 per cent of members of Merched y Wawr, 14.2 per cent of members of Women in Agriculture and only 3 per cent of WRVS members. Interestingly, almost one-third of trade union members (32.2 per cent) and over 40 per cent of Royal College of Nursing members claimed strong or good working relations with the National Assembly despite the fact that only very few members of these groups felt that the National Assembly had made a difference to their organization (12.9 per cent and 12.8 per cent respectively).

In order to continue to explore members' broad views on the impact of devolution on their organization, respondents were asked about lobbying activities. The majority reported that their organization had 'lobbied' the National Assembly, but here too there were significant differences between groups. The 'promotional' groups, not surprisingly, figured significantly in this activity with well over three-quarters of members of these groups saying that their organization had lobbied the National Assembly. Similar results were found among members of the 'political' groups: 85.7 per cent of Women in Agriculture members, 64.4 per cent trade union members and 60 per cent of Royal College of Nursing members reported that their organization had been involved in lobbying. However, members of these organizations did not feel that the National Assembly had made much difference to their organization and this could perhaps indicate that they felt their lobbying had been unsuccessful. Women in Agriculture are a case in point here: 87.5 per cent claimed that they had lobbied the National Assembly, but only 14.2 per cent spoke of a good or strong working relationship with the National Assembly and only 15 per cent felt that the National Assembly had made a difference to their organization. Lobbying the National Assembly appeared not to be a major activity of social/service organizations at least in terms of the understandings of their grass-roots members. A significant majority of members of WRVS and the Women's Institute said they did not know if their organization had lobbied the National Assembly.

Looking at the first term of the National Assembly, our evidence suggests that there were very mixed views among grass-roots members of women's groups and organizations about the impact that devolution was having. Members of promotional, campaigning organizations displayed the most enthusiasm for and involvement with the Welsh Assembly Government. Members of organizations which focus on service provision and/or social activities felt that the National Assembly had made little or no difference to their organization and members of 'political' organizations did not feel that the National Assembly had made much difference to their organization despite the fact that they had been active in lobbying and claimed to have a reasonably good working relationship with the National Assembly. These findings parallel evidence concerning women's perceptions of their ability to influence political decisions. Among members of 'promotional' groups just over 60 per cent felt that they could influence decisions affecting Wales. This compares to only 33 per cent of members of 'political' groups and 29 per cent of members of 'social/service' organizations.

On one level the evidence presented so far is not surprising. It might have been anticipated that 'promotional' and 'political' groups would be more involved with the National Assembly than 'social/service' groups. By definition such groups are seeking to advance a particular cause or promote a particular policy within Wales. To do this they need to engage with political structures. In this sense, such groups were continuing to do what they had always done but within the framework of a new structure. It would appear that some were more satisfied than others with the new system. But a guiding principle of devolution was 'inclusiveness', involving and consulting under-represented groups and increasing the participation – particularly of women – in decision-making. The evidence discussed so far does not indicate much progress towards the achievement of this goal. Groups and organizations already involved in policymaking and engaged with political structures, continue to be so albeit with varying degrees of success, but other groups appear to remain marginalized or disen-gaged with large numbers of members of these groups, at least at grass-roots level, feeling that they have no influence over decisions affecting Wales (48 per cent of social/service group members and 56 per cent of 'political' group members).

A particularly significant finding of this research was the large number of grass-roots members of social/service organizations, and to a lesser extent of political organizations, who fell into the 'don't know' categories of questions about the impact of the National Assembly, relationships with the National Assembly and lobbying the National Assembly. This raises questions about knowledge and access to information. Had the invitation to participate and be included been received? Were women aware of how to take up the invitation?

Information and communication

Devolution involved the setting up of a variety of structures and mechanisms aimed at bringing governance closer to the people. Thus there are both local and regional Assembly Members, regional committees, a National Assembly website, televised proceedings of National Assembly debates and numerous councils and committees which deal with particular issues, for example, Wales Council for Voluntary Action (WCVA),[4] the Equal Opportunities Committee and various Subject committees. We sought the views of respondents on whether all or any of these institutional developments had facilitated communication between government and their organization. Overall, responses were negative and many members were not aware of the existence and function of such structures and mechanisms, let alone how to access them. It was only having a local Assembly Member (AM) which achieved anything approaching a positive response (36.9 per cent women). One-fifth valued the televised proceedings, but no other mechanism for communication rated significantly among responses in the women's sector as a whole. Once again, there were some differences apparent on the basis of organizational grouping. The role of the local Assembly Member was most valued by members of 'promotional' and 'political' organizations and members of 'promotional' groups were the only ones who showed any support for, or indeed knowledge of, innovations such as the regional committees, the Voluntary Sector Partnership Council, the Equal Opportunities Committee and the subject committees. Interestingly, just over 30 per cent of Merched y Wawr members felt that televised proceedings had improved communications and 42.9 per cent of members of Women in Agriculture approved of the website along with 40.5 per cent of Chwarae Teg members and 30.4 per cent of WAW (Wales Assembly of Women) members.

As was discussed earlier in this chapter, a key way in which the National Assembly has sought to encourage participation by marginalized groups in the decision making process has been by funding and supporting a number of equality policy networks of which WWNC (Wales Women's National Coalition) is a major example. It is the gender representative on the Wales Voluntary Sector Partnership Council. It works with the Welsh Assembly Government as a forum for consulting with women to ensure that women's voices are heard at the highest levels of policymaking in Wales.

Respondents in our survey were asked whether their organization belonged to WWNC and what sort of communication they had had with this forum. The results indicated that the profile of WWNC was not very high amongst grass-roots members of women's organizations in Wales and that during the first term of the National Assembly the coalition had failed to make much impact on the majority of grass-roots members of women's organizations. Over 80 per cent of respondents did not know if their organization belonged to WWNC. Once again variations existed between the organizations studied, with significantly more respondents from the 'promotional' groups (WAW,

Chwarae Teg and WWA) being aware of the umbrella network and of their organization's membership of it. Knowledge of membership of WWNC among members of the 'political' organizations was patchy. Nearly one-quarter of Women in Agriculture members were aware of their organization's membership of WWNC, but this was the case for only 13 per cent of trade union members and 3 per cent of Royal College of Nursing members. The overwhelming majority of respondents from the 'social/service' organizations were not aware of the existence of WWNC and certainly did not know if their organization belonged to it (96.9 per cent, WRVS; 94.4 per cent, WI; 77 per cent, Merched y Wawr).[5] Given the overall lack of knowledge concerning WWNC it was not surprising that very few respondents said that they had received a newsletter, stood for office, attended a meeting or conference, or been asked for their opinion on a policy issue by WWNC. The only affirmative answers to any of these questions came from members of the 'promotional' groups and even here the numbers were very small. Only 19 per cent of Chwarae Teg members, 11 per cent of WAW members and 9 per cent of WWA members had ever received a newsletter from WWNC and less than 10 per cent of members from any of these organizations had ever been asked their opinion on a policy issue.

Increasing participation: the first term

The results of this survey of grass-roots members of women's organizations in Wales, undertaken during the first term of the National Assembly, revealed very mixed results with respect to the success of the devolution experiment in engaging women in the political process. There was evidence that an 'elite' subgroup of organizations was developing that was achieving a generally effective relationship with the National Assembly. This comprised the 'promotional', campaigning organizations such as Chwarae Teg, Wales Assembly of Women and Welsh Women's Aid. Members of these organizations were involved in the new policy agenda, enthusiastic about devolution, and reasonably knowledgeable about the new structures and mechanisms of consultation and communication. Interestingly, these members belonged to groups and organizations that had pre-existing ties with policymakers, bureaucrats and politicians prior to devolution. They represented organizations that were reasonably well resourced, well informed and knowledgeable and that were already 'connected', knew the 'right' people and knew their way around the political structures. For members of these groups and organizations there were few barriers or information deficits to prevent them making the most of the devolutionary experiment. This was not the case for members of other organizations.

Members of what have been termed here 'political' organizations shared a common concern to influence politicians and policy. They wanted to be involved and to participate in policymaking and they showed some level of approval for the innovations of devolved governance. However, overall they did not feel that the National Assembly had made much difference to their organizations despite the fact that they had been active in lobbying and claimed to have a reasonably good working relationship with the National Assembly. They appeared not to have much knowledge, information or experience of potential access routes to political involvement and not to have personal and political links with politicians and/or officials. Whilst they felt that they had, or ought to have, some influence over decisions affecting Wales, they are best described as 'aspirant but frustrated' due to their lack of sufficient information, resources or access. This response was characteristic of the trade unions, the Royal College of Nursing and Women in Agriculture.

Members of organizations that focused primarily on service provision and/or social activities were largely 'disengaged' from the political process. They included the WI, Merched y Wawr and WRVS. These members felt that the National Assembly had made little or no difference to their organizations and above all they lacked any knowledge of or information about the new mechanisms designed to improve, encourage and develop participation in the political process. However, the 'disengagement' of these members should not be taken as evidence of lack of interest. There were indications that members of these organizations did have an interest in and some desire to participate in the policy process of the National Assembly. They were the most likely to know the name of their local AM, felt that the National Assembly was, or should be, accountable to their organization and were forthcoming with views on how the National Assembly could improve its working relationship with their organization in the future. In particular, they wanted more opportunities to meet with Assembly Members locally, provision of better information on Welsh Assembly Government policies, more media coverage on how to get involved in the National Assembly's work and more local 'workshops' and training sessions telling them how to become involved. These responses point to a desire or a willingness on the part of grass-roots members of what might be called 'traditional' women's organizations, such as the WI, WRVS and Merched y Wawr, to participate in post-devolution policymaking. The expressed demand for local workshops, training sessions and meetings with AMs highlights an information and skills deficit among members of such organizations. It also draws attention to the need for more responsive and flexible opportunity structures to be developed if genuinely inclusive and participatory governance is to be achieved.

According to Lowndes and Wilson (2001), the design of political institutions is a crucial variable in determining whether social capital becomes an actual rather than a potential resource for democracy and governance. They point to the need for a range of responsive and inclusive participation methods and political institutions to increase public participation. It may be that regional committees and equality policy consultation networks are not the most appropriate mechanisms for engaging and mobilizing grass-roots members of all women's organizations. They are too centralized and too 'top-down'. There is a need for more local and informal methods of participation. Lowndes (2004) refers to women's social capital as 'really useful social capital'. It is embedded in the community and in neighbourhood-specific networks of informal sociability, but it may not spill over into the political domain unless political institutions are redesigned in such a way as to maximize women's opportunity to 'convert' their social capital into political involvement. Maloney et al. (2000) make a similar point when they argue that political opportunity structures affect the ability of different groups and associations to engage with democracy and with political elites. The evidence of the research reported here lends support to these arguments. A more flexible range of political structures and more locally based access routes may well be required if greater inclusiveness is to be achieved.

Many grass-roots members of women's organizations lacked knowledge of the National Assembly, its workings, its mechanisms and its policies and had little or no information about how to acquire knowledge or how to become involved. It is perhaps not surprising that women's organizations that had been part of the political scene in the pre-devolution era – groups that had knowledge, resources and contacts, that had been involved in varying ways in discussions leading up to devolution and that now had 'friends in high places' – were the most positive about the early days of the National Assembly and were successfully negotiating their path through the new political structures. Indeed, it could be argued that these were organizations that had been incorporated into the new political opportunity structures (see also discussions in chapter 4). Other organizations were not in this position. Some saw opportunities but seemed to lack the knowledge or resources to access or exploit them, others seemed not to be aware of the opportunities or that they were being 'invited' to take part. Some NGOs possessed the skills, the capacity and the internal structures and systems to meet the challenge of devolution. Others needed greater training and capacity building in order to enable their full participation. Chaney draws attention to some of the factors involved in extending the participation of women's groups and organizations in policymaking in the early days of the National Assembly.

> Starting from a 'low base' managers have often been on a steep learning curve in developing lobbying and consultation skills in order to focus on the Assembly's policy-making structures. Limited organizational capacity and resources in women's NGOs have been a pressing issue during the first years of devolved governance, one that has created tensions between conducting extensive consultation with NGOs entire grassroots membership and the expedient use of an 'executive' response by a limited number of managers on behalf of members. (Chaney, 2007: 156)

But, whilst most organizations have had to adapt to the ever increasing demands of consultation, and whilst many managers complain of 'consultation overload', some organizations have been better equipped than others to deal with this. Some women's groups were better equipped to face the 'technocratic' challenge of devolution and better equipped to consult their membership. Other groups, in particular the social/service organizations, lacked the capacity, skills and the organizational mechanisms to respond to consultations and to involve their grass-roots members.

Beetham argued that 'extending participation . . . can simply mean more power for already advantaged groups' (Beetham, 1996: 32). There is evidence that this may have been happening as far as women's organizations were concerned in the early days of the National Assembly. The danger is that the wholesale marginalization of women's organizations in the policy process that existed in the pre-devolution era is replaced by a system characterized by neo-corporatist, elite participation in the work of Welsh government for some women's organizations and continued marginalization for the rest. More recently, Hodgson (2006) has drawn attention to some of the problems that arise when those concerned with issues of governance seek to draw civil society into policy development and policy implementation and the way in which this can adversely affect or hinder the operation of some voluntary organizations.

> Questions need to be asked as to whether the Assembly is assisting capacity-building or whether it is in fact moulding a new breed of bureaucrats (Jones, 2005). There is also the question as to whether civil society organizations are becoming more accountable to, and representative of, their own stakeholders or simply to state bodies. (Hodgson, 2006: 177)

The question remains as to whether genuine participation and inclusion can be attained through 'top-down', technocratic mechanisms and procedures. The new measures may have served to encourage the involvement of the 'managerial elite' of some women's NGOs, particularly those who were well placed to take advantage of the innovations, but they appear to have made little progress in widening participation to the grass-roots members of women's organizations across Wales. Further efforts are required and alternative mechanisms needed to engage more directly with grass-roots members of women's organizations. It is here that the women's equality policy network – WWNC – has a key role to play.

The Wales Women's National Coalition

From the outset the Wales Women's National Coalition was charged with the duty of consulting with women's organizations and ensuring that women's voices were heard at the highest levels of policymaking. Arguably, this was a massive task, given the diversity of women's organizations, and it is clear that in the first term of the National Assembly WWNC struggled to achieve its brief. Very few grass-roots members of women's organizations were aware of its existence and its public profile was sparse. There were plans to develop a website but no finished product was in existence. There was no newsletter that was circulated to all organization members and few ways of consulting with grass-roots members of organizations. There was some communication with officers and elected officials of member organizations, but WWNC was reliant on those officers to channel such communications and consultations to their own membership and, as was suggested earlier, some organizations lacked the capacity or mechanisms to do this. It is difficult to see how WWNC was being an effective 'voice for women' in this early period of devolution in the sense of representing all women across all regions of Wales and from all types of organizations. It may be that equality policy networks, such as WWNC, have been set an impossible task, but before coming to that conclusion we should look at how WWNC has developed in recent times in an effort to meet the challenges set by its experiences in the early years.

Extending participation: new developments

The Wales Women's National Coalition now calls itself Women's Voice (Llais Merched).[6] This change took place in 2006, partly because it was felt that the old name was causing some confusion in that it was too similar to names of other organizations, and partly as a 'rebranding' exercise. The new name is seen to be shorter, sharper and more appropriate to the aims of the organization. Women's Voice now has an impressive and informative website (*www.womensvoice.org.uk*) that describes its role, aims and activities, advertises events and invites contact. This goes a long way towards raising its profile and disseminating information.

Women's Voice describes itself as 'an independent umbrella organization committed to taking women's concerns and interests to the very heart of government. It campaigns on the key issues affecting women's lives in 21st Century Wales.' It continues to represent gender issues on the VSPC (Voluntary Sector Partnership Council) and responds to consultation documents from all departments of the National Assembly and other public sector bodies. It has a membership of thirty-three organizations representing over 750,000 women across Wales and, whilst it is recognized that these organizations encompass a diverse range of viewpoints, it is felt that all are agreed on the promotion of women's concerns and interests in one way or another. Women's Voice thus claims to be a 'progressive authority on gender issues in Wales'.

The title Women's Voice is important in at least two ways. First, it indicates a desire and concern to listen *to* women's voices, to hear what they have to say. Secondly, it draws attention to the fact that it is an organization that can be a voice *for* women in policymaking and decision-making in Wales. According to the home page of the website,

> we endeavour to vocalize the needs, opinions and struggles of women in Wales. Women's Voice provides a vocal point for women of all ages, ability and ethnicity living in Wales . . . We ensure women are heard by ensuring we listen to women both in their organizations and individually.

The importance of consulting, and listening to, a wide range of women is recognized in these statements. All women need to be included. Developments such as regular member mailings, an annual review and monthly e-newsletters seek to contribute to this. Conversations with the chair of Women's Voice in the summer of 2008 revealed that the organization was very aware of issues of communication and information flow. The problem for an umbrella organization, such as Women's Voice, is how to reach the grass-roots members of those groups that come under its umbrella and how to involve people on the ground and not just their officers and officials. Women's Voice is largely reliant on member organizations to disseminate information and to feed down to, and up from, grass-roots members. It was recognized that there was still a gap here that needed addressing. The hope was that electronic communications and mailings and a more public profile and presence might go some way towards tackling this. Member organizations are strongly encouraged to 'tell your members they now belong to Women's Voice and put a link to Women's Voice on your website'. A further development is the introduction of individual membership of Women's Voice. It is recognized that not all women either are, or want to be, members of groups and organizations but may wish to make their voice heard on an individual basis.

The recognition of the need to be a voice for a broader and more inclusive range of women is further evidenced by recent projects that Women's Voice has initiated or in which it is involved. One such project is a mentoring project coordinated by the WI (which is the grant recipient) and supported by Wales Council for Voluntary Action (WCVA). The aim of this project is to recruit mentors who will support other women in reaching a range of personal goals. These may include standing for election at local or national level, becoming a magistrate, setting up a business, being involved in community regeneration or acquiring language skills. Women's Voice is responsible for recruiting mentors through networking, advertising and highlighting the project at its meetings and events. This project is seen to be effective and successful. According to the chair of Women's Voice, it is playing a significant role in reaching out to a wide range of women, both mentors and mentees. 'There is so much talent and potential that goes untapped and projects such as this are enormously important' (personal communication, 2008).

Another way in which Women's Voice will be seeking to reach out to and include a wider range of women in its activities is through a series of roadshows for which it has recently received Welsh Assembly Government funding. The purpose of these is to take Women's Voice to women around Wales; to reach out to women in all parts of Wales – north, south, west and mid – to involve and get the views of as many women as possible. It was anticipated that there would be guest speakers at each event and also 'breakout' groups that would give women the opportunity to raise issues with Women's Voice that could be fed into National Assembly Ministerial meetings.

> It will be very important to publicize the road shows really well and attract women who do not belong to organizations and may be put off by such events. We want to attract women who don't usually attend meetings such as this and who feel their voice is not heard or who perhaps need support. (personal communication, 2008)

Arguably, this type of development may go some way towards meeting the need, voiced by a large number of the grass-roots members of women's organizations surveyed in the study reported here, for a wider range of responsive and inclusive participation methods and for more local and informal methods of participation (Lowndes and Wilson, 2001).

However, the most recent meeting to take place in north Wales under the auspices of Women's Voice was advertised as a 'Conference', was geared towards 'representatives of public, private and voluntary sector organizations, groups or individuals who have an interest in women's issues, gender equality or equality and diversity generally', and had a significant 'academic' bent both in terms of the speakers and the discussion group themes. Clearly there is a role for such conferences, but they do little to draw in a wide range of women or to encourage greater participation in policymaking or in the political system on the part of women who are not comfortable with or are put off by formal meetings. It is to be hoped that the 'roadshow' idea is put into practice on an all-Wales basis and that information can be disseminated and consultation take place at local levels within contexts, settings and structures that are accessible to all women. If Women's Voice is to be an effective organization, listening to and speaking on behalf of all women in Wales, it must to do more than just talk about inclusivity, it must actively reach out to women in ways that acknowledge diversity and difference. It needs to do more than just invite women and their organizations to come under their umbrella. It needs to modify the umbrella to take account of the different skills, resources, capacities and ways of working of different organizations. Sarah Batterbury, discussing the shift in discourse towards inclusivity and partnership, suggests that we reflect on the meaning of the word 'inclusion'. She notes that,

> Carlos Skliar (2002) in his research on deaf and other minority groups has observed that inclusion is a term that in fact requires change by those being included and is anything other than a genuine acceptance of our mutual diversity. He noted that inclusion is about inviting 'the other' in but only on our own terms. This effectively perpetuates ongoing exclusion and division. (Batterbury, 2006: 333)

If the mechanisms of communication remain bureaucratic and technocratic, if assumptions are made that all women will want to share in conferences, papers, agendas, discussion groups and motions or will access their information and newsletters electronically, if inclusion can only ever be achieved on the terms set by the host organization, then it will remain a myth and the devolution goal of bringing marginalized sections of society into decision-making in order to increase the legitimacy and efficiency of government is doomed to fail. Furthermore, there exists the very real risk of undermining rich sources of social capital rooted in networks, trust and relationships that characterize many of the organizations whose membership is concerned, above all, to help others and give something back to society.

Conclusion

The introduction of devolved government appeared to provide an opportunity for previously marginalized groups, such as women, to be more included within the democratic process. In Wales the inclusive approach was embraced enthusiastically by politicians and by many NGOs. New mechanisms sponsored by the Welsh Assembly Government were introduced in order to extend representation, and the desire to increase participation, to re-engage citizens in politics and to create a more inclusive and participatory democracy was a genuine one. Much of the onus was placed on the umbrella organizations or policy networks, such as WWNC/Women's Voice, that act as an intermediary between the Welsh Assembly Government and the organizations of marginalized groups. In the early years of devolution the results were mixed. There was substantial approval for the new mechanisms on the part of some NGOs and their members, but these tended to be groups that had previously established strong informal networks with the decision makers and that had been well placed and blessed with the capacity to take advantage of the innovations. Members of other women's NGOs were either frustrated in their attempts to participate and be included or were generally uninformed about or indifferent to their organization's new role. This was particularly true of those who had joined their organization through social networks and/or from a sense of civic duty – to help others, to be of service. These women tended not to define their activism as political. Attempts to draw on and use the substantial reserves of social capital created by groups such as these need to recognize the importance of social networks and social ties between ordinary members of these groups and the local focus of such networks. New, more responsive and more inclusive participation methods and mechanisms may need to be established, particularly at the local level, if substantial progress is to be made in widening participation and creating a truly inclusive democracy.

Notes

1 Social Capital and the Participation of Marginalised Groups in Government. ESRC: R000239410. Research project led by Professor Ralph Fevre and Dr Paul Chaney at the University of Cardiff, which also included Dr Charlotte Williams and Sandra Betts at Bangor University.
2 Members of ten organizations returned completed questionnaires. The four respondents from TGWU (Transport and General Workers' Union) were combined with those from Unison Wales/Cymru to form one group – trade unions.
3 Chwarae Teg (Fair Play) works in partnership with other organizations in the public, private and voluntary sectors to promote the economic development of women in Wales through employment practices, education and skills, enterprise and public policy. Wales Assembly of Women (WAW) was established in 1984. Its aims are "to provide a voice for the

women of Wales enabling them, through their own languages, to participate fully in local, national and international affairs" (WAW, 1994). Merched y Wawr (Women of the Dawn) is a women's voluntary organization with over 6,000 members and hundreds of branches across Wales. It operates through the medium of the Welsh language. Local branches hold social and cultural activities.

4 WCVA (Wales Council for Voluntary Action) represents and campaigns for voluntary organizations, volunteers and communities in Wales. It seeks to develop and promote policies that create opportunities for voluntary and community involvement.

5 Each of these organizations was in fact a member of WWNC.

6 Women's Voice continues to use its old name alongside its new one for legal reasons.

References

Baron, S., J. Field and T. Schuller (eds) (2000). *Social Capital: Critical Perspectives*, New York: Oxford University Press.

Batterbury, S. (2006). 'Evaluating policy initiatives to enhance civil society', in G. Day, D. Dunkerley and A. Thompson (eds), *Civil Society in Wales: Policy, Politics and People*, Cardiff: University of Wales Press, pp. 313–35.

Beetham, D. (1996). 'Theorising democracy and local government', in D. King and G. Stoker (eds), *Rethinking Local Democracy*, London: Macmillan, pp. 28–49.

Betts, S. and P. Chaney (2004). 'Inclusive and participatory governance? The view from the grass roots of women's organizations in Wales', *Wales Journal of Law and Policy*, 3, 2, 173–87.

Cabinet Office (1999). *Modernising Government*. Cm 4310, London: The Stationery Office.

Chaney, P. (2003). 'Increased rights and representation: women and the post-devolution equality agenda in Wales', in A. Dobrowolsky and V. Hart (eds) *Women, Politics and Constitutional Change*, Basingstoke: Palgrave, ch. 8.

——, T. Hall and A. Pithouse (eds) (2001). *New Governance – New Democracy? Post-Devolution Wales*, Cardiff: University of Wales Press.

——, F. Mackay and L. MacAllister (2007). *Women, Politics and Constitutional Change: The First Years of the National Assembly for Wales*, Cardiff: University of Wales Press.

Dahl, R. A. (1989). *Democracy and its Critics*, New Haven: Yale University Press.

Day, G., S. Dunkerley and A. Thompson (2006). *Civil Society in Wales: Policy, Politics and People*, Cardiff: University of Wales Press.

Hodgson, L. (2006) .'Civil society in action: network building and partner-ships in Wales', in G. Day, D. Dunkerley and A. Thompson (eds), *Civil Society in Wales*, Cardiff: University of Wales Press, pp. 163–80.

Jones, B. (2005). 'Concluding remarks', ESRC Local and Regional Governance: Bringing the Voluntary Sector in, Research Seminar series 2004–6, University of Bath, 13 May.

Lowndes, V. (2004). 'Getting on or getting by? Women, social capital and political participation', *British Journal of Politics and International Relations*, 6, 1, 47–56.

—— and D. Wilson (2001). 'Social capital and local governance: exploring the institutional design variable', *Political Studies*, 49, 4, 629–47.

Maloney, M., G. Smith and G. Stoker (2000). 'Social capital and urban governance: adding a more contextualized "top-down" perspective', *Political Studies*, 48, 4, 802–20.

National Assembly Advisory Group (NAAG) (1998). *Recommendations*, Cardiff: NAAG.

Parry, G., G. Moyser and N. Day (1992). *Political Participation and Democracy in Britain*, Cambridge: Cambridge University Press.

Pateman, C. (1970). *Participation and Democratic Theory*, Cambridge: Cambridge University Press.

Patterson, L. and R. Wyn Jones (1999). 'Does civil society drive constitu-tional change?', in B. Taylor and K. Thompson (eds), *Scotland and Wales: Nations Again?*, Cardiff: University of Wales Press, pp. 169–97.

Portes, A. (1995). 'The economic sociology of immigration', in A. Portes (ed.), *Economic Sociology and the Sociology of Immigration: A Conceptual Overview*, New York: Russell Sage Foundation, pp. 1–41.

—— (1998). 'Social capital: its origins and applications in modern soci-ology', *Annual Review of Sociology*, 24, 1–14.

Putnam, R. (1993). *Making Democracy Work: Civic Traditions in Modern Italy,* Princeton, NJ: Princeton University Press.

—— (2001). *Bowling Alone: The Collapse and Revival of American Community,* London: Simon and Schuster.

Sklair, C. (2002). *Y Si El Otro No Estuviera Ahi?*, Buenos Aires: Mino y Davila.

Verba, S. and N. H. Nie (1972). *Participation in America: Political Democracy and Social Equality*, New York and London: Harper Row Publishers.

——, N. H. Nie and J. O. Kim (1978). *Participation and Political Equality: A Seven Nation Comparison*, Cambridge: Cambridge University Press.

——, L. L. Schlozman and H. E. Brady (1995). *Voice and Equality: Civic Volunteerism in American Politics*, Cambridge: Harvard University Press.

Wales Assembly for Women (1994). *Action for Equality, Development and Peace: a Report for the Fourth United Nations World Conference on the Status of Women, Beijing 1995*, Cydweli, WAW.

Welsh Office (1997). *Llais Dros Gymru – A Voice for Wales*, Cardiff: Welsh Office.

Woolcock, M. (1998). 'Social capital and economic development: toward a theoretical synthesis and policy framework', *Theory and Society*, 27, 151–208.

II

SOCIAL JUSTICE FOR WOMEN?

4

Devolution, Gender and Childcare: A Distinctive Agenda for Wales?

WENDY BALL

Devolution and the creation of the National Assembly for Wales (NAW) created a space for the making of childcare policy at national level in Wales and with the involvement of actors and organizations interested in the needs and preferences of mothers, fathers and children in Welsh communities. Childcare policy could also be allied with the Assembly's inclusion, social justice and children's rights agenda (WAG, 2004a; 2004b; 2005) and its commitment to mainstreaming equality of opportunity and gender equality across all policy developments (Chaney and Fevre, 2002; NAW, 2004; Charlotte Williams, 2001).

In this chapter I address two questions. First, how has childcare policy connected with those key political values and policy commitments claimed by the Assembly? Secondly, has devolution facilitated an agenda that is *distinctive* and *responsive* to the ways in which mothers and fathers in Welsh communities wish to manage childcare? These questions will be pursued by tracing the history of childcare policy in Wales since devolution and by examining the perspectives of key stakeholders in policy: policymakers, practitioners and parents.

The research on which this chapter is based was conducted between 2002 and 2006.[1] It explored childcare policies in Wales in relation to feminist questions about their implications for gender equality and social constructions of motherhood and fatherhood. The study is based on an analysis of public policies and qualitative interviews with policy actors at the national and local levels in Wales. It also included interviews with mothers and fathers living in three neighbourhoods of Swansea about their childcare and domestic practices, their use of informal and formal childcare provision and their perspectives on the range of local services for parents and children.

Childcare policy in Wales

Childcare policy in Wales has been shaped by New Labour's agenda for childcare. In May 1998 the UK government announced the national childcare strategy (DfEE, 1998) and in October of the same year the green paper, *Supporting Families* (Home Office, 1998), was issued for consultation. Both these papers reflected some of the wider priorities of New Labour in relation to combating poverty, promoting social inclusion and investing in children (Millar, 2003). Indeed, the national childcare strategy is an essential component of the agenda for welfare reform alongside other government strategies. Following devolution, policymakers in Wales have been free to develop their own agenda for childcare but within limits. Some of these limits are a result of the reserve powers of the UK government in areas such as taxation, benefits and maternity rights. Other limits come from the power of dominant discourses to shape what can be imagined.

By tracing the process of policy change in this area it is possible to identify which social movement organizations sought to influence policy and how the political and discursive opportunity structures influenced their framing of claims in relation to childcare and associated agendas. The analysis of childcare policy in Wales is based on Welsh Assembly Government (WAG) policy documents and debates pertaining to gender equality, social justice and childcare. The proceedings of the Welsh Affairs Select Committee on *Childcare in Wales* (1999) also provided a starting point in illuminating potential tensions in the policy processes surrounding this issue.

In June 1998 *The National Childcare Strategy in Wales* (Welsh Office, 1998) was published. This consultation document attracted considerable criticism from interested parties and, according to the Welsh Affairs Select Committee, 'was a disappointment to many' (1999: Introduction, para. 1). Critics claimed that it remained too close to the English strategy in the proposals, did not reflect Welsh differences and did not incorporate views put forward during consultation in Wales and by the Childcare Strategy Task Group that had been set up by the Welsh Office. As a consequence the Select Committee on Welsh Affairs undertook an inquiry into childcare in

Wales. Its report was published in May 1999. The select committee provided an opening in the political opportunity structure at a crucial point in the history of Wales – shortly before the transfer of power to the National Assembly. Social movement organizations with an interest in childcare had an unprecedented opportunity to express their views at a time of considerable optimism about the future of Welsh politics. Here I consider those organizations which gave evidence, how their arguments were framed and their subsequent involvement in the policymaking process.

A wide variety of organizations took the opportunity to submit evidence, including organizations from the voluntary sector, industry and employment, early years education and childcare. There were three submissions from bodies with an obvious concern with gender equality issues. These were the Equal Opportunities Commission (EOC) in Wales, Chwarae Teg (Fair Play) and the Minority Ethnic Women's Network (MEWN). The Equal Opportunities Commission was set up by the sex discrimination legislation in the 1970s and was a quasi-governmental organization that was replaced by the Equality and Human Rights Commission in October 2007. Chwarae Teg was established in 1992 with the aim of improving the economic circumstances of women in Wales (see also chapter 1). It has sought to expand childcare provision and has been involved as a manager of various childcare projects. MEWN was established in 1991 on the initiative of the then director of EOC Wales and the Welsh Women's European Network in order to redress the low representation of minority ethnic women in the voluntary sector. The other organization which was very influential in the development of childcare policy was the Welsh Local Government Association (WLGA). Feminist activists were key to these organizations, either because they had been involved in setting them up (as with Chwarae Teg) or because they occupied key positions within them. And, with the exception of WLGA, there is a sense in which they emerged from social movement organizations or were established as a result of social movement activity; thus, although they play key political roles, they are positioned within the political opportunity structure as both insiders and outsiders.

The EOC's submission framed childcare within equal opportunities discourse and related it to economic needs; its main focus was on the achievement of gender equality through participation in the labour market. This can be seen as an example of strategic framing, with arguments being articulated in a way that will resonate with dominant cultural frames and, consequently, have a chance of influencing policy development. Chwarae Teg's submission concentrated on making an economic case for childcare and its interest in gender equality is expressed in terms of removing barriers to women's entering paid work. In both these submissions childcare is framed within a role equity discourse in relation to paid work and the needs of the economy. MEWN was the only organization that framed childcare in relation to the specific and different needs of women. Whilst the organization would not describe itself as feminist, it does support and provide women-only training as part of a positive action strategy. In its submission it outlined its interest in the provision of women-only training in childcare to meet the cultural and religious preferences of some Muslim women. Its arguments were, therefore, framed in a way that did not resonate with the dominant discourse of gender equity and mainstreaming. The framing of childcare needs in terms of gender difference and separatism poses a challenge to dominant discourses of equality and MEWN encountered some resistance from members of the select committee. In this instance MEWN were only able to sustain an argument that women may have needs that are different from men through reference to cultural and religious differences. The WLGA argued for a child-focused policy which located childcare within a wider package of initiatives for children. The discourse they mobilized was one of children's rights.

In most of the other submissions childcare was not linked to questions of gender equality and/or the needs of women and those organizations that did state this as a priority were more likely to be taken seriously where the link between childcare and gender equality was located in a role equity and economic efficiency discourse. It is significant that feminists who had been active in the women's movement of the 1970s were amongst those framing the arguments for childcare both in terms of equal opportunities and economic efficiency and in terms of children's rights. Arguments framed in terms of difference, such as those advanced by MEWN, were subsequently marginalized.

Following devolution, the National Assembly for Wales had to take the national childcare strategy forward and in February 2001 the minister for health and social services established a National Childcare Strategy Task Force with a brief to develop a new childcare action plan. A significant number of those organizations that had submitted evidence to the select committee were represented as members of the task force. Hence there is a sense of continuity in the kinds of organizations that have been able to influence policy development; those that framed childcare in ways that resonated with a role equity discourse were rewarded with further incorporation into policymaking arenas.

The National Childcare Strategy Task Force presented its report in November 2001 and this laid the foundation for subsequent childcare policy in Wales (NAW, 2002, 2005). The report placed emphasis on putting the needs of children first as part of an extensive programme of measures for children. This suggests that the political and discursive opportunity structure has been open to organizations which framed their arguments in terms of children's rights and/or in terms of economic efficiency. This resonated with the discourse of equality institutionalized within the Assembly. Thus the minister for health and social services, in her forward to the report, writes:

> we continue to recognise that an effective strategy for childcare can improve the opportunities of many people to access employment and training. *Women in particular – although not exclusively – are likely to benefit in this respect. An adequate supply of good quality childcare therefore helps to meet the Assembly's economic aspirations and promotes equality of opportunity.* (NCSTF, 2001: 2, my emphasis)

Here childcare is seen as enabling women to participate in the workforce. The link between expanded childcare and opportunities for women is taken to be so self-evident that the difficulties and challenges involved are glossed over. Childcare is seen as a means of enabling mothers to combine caring for children with paid employment and as a means of social inclusion. It is framed as an economic issue and as part of the welfare-to-work agenda of New Labour.

The discourses that have resonance within the new political and discursive opportunity structure in Wales, therefore, are those of children's rights, equal opportunities and social inclusion through economic opportunity. The alternative discourse of women's rights and gender difference has been abandoned.[2] Thus demands for childcare are now framed in terms of children's rights, equal opportunities and the economic benefits of childcare by both femocrats within the Assembly and by organizations external to it. The voices of those, such as MEWN, who mobilize a discourse of difference, are marginalized and a more radical framing of childcare which challenges domestic divisions of labour and the gendering of care work has been replaced by one which resonates with liberal notions of equality and equal rights. Thus there is little sense that either devolution or the statutory duty has encouraged childcare policy in Wales to be thought about in ways that are distinctive from the New Labour vision. In the following section I explore these claims further with reference to my interviews with policy actors.

Childcare policy arenas

Reference has been made to the Assembly's commitment to a different style of politics based on inclusivity, accessibility and openness (Laffin and Thomas, 2000; Catriona Williams, 2003; see also chapter 3 this volume). According to Catriona Williams, the 'working methods of the Welsh Assembly Government have been extremely conducive to the involvement of outside bodies in the development of policies' (2003: 250), including early years provision and childcare. It was, therefore, important for this research to include national policy actors inside and outside the Assembly and six national policy actors were selected for interview. The sample included two actors located within the Assembly, three from regional public bodies that had been active in the childcare policymaking process and one from a public body representing children. At the local level eight policy actors involved in children's services were interviewed and this was supplemented with meetings with local practitioners in early years education and child-care provision. This is evidently a small sample and cannot be assumed to represent the full range of political and policy interests in this regard. However, all fourteen actors were well placed as 'key informants' (Burgess, 1984) to provide some important insights into national or local level policy agendas.

My interviews with policy actors ranged over a variety of themes but in this chapter I confine attention to how they framed childcare and their understanding of its relationship to gender issues. The *national* policy actors tended to draw mainly on the economic regeneration and children's needs/social inclusion frames in discussing childcare. As Keith Hall,[3] an Assembly member, observed:

> I think as well in Wales, from an economic point of view, although I don't think we have cracked unemployment, we have got as close to cracking unemployment as we are likely to get if we continue the present

trajectory. But the area we haven't really cracked is economic inactivity so we thought childcare is an integral part of dealing with the economic inactivity.

Mike Davies (Assembly advisor) believed there was the potential for those who were economically inactive as a consequence of unpaid caring duties to be persuaded to convert their skills into something of value in the labour market:

> One of the things that I think that we have to do is to persuade people in that position is that actually the things that they have been doing when they have not been formally working give them skills and experiences and are very directly relevant to what the marketplace needs. Most often they seem to me to be in the caring type areas.

He continued:

> So, from an economic development perspective, the interest in childcare is both because we need it in order to persuade people who are economically inactive to become active, but also because I think those people represent an untapped pool of talent that means some of those people will be able to become the providers of childcare.

This is far removed from the vision of an 'ethics of care' (F. Williams, 2001) in which care within the domestic realm is valued in its own right, thus meeting claims for cultural recognition. Those who provide the bulk of unpaid care are merely to be encouraged into a social care sector characterized by gender inequalities and low pay (Osgood, 2005). There is little evidence here that childcare policy has been examined through the lens of gender mainstreaming despite the involvement of actors from gender equality organizations in the national policy process and partner networks in Wales.

Concerns with gender equality appeared subservient to the economic frame meaning that full attention to the interaction between gender, care and work was lacking in understandings of policy. Policy actors were asked to comment on how childcare could connect with the Assembly's gender mainstreaming agenda. Alison Connor (equality body 1) argued that gender mainstreaming had not happened in the childcare policy arena. When asked if the gender equality agenda was integrated with childcare policy, she replied:

> No, I don't think they are and I think there is a general lack of awareness of the issues between the two and there is a general lack of understanding of child poverty and the gendered nature of child poverty . . . I think the lack of understanding of how those things interconnect has seriously damaged policy.

Whilst those with gender expertise raised some concerns, it was evident that some of the insiders to the Assembly were not confident in discussing the issue of gender equality. Keith Hall (Assembly Member), for example, claimed that the issue was dealt with by the fact that the membership of the Childcare Working Group was predominantly made up of women, some of whom had a 'track record' in this area:

> *I think we just take it as read*, it is not an issue of contention, really. And I'd say, it does not guarantee anything but two thirds of the group are women, if not more, so I mean, many have a long track record on equal opportunities activity. So people who are involved on the Committee have probably spent their political life dealing with gender issues and equal opportunities issues . . . (my emphasis)

However, Chwarae Teg was the only organization represented on the Childcare Working Group that has a specific brief to address gender equality and its focus is on economic development. The track record referred to here does not appear to have helped generate a focus on how gender, care and paid work interact; rather, it has been *taken for granted* that women will benefit from an expanded childcare market.

Alison Connor (equality body 1), Liz Spencer (equality body 2) and Lesley Thomas (public service body) all had particular expertise in the field of gender equality. Yet they considered equality primarily in relation to an economic frame and publicity and policy texts produced by their organizations utilize a discourse that focuses on the business case for childcare and issues of work–life balance. This is a limited view of the connections between childcare and gender equality and ties in with the emphases of New Labour and Assembly policy texts. In this sense it is possible to identify how dominant textual discourses regulate and set limits to social action and tie social action in different localities to the economic apparatus (Smith, 1990). Those partners that achieve access to regional policymaking are those that support favoured discourses and are able to use them effectively to further their particular interests (Ball and Charles, 2006).

With regard to the two policy actors from the Assembly, neither had spontaneously used a gender equality frame when talking about childcare and when questioned directly about this appeared uncertain. Mike Davies (Assembly advisor) shifted the discussion immediately to equality in general:

One of the ways in which I think this Assembly Government tries to think about, talk about, equality is that we want to move on from simply talking about equality of opportunity and to talk about equality of outcome . . .

It is about trying to say that over time we narrow down some of the inequalities that exist in our society and give a sense of cohesion.

Keith Hall interpreted the link in terms of removing barriers to paid work for all:

We will take the view that certainly everybody who wants to be able to partake in the labour market should have all the obstacles that can affect that removed from them. So, I think we are coming at it from that way. I mean obviously the Assembly is completely signed up for the equal opportunities agenda.

In this sense gender was viewed as one of a range of possible factors leading to inequality and it could be argued that the statutory duty encourages this broad perspective. However, there was little indication that gender mainstreaming had captured the imagination of either policy actor. The strong commitment of the Assembly to promoting equality was taken for granted and as something to be welcomed. Those policy actors without a specialist interest in gender equality are able to celebrate it as another marker of 'inclusion' but are less confident about how this is worked through in specific policy arenas. Kim Hoque and Mike Noon have considered claims that equal opportunities policies can sometimes be merely 'empty shells' and 'exercises in image management' (2004: 482). Simon Duncan has argued that gender mainstreaming can be rhetorical and can result in gender policies that are '"broad and shallow" rather than "narrow and deep"' (2002: 312). My interviews with national policy actors lend some support to these fears.

Local policy actors understood childcare policy in terms of meeting the needs of families, especially those living in poverty, and enabling community regeneration. There was also a different understanding at the local level of the links between childcare and *gender* issues. While the regional policy actors mainly connected gender and childcare in terms of providing equal opportunities to access paid work, the local policy actors understood childcare policy as providing support for (vulnerable) mothers and their children. This also incorporated recognition that women in minority ethnic communities might have particular needs for support thus echoing some of the concerns presented by MEWN to the select committee.

Many of the local policy actors talked about the relationship between parenting and childcare in terms of some of the difficulties facing mothers and fathers. The traditional division of labour between mothers and fathers was generally taken for granted but this did mean that some recognized the stresses that mothers confined to the home or seeking to balance too many responsibilities could face. There was an appreciation that childcare did not provide an automatic route to equality for women and that, where women do work, this can be a double burden and a source of guilt:

> I think childcare can only assist women with a career but equally ... I think it is one in five children is raised without a Dad and here the woman has to be in a high enough job to be able to access childcare. But more and more women are, I suppose, career-minded and I think they are caught in the middle, really. They would like to stay at home to care for their children but equally they have got all the other areas ... (Debra Mason, Early Years Development and Childcare Partnership)

> Well, I suppose (childcare can help equal opportunity) in as much as women can go out to work but for a number of reasons they are probably still limited to part-time sort of jobs ... women still predominantly take over responsibility for childcare, whether they are doing themselves or organizing it and also a lot of domestic ... sometimes organizing the childcare as well as going out to work as well as doing all the domestic, sometimes it is just one more burden. (Sarah Wilson, Early Years Development and Childcare Partnership)

This understanding of how women, especially those with access only to low-paid employment, may experience the pressures to combine work with childcare seemed to be missing at national level and this ties in with the strategic and operational split in policymaking. It also relates to professional and social class differences between women. National policy actors, although claiming to act on behalf of all women, seemed to be articulating a role equity discourse that may speak more to the interests of middle class, professional women. In contrast, local policy actors, focusing their work on families living in poverty and low-income households believed this discourse may not seem to be relevant to their circumstances. There was also some recognition that there was a need to consider the role of men, including those fathers caring alone or living apart from their children, and the local Sure Start Partnership had facilitated work in this regard.

Whilst some local policy actors did refer to the gendered nature of care in their responses, there was no evidence that this was in the context of a strong gender equality policy or commitment to further the Assembly's mainstreaming agenda at the local levels. As one member of the Early Years Development and Childcare Partnership (EYDCP) observed, attention to gender equality 'hasn't been a role that it [EYDCP] has taken on and I'm not sure I could see it doing so in the near future' (Sarah Wilson). Although the Assembly has placed gender equality as a key political value on the map in Wales, it cannot be assumed that this has encouraged a shift at the local level of governance where social justice interests focus on issues of social class and deprivation.

The foregoing analysis of policy texts and interviews with policy actors reveal the role of childcare policy is framed with reference to gender equality, economic regeneration and children's needs and these are harnessed to the economic frame in terms of social investment for the future. In Wales, childcare policy is thus framed in ways that reflect the New Labour vision in London but some differences were revealed both through policy analysis and in discussion with policy actors. The emphasis on framing childcare in relation to *children's needs/rights* is more pronounced. The idea of children having rights of citizenship is stronger than at the UK level and the creation of the Office of the Commissioner for Children for Wales is of huge symbolic importance in this regard (Clarke, 2002; J. Williams, 2005). This framing has provided a space in the *discursive opportunity structure* through which children's organizations in Wales have been able to press for childcare as a *universal right* for all children rather than merely a means to support the welfare-to-work agenda. There is also evidence that issues of tackling poverty, promoting social inclusion and advancing social justice are understood in different ways in Wales. The policy agendas (for example, social inclusion, tackling child poverty) remain the same but the *discursive framing* is more tied in with concerns over inequality and the need to redistribute resources. This alternative framing is significant because it leaves open a door within the discursive opportunity structure as social movement organizations continue to press their demands.

Whilst this greater awareness in Wales of the need to tackle social class inequalities is to be welcomed, there is the danger that gender has fallen out of the picture. Despite the statutory duty, support for gender mainstreaming and the entry of femocrats into the Assembly, my research found little evidence that the connections between childcare and gender relations had been addressed. Childcare policy is *assumed* to improve gender equality because it enables women to do paid work. At best this ties in with a liberal feminist agenda for equal rights in the public realm. This ignores the connections between women's place in the private realm and their capacity to enjoy the achievements of liberal feminism in the public realm. The *differences* between women in relation to this capacity are sidelined. It has been possible for some women to gain from gender equality legislation and policy whilst leaving the gender order and local gender cultures intact. It is thus possible to see how feminism may have failed in its capacity to speak for 'ordinary women'. In this sense the statutory duty and gender mainstreaming in Wales are not being pushed to their full potential so that cultural and economic recognition for unpaid care is secured. In order to challenge prevailing policy frames in this regard, the study conducted interviews with mothers and fathers in different socio-economic circumstances about their childcare practices and drew on this material in subsequent meetings with policy actors. This is the focus of my final section and I confine my attention to the mothers' accounts because cultural constructions of what counts as being a 'good mother' were revealed to be significant.

Hearing mothers, disrupting policy?

The mothers' accounts pointed to gaps between their preferences and needs and what was being offered through childcare policy. This was further complicated in that maternal preferences were sometimes expressed in ways that could reinforce current gender inequities and suggests that feminist definitions of childcare needs would be contested. The connections between government agendas, feminist challenges to those agendas and maternal choice is thus highly complex. The policy interviews provided an opportunity to discuss some of these complexities with reference to themes from the mothers' interviews. Policy actors occupy an interesting position in that they have some power to reshape policy and yet they may also be tied into wider relations of ruling through their location within the state, political parties and professional organizations.

It has been argued that policy discourses frame the childcare agenda in particular ways and policy actors appeared to be operating within dominant frames whilst drawing from them in ways that resonated with their role and professional/political values. However, by using data from the mothers' interviews, it was possible to reveal gaps between particular ways of framing policy and what is happening in practice. In this way I was using the method of 'institutional ethnography' (Smith, 1988; 1990) to grasp mothers' daily experiences and to use this to disrupt childcare policy frames.

Following Marshall's call for feminist critical policy analysis to consider 'marginalized populations' (1997: 19) I was concerned that parents represent a largely silent interest group in the making of child-care policy in Wales. Whilst new partnership arrangements and duties to consult may have started to resolve this and there are localized efforts to secure user involvement, the mothers in this study did not feel there were any avenues to make their voices heard.

One theme from the mothers' interviews that I discussed with the policy actors concerns mothers' value systems and dominant constructions of what it means to be a 'good mother'. There is a substantial body of research that reveals how mothers' value systems or *gendered moral rationalities* (Duncan and Edwards, 1999; McDowell et al., 2005) may impact on their approach to managing childcare and that this may vary geographically and in relation to social class (Vincent et al., 2004) and ethnicity. Childcare has been explored as part of the domestic division of labour (Graham, 1993) and comprising three forms of work: practical care, educational development and emotional support (Reay, 2005). With regard to all three forms of work, it is well documented that this labour is gendered and that mothers are most intensely involved in performing it (Lawler, 2000). In order to explain this we need to examine mothering 'as a historically constructed ideology' (Hays, 1996: x) and as an arena that shapes the identity of many women (Graham, 1993). Whilst women may mother under different social and economic conditions, there are powerful cultural expectations regarding how mothering is performed (Hays, 1996). Sharon Hays has explored contemporary expectations of mothers through the concept of 'intensive mothering': 'The ideology of intensive mothering is a gendered model that advises mothers to expend a tremendous amount of time, energy, and money in raising their children' (1996: x).

Childcare involves more than the routine practical care of children. It also embraces educational support (Reay, 1998; 2000; Standing, 1999) and 'emotion work' (Duncombe and Marsden, 1999) and mothers are the central players in this. The mothers in Hays's study were all aware of what was expected in the performance of 'intensive mothering' based on a child-centred model and informed by the advice of experts. Whilst Hays developed this model on the basis of interviews with mothers in the United States of America, 'intensive mothering' is recognized as an international ideology that 'is found in any society where the dominant culture stresses collective progress based on individual effort and achievement' (Cheal, 2002: 105).

My evidence showed that *all* mothers in the sample made choices in relation to moral codes and that these choices reproduced (more or less) gendered divisions of labour. Similarities between mothers from different social class and ethnic backgrounds in wanting to 'be there' for their children were striking. This notion of 'being there' emerged repeatedly during the interviews and in a variety of contexts. Fiona Williams (2004) argues that 'being there' for children is one possible preference expressed by mothers in an effort to 'do the right thing' for them. This was also true of the mothers whom I interviewed and, for example, those mothers who had changed their conditions of paid employment following childbirth would often justify this in terms of wishing to give time to their children:

> I've been there for them! You know, see them off in the morning, pick them up at night and nobody else is doing that. It has been quite lucky that since [youngest child] has gone to school I haven't had to rely on anyone else to pick her up or drop her off. (Gail)

The interviews with mothers revealed that powerful moral codes shape their attitudes to paid work, the gendered division of labour at home and their perspectives on using formal childcare. However, the similarities in moral codes mask important differences in their access to material wealth (economic capital) and social support from family, friends and neighbours (social capital). These resources do make a difference to mothers' childcare strategies, their use of informal and formal childcare and thus their capacity to care for their children in a way that resonates with their moral codes.

Mothers' values and cultural practices are shaped by the ideology of intensive mothering yet this ideology may conflict with the economic framing of childcare, incentives provided through tax credits to use formal care and encouragement for women to enter the labour market. Policy texts approach gender roles only in relation to role equity and work–life balance considerations. Yet the moral economy of care and the contribution of unpaid caring labour to the political economy are not addressed.

The two actors from regional gender equality bodies appeared uneasy in talking about the issue of mothers' own preferences. Alison Connor (gender equality body 1) did not accept a preference to be home as a credible position for mothers to adopt. Whilst explaining that her organization was 'centring the agenda round choice', her own view was that there should not be a choice because:

> While there is a choice and men earn more than women, it will always be a choice that the women stay at home . . . and you are never going to break the cycle . . . when you compare with international experience, it is a cultural thing, where it has become the norm that all children go into some kind of formal childcare . . . there is much wider acceptance that is how children grow up.

This is a perspective that is, perhaps, to be expected from a policy actor campaigning for improved formal childcare provision. Simon Duncan and his colleagues comment on the validity of arguments from reformers 'that child care preference is a circular process where, if mothers had more experience of formal provision, they would rate it more highly' (Duncan et al., 2004: 263). They argue that their interviews with mothers about childcare revealed that these claims oversimplify how choices are reached. Rather, 'Child care evaluations are one part of mothers' value systems, and in turn these emerge in specific social and geographical contexts" (ibid.). In this interview I provided some examples from my own data to illustrate this point. I referred to mothers who had been in professional jobs and yet stated a preference to stay home for a time with their children either because they felt morally obliged to do so or because they had found this to be more enjoyable than work. Alison Connor responded: 'Saying that, it is needs driven, isn't it?', citing the lack of access to well-paid employment and affordable childcare as the reason why these preferences were expressed. However, this argument conflicts with my evidence that some women in well-paid professional jobs living in areas that were well provided for in terms of formal childcare or with access to generous informal care *still* stated a preference to be at home. This policy actor held strong views that paid work was good for women and would not accept that my evidence was valid. She viewed the 'gendered moral rationalities' revealed in my research as merely outmoded attitudes: 'because the Government has said you will go out to work and here is the provision and actually we are still caught in this trap of it is best for children to be home with mummy'.

Alison Connor was also in disagreement with work–life balance initiatives that enabled some mothers to choose part-time work on the grounds that this was in conflict with advancing gender equality: 'A lot of that is arguments around the business case . . . my personal view is actually that part-time working is a big contributor to the pay gap and actually providing choice has not solved the problem.' This view sees the extension of 'choice' for parents as a barrier to achieving gender equality and redistribution of care between women and men. Yet, surely this example points to the need for more vigorous policies to ensure part-time working does not lead to disadvantage in pay and conditions, rather than to suggest that the choice to work part-time should be limited. This policy actor's view is that if women are to achieve claims that connect with a politics of redistribution this will mean sacrificing claims based on a politics of recognition (Fraser, 1997, 2001). The problem is that claims for recognition and claims for redistribution are treated as mutually exclusive.

Liz Spencer (gender equality body 2) believed policy should provide choice for parents and stressed that the role of her organization was to ensure a genuine choice was available for women:

> So anybody who wants to stay at home with one child or however many children for whatever period of time, fantastic. If there is an opportunity to keep in touch with the world of study, the world of work, the wider community, then those are the sorts of things that [my agency] would be interested in making sure to offer as much choice and as many options as possible to women . . .

Liz Spencer's organization is geared towards achieving role equity for women and men and enabling women to return to the labour market, and fulfils a very valuable role in this regard. This, however, means that the main focus is on those women who do paid work outside the home and does not engage with those mothers who may value recognition for work done at home in terms of financial support, respite and advice.

Other policy actors believed that there should be choice and respect for cultural preferences. Some were in favour of providing support through a redistribution of resources for those wishing to extend the time they stayed home with their children:

> there is a substantial minority of women that, and it is women predominantly, that feel bad about going to work, certainly for the first 12 or 18 months and that an awful lot of women are going to work earlier and that is simply because of pure economic pressure. You know it isn't their

preferred choice but they just have to do it because of the reality of their economic circumstances.

So, I do think ideally, and whether there is an issue of affordability . . . there is a need for more extended maternity leave that would take some pressure off parents. I think there is a political argument, there is an evidence based argument for children. (Keith Hall, Assembly Member)

I firmly believe that if parents want to stay at home and look after their children then there should be an incentive. (Rita Daniels, EYDCP)

A further issue that was raised in relation to themes from the mothers' interviews concerned whether formal childcare was good for children and some mothers expressed this in terms of anxieties over child safety. Some policy actors saw these anxieties and the preference for informal care over formal care as a cultural peculiarity whilst others believed that too much reliance on formal childcare may not be in children's best interests. Policy actors thus held a variety of perspectives. Some wanted cultural recognition and resources such as extended maternity/paternity leave for parents caring for their children at home. They wanted parents to be enabled to stay home with their children and to limit the use of formal childcare if this was their preference. Others believed that cultural preferences that leave the gendered division of labour intact needed to be challenged and that this may mean limiting choice. Yet all perspectives operate by favouring either claims for cultural recognition of unpaid care or claims for a redistribution of resources. What is needed is a way of integrating these claims.

Conclusion: disconnections in policy?

Despite the emphases of policy texts and some of the discursive frames initially used by actors, the discussion of the material from the interviews with mothers' pointed to areas where some actors had reservations about certain aspects of policy, were aware of some of the significant gaps in what was on offer for parents and knew that the frames that they were adopting could be contested.

Given the commitment of the Assembly to gender mainstreaming and the entry of 'femocrats' (Charles, 2004) into the political apparatus, it is disappointing that childcare policy has not been fully connected to gender issues. There is little evidence at either the national or the local level of a sophisticated understanding of how childcare connects with 'recognition' and 'redistribution' claims in relation to gender parity. In terms of now suggesting a feminist agenda for childcare in Wales it must be acknowledged that Wales is achieving distinctiveness in its style of governance and political values (Chaney and Fevre, 2001) providing a 'policy window' (Marshall, 1997) for social movement organizations seeking to influence change. The adoption of the statutory duty, the gender balance within the Assembly and the efforts to work in partnership with the voluntary sector and local government exemplify this point (see chapter 2). Yet there is little evidence of feminist movements pressing for change in the childcare arena, which means that femocrats within the Assembly and partner organizations may be the only ones considering gender at all. My interviews with national policy actors revealed that they were mainly working within the terms defined by New Labour and were focused on role equity considerations in terms of gender. However, by pressing for role equity and independence through paid work for women, reformers do not engage with how many mothers experience combining paid work and care. Mothers' values, preferences and experiences do need to be understood as a basis for moving policy forward. It is not acceptable and is in fact incorrect merely to treat those preferences as old-fashioned cultural norms that must be eroded. Indeed, there are aspects of parenting and education policy that may be reinforcing mothers' feelings that they must be there for their children (Gillies, 2005; Standing, 1999) and all the mothers interviewed stressed their educational role. Among local policy actors, on the other hand, there was little evidence that gender was a major concern, although there was awareness of the pressures facing mothers, fathers and children in poor communities and the need to be responsive to cultural diversity and its interaction with gendered norms. In this case, gendered cultural preferences are taken for granted and some professionals may reinforce this through their own gendered values. This is also problematic.

Childcare policy in Wales has thus been limited by a very narrow understanding of the connections between gender and childcare, based on role equity in paid work. The value of unpaid care has been neglected and the adoption of a gender-neutral discourse evades attention to the discourses and social conditions of motherhood and their implications for policy. There needs to be much deeper engagement with what needs to be done to advance gender equality. This will mean moving beyond the narrow liberal feminist agenda focused on providing routes into paid work to grasping the complexities involved in marrying claims for recognition and redistribution.

Policy should be informed by an 'ethics of care' (F. Williams, 2001) that acknowledges both claims for redistribution and claims for recognition and how these interact. If care was to be culturally recognized and valued, this would involve a debate about who does it, why it is distributed unequally and why society could not function if those who care informally chose not to continue. On this basis the preferences of carers could be respected and taken into account in policies to redistribute resources accordingly. Policies must simultaneously improve support for carers whilst providing this in a variety of ways so that there are genuine choices.

Feminist claims for redistribution of labour at home and in paid work cannot be 'top-down', imposed or assumed to be furthered simply by enabling more women to do paid work. There is a need to engage with cultural preferences and the ideologies and discursive frames that continue to inform those preferences whilst simultaneously providing a range of policy options and benefits that mean the choice to care is a respected pathway and can be conducted in a variety of ways. If devolution and the difference of style and vision emerging in Wales mean anything, they will mean offering opportunities to explore these complex options.

Notes

[1] The study was undertaken for my doctorate while I was a Ph.D. student in sociology and I am grateful to the University of Wales Swansea for the award of a post-graduate bursary during the period 2002 to 2005. I would also like to thank Professor Nickie Charles and Dr Charlotte Davies for their support and encouragement in their role as supervisors.
[2] See also Dobrowolsky and Jensen, 2004, for an account of similar processes in Canada.
[3] The names and institutional affiliation of all policy actors have been changed to protect anonymity.

References

Ball, W. and N. Charles (2006). 'Feminist social movements and policy change: Devolution, childcare and domestic violence policies in Wales', *Women's Studies International Forum*, 29, 2, 172–83.

Burgess, R. G. (1984). *In the Field: An Introduction to Field Research*, London: Allen and Unwin.

Chaney, P. and R. Fevre (2001). 'Ron Davies and the cult of "inclusiveness": devolution and participation in Wales', *Contemporary Wales*, 14, 21–49.

—— (2002). *An Absolute Duty: Equal Opportunities and the National Assembly for Wales*, Cardiff: Institute of Welsh Affairs.

Charles, N. (2004). 'Feminist politics and devolution: a preliminary analysis', *Social Politics*, 11, 2, 297–311.

Cheal, D. (2002). *Sociology of Family Life*, Basingstoke: Palgrave.

Clarke, P. (2002). 'The Children's Commissioner for Wales', policy review, *Children and Society*, 16, 4, 287–90.

Department for Education and Employment (DfEE) (1998). *Meeting the Childcare Challenge: A Framework and Consultation Document*, Cm. 3959, London: The Stationery Office.

Dobrowolsky, A. and J. Jenson (2004). 'Shifting representations of citizenship: Canadian politics of "women" and "children"', *Social Politics*, 11, 2, 154–80.

Duncan, S. (2002). 'Policy discourses on "reconciling work and life" in the EU', *Social Policy and Society*, 1, 4, 305–14.

—— and R. Edwards (1999). *Lone Mothers, Paid Work and Gendered Moral Rationalities*, London: Macmillan.

——, R. Edwards, T. Reynolds and P. Alldred (2004). 'Mothers and child care: policies, values and theories', *Children and Society*, 18, 4, 254–65.

Duncombe, J. and D. Marsden (1999). 'Love and intimacy: the gender division of emotion and "emotion work"', in G. Allan (ed.), *The Sociology of the Family: A Reader*, Oxford: Blackwell, pp. 91–110.

Fraser, N. (1997). 'From redistribution to recognition? Dilemmas of justice in a "postsocialist" age', in N. Fraser, *Justice Interruptus*, New York: Routledge, pp. 11–40.

—— (2001). 'Recognition without ethics?', *Theory, Culture and Society*, 18, 2–3, 21–42.

Gillies, V. (2005). 'Meeting parents' needs? Discourses of 'support' and 'inclusion' in family policy', *Critical Social Policy*, 25, 1, 70–90.

Graham, H. (1993). *Hardship and Health in Women's Lives*, London: Harvester Wheatsheaf.

Hays, S. (1996). *The Cultural Contradictions of Motherhood*, New Haven, CT: Yale University Press.

Home Office (1998). *Supporting Families*, Cm.3991, London: The Stationery Office.

Hoque, K. and M. Noon (2004). 'Equal oportunities policy and practice in Britain: evaluating the 'empty shell' hypothesis', *Work, Employment and Society*, 18, 3, 481–506.

Laffin, M. and A. Thomas (2000). 'Designing the National Assembly for Wales', *Parliamentary Affairs*, 53, 3, 557–76.

Lawler, S. (2000). *Mothering the Self: Mothers, Daughters, Subjects*, London: Routledge.

McDowell, L., K. Ray, D. Perrons, C. Fagan and K. Ward (2005). 'Women's paid work and moral economies of care', *Social and Cultural Geography*, 6, 2, 219–35.

Marshall, C. (ed.) (1997). *Feminist Critical Policy Analysis: A Perspective from Primary and Secondary Schooling*, London: Falmer Press.

Millar, J. (2003). 'Squaring the circle? Means testing and individualisation in the UK and Australia', *Social Policy and Society*, 3, 1, 67–74.

National Assembly for Wales (NAW) (2002). *Childcare Action Plan*, Cardiff: NAW.

—— (2004). *Report on Mainstreaming Equality in the Work of the National Assembly*, Equality of Opportunity Committee, Cardiff: NAW, July.

—— (2005). *Sixth Annual Equality of Opportunity Report: 2004–2005*, Cardiff: NAW.

National Childcare Strategy Task Force (Wales) (NCSTF) (2001). *National Childcare Strategy Task Force Report*, independent report submitted to National Assembly for Wales, Health and Social Services Committee, Cardiff: NAW, 21 November.

Osgood, J. (2005). 'Who cares? The classed nature of childcare', *Gender and Education*, 17, 3, 289–303.

Reay, D. (1998). *Class Work: Mothers' Involvement in Children's Schooling*, London: University College Press.

—— (2000). 'A useful extension of Bourdieu's conceptual framework?: emotional capital as a way of understanding mothers' involvement in their children's education?', *The Sociological Review*, 48, 4, 568–85.

—— (2005). 'Gendering Bourdieu's concepts of capitals? Emotional capital, women and social class', *The Sociological Review*, 52, S2, 57–74.

Smith, D. E. (1988). *The Everyday World as Problematic: A Feminist Sociology*. Milton Keynes: Open University Press.

—— (1990). *Texts, Facts and Femininity: Exploring the Relations of Ruling*, London: Routledge.

Standing, K. (1999). 'Lone mothers' involvement in their children's schooling: towards a new typology of maternal involvement', *Gender and Education*, 11, 1, 57–73.

Vincent, C., S. J. Ball and S. Kemp (2004). 'The social geography of childcare: making up a middle-class child', *British Journal of Sociology of Education*, 25, 2, 229–44.

Welsh Affairs Select Committee (1999). *Childcare in Wales*, third report of the committee, session 1998–99, HC156, London: The Stationery Office.

Welsh Assembly Government (WAG) (2004a). *Social Justice Report 2004*, Cardiff: NAW.

—— (2004b). *Children and Young People: Rights to Action*, Cardiff: NAW.

—— (2005). *The Childcare Strategy for Wales: Childcare is for Children*, DfTE information document no. 047–05, Cardiff: NAW.

Welsh Office (1998). *The National Childcare Strategy in Wales: A Consultation Document*, Cm. 3974, London: The Stationery Office.

Williams, Catriona (2003). 'The impact of Labour on policies for children and young people in Wales', *Children and Society*, 17, 3, 247–53.

Williams, Charlotte (2001). 'Can mainstreaming deliver? The equal opportunities agenda and the National Assembly for Wales', *Contemporary Wales*, 14, 57–79.

Williams, F. (2001). 'In and beyond New Labour: towards a new political ethics of care', *Critical Social Policy*, 21, 4, 467–93.

—— (2004). *Rethinking Families*, London: Calouste Gulbenkian Foundation.

Williams, J. (2005). 'Effective government structures for children? The UK's four children's commissioners', *Child and Family Law Quarterly*, 17, 1, 37–53.

5

Developing a Domestic Abuse Strategy

NICKIE CHARLES AND STEPHANIE JONES

The Welsh Assembly Government launched its domestic abuse strategy on 30 March 2005. This was the culmination of several years of work which had been set in motion with the establishment in 2002 of the Working Group on Domestic Violence and Violence against Women in Wales by Jane Hutt, then minister of health and social services. Prior to this there had been some debate on domestic violence in the Assembly chamber but a coherent policy had not emerged. This must partly be due to the fact that domestic violence is defined as a criminal justice issue by the UK government and, despite devolution, responsibility for criminal justice remains with the Home Office. The legal and policy framework within which the Assembly operates in relation to domestic violence is therefore circumscribed by Westminster and policy development in Wales reflects this. Many of the Assembly's priorities in relation to domestic violence are those set out by successive Labour administrations since 1997.

Background

The way in which domestic violence has become an integral part of government policy is one of the success stories of second-wave feminism. In the 1970s, local refuge groups were established and, in Wales, the first to be set up was Cardiff Women's Aid in 1975. By the end of the 1980s there were twenty-nine refuge groups in Wales 'providing refuge accommodation in 32 refuges and running 12 information centres' (Charles, 1991: 1). Welsh Women's Aid, founded in 1978, now has thirty-four member groups, there are women's refuges in all but one local authority area[1] and many other agencies and services are dealing with the problem of domestic violence. As well as setting up refuges, which can be seen as a form of feminist welfare provision (Charles, 1995), the women's movement also demanded that the government take the issue of domestic violence seriously. Feminist involvement in the Labour Party in the years when it was out of office resulted in both a political commitment to tackling domestic violence and its incorporation into the criminal justice agenda when the Labour Party was returned to power at Westminster in 1997 (Charles, 2000; Charles, 2004). In this process of incorporation, however, more radical feminist voices and framing of domestic violence seem to have been marginalized while others have come to the fore (Ferree, 2003; Charles, 2004; Ball and Charles, 2006). Thus the feminist definition of domestic violence as a 'structural problem deriving from unequal gendered power relations and unequal access to resources' (Charles, 2004: 300) has been replaced by one which sees domestic violence as family or individual violence, that is, violence which takes place within or relates to the domestic sphere, but which has no gendered dimension. This definition can be found in government policy documents where domestic violence is seen primarily as a criminal justice issue and, arguably, it is this reframing of it that has made possible its move up the political agenda. There are now signs that attempts are being made to redefine it as an equality issue and establish it as part of the equalities and human rights agenda (Horvath and Kelly, 2007). Such attempts acknowledge that it is the voice of liberal feminism which has become assimilated into the discursive opportunity structure and that it is this discourse that may permit a reframing of the issue. In this process of struggle over definitions and meaning, however, a more radical framing of domestic violence as an issue of unequal, gendered power relations is in danger of being sidelined.

As well as being defined as a criminal justice issue and, in the process, being depoliticized, domestic violence is increasingly being seen in terms of its effect on children. The focus on children is not peculiar to this field and has been linked to the emergence of the social investment state (see also chapter 4). This has 'the child and the community' as its 'emblems' (Lister, 2003: 437) with the child being seen as 'the citizen-worker-of-the-future' and, therefore, meriting state investment (Williams and Roseneil, 2004: 185). The focus on the child, however, has the effect of 'undermining women's inclusion and full access to citizenship' because the gender dimension of issues such as domestic violence are no longer recognized (Dobrowolsky and Jensen,

2004: 174). These different definitions and framings of issues have implications not only in terms of policy prescription and access to resources, but also in terms of social justice. This is because they involve a struggle over recognition of the gendered nature of domestic violence and the fact that it affects women as a group; women's greater vulnerability to violence affects their status in society and diminishes their agency. A failure to recognize this amounts to misrecognition and has implications in terms of inequalities, women's human rights and social justice. In practical terms this means that the effects of policies on women and on gender relations are not taken into account, equality is taken to imply similar treatment and gender neutrality, and substantive inequalities and differences are no longer seen as legitimate grounds for making claims on the state. Furthermore, organizations that retain a gendered discourse run the risk of being marginalized and as a result many adopt a language of gender neutrality (Williams and Roseneil, 2004). An example of these different ways of framing an issue can be found in the way policies on domestic violence have developed. In what follows we outline the development of policies since devolution and the relationship between policy development in Wales and England. We then explore the mechanisms of policy development and implementation within and without the Assembly, investigating the part played by key actors within the Welsh Assembly Government and the participation of civil society organizations. Our focus is on the way the all-Wales domestic abuse strategy was developed at the level of the Assembly and how a local strategy was developed in a particular local authority area. Finally, we look at the shifts in the discursive framing of domestic violence, exploring the issue of gender neutrality and its implications in terms of resource allocation and social justice.

Domestic violence policies since devolution

Since the 1997 general election domestic violence has had a higher profile in public policy. The UK Labour government published the policy document, *Living Without Fear*, in 1997 and, in 2003, produced a consultation paper on domestic violence (Home Office, 2003). This led directly to the passing of the Domestic Violence, Crime and Victims Act 2004 which applies in England and Wales. Apart from introducing the first major legislation on domestic violence in almost thirty years, the Labour government published a guidance manual for dealing with domestic violence for healthcare workers in 2000 and, in 2004, a report that explains how health professionals can make an impact on this issue (Department of Health, 2000; Taket, 2004). It is not only the Westminster government that has taken initiatives on domestic violence. Health professionals produced their own guidelines: for example, the Royal College of Midwives produced a position paper on domestic violence during pregnancy in 1997, the BMA published a report on domestic violence in 1998 and the Royal College of General Practitioners issued guidance on domestic violence in relation to primary healthcare in 2002 and 2003 (RCM, 1997; BMA, 1998; RCGP, 2002, 2003). Similarly, trade union organizations such as the Trades Union Congress and public sector workers' union, UNISON, have developed campaigns and guidelines which attempt to place domestic violence on the workplace agenda and negotiate workplace policies to support staff experiencing domestic violence (TUC, 2002; UNISON, 2003), while the general workers' union, GMB, held its Stop the Beatings: Suffering in Silence conference in March 2005. Thus, although domestic violence is a 'hidden' crime, associated with stigma and under-reporting,[2] since 1997 it has had a much higher profile and, as well as the Domestic Violence, Crime and Victims Act coming onto the statute books in 2004, the Sexual Offences and Female Genital Mutilation Act became law in 2003 and, in 1997, the Protection and Harassment Act was passed.

Because domestic violence is defined as a crime which has to be dealt with by the criminal justice system, the legislative framework within which the Welsh Assembly Government operates is laid down by Westminster and policies are implemented by the Home Office in Wales in the form of the Assembly's Crime Reduction Unit. The Welsh Assembly Government and the Crime Reduction Unit work together in implementing policies which are developed at Westminster and, currently, the Assembly's Community Safety Division and the Wales Home Office Crime Team are located in the Assembly offices in Merthyr Tydfil and 'cooperate on a wide range of initiatives to respond to domestic abuse' (CC(3)–06–08: paper 1)

The overarching framework for domestic violence policy is, therefore, largely decided by Westminster, although, given the Assembly's jurisdiction over areas such as housing, health and education, there is some room for the development of a particularly Welsh approach to domestic violence. This was recognized in the first Assembly when the minister for health and social services set up a Working Group on Domestic Violence and Violence against Women to advise on the development of a domestic abuse strategy This group brought together statutory and voluntary agencies working in the area of domestic violence. Welsh Women's Aid and other voluntary sector domestic violence organizations were represented on it as were criminal justice agencies, minority ethnic organizations, health and social services, local government and voluntary organizations such as the National Society for the Prevention of Cruelty to Children (NSPCC) (WAG, 2005: 29). The working group provided an opportunity for women's organizations to influence policy and recognized their expertise in this area. It also institutionalized both the presence of women's organizations within the policymaking process and an engagement with civil society organizations.

Soon after the working group was established, a commitment was made by the Welsh Assembly Government to set up an all-Wales domestic violence helpline for which Welsh Women's Aid successfully bid and which is funded by the Welsh Assembly Government. The sequence of events which led to the development of the all-Wales domestic abuse strategy can be seen in figure 5.1.

The domestic abuse strategy recognizes the seriousness of domestic violence and sets out policy guidelines to deal with it and its repercussions in a 'joint agency' approach. It follows UK government guidelines, such as those in the 1998 Crime and Disorder Act which required that police and local authorities form partnerships with the aim of reducing crime in the local area. To meet this requirement, community safety partnerships were set up in Wales and some of them have developed their own domestic abuse strategies. In what follows we consider how the all-Wales strategy was developed and how one local authority area in Wales drew up its own domestic abuse strategy. We draw on two pieces of research: a project[3] that was commissioned by the domestic abuse coordinator in Swansea as part of the development of the Swansea domestic abuse strategy, and a study entitled 'Gender and political processes in the context of devolution' which was funded by the Economic and Social Research Council.[4]

Developing the all-Wales strategy

The development of an all-Wales strategy marks Wales off from England which, rather than a strategy, has a national delivery plan

1999	Break the Chain Campaign – Assembly supports it
2001	Domestic violence manual for health care professionals launched
2002	Working Group on Violence against Women in Wales chaired by senior civil servant set up
2003	Supporting People programme launched Domestic abuse funding stream established – Assembly funding increased from £450,000 to £1.17m
2004	Telephone helpline, 12 hours a day, launched Gwent Criminal Justice Board funds pilot scheme, SDVC in Caerphilly *Good Practice on Domestic Abuse* guidance booklet for schools launched Domestic Violence, Crime and Victims Act 2004 Workplace policy on domestic violence launched by Wales TUC Women's Committee, supported by minister for social justice and regeneration, part of '16 Days of Activism' *Tackling Domestic Violence: Providing Support for Children who have witnessed Domestic Violence* published by Home Office
2005	Tackling Domestic Abuse: All Wales National Strategy launched Working group's terms of reference revised and name changed to Working Group on Domestic Abuse All-Wales network of domestic abuse coordinators set up All-Wales pathway training pack for use in all NHS Trusts produced Increase in Assembly funding of £1.1m between 2005–8 announced The Dyn project set up Home Office publishes national delivery plan for domestic violence
2006	Assembly guarantees recurring funding for all community safety partnerships in Wales for domestic abuse coordinators Refuge for men opened in Montgomeryshire All-Wales schools programme has module on domestic abuse – 97 per cent of primary and secondary schools are covered Assembly funding for domestic abuse increased to £3.8m Piloting of All-Wales routine enquiry about domestic abuse in A&E departments
2007	All-Wales 24-hour helpline launched Assembly establishes rolling evaluation of domestic abuse projects
2008	Key performance indicators for domestic abuse coordinators issued Dyn project sets up all-Wales helpline WAG domestic abuse budget for 2007–8 and 2008–9 £3.774m*

Figure 5.1: Domestic abuse policy timeline and selected key policy achievements

Source: The Record, 4 February 2004, 21 January 2004, 18 April 2002; Minutes of the Social Justice and Regeneration Committee 12 January 2006, 22 March 2007, various WAG press releases

* EHRC; 'Domestic abuse: the facts', a secondary research report, evidence presented to the Communities and Culture Committee inquiry into domestic abuse.

which was published in 2005. This plan applies to both England and Wales and its seven key objectives are part of the crime reduction agenda: they range from reducing the prevalence of domestic violence, through increasing the rate of reporting domestic violence offences and ensuring adequate protection and support for 'victims of domestic violence', to reducing the 'number of domestic violence related homicides' (Home Office, 2005: 25). The definition of domestic abuse in this document is gender neutral and was developed from one used by the Association of Chief Police Officers. Domestic abuse is: 'Any incident of threatening behaviour, violence or abuse (psychological, physical, sexual, financial or emotional) between adults who are or have been intimate partners or family members, regardless of gender or sexuality' (Home Office, 2005: 7).[5]

Given that the criminal justice framework was already in place, the focus of the Welsh strategy was of necessity on the social policy dimensions of domestic violence and 'its impacts on the health and well being of people' (WAG, 2005: 7). The strategy document notes that 'social services, children's services, welfare, health, housing, education and training are all responsibilities that are devolved to the Assembly' (ibid.: 7) and that the new Supporting People programme (introduced in 2003) would result in approximately £6.5m 'being devoted to over 500 units of accommodation for women escaping domestic abuse' (ibid.: 8). The principles underlying the strategy are equality, which, because of the equality duty, threads through all WAG policy development, 'protection and support for victims, perpetrator accountability' and 'prevention' (ibid.: 3). Protection is properly a matter for the criminal justice system whereas prevention and support involve health, social services, children's services and education which are areas where the Assembly has devolved powers.

Community safety partnerships are identified as the 'key local partnership' for delivering the domestic abuse strategy. This is in line with the UK government requirement that local authorities and police establish partnerships to reduce the levels of crime and disorder in their area. Membership of these partnerships is drawn from the police, police authorities, local authorities, local health boards and the fire service: all statutory agencies. It is also recommended that local domestic abuse fora be invited to contribute to the development of local domestic abuse strategies in order that the voices of 'victims' be heard, and that domestic violence agencies may be invited to participate in community safety partnerships (ibid.: 23–4). The key objectives of the strategy are those set out in the national plan (Home Office, 2005) and it is to be monitored by the Assembly's Working Group on Domestic Abuse.

Within the strategy document a considerable amount of evidence is presented showing that domestic violence is overwhelmingly perpetrated against women; however, the definition of domestic abuse is, like its English counterpart, gender neutral. Domestic abuse is defined as: 'the use of physical and/or emotional abuse or violence, including undermining of self confidence, sexual violence or the threat of violence, by a person who is or has been in a close relationship' (WAG, 2005: 6). It appears that there had been some discussion of the definition in the working group (working group minutes, 16 December 2003) but this had been halted, possibly because it needed to fall in line with the gender-neutral UK definition (Home Office, 2005). Unlike its Home Office counterpart, however, there is an important dimension to the definition which, as well as being longer and more detailed, states that 'Domestic abuse is not a "one-off" occurrence; it is frequent and persistent' (WAG, 2005: 6); the strategy goes on to state that 'the great majority of domestic abuse is perpetrated against women and their children' (WAG, 2005: 7).

The strategy follows the national plan in claiming that the definition of domestic abuse needs to be wide enough to include such things as 'honour crimes'. This seems to suggest that the definition of domestic violence in the all-Wales strategy was expected to conform to that in the national plan, something that was also facilitated by the involvement of WAG representatives with the Inter-Ministerial Group on Domestic Violence which had been set up in 2003 and which brought together representatives from England, Wales and Northern Ireland.

There was also a shift to gender neutrality in the renaming of the working group. Within the strategy document it is referred to both as the Working Group on Domestic Violence and Violence against Women, which was its name when it was set up, and as the Working Group on Domestic Abuse, which it became once the domestic abuse strategy had been launched. When its name was changed, in December 2005, its remit also changed, becoming oversight of the implementation of the all-Wales strategy. With this renaming, violence against women is replaced by domestic abuse; this has the effect of reducing the visibility of gender and gendered power as a crucial dimension of domestic violence. In other words, although domestic abuse is to be tackled, there is no longer any suggestion in this definition, or in that of the Westminster government, that it has anything to do with unequal and gendered power relations. This is despite the fact that equality is one of the strategy's underlying principles and its recognition that it is overwhelmingly women who experience domestic violence. Furthermore, the strategy is set very firmly within the purview of the crime reduction strategy and it is the community safety partnerships which are defined as the key actors. In this sense it does not differ significantly from the national plan and, indeed, shares the principles of prevention, protection and justice, and support (Home Office, 2005: 4). The only difference is that it adds the additional principle of perpetrator accountability and does not mention justice. Thus, although Welsh Women's Aid was involved in drawing up the all-Wales strategy, with the support of key woman-centred women in the Assembly, the criminal justice agenda means that neither they nor their definition of domestic violence as gendered are central to its delivery.[6]

As part of the strategy, funding to Welsh Women's Aid and its member groups, as well as to other organizations working in the domestic violence field, was increased. Prior to launching the strategy, the Welsh Assembly Government had streamlined and increased funding for domestic violence projects and organizations with funding increasing from £450,000 to £1.17m per annum in 2003; by 2008 it had reached £3.7m. Welsh Women's Aid receives its core funding from the Welsh Assembly Government and funding for local refuge groups is through the Supporting People Revenue Grant.[7] The Supporting People revenue funding has placed refuge groups on a more secure financial footing as they do not have to apply for it annually; some other sources of funding are, however, less secure. This means that funding for both Welsh Women's Aid and local groups is still problematic, with several of those we interviewed feeling that their future was uncertain. At the time of interview some refuge groups were experiencing difficulties with the conditions placed on them by the Supporting People funding which restricts the type of service they can provide. The other difficulty they experience is that the equalities agenda and particularly the gender equality duty has led some local authorities to argue that there is no longer a need for specialist services for women or for other 'minority' groups; in some cases this has led to women's refuge groups' experiencing pressure to open their doors to men (WWA, 2008).[8]

Thus far we have discussed the all-Wales domestic abuse strategy and its relation to the national plan which covers England and Wales. The fact that an all-Wales strategy exists at all, however, is something that is in need of explanation, given the fact that the criminalization of domestic violence and the retention by the Home Office of responsibility for the criminal justice system means that domestic violence policy is largely decided at Westminster and implemented in Wales. In what follows we argue that this can be explained by the presence of key actors in the Welsh Assembly who have a background in feminist social movement politics and their commitment to involving civil society organizations, such as Welsh Women's Aid, in the development of a 'made-in-Wales' strategy.

Key actors – domestic violence champions

As we have already noted, the Working Group on Domestic Violence and Violence against Women was set up by Jane Hutt when she was minister of health and social services. She was a founder member of Welsh Women's Aid in the 1970s and, like other women AMs, maintains her connections with women's organizations which operate 'as a reference group'. The working group, as well as including statutory agencies, drew in what can be seen as social movement organizations, such as Welsh Women's Aid, and other women's organizations working in the domestic violence sector such as Black Association of Women Step Out (BAWSO), Cardiff Women's Safety Unit and Cymdeithas Tai Hafan (WAG, 2005: 29). According to Edwina Hart, 'Jane Hutt's approach to the all-Wales strategy was to bring everybody together, get organisations working together and create a policy initiative that drew together all interested elements of society and all Welsh Assembly Government departments to discuss the issue' (The Record, 21 April 2004). The draft strategy was sent out for consultation, providing an opportunity for local Women's Aid groups as well as Welsh Women's Aid to respond to it. The strategy itself was drafted by a subgroup of the working group, primarily by a secondee from Swansea University, and was overseen by the working group. The establishment of the Working Group on Domestic Violence and Violence against Women was key to the development of the all-Wales strategy and in its renamed form, as the Working Group on Domestic Abuse, it continues to advise on policy in this area.

At the time the working group was set up, Jane Hutt, as minister for health and social services, had responsibility for domestic abuse, but by the time the strategy was launched this had passed to Edwina Hart as minister for social justice and regeneration. She too was very committed to prioritizing domestic violence. A senior civil servant told us:

> But for instance domestic abuse, the previous minister took a particular interest in that, really because although sentencing and the law is non-devolved, how you actually treat, you know deal with the victims of domestic abuse is very much devolved. So it comes down to things like housing, support services, and lawyer services and all the rest of it. I suppose on that one there was, you know the minister herself was very committed. [That was Edwina?] Edwina, yes, was very committed to those particular issues, was willing to put resources in and took a very active interest in it, and we have the structures in Wales to actually help with that. (interview with a Welsh Assembly Government civil servant)

In the third Assembly, responsibility for domestic violence lay, initially with Brian Gibbons, minister for social justice and local government, and the Communities and Culture Committee was the one that scrutinizes policy in this area. At the time of writing this committee was currently investigating provision for domestic violence in Wales and collecting evidence.[9]

There appears to be a cross-party consensus within the Assembly that it is important to tackle domestic violence and give it a high priority; however, there is also a view, both inside and outside the Assembly, that without women AMs and ministers who were particularly committed to this issue, it might not have received such attention. During the first and second Assemblies, the minister for health and social services and the minister for social justice and regeneration respectively issued many press releases detailing the Assembly's work on domestic violence and making public appearances supporting work in this area; this helped to raise its public profile. Having said that, however, it has also been prioritized by the Westminster government and is a policy area that has undergone considerable development and elaboration since 1997. These developments include the establishment of specialist domestic violence courts (SDVCs), multi-agency risk assessment conferences (MARACs), independent domestic violence advisers (IDVAs) and sexual abuse referral centres (SARCs). Cardiff Women's Safety Unit developed the prototype for MARACs which was subsequently taken up by the British government and one of the pilot SDVCs was located in Caerphilly. These initiatives are all part of the criminal justice agenda and are happening in England as well as in Wales. At a local level the community safety partnerships are, as we have seen, entrusted with taking the strategy forward and with appointing domestic abuse coordinators for which the Assembly provides a recurring funding stream. There is now a domestic abuse coordinator in every local authority area and they are currently developing key performance indicators so that their work can be monitored by the Assembly and can be more effectively coordinated across Wales. These key performance indicators will form the basis of a strategic action plan which is being developed by the WAG Working Group on Domestic Abuse in consultation with one of the domestic abuse coordinators.

Defining domestic violence

As we have already seen, the definition of domestic violence contained in the all-Wales strategy is gender neutral and, although it includes the important qualification that domestic violence 'is not a "one-off" occurrence', it no longer emphasizes the fact that women are overwhelmingly the ones who experience domestic violence. Indeed, the strategy document makes explicit that 'any person can be the victim of abuse', although it draws attention to the fact that 'the great majority of domestic abuse is perpetrated by men against women and their children' (WAG, 2005: 6–7). The broadening out of the definition enables all types of violence that occurs between family members and intimate partners to be included. Thus child abuse is included as are 'honour crimes'. The inclusion of child abuse marks off the definition in the Welsh strategy from that in the national plan where it 'incorporates violence between family members over 18 as well as between adults who are, or were, intimate partners' (Home Office, 2005: 7). In this definition those under the age of eighteen are excluded but in the Welsh definition children are explicitly included. The widening of the definition of domestic violence to include almost every form of violence that takes place within or related to the domestic sphere is significant when we consider that domestic violence was put on the political agenda by second-wave feminism and was seen primarily as male violence against women. Indeed, in their submission to the Communities and Culture Committee, Welsh Women's Aid discusses the strategy's definition of domestic abuse, pointing out that: 'Domestic abuse is a crime committed predominantly against women, with 77 per cent of victims of domestic violence being women, and the government's definition should recognize this. Almost half of women in England and Wales experience domestic violence, sexual assault or stalking during their lifetime' (Welsh Women's Aid, 2008). They also point to the UN Declaration on the Elimination of Violence against Women which defines domestic abuse as

'Any act of gender-based violence that results in, or is likely to result in, physical, sexual or psychological harm or suffering to women . . .' This definition incorporates the fact that domestic abuse concerns the misuse of power and it highlights that it enhances the inequality against women. (Welsh Women's Aid, 2008)

The fact that a gendered definition has been abandoned within Wales and at Westminster (although significantly not in Scotland) represents a change in the way domestic abuse is understood and framed. Instead of being understood as an aspect of a patriarchal society which is in need of transformation in order that gender equality may be achieved and women may live free of the fear of abuse – whether physical, sexual or psychological – it removes any idea of patterned and systemic inequalities from the understanding of domestic violence. The only thing that distinguishes domestic violence from any other form of assault is that it takes place in and around the domestic sphere; it is no longer seen as an abuse of male power over women.

Developing a domestic abuse strategy in Swansea

In 2004, while the all-Wales strategy was still in the drafting phase, domestic violence was gaining a higher profile in Swansea through the local authority's community plan where it was identified as a key element of two strategic themes: the Safer Swansea Partnership and the Health, Social Care and Wellbeing Strategy Board; its importance was also recognized by the Substance Misuse Action Team in their plan (City and County of Swansea, 2004). The impetus for developing a local strategy came from a position paper which had arisen from a series of 'evidence sessions' on domestic violence held by the Social Services Cabinet Advisory Committee in 2005. These 'evidence sessions' included presentations from the head of mental health and learning disability, Swansea Women's Aid, the local domestic abuse unit of the South Wales Police, the Safer Swansea Partnership, the Minority Ethnic Women's Network (MEWN Swansea) and the Swansea Domestic Abuse Forum. The position paper recognized that domestic violence was an issue which is relevant to child protection, substance misuse, mental health, protection of vulnerable adults, youth offending and vulnerable groups including minorities. It also recognized the importance of developing a human resources policy on domestic violence for employees of the local authority and argued for the development of a Swansea domestic abuse strategy for 2006–8 (City and County of Swansea, 2005).

Swansea has had a Domestic Abuse Forum since the mid-1990s although it had not been very active until the domestic abuse coordinator was appointed in 2004; it did, however, have an action plan prior to the development of the Swansea strategy. The forum is a subgroup of the Safer Swansea Partnership (which is the community safety partnership in Swansea) and its role is to raise awareness of issues amongst the public and professionals; develop policy and practice; campaign for increased service provision such as refuges, safe houses and counselling; and advise and support organizations dealing with those experiencing or threatened with domestic violence.

The Safer Swansea Partnership, which the Domestic Abuse Forum advises on domestic violence policy, includes both statutory and voluntary organizations in line with UK government policy. Thus criminal justice agencies as well as representatives from education and health are involved as are women's organizations such as Swansea Women's Aid, BAWSO, Cymdeithas Tai Hafan and MEWN. Moreover, prior to the development of the Swansea domestic abuse strategy, the local authority had already taken a number of initiatives on domestic violence. These involved, inter alia, the homelessness strategy identifying domestic violence as one of the three main causes of homelessness; funding being provided for an outreach worker for Swansea Women's Aid; safe houses being provided in partnership with BAWSO and Swansea Women's Aid; and research being carried out into the needs of and barriers facing minority ethnic communities in relation to domestic violence.

The audit

It was also in 2004 that the newly appointed domestic abuse coordinator commissioned an audit of existing service provision for survivors and perpetrators as part of the development of the Safer Swansea domestic abuse strategy. Its aim was to generate information about the range of provision in Swansea and any gaps that might exist and it took the form of a questionnaire survey for agencies and organizations and two focus groups with women survivors. It also aimed to raise awareness of domestic violence across a wide range of agencies in the area. A total of 438 organizations were identified by the domestic abuse coordinator and questionnaires were sent out to them. The questionnaire asked about the services they provided, awareness of domestic violence, record keeping, how the organization worked with vulnerable and marginalized groups, domestic violence policies, views on multi-agency working, project development and, finally, training requirements and the possibility of developing links with the domestic abuse coordinator.

Seventy-two organizations returned completed questionnaires, which represents a response rate of 16 per cent. The main finding was that there was widespread recognition of the seriousness of domestic violence and its impact on people's lives but that there were problems with existing service provision and that there was much that could be improved. Particular difficulties related to access, funding and inter-agency working. Thus marginalized groups were seen as experiencing difficulties in gaining access to services due to a reluctance to disclose, language barriers and a lack of understanding of cultural differences by mainstream agencies. Respondents suggested that an increase in funding was needed to provide more refuges and to support inter-agency working although the survey also showed that experiences of inter-agency working were not always positive. Some respondents cited time delays and competition between agencies as problems while others regarded information sharing as problematic because of issues of confidentiality; still others stated that information sharing was vital for protection. There was support for the idea of a single access point service model which would make contacting service providers easier for those experiencing domestic violence.

The two focus groups highlighted the need for improvement in service provision. One focus group was held with women from black and minority ethnic groups in central Swansea, the other with members of a Sure Start support group in east Swansea. In total fourteen women participated in the focus groups. The participants had between them experienced a wide range of service provision, but considered few to have been really helpful. Several areas of concern were discussed: notably inconsistent and insensitive responses, lack of service provision and a lack of 'joined-up' working between agencies or even within departments. Some good practice was identified, however, notably in specialist agencies dealing with domestic violence and amongst individuals in statutory agencies who had been particularly helpful and supportive, such as some female police officers and health visitors.

The findings of the audit informed the development of the strategy which was drafted by the Domestic Abuse Forum's Strategy Coordination Group, a subgroup of the Domestic Abuse Forum, after a series of workshops with 'stakeholders'.

The Swansea strategy

The 2006–8 Swansea strategy is a substantial document which situates the domestic abuse strategy within the framework laid down by the Home Office and elaborated for Wales in the all-Wales strategy. It focuses on four key areas: prevention; protection and support; perpetrator accountability; and accommodation and support. The first three are the principles identified in the all-Wales strategy while the fourth has been added in recognition of the fact that domestic violence is associated with homelessness and that a major way of supporting survivors is to provide alternative safe accommodation, usually in the form of women's refuges, or to make their own homes safe by ensuring that the perpetrator no longer has access. As with the all-Wales strategy, the principle of equality is central to it. The strategy (Safer Swansea Partnership, 2006) provides a detailed discussion of what it intends to do in order to meet its aims of

- Increasing women and children's/young people's safety
- Holding abusers accountable
- The prevention of abuse
- Supporting and informing children and young people

It also includes an action plan with detailed tasks and the groups, organizations and agencies in both statutory and voluntary sectors that are to carry them out, and a comprehensive list of those organizations and agencies which provide support to survivors. The action plan was to 'enable the Safer Swansea Partnership to begin to fulfil the aims of the All Wales National Strategy' (Safer Swansea Partnership, 2006: 17).

The strategy is an impressive document which demonstrates that the Safer Swansea Partnership is taking domestic violence seriously and has set up a series of measures to ensure that domestic violence is detected, survivors are protected and perpetrators are brought to justice and given the opportunity of re-education. It also discusses the need to address the causes of domestic violence, but the measures included here are limited to educating children and young people (ibid.: 22).

The overall aim of the strategy is to 'make a **significant** and **measurable difference** to the lives of people in Swansea who are experiencing or have experienced domestic abuse' (ibid.: 18, emphasis in original). It is to be monitored through the use of key performance indicators which are the seven key objectives of the national plan discussed earlier and are an integral part of the criminal justice agenda. Monitoring will be carried out by the Domestic Abuse Forum Strategy Coordination Group which oversaw the strategy's development. Monitoring 'will also need to make central reference to the issue of equalities and to ensuring that the work which results from the Action Plan fully addresses the needs of all those affected by domestic violence, on a consistent and long-term basis' (ibid.: 19–20). It is the Domestic Abuse Forum rather than the Safer Swansea Partnership that has ownership of the action plan and is responsible for ensuring that it is carried out and monitored.

The development of this strategy and the commitment at local level to putting in place measures to combat domestic violence is an important example of the implementation of policies developed at national UK level and, to a lesser extent, at the level of the Welsh Assembly Government. And it clearly has implications in terms of the resources that are to be allocated to a whole range of domestic violence services which should make a real difference to the experience of survivors. One of the commitments was to develop two new women's refuges in Swansea, one specifically for black and minority ethnic women. The latter was opened in May 2007 and, at the time of writing, the other has been given the go-ahead and capital funding has been approved but suitable accommodation has not yet been found. Each new refuge has eight family places.

Having said that, however, the strategy appears fundamentally to misrecognize the nature of domestic violence and violence in general.

The definition that it adopts is gender neutral, it very deliberately removes all references to gender when discussing survivors and their experiences, even when using individual quotes, and emphasizes again and again that domestic violence can be experienced by anyone. It defines domestic abuse as:

> Any incident of violence or aggression, wherever and whenever it occurs. The abuse may include physical, sexual, emotional or financial abuse of an individual by a family member, partner or ex-partner, in an existing or previous relationship, regardless of gender, culture or sexual orientation. (ibid.: 9)

This is similar to the Home Office definition and is the one used by the South Wales Police. In this document, therefore, as well as in the UK government's national plan, it is a gender-neutral definition derived from the criminal justice system which is used. In the all-Wales strategy, although the definition is gender neutral, there is recognition that domestic violence is not a one-off occurrence and that it is gendered.

Furthermore, the Swansea strategy says that it uses gender-neutral terminology '(such as "*people who are abused*, rather than "*women who are abused*"), because it is recognized that men as well as women can be abused' (ibid.: 10, emphasis in original). It also asserts 'that domestic abuse occurs amongst people of all ages, classes, races, cultures and religions, and can affect anyone, whatever their gender or sexual orientation' (ibid.: 5) and that 'domestic abuse does not affect any one group or sector of people in society' (ibid.: 17). This commitment to gender neutrality does not sit easily either with the evidence presented in the all-Wales strategy or with evidence (albeit much more scarce) in the Swansea strategy itself that 'the majority of reported incidents of physical violence within intimate relationships are perpetrated by men upon women who are, or have been, their partners or wives' (ibid.: 9). It also does not sit easily with evidence presented under the section on prevention where it is claimed that the causes of domestic violence must be addressed. The only preventative measure mentioned here is the education of children and young people and research evidence is cited which shows that even amongst children the gendering of domestic violence is apparent. Thus

- Over 75 per cent of 11–12 year old boys thought that women are hit if they make men angry

- More boys than girls of all ages thought that some women *'deserve'* to be hit
- A survey of young people aged 14–21 showed that almost half the young men surveyed and a third of the young women thought that there could be circumstances in which it could be acceptable for a man to hit a female partner
- 1 in 8 of the young men thought that *'nagging'* is a sufficient justification for violence (ibid.: 22)

The significance of gender to these findings is not commented upon and no attention is paid to the social and cultural underpinnings of domestic violence, particularly its relation to masculinities and male identity (Horvath and Kelly, 2007). Moreover, despite the importance attached to equality, there is no mention of the link between domestic violence and gendered inequalities or of domestic violence being 'both cause and consequence' of such inequalities and representing an infringement of women's human rights (ibid.: 2).

This misrecognition of the nature of domestic violence has occurred despite the involvement of organizations such as Swansea Women's Aid, Tai Hafan and MEWN in the development of the Swansea strategy. These organizations have neither been able to counter the criminal justice framing of domestic violence nor have they been able to press the point that equality implies neither sameness nor gender neutrality. Indeed, if groups with different needs and requirements are treated the same, that is, equally, the outcome will simply reproduce existing inequalities rather than reducing them. Clearly, the incorporation of domestic violence into the criminal justice system and subsequent policy development has fundamentally influenced both the way the problem is understood and policy implementation at local level.

Many of those working in the domestic violence sector expressed their unhappiness with the strategy precisely because of its gender neutrality. One of the members of the Swansea Domestic Abuse Forum told us that, in her view, it tended to be people who had never worked with victims of domestic violence who insisted on an emphasis on gender neutrality. She spoke about the definition in the Swansea strategy.

> Ours is gender – well it is gender neutral in the sense that obviously we acknowledge that there is domestic abuse towards men, and everybody acknowledges that. It has been very difficult because some of us,

especially people with a sort of Women's Aid background or specifically women focused services, have always said 'well, it's not gender neutral is it?' and obviously it is not gender neutral in severity and percentage. (interview with Domestic Abuse Forum member)

The successor strategy, launched in October 2008, is much shorter, consisting of an action plan, which is similar to that of 2006–8, and contact details of local domestic violence agencies. This action plan was influenced by the key performance indicators which have recently been developed by domestic abuse coordinators in Wales. They include a range of tasks that community safety partnerships are expected to undertake such as producing a directory of local domestic violence services, developing a multi-agency strategy, supporting a domestic abuse forum, having an information-sharing protocol, linking with the all-Wales schools programme on domestic abuse, providing training, raising awareness of the twenty-four-hour helpline, undertaking perpetrator programmes, running MARACs, collecting multi-agency data, establishing links with the local safeguarding children boards, taking on board diversity issues and addressing the issue of forced marriage. Although meeting the key performance indicators is not a statutory requirement, the domestic abuse coordinators assume that it will be so in the future.

One of the Swansea Domestic Abuse Forum members told us that, as well as being based on the key performance indicators, the action plan had to be achievable within a year:

the action plan of the strategy that we have just written is only a year. We wanted to be realistic, because there is no point in writing an action plan that says things we are not going to achieve, because then, obviously, you get very negative feedback from service users and providers. So the things we have taken out are things . . . we knew we weren't going to achieve in a year. (interview with Domestic Abuse Forum member)

Gender neutrality and men

The commitment to gender neutrality that characterizes the Swansea strategy has been evident for some time and is linked discursively to the need to recognize that men may also experience domestic violence. Thus, the response of the Swansea Domestic Abuse Prevention forum, the forerunner of the Swansea Domestic Abuse Forum, to the Welsh Assembly Government's consultation on the all-Wales strategy pointed to the need for services for men who had experienced domestic violence:

> Although it [the draft strategy] acknowledges male victims by statement, the document's general use of the female gender for the victim does not point to the development of appropriate service responses for men. We would like to see strengthened the resources to make provision for victims of abuse who are not women – men in hetero and homo sexual relationships which are abusive.[10]

Responses like this were incorporated into the strategy which, while recognizing that it is women and children who overwhelmingly experience or are threatened with domestic violence and citing evidence in support of this, also points to the possibility that men may be victims (WAG, 2005: 7, 8, 15, 21). It is in this context that services for men who are experiencing domestic violence have been developed. Thus in Wales a service for men who have experienced domestic violence, the Dyn Project, was set up in 2005 and a refuge for men was set up in Montgomeryshire in 2006.

Misrecogntion and misleading statistics

While it is evident that some men do experience domestic violence, the scale of the problem appears to be exaggerated by the way in which government statistics are being used. Thus, until mid-2009 on both the Dyn Project and the Assembly websites, as well as in WAG press releases, the following statistics could be found: 1 in 4 women and 1 in 6 men experience domestic violence (see, for example, *http://www. dynproject.co.uk/default.asp?contentID=537*). This gives the impression that we are talking about a comparable phenomenon and, by implication, that services for women should be balanced by the provision of services to men, not equally but to a much greater extent than is the case at present. In the Swansea strategy these figures are used to extrapolate the numbers of women and men in Swansea who may be experiencing or threatened with domestic violence. These extrapolations suggest that '17,120 women and 10,773 men in Swansea may have been the victims of domestic abuse' and that '3,966 women and 2,920 men' may have experienced domestic violence in the past year (Safer Swansea Partnership, 2006: 14). If we look at how these statistics have been generated, however, we find that they are extremely misleading and that using them in this way amounts to a misrecognition and misrepresentation of the problem.

The figures come from a report into domestic violence conducted on behalf of the Home Office and published in 1999 (Mirrlees-Black, 1999). In this report domestic violence was defined as 'those incidents involving partners, ex-partners, household members or other relatives regardless of where they took place' (ibid.: 8). Using this measure the findings from the British Crime Survey showed that 23 per cent of women and 15 per cent of men aged between sixteen and fifty-nine had 'ever' experienced domestic violence. However, 'ever' experiencing domestic violence includes one-off incidents as well as repeated incidents of domestic violence and, if we remember the definition of domestic abuse in the Welsh strategy, one of the defining features of domestic abuse is that it is 'frequent and persistent' (WAG, 2005: 6). Like is not, therefore, being compared with like, especially when we take into account that the 'experiences of female victims are qualitatively different from that of most male victims. Not only are they more likely to be injured in assaults, they are also far more likely to be living in fear of their partners' (Mirrlees-Black, 1999: 20). And women were much more likely to

> be classified as chronic victims [i.e. those who had been assaulted three or more times] than men. A far larger proportion of women victims of domestic assault had suffered repeated victimisation. In total, three-quarters (73 per cent) of the chronic victims were women. (ibid.: 25)

Furthermore, 'women are far more likely than men to be repeatedly assaulted' (ibid.: 28) with '89 per cent of those who suffer sustained domestic violence' being women (EVAW, 2007). The Home Office study shows too that men in Wales are at a lower risk of assault than men in England so the bald statistics, misleading as they are, do not even apply in Wales. These findings, therefore, give the lie to the statistics that appear on official websites and in domestic abuse strategies.

In Scotland follow-up research into men who reported experiencing domestic violence to the British Crime Survey was carried out and showed that some of the men had reported being assaulted when they were themselves perpetrators, others had included non-domestic assaults and a quarter had not experienced domestic violence at all (Gadd et al., 2002). And, indeed, the Dyn Project, which provides a service for men who have experienced domestic violence, has to screen men who come to it very carefully in order to ensure that they provide services only to those who are genuinely in need of them. A report into the Dyn Project explains why this is necessary:

> Screening is not commonplace within services for women because women constitute the overwhelming majority of those abused; however, when working with *heterosexual* men it is not possible to rely on a statistical probability that they will be a victim. It has been established that perpetrators of domestic violence use the language of victimisation in order to minimize or excuse their actions. When working with *gay, bisexual and transgender* men, screening is essential because the dynamics of the relationship may not make it possible to easily identify the role of each partner or there may be a history of counter-allegations. (Robinson and Rowlands, 2006: 5 emphasis in original)

Furthermore, for heterosexual men who constitute 'the overwhelming bulk of cases coming to the Dyn Project', 'the distinction between "victim" and "perpetrator" is often blurred' (ibid.: 6). Many of these men are perpetrators or involved in 'common couple violence' where both partners are abusive and where, in a 'substantial number of cases', the man will have been the 'primary aggressor' (ibid.: 59).

Given these observations and the experiences of those working with men who claim to be victims of domestic violence, the figures for men's experiencing domestic violence derived from the British Crime Survey must be viewed as, at the very least, problematic. They can certainly not be used legitimately to claim that resources for men need to be on a par with those for women and it is disturbing that, until recently, they were used on the official WAG website (*http://wales.gov.uk/topics/housingandcommunity/safety/domesticabuse/?lang=en*, accessed 18 October 2008).[11]

The question of services for men and the gender-neutral definition of domestic abuse was raised as a matter of concern by several of the local domestic violence organizations and coordinators whom we interviewed. They do not wish to deny that some men experience domestic violence and require provision, but what they are concerned about is that resources will be diverted from women-only organizations and the provision of services to women will decline. Their fears are justified, given the pressure that some women's refuges are experiencing from local authorities to open their doors to men in the name of equality or risk losing their funding. This is despite the statement in the code of practice which is part of the gender equality duty which emphasizes the importance of gender-differentiated provision in relation to domestic violence.

Women make up the majority of victims of domestic violence and rape. It would not be appropriate, therefore, for a local council to seek to fund refuge services on a numerically equal basis for men and for women. The promotion of equal opportunities between men and women requires public authorities to recognize that the two groups are not starting from an equal footing and identical treatment would not be appropriate. (EVAW, 2007)

The misinterpretation of equality as implying sameness or gender neutrality is something on which the Equalities and Human Rights Commission (incorporating the Equal Opportunities Commission) Wales has taken a stand and it has recently written to all local authorities reminding them that 'domestic abuse is one of the most serious forms of gender inequality' (Jenkins and Dunne, 2007: 19). What is significant about the language used here is that domestic abuse is defined as an equality issue and linked to gender inequalities in particular, thereby reasserting its gendered nature and attempting to reframe it in terms of gendered power relations. This position not only re-emphasizes the gendered nature of domestic violence but also reframes it as a feature of male power and masculinity. It also links domestic violence to women's human rights (Horvath and Kelly, 2007). As such it is part of an ongoing struggle about defining domestic violence which has implications in terms of resource distribution, recognition and social justice.

Making a difference?

The evidence presented here shows the way in which policy developed at national UK level has been taken up at an all-Wales and local level. It is demonstrably the case that service provision for survivors of domestic violence has been improved. Resources have increased and been streamlined, with many projects being funded by the Welsh Assembly Government and more multi-agency working at local level. This improvement was reflected in the accounts of those working in the field. They spoke of the way that special domestic violence courts had improved women's experiences of going to court and how the introduction of multi-agency risk assessment conferences had led to better protection for those women most at risk from domestic violence. Along with these improvements, and particularly as a consequence of increased levels of funding and greater accountability,

Welsh Women's Aid and local Women's Aid groups have adopted more bureaucratic forms of organization. They have become service providers rather than feminist forms of welfare (Charles, 2004). The very real improvements, therefore, have come at the price of a reduction in autonomy for feminist-inspired organizations such as Welsh Women's Aid and their member groups, and the declining influence of feminist definitions of domestic violence on the domestic violence agenda. Taken together this represents a marginalization of more radical feminist voices within the domestic violence field (see also chapter 4). There also seems to be more central control exerted over the activities in which local groups can engage and some groups have experienced difficulties due to the interpretation of the gender equality duty at local level. Thus some local authorities have interpreted the gender equality duty as implying the need for equal treatment regardless of different need. This is reflected in the Swansea strategy where, although some groups are recognized as having special needs, such as travellers, BME groups and children, others, such as women, are not.

There are, however, some interesting tensions between the all-Wales strategy and the strategy that has been developed within Swansea which, we suggest, reflect the influence of key, strategic women within the Welsh Assembly Government. Both the all-Wales strategy and the Swansea strategy are situated within the national UK criminal justice framework and there is little leeway within this framework to dissent from a gender-neutral approach. There are, however, differences in emphasis between the two strategies, with the all-Wales strategy more clearly emphasizing the gendered nature of domestic violence. This contrasts with the Swansea strategy and may relate to the presence of key strategic women within the National Assembly as well as the presence of feminist organizations on the Working Group on Domestic Violence and Violence against Women; as a result the all-Wales strategy is not so militantly gender neutral as the local one. At local level, in contrast, there are no key feminists in powerful positions and especially not in the criminal justice agencies that appear to be controlling the agenda. This may partly explain the difference between the all-Wales and the local strategies. Furthermore, at local and UK level, criminal justice agencies have been able to impose the idea of gender neutrality which has implications both for resource distribution and in terms of recognition. In terms of recognition it means that the gendered dimensions of domestic violence are no longer recognized and that pressure on local refuge groups to open their doors to men is legitimated. It also means that there is pressure for resources to be distributed more evenly between services for women and men survivors; something which is highly problematic given that domestic violence is overwhelmingly experienced by women and that resources are limited. Thus the commitment to gender neutrality, which is how gender equality is being interpreted, is serving to mask the gendered dimensions of domestic violence. Gender equality is interpreted as implying gender neutrality. There appears to be no realization that the same treatment of groups which are differentially positioned with different needs reproduces inequalities rather than producing equality.

The way in which statistics on domestic violence are presented also gives cause for concern. As we have seen, high figures for 'ever experiencing' domestic violence conflate intimate partner violence with any violence, implying that men experience violence at the hands of women, whereas in fact it is more likely to be at the hands of other men. This underlines the fact that it is overwhelmingly male violence that is the problem and that it is not a phenomenon that is gender neutral. Violence is associated with masculinity in British culture, and it is this which needs to be changed if domestic violence is to be eradicated. Education programmes in schools are extremely important in this context and, although they are highlighted in the local and national strategies, not nearly as much resourcing is going into this as into other measures which actually 'mop up' after domestic violence rather than try to prevent it.

There seems to have been a shift in policy from the recognition that women – as a status group – are disproportionately disadvantaged by domestic violence to a view that domestic violence can affect anyone and *therefore* is not gendered. This view disregards the evidence that, on the whole, domestic violence is perpetrated by men on women, and that although individual men may experience domestic violence, men *as a group* do not. Thus, although services to those experiencing domestic violence have improved since devolution, a dangerous misrecognition of the nature of domestic violence has become dominant in WAG policy and in domestic violence strategies at local level. This can be related to the dominance of the criminal justice agenda and to the insistence on gender neutrality. This, we suggest, is in danger of rendering invisible the profoundly gendered nature of domestic violence which, in turn, will have implications in terms both of resource distribution and of social justice for the some of the most disadvantaged groups of women in Wales.

Notes

1. There is currently no refuge in Blaenau Gwent CBC, however a refuge is being developed there for people with complex needs and is due to open towards the end of this year.
2. The British Crime Survey (Home Office, 2000) reports that domestic violence is the least likely violent crime to be reported, with just under one-third of all cases reported to the police.
3. This culminated in the publication in (2005) of S. Jones, N. Charles and H. Edwards, *An Audit of Domestic Abuse in Swansea*, for the City and County of Swansea and the Safer Swansea Partnership.
4. ESRC grant number RES-000–23–1185 awarded to Nickie Charles (principal investigator), Charlotte Davies and Stephanie Jones.
5. Such a broad definition is in use only in England and Wales and differs not only from the one in use in Scotland but also from the one to be found in the UN Declaration on the Elimination of Violence Against Women which defines violence against women as 'any act of gender-based violence that results in, or is likely to result in, physical, sexual or psychological harm or suffering to women, including threats of such acts, coercion or arbitrary deprivation of liberty, whether occurring in public or in private life' (Horvath and Kelly, 2007: 3).
6. Welsh Women's Aid's definition of domestic abuse can be found on their website and is

   > the actual or threatened physical, emotional, psychological, sexual or financial abuse of a woman by a partner, family member or someone with whom there is, or has been, a close relationship. This abuse also relates to the perpetrator allowing or causing a child to witness, or be at risk of witnessing domestic abuse.

   They add that domestic abuse 'essentially involves the misuse of power' and that 97 per cent of reported 'incidences [*sic*] of domestic abuse are perpetrated by men against women' (*http://www.welshwomensaid. org/index.html*, 4 October 2008).
7. Welsh Women's Aid currently receives £1,019,261 from the Welsh Assembly Government to fund the organization's ten full-time workers, its children's services and the twenty-four-hour helpline. However, this does not cover the organization's running costs (WWA, 2008: 21). The Supporting People revenue grant provides funding for refuges indirectly as it is paid to an accredited support provider: these can be housing associations, local authorities and recently Welsh Women's Aid has itself

become an accredited support provider. Local refuge groups have a contract with an ASP to provide services to women and children fleeing domestic violence and it is via them that they receive the Supporting People revenue grant funding.

[8] Southall Black Sisters had to take Ealing Council to court because Ealing was arguing that a service specifically for minority ethnic women was no longer permissible in the light of the various equality duties. The council settled before a judgment was reached which is unfortunate as it means that this case does not set a precedent.

[9] See *http://www.assemblywales.org/bus-home/bus-committees/bus-comm ittees-third1/bus-committees-third-ccc-home/cc_inquiries/nafw_domestic_ abuse_-_home/domestic_abuse/cc_3_da_responses.htm.*

[10] Swansea Domestic Abuse Prevention Forum: *Response to Tackling Domestic Abuse: the All Wales National Strategy*, item 10, 17 September 2004.

[11] These statistics were removed from the websites of the WAG and the Dyn Project in the summer of 2009. Earlier that year there had been wide-spread dissemination of research findings from the project 'Gender and political processes in the context of devolution' which pointed out the problems in the way these statistics were being used. It is possible that these developments were linked (for details of the research findings document see *http://www2.warwick.ac.uk/fac/soc/sociology/rsw/resear ch_centres/gender/gppcd/dissconf*).

References

Ball, W. and N. Charles (2006). 'Feminist social movements and policy change: devolution, childcare and domestic violence policies in Wales', *Women's Studies International Forum*, 29,172–83.

British Medical Association (BMA) (1998). *Domestic Violence: A Healthcare Issue?*, London: BMA.

CC(3)–06–08: paper 1 (2008). Inquiry into domestic abuse: evidence to the Communities and Culture Committee, presented by the minister for social justice and local government, p. 2, *http://www.assemblywales.org/ bus-home/bus-committees/bus-committees-third1/bus-committees-third-ccc -home/cc_inquiries/nafw_domestic_abuse_-_home/domestic_abuse/cc_3_ da_responses.htm*, accessed 12 October 2008.

Charles, N. (1991). *The Funding of Women's Aid Services to the Community: A Research Report*, Cardiff: Welsh Women's Aid.

—— (1995). 'Feminist politics, domestic violence and the state', *Sociological Review*, 43, 4, 617–40.

—— (2000). *Feminism, the State and Social Policy*, Macmillan: Basingstoke.

—— (2004). 'Feminist politics and devolution: a preliminary analysis', *Social Politics*, 11, 2, 297–311.

City and County of Swansea (2004). *Ambition is Critical: Making a Better Swansea*, Swansea : City and County of Swansea.

—— (2005). 'Domestic abuse position paper', Directorate of Social Services and Housing, Swansea: Social Services Cabinet Advisory Committee.

Department of Health (DoH) (2000). *Domestic Violence: A Resource Manual for Health Professionals*, London: DoH.

Dobrowolsky, A. and J. Jensen (2004). 'Shifting representations of citizenship: Canadian politics of "women" and "children"', *Social Politics*, 11, 2, 154–80.

End Violence Against Women (EVAW) (2007). *Making the Grade? 2007: the Third Annual Independent Analysis of UK Government Initiatives on Violence against Women*, London: End Violence Against Women Coalition, *www.endviolenceagainstwomen.org.uk*.

Ferree, M. M. (2003). 'Resonance and radicalism: feminist framing of abortion in the United States and Germany', *American Journal of Sociology*, 109, 2, 304–44.

Gadd, D., S. Farrall, S. Dallimore and N. Lombard (2002). 'Domestic abuse against men in Scotland', research finding no. 61/2002, *www.scotland. gov.uk/Publications/2002/09/15160/9339*, accessed 18 September 2008.

Home Office (2000). *British Crime Survey*, London: Home Office.

—— (2003). *Safety and Justice: the Government's Proposals on Domestic Violence*, London: Home Office.

—— (2005). *Domestic Violence: A National Report*, London: Home Office.

Horvath, M. and L. Kelly (2007). *From the Outset: Why Violence should be a Priority for the Commission for Equality and Human Rights*, London: End Violence Against Women.

Jenkins, T. and J. Dunne (2007). *Domestic Abuse: the Facts*, a secondary research report, Manchester: Equal Opportunities Commission, August.

Jones, S., N. Charles and H. Edwards (2005). *An Audit of Domestic Abuse in Swansea*, for the City and County of Swansea and Safer Swansea Partnership.

Lister, R. (2003). 'Investing in the citizen-workers of the future: transformation in citzenship and the state under New Labour', *Social Policy and Administration*, 37, 5, 427–43.

Mirrlees-Black, C. (1999). *Domestic Violence: Findings from a new British Crime Survey Self-completion Questionnaire*, Home Office research study 191, London: Home Office.

Robinson, A. and J. Rowlands (2006). *The Dyn Project: Supporting Men Experiencing Domestic Abuse: Final Evaluation Report*, Cardiff: Cardiff University and the Dyn Project.

Royal College of General Practitioners (RCGP) (2002). *Domestic Violence: the General Practitioner's Role*, London: RCGP.

—— (2003). *Domestic Violence in Families with Children: Guidance for Primary Healthcare Professionals*, London: RCGP.

Royal College of Midwives (1997). *Domestic Abuse in Pregnancy*, Position Paper 19, London: Royal College of Midwives.

Safer Swansea Partnership (2006). *The Swansea Domestic Abuse Strategy 2006–08 Laying the Foundations*, Swansea: Safer Swansea Partnership.

Taket, A (2004). *Tackling Domestic Violence – The role of Health Professionals*, London: Home Office.

The Record, 21 January 2004, offical record of National Assembly plenary sessions.

Trades Union Congress (TUC) (2002). *Domestic Violence: A Guide for the Workplace*, London: TUC.

UNISON (2003). *Raise the Roof on Domestic Abuse*, London: UNISON.

Welsh Assembly Government (WAG) (2005). *Tackling Domestic Abuse: The all-Wales National Strategy: A Joint-Agency Approach*, Cardiff: WAG.

Williams, F. and S. Roseneil (2004). 'Public values of parenting and part-nering: voluntary organizations and welfare politics in New Labour's Britain', *Social Politics*, 11, 2, 181–216.

Working Group Minutes (16 December 2003), minutes of the Working Group on Domestic Violence and Violence Against Women in Wales, WAG document.

Welsh Women's Aid (WWA) (2008). Communities and Culture Committee, Scrutiny Enquiry: Domestic Abuse, response from Welsh Women's Aid, *http://www.assemblywales.org/cc_3_dall_._welsh_women_s_aid_response. pdf*, accessed 12 October 2008.

6

Mainstreaming Across the Equality Dimensions: Policy on Sexual Orientation in Wales

ALISON PARKEN

The statutory equality duty within the Government of Wales Act 1998 (s.120) required the National Assembly to ensure that 'functions are exercised with due regard to the principle that there should be equality of opportunity for all people'. The duty, now superseded by the Government of Wales Act 2006 (s.77) such that its requirements now rest expressly with ministers, is unique through its inclusion of 'all people'. As a result, sexual orientation has been included within the equality infrastructure of government in Wales from the inception of devolution.

The statutory duty, interpreted as a requirement to promote equality, has provided a platform to equate it with the potentially transformative approach to equalities work known as 'gender main-streaming' (Rees, 1998, 2005) which is discussed and evaluated by Chaney (chapter 2, this volume). Gender mainstreaming has a legal basis within the Treaty of Amsterdam 1997. As adopted by the European Commission, it is defined as: 'mobilising all general policies and measures specifically for the purpose of achieving equality by actively and openly taking account at the planning stage of their possible effects on the respective situations of men and women' (Commission of the European Communities, 1996).[1] Thus actions to eliminate inequalities and to promote equality, for women and men, are not limited to discrete equality legislation or restricted to anti-discrimination measures. Following this, the Wales equality duty can be interpreted as an 'absolute duty' (Chaney and Fevre, 2002) that equality should be promoted, in all policies, and for all people.

The National Assembly for Wales Standing Committee on Equality of Opportunity has reinforced this interpretation through its definition of equality mainstreaming: 'equality issues should be considered from the outset as an integral part of the policy making and service delivery process' (NAW, 2003a). Indeed, the cross-party, cross-cutting, equality committee included sexual orientation within its remit for promoting equality prior to the existence of any UK anti-discrimination legislation on that basis (NAW, 1999). In theory, this action pre-empted and exceeded the scope of the subsequent Employment Equality Regulations (Sexual Orientation) 2003 and Sexual Orientation Regulations 2007. The committee's aim has been an evidence-based mainstreaming approach for all equality strands.

As a result there has been a growing interest in trying to understand how to promote equality in ways that encompass all the 'strands' of equality as well as providing evidence of intersectional inequalities in Wales, at a European level (Yuval-Davies, 2006; Verloo, 2006) and within the UK, following the government's proposal for a single equality duty, to be 'known as the public sector duty' (Government Equalities Office, 2008: 105). Whether the principles and tools of gender mainstreaming can be transferred to mainstreaming equality more generally has, however, been questioned (Rees, 1998; Walby, 2005) and Wales has led the way in this enquiry through research designed to establish a 'multi-strand' approach to promoting equality and human rights within equality impact assessments (Parken and Young, 2007, 2008; Parken, 2010). This research was limited, however, by the adoption of existing constructions of equality within the policy frames of sexual orientation and gender mainstreaming. It was not within its remit to consider how the gender mainstreaming frame might limit enquiry into social justice on grounds of gender by not considering sexual orientation, or how the framing of sexual orientation legislation might not take gender into account.

In this chapter, I examine the legacy of the 'single strand' approach to equal treatment legislation dominant at European Union and nation-state level, and show how both gender mainstreaming and sexual orientation policies need to be reframed to recognize their intersectionality. I then review some examples of how sexual orientation has been included within policies and strategies in Wales. These examples reveal that the 'single strand' equal treatment paradigm remains dominant but also point to education policy in Wales as having the potential for an intersectional frame that could promote equality on grounds of gender and sexuality. First, however, I look at how sexuality and gender have been understood and the implications of such understandings for policy development.

Intersectionality – the case for a hetero-gendered policy frame

In the social sciences, sexuality is understood not as biologically determined or fixed but as a potentially fluid interrelationship between subjectivity, society and the body (Duncan, 1996; Nye, 1999).[2] Being socially constructed, and varying by ethnicity, gender and over place, time and lifespan (Simon and Gagnon, 1998; Weeks, 1985; Vance, 1992), should not imply that an individual's sexuality is any more easily changeable than if it were to be conceived of as biologically determined. However, many lesbians and gay men endorse a biological stance and resist discussion of sexuality as socially constructed. Their fear is that in societies where heterosexuality is reified as the 'natural norm', they may be asked to 'choose' differently (Rahman and Jackson, 1997; Power, 1998). An examination of the social and economic institutions that construct heterosexuality, and its place in defining gender roles, is thus required. In particular, the power to define sexuality has significant consequences for all women in relation to policymaking.

The way in which gender and sexuality are defined within activism and in the academy, amongst proponents of feminist, lesbian and gay and queer sociology, is contested and has changed over time.[3] In the wake of the 'sex-wars' (see Caplan, 1987; Hawkes, 1996; Jackson and Scott, 1996; Vance, 1992) there has been a movement from a radical gender politics to a politics of sexual plurality (Parken, 2003) while over the past four decades the political agendas of gender or sexuality-based social movements have been variously in concert or in conflict (Jackson and Scott, 1996; Plummer, 2000). This history affects how lesbian, gay and bisexual people situate their identities in relation to gender, sexuality, age, class and ethnicity, and thus how they interpret their circumstances in changing situations in relation to equalities policies. It raises the question of when, and in what circumstances, gender or sexual orientation is the more relevant, as well as how they might interact.

In what follows I argue that sexual orientation policy is gender blind and that gender mainstreaming is sexuality blind. This means that in order to develop a coherent policy framework these two aspects of inequality need to be brought together. I do this by looking first at sexual orientation then gender equality policies.

Existing policy frameworks – sexual orientation

Within UK legislation, sexual orientation has been conceived narrowly as an issue of individual personal identity, requiring remedy only through 'recognition' (Fraser, 1997) or inclusion in an anti-discrimination approach. The Employment Equality (Sexual Orientation) Regulations 2003 prohibit discrimination in education, training and employment, and define sexual orientation as:

- orientation towards persons of the same sex; or
- orientation towards persons of the opposite sex; and
- orientation towards persons of the same and the opposite sex.

The term sexual orientation covers heterosexuals, lesbians, gay men and bisexuals and is not limited to sexual activity. The term 'sexual identity' is preferred by an Office for National Statistics working group set up to examine how to include a measure in national datasets, excluding the census (Wilmot, 2007). Questions about sexual identity will be included in all major household surveys such as the Annual Population Survey and Labour Force Survey from 2009, with first reports available in 2010. Through self-identification, this term allows for a definition expanded beyond sexual activity, to include issues of culture and potential inequalities that are shared within a 'community of interest' (Stonewall Cymru, 2004).[4]

Both terms, however, leave vague the question as to whether the legislation includes protection against discrimination for outward 'display' that might indicate that someone is lesbian or gay (*Equal Opportunities Review*, 2003: 22).[5] In a research interview that I conducted in 2001 with the organization Lesbian and Gay Employment Rights (LAGER), the interviewee recalled advocating in a case brought under the Sex Discrimination Act 1975, where a male employee was dismissed for perceived 'effeminacy'. The way that the employee walked on the shop floor, described as 'wiggling' by managers in company memos, was said to be 'putting customers off' (Parken, 2003: 266). The employee was being censured for not 'doing gender' appropriately (West and Zimmerman, 1987), that is, as a heterosexual performance of masculinity. Thus it is to the naturalized ways of 'doing gender' as 'doing heterosexuality' (Parken, 2003), or hetero-gender, that we must look to link gender, sexuality and inequality.

Moreover, prior to the introduction of the Employment Equality (Sexual Orientation) Regulations 2003, other, unsuccessful attempts had been made to extend protection to lesbians and gay men under sex discrimination law. That the arguments were not accepted reveals how lesbians and gay men were divorced from their gender by their sexual orientation and, by this means, denied protection under the sex discrimination legislation.

In the case of Pearce v Governing Body of Mayfield Secondary School (2001) IRLR 669, for instance, it was argued that the abuse to which school teacher Shirley Pearce was subject from pupils was gender specific; she was called 'lesbian shit', 'lemon', 'lezzie', 'dyke' (Monaghan, 2002: 1). However, under the requirement for 'comparators', peculiar to UK law, employment tribunals have held that the proper comparator for a lesbian is a gay man and vice versa (heterosexuals bringing sex discrimination cases were not required to know the sexuality of their comparator). Further, tribunals have argued that if their comparator would also have been discriminated against (although the abuse would have been differently gendered), then there was not sex discrimination but sexual orientation discrimination. As the discrimination lawyer, Karen Monaghan argues,

> The fact that a pupil might subject a lesbian teacher and a gay man teacher to gender specific homophobic abuse does not mean that neither are discriminated against on the grounds of sex – *it means they are both discriminated against on grounds of sex.* The CA apparently confuse motive with grounds. (2002: 2, my emphasis)[6]

The connection between gender and sexuality is revealed where complainants are 'policed' for not 'doing gender' as a heterosexual performance of femininity or masculinity (West and Zimmerman, 1987). In this way, sexual orientation policy divorces sexuality from gender whilst, in relation to gender discrimination, heterosexual men's and women's sexuality is so naturalized (assumed) as to have become invisible. In other words, sexual orientation legislation is gender blind while gender mainstreaming policy, although structured by heterosexuality, is sexuality blind.

Existing policy frameworks – gender equality

In reality, gender and sexuality are deeply imbricated and have profound material consequences in terms of access to employment. This, however, is not necessarily recognized, either in academic analysis or in policy development. It has been argued, for example, that jobs are not gender neutral (Acker, 1990) but, rather, are spaces where we 'play out' or construct our gender. The particular ways in which masculinity and femininity are performed in different locations in the labour market have been described for the printing industry (Cockburn, 1985), retail services (Cockburn, 1991; MacEwen Scott, 1994), engineering (Breakwell, 1985), the airline industry (Taylor and Tyler, 2000), tourism and services more generally (Adkins, 1995; 2000), the media (Parken, 2003) and in various locations within 'the city' (McDowell, 1997). Such gender performances are, however, narrowly conceived within the inequitable heterosexual gender binary.

Lesbian, gay and bisexual (LGB) people may experience the requirement to produce such a *hetero-gendered* performance (Parken, 2003) as 'chill factors' leading to occupational ghettoization (Hall, 1989). Moreover, discomfort with gender 'fit' and discrimination in employment can contribute to the risk of poverty for LGB people (John and Patrick, 1999). Bellis and Boyce (2005) suggest that, because of this, targeted pre-employment support, often via LGB community groups, may be necessary to build sufficient confidence before some LGB people can join mainstream training and employment programmes.

This suggests that it is important to analyse gender and sexuality as intersectional and as relating to all people. This has been done by considering how the labour market is structured by both gender and sexuality. A material analysis of how gender is constructed within the social and economic institutions of heterosexuality (see Delphy, 1984; Delphy and Leonard, 1992; Adkins and Leonard, 1996; Adkins and Lury, 1996) argues that, contrary to dominant economic models where gender, because it is both biological and sociological, is said to create the division of labour (Becker, 1981), the division of labour creates gender (Giddings, 1998: 98). Here, the organization of labour markets is analysed as situating men, unfettered by caring responsibilities, as the 'ideal workers' of capitalism (Pateman, 1988). The 'employment contract' is underpinned by a marriage contract, wherein women's unpaid childcare and adult dependent care work, is assumed and reinforced by welfare and employment programmes, income tax and national insurance rules. This formulates a 'bread-winner ideology' or 'gender contract' (Rees, 1998). Gender and sexuality become anything but a private matter and their 'public' organization is detrimental to women:

> If men's ability to retain their labour market advantage rests largely on their capacity to appropriate the unwaged labour of women (Pateman, 1988), then we need to recognise the centrality of heterosexuality for providing the logic that translates women's labour into men's material advantage . . . [accusations of privilege often] levelled at heterosexual feminists can be seen as contradictory. (Dunne, 2000: 137)

Addressing the 'gender contract' is the focus of the gender main-streaming approach to equality, as it seeks to 'undo' the ways in which gender has become a key distributor of who works, where they work, under what conditions and for how many hours (Rees, 1998, 2005). However, gender mainstreaming is silent on the construction of the inequitable gender binary within heterosexual systems. It does not acknowledge that the 'gender contract' is an economic and social 'heterosexual gender contract'. It is still lesbian, gay and bisexual people who are seen to have 'brought sexuality into' policymaking as an 'issue'.

Lesbian and gay economists have also identified the assumption of heterosexuality in dominant economic models.[7] As a result of studies, which have mostly taken place in North America, authors call for the discipline of economics to engage with this critique, such that Allen argues that lesbian women's rejection of 'that primary form of obliga-tion, obligation to men' (1986: 37) brings a lesbian economics into being. Lesbians' need for financial independence, without the construction of their femininity being 'played out' with the expecta-tion of inclusion in the breadwinner/homemaker framework, means that it is not possible to 'add lesbians in' to current gender main-streaming frameworks, just as it has not been possible to secure change by 'adding women in' to existing androcentric institutions and their hierarchies.[8] I suggest the way forward for all women is an under-standing of economic and social systems as *hetero-gendered* (Parken, 2003), thus bringing together an intersectional analysis of gender and sexuality.

Such an analysis would mean that, when considering women's economic position more widely, we would consider the ways that gender is informed by heterosexual household organization. The recently revised Welsh Assembly Government (WAG) Communities First strategy (WAG, 2008a) provides an illustration of this. It defines tackling child poverty as its main aim and posits employment as the main route out of child poverty. Yet it is silent on the question of gender, beyond an indication that most lone parents are women. An investigation into relative incomes within heterosexual families, however, reveals that only one in ten men on low incomes earn sufficient to keep their families out of poverty (Millar and Gardiner, 2004), and that in 2004–5, for 39 per cent of couples, less than a quarter of total family income came from the individual incomes of women (Department for Work and Pensions, 2006). More significantly, research shows that it is often the second earner's income (most often a woman's) that can make the difference between falling into or, getting out of, poverty (Millar and Gardiner, 2004). By not examining income disparity by gender within heterosexual couple households the policy assumes resources are shared equally. A different, *hetero-gendered* analysis could have led to the production of a gendered employment strategy designed to assist women in couples to join the labour market.

An analysis of unequal pay within the WAG Equal Pay campaign which has been running for several years, with partners in the TUC and Equal Opportunities Commission, may also look different through a hetero-gendered analytical lens. Here we see the particular struggle lesbians have for financial independence in labour markets defined by the hetero-gendered breadwinner ideology. Siltanen's (2002) analysis of occupational segregation (including part-time working), describes a 'full wage' as sufficient to support a financially independent household and other household members not in waged work. Her study of postal workers demonstrated that 'typical' gendered work patterns mean that 'women's jobs' are characterized by 'component wages', which are insufficient to maintain a financially independent household or support a dependent. Age, ethnicity and marital status also affected the times at which men and women might be in 'full wage' jobs. For women, a move to 'full wages' often meant taking up 'men's' work and overtime working (Siltanen, 2002).

Dunne's (1997) research with lesbians in senior management and the professions also showed how coming to identify as lesbian in later life led many who had previously identified themselves as heterosexual to a renewed interest in education or careers and/or attempts to find routes into 'men's work' so that they might attain individual financial independence. There may be similarities for single and divorced women who have not been in, or find themselves one step removed, from the heterosexual breadwinner/homemaker framework.

Several studies also point to gender disparity in pay between gay men and lesbians (Badgett, 1995; Brown, 1998; Arabsheibani et al., 2002; 2003). The most recent figures, coming as part of the Stonewall Cymru Survey *Counted In!* (Williams and Robinson, 2007), which is funded by WAG, show that 'although women were more likely to have university degrees [than gay men in the study], they were less likely to hold managerial or supervisory positions within organisations' (p. 46), and that as a consequence 'average annual earnings for men was £25,500 compared to £21,600 for women'.

A policy perspective that examined how gender is constructed within heterosexually defined economic and social systems might also challenge calls under gender mainstreaming for working hours, transport, health and social care systems and employment contracts to reflect what women do as well as men (Parken, 2003). These policies tend to assume and reinforce the heterosexual household division of labour by seeking to make it easier for (heterosexual) women to 'marry' working and caring. They do not upset the gender hierarchy and so may not ultimately benefit heterosexual women, and they may not tackle issues of concern for lesbian women in employment.

Bringing gender and sexuality together

Sexual orientation policy too is a long way from adopting such an analysis of gender, anywhere in the UK. The policy frame does not allow examination of the material consequences and inequalities of hetero-gendering for lesbians and gay men, and leaves us at the 'recognition' end of Fraser's (1997) recognition versus redistribution social justice dichotomy. The result is a loss of focus on gender not only for lesbians in relation to gay men but on the intersection of gender and sexuality in equality policy for all.

There are obvious implications here for future cross-strand or intersectional working. Currently, cross-strand working operates on an 'additive model' (Crenshaw, 1994), but is criticized for beginning from one strand and then adding on another, or several strands, without taking into account the differing origins of, or mechanisms that reproduce, different inequalities (Verloo, 2006). As we have seen this leaves unaddressed the structural connections and consequences of inequalities. It is necessary to move beyond the single-strand approach.

It is encouraging that some early stage thinking on these issues has recently been championed by the National Assembly for Wales through the 'multi-strand project' (Parken and Young, 2007; Parken, 2010).[9] However, I have argued that we should now progress to an intersectional analysis of gender and sexuality that examines the roots or origins of each apparently separate equality strand for the deep connections that build and sustain inequalities. Such an analysis would also bring transgender people within the scope of analysis of both gender and sexuality.

In the next section, I review the development of sexual orientation policy and the equality infrastructure since devolution within the existing policy frame, one which separates gender and sexuality. I also consider education policies in Wales which show the potential of an intersectional approach.

Equality infrastructure for sexual orientation in Wales

The current equality duty requires the Welsh ministers:

> after each financial year, to publish and lay before the Assembly a report containing a statement of the arrangements made under subsection (1) which had effect during that financial year and an assessment of how effective they were in promoting equality of opportunity. (Government of Wales Act, s.77, 243)

By aiming for equality of opportunity for all, the duty exceeds the scope of the 'six strand' approach prevalent since the Equal Treatment Directive (2000) and the legal duties to promote equality (Race Equality Duty, 2000; Disability Equality Duty, 2005; Gender Equality Duty, 2006). In the extract above we see that equality of opportunity is clearly interpreted as promoting equality.

To support the operation of the duty, the Labour administration of the first Assembly (1999–2003) created an equality infrastructure. At this time there was little community capacity to support engagement with people not covered by equality legislation including lesbian, gay and bisexual (LGB) people. The government recognized the need to hear directly the voices of the marginalized on issues regarding disability, sexual orientation, ethnicity and gender. As a result the Welsh Assembly Government provided core funding to four 'all-Wales' consultative groups, so that they may garner information on equality issues to inform policymaking and service delivery. The LGB Forum/Stonewall Cymru was one of these groups (see also Sandra Betts's chapter in this volume on the gender equality policy network).

The Stonewall equality lobbying group was formed initially in 1989 to 'fight the clause', section 28 of the Local Government Act 1986 (enacted 1988), which suggested that local authorities in England and Wales had been 'promoting' homosexuality. It was interpreted, wrongly, to suggest that there could be no discussion of lesbian and gay lives within schools, particularly in personal and social education.

Drawing upon Stonewall's lobbying experience, the fledging LGB Forum – at the time with two part-time staff and an active voluntary council (gender balanced and with representatives of other 'strands') – established campaigning in Wales to include equality issues in legislation, employment, civil partnerships, goods and services, education, employment, community safety, health, community development and fair portrayal of LGB people in the Welsh media. The LGB Forum became Stonewall Cymru in 2003, in recognition of the operational support provided by Stonewall and the need for greater cross-border links. Indeed, at the Stonewall Cymru 2006 annual conference, where the minister for business and equality, Jane Hutt, gave the keynote speech (ministers have regularly spoken at these events on, for example, education, health and mainstreaming equality), Ben Summerskill, chief executive of Stonewall, stated that the stance taken by the minister, the National Assembly for Wales and the all-party, cross-cutting, Equality of Opportunity Committee (to refuse a delay in sexual orientation anti-discrimination legislation for goods, facilities and services until a single equality act was prepared) had been vital in gaining commitment to legislation in the Equality Act 2006.

Funded by, and working with, the government of Wales as a 'critical friend' enabled Stonewall Cymru to become a valuable partner to government and service providers in Wales. Central to this integration was the decision by the first and second National Assembly Standing Committee on Equality of Opportunity specifically to include sexual orientation in its remit:

> The Committee's terms of reference are set out in Standing Order 14, which requires it to have particular regard to the need for the Assembly

to avoid discrimination on grounds of gender, race or disability. While maintaining this focus, the Committee also considers other sources of discrimination, for example, age, sexual orientation, faith or religious belief. (NAW, 2003a)

Further, the decision of the Equality of Opportunity Committee, supported by the directors of the statutory equality commissions in Wales, to invite Stonewall Cymru to act, alongside representatives from the commissions, as a 'standing invitee', can be said to have put sexual orientation equality issues on a par with race, disability and gender.

As a cross-party and cross-cutting committee, the Equality of Opportunity Committee is required by

Standing Orders to scrutinise the Assembly's Annual report on equality, which includes the details of all actions by government departments; primary equality legislation that is remitted to the Business Minister (following a change to Standing Order 6.6iv on 22 February 2005), and the annual reports of . . . 'public bodies concerned with the promotion of equal opportunities' (the statutory equality commissions and WLGA Equalities Unit) (NAW, 2003a)[10]

In this regard, recommendations from two Stonewall Cymru surveys have been adopted by the National Assembly, successfully embedding consideration of sexual orientation, on a wider social justice footing, into the policy areas outlined above. The first all-Wales LGB survey (Robinson and Williams, 2003)[11] also considered criminal justice (although not devolved) and media, as well as measuring how comfortable LGB people in Wales felt about being 'out' in various public service settings such as in interaction with GPs. The second, *Count us In!* (Stonewall, 2004), which reported on the participation of LGB people in Wales in their geographical communities and in their 'community of interest', with a particular focus on those living in rural areas, was extensively discussed at committee. Stonewall in Wales has chosen a community development focus so that through regional LGB forums local issues are communicated to local authorities, police and public sector service providers.

Following the adoption of the recommendations, the minister with responsibility for equality reports annually to the equality committee on the progress made by government and service providers towards meeting the recommendations. This has created time for discussion of sexual orientation issues at the heart of government that is perhaps unique to the devolved nations. It has also provided for Stonewall Cymru to be present to argue for LGB equality, and mainstreaming equality more broadly, in policy forums such as the Census Advisory Group, the Wales Equality Reference Group and the Mainstreaming Equality Task and Finish Group (2005–6). The latter sought to implement the recommendations of the equality committee's *Report on Mainstreaming* (NAW, 2004), in which sexual orientation was again included under the rubric of promoting equality.

One of the key recommendations from this review was the need to address the evidence base for equality, to inform policymaking and make it possible to measure policy outcomes. This is vital for progress towards promoting equality for LGB people. Sexual orientation does not appear in the Census of Population. As a consequence, there is no national population baseline for LGB people, and no opportunity to consider gender and sexuality intersectionally. Despite the efforts of Stonewall Cymru and other lobbying groups, the equality committee and service providers in Wales (and England) who argued for its inclusion (placing it third in an Office of National Statistics consultation on new topics for inclusion), it will not be included in 2011. The opportunity to consider gender and sexuality in relation to pay, income, unpaid work and employment will be missed.

Such a data hierarchy hampers the operation of equality impact assessments (EIAs) and creates inequality between equality strands (Parken and Young, 2007). However, a Welsh Assembly Government Equalities Evidence Review is currently underway with the aim of formally identifying data gaps. A Data Asset Register for Equality Strands is then to be compiled with the aim of assisting officials to carry out EIAs. This review will include sexual orientation in its remit although it will find little quantitative data to detail.

Wales's equality infrastructure also enjoins former National Assembly-sponsored public bodies and service deliverers to gain insight into LGB lives in Wales; this means that Stonewall Cymru is asked to represent their interests on a host of committees. To list just a few: the SME Equality Project (Welsh Development Agency, now part of the Welsh Assembly Government); the LGB committees of the four separate police forces in Wales (although policing is not devolved); the equality officers network for all twenty-two local authorities; voluntary sector advice provider forums; equality committees of NHS trusts; the steering group of the NHS Centre for Equality and Human Rights; and the Welsh Assembly Government Anti-Bullying Network.

Given this descriptive review of the equality infrastructure in Wales, I conclude that the systems and structures of the devolved government, and exceptional access to ministers and senior officials, provide a rare opportunity to discuss issues of sexual orientation inequality. Given this level of inclusion, I turn to consider how this has influenced policy.

Policy and legislative change

It is not possible to review all Welsh Assembly Government policies. This overview will describe where sexual orientation has been included, at least in name, in policies and high-level strategies. However, I will also discuss polices that aim to tackle homophobic bullying in schools in Wales, which appear to incorporate some understanding of the connections between gender and sexuality.

Welsh Assembly Government core strategies and policy documents have long referred to their commitments to section 120 (now section 77 of the new Government of Wales Act 2006). However, sexual orientation was not mentioned by name in several key programme documents in the first and second Assemblies. Although not an exhaustive list, sexual orientation is named in the following strategies: the *Black, Minority, Ethnic Housing Action Plan* (2002); *Community Safety Strategies* (2005–8); *Creative Futures: A Culture Strategy* (2000); *Designed for Life* (WAG, 2005a); *Health Care Standards for Wales* (WAG, 2005b); *Rural Development Plan for Wales* (WAG, 2006a); *Making the Connections* (WAG, 2004a); *Delivering the Connections* (WAG, 2005c); *Communities Next* (WAG, 2008a).[12]

In strategies and action plans, sexual orientation most often appears as part of the now familiar 'six strand' equalities list. The Welsh language is sometimes included in such lists with sexual orientation, age, gender, disability, ethnicity and religion and belief. However, this equality terminology displays adherence to a compliance model providing only for the negative right not to be discriminated against. The language used suggests that services are available to all 'regardless of' or 'irrespective of' sexual orientation. This homogenizes lesbians and gay men and makes the gender inequalities they experience invisible. It also falls short of the positive and proactive approach to mainstreaming equality envisioned through the statutory duty.

148

Examples of exceptions to this negative codification of equality in Welsh Assembly Government policy include: *The Carers' Strategy* (WAG, 2007a), *Communities First Guidance* (NAW, 2001), *The Learning Country 2: Delivering the Promise* (WAG, 2006b), *Fulfilled Lives, Supportive Communities: A Strategy for Social Services in Wales* (WAG, 2006c), and *The Wales Spatial Plan* (WAG, 2004b). In these strategies the content and language displays concern with understanding subjective specificities in regard to an individual's difference, barriers they may face and contributions they make, by designing services to include, rather than ensure they are not excluded, as compliance with the equal treatment paradigm suggests.

A good example of moving beyond this approach is the recent ministerial health guidance circular, *Raising Awareness of the Needs of Lesbian, Gay and Bisexual People when Accessing Health Services*, which states:

> The commitment of organisations within NHS Wales that all patients will receive services that are sensitive to their individual health needs should ensure that LGB people whether single or in a relationship, are treated with dignity and respect because of their differences and not in spite of them. (NAW, 2008a: 3)

Significantly, *One Wales* (WAG, 2007b), the current Labour/Plaid Cymru coalition government's four-year programme document, focuses extensively on equality and social justice, and includes sexual orientation under promoting equality. There is perhaps room in its characterization of discrimination as not only affecting individuals but also groups, to the extent that their life chances may be damaged and that they need to feel valued (2007b: 26), to broaden equality efforts beyond compliance with anti-discrimination measures. There are also further signs of cross-strand, if not intersectional approaches in the new WAG *Strategy for Older People in Wales* for 2008 to 2013. Older LGB and transgender people were considered in the research design and included in the consultation and engagement elements of policy formation (WAG, 2008b: 12–13, 47).

This theme is taken up in the consultative document for the Welsh Assembly Government *Single Equality Scheme*. The plan demonstrates a commitment to identifying and addressing cross-strand issues (WAG, 2008c: 4) and to ensuring that any one of the 'six strands' are not 'diluted within a single scheme' to promote equality (ibid.: 5).

Such initiatives may not move policymaking beyond a cross-strand equal treatment model but there are some examples within education policy in Wales that demonstrate an understanding of how gender and sexuality can intersect to create inequality.

Integrating gender and sexuality: the case of education policy

Education policy is fully devolved in Wales. National Assembly circulars, although not enforceable, effectively repealed section 28 of the Local Government Act 1986, a year before it was removed from the UK statute book. National Assembly Circular (11/02) on *Welsh Assembly Guidance, Sex and Relationships Education in Schools* stated that section 28 of the Local Government Act 1986 did not prevent 'objective discussions of homosexuality' in the classroom.

Subsequently, *Respecting Others: Anti-bullying Guidance* included express reference to the intersectionality of gender and sexuality:

> Gender, racial and sexual bullying often come together in particular ways. For example Connolly (1998) describes how some South Asian boys are often 'feminised' and some Afro-Caribbean boys are overtly 'sexualised'. Research suggests that gender and sexual bullying often intersect where homophobic insults are used to police traditional gender roles. (NAW, 2003b: 13)

Here there is acknowledgement of how heterosexual gender roles can be used to 'police' girls and boys into heterosexual presentations of self but also that the manifestation of this opprobrium can look like homophobia. There is recognition too that teachers must take active steps to address what appears to be homophobic bullying, in its different manifestations, for all pupils:

> Sexual bullying can also be related to sexual orientation. Pupils do not necessarily have to be lesbian, gay or bi-sexual to experience such bullying. Just being different can be enough. A survey of 300 secondary schools in England and Wales found 82% of teachers aware of verbal incidents, and 26% aware of physical incidents. Almost all schools had anti-bullying policies, but only 6% referred to this type of bullying. Factors hindering schools in challenging homophobic bullying include staff inexperience and parental disapproval (ibid.: 14).

The pressure to display heterosexual masculinity or femininity has been observed in an ethnographic study of primary school children (Renold, 2001). This must have an effect on gendered subject choice; school subjects, like jobs, are not gender neutral but, rather, can serve to demonstrate heterosexual femininity or masculinity. Through such an analysis these policies could go even further in their consideration of the effects of intersecting gender and sexuality inequality, perhaps tracing them through to the labour market and pay systems.

The education minister followed up *Respecting Others* by requesting all schools to submit their anti-bullying policies to the National Assembly for inspection. She commissioned Cardiff University (WAG, 2006d), to undertake an evaluation of the policies, and required Estyn, the schools inspectorate, to find examples of good practice. In the Cardiff University report only those policies which adopted a 'whole-school' approach to tackling bullying and which expressly discussed efforts to address homophobia got top marks.

Estyn's findings and recommendations are included in their *Guidance for Inspection of Secondary Schools*. Inspection for a policy on homophobic bullying is a requirement and, beyond the sexual orientation approach, although not named as hetero-gendering, the guidance distils an understanding of gender and sexualities in interaction:

> Pupils and teachers may be the victims of bullying on the grounds of their sexual orientation. Boys or girls who are, or whose behaviour in any way suggests that they might be gay, lesbian or bisexual, or whose behaviour is different in any way from accepted group norms, can be vulnerable to homophobic bullying. Inspectors should consider whether schools' anti-bullying policies and strategies deal adequately with these issues. If school policies and practices are not dealing adequately with issues of homophobia, inspection reports should say so. You should report on more than the existence of an anti-bullying policy and procedures. (Estyn, 2008: 101)

These examples demonstrate the value of acting upon qualitative understandings of the ways inequalities are experienced in different settings. Indeed, qualitative research, with its rich detail of how people experience inequality and how class, gender, sexuality and age can combine to create particular inequitable outcomes, may be the only method for reaching intersectional understanding. It may be vital for informing policy that can mainstream all the equality dimensions.

Conclusions

In Wales, the unique equality duty, the equality infrastructure and continued (cross-party) political will has provided an exceptional space for advocacy by, and on behalf of, LGB people in Wales. However, the policy frame established for sexual orientation at European and UK level has restricted the focus to the personal characteristics of lesbian, gay and bisexual people requiring protection in an anti-discrimination paradigm. As such, analysis of gender and of heterosexuality is excluded.

Similarly, gender mainstreaming strategies have neglected analysis of sexuality by missing the opportunity to analyse how heterosexual socio-economic systems and structures construct an inequitable gender dualism. The examples given in this chapter, on community regeneration, equal pay and education, show how such an intersectional analysis could lead to different policy outcomes. There is potential to bring such analysis to bear on policy in Wales and the equality infrastructure exists to facilitate such work. However, there needs to be debate about how this is to be achieved, and how policy-making can be moved from a default compliance model to the more proactive project of mainstreaming equality across the equality dimensions for all.

Notes

1. Gender mainstreaming was given legal status by the Treaty of Amsterdam 1997 and became one of the specific tasks of the Community (Article 2) DG Employment and Social Affairs, EC unit DG5 ('Beijing +5: An overview of the EU follow up and preparations', EC 2000 ISBN 92–828–9418–5).
2. For a review of the historical changes in usage of the term 'sex' to denote biological and gender difference in recent times, including 'the rise of a two sex model', see Oudshoorn (1999). For the linguistic confusion of anatomical sex, and sex as *the* 'sex act' see Jackson (1996). For contestation of the continued search for biological determinants of sexualities, see LeVay on the 'Sexual brain' (1999: 290–3), Hamer and Copeland on 'the gay gene' and the difficulties of linking genes to behaviour (1999: 285–90).
3. See Parken (2003) for a review of the ways these academic disciplines have defined gender and sexuality and the consequent political positions that flow from the varying conceptions.

[4] McManus (2003) argues that the subject matter should define the category, for example, 'men who have sex with men' may be more inclusive for sexual health research (p. 7), where those engaged in same-sex activity may not link this to a specific identity.

[5] *Equal Opportunities Review (EOR)* asks whether the definition covers orientation and behaviour. Coverage only for a state of mind, they argue, could result in the different conduct (i.e., outward manifestations of identity) of homosexuals in comparison to heterosexuals not being covered (*EOR*, 95). Could an employer in a case such as Boychuck v H J Symons [1977] (IRLR, 395) still argue 'that it has no objection to employing lesbians but to "display"' (in this case a badge) and is concerned about the (alleged) negative effect that has on its business interests (*EOR*, 95: 35)?

[6] CA – Court of Appeal. See also Bamforth (1994, 1997) and Wintemute (1994).

[7] See, especially, the 'Explorations' edition of the journal *Feminist Economics* (1998).

[8] See also Dunne (1999) and Gabb (2001) on the division of labour in lesbian households, particularly the effect of social class.

[9] The research undertaken in 2006–7 was jointly funded by the Welsh Assembly Government and the Department for Communities and Local Government.

[10] *http://www.assemblywales.org/hom-pdfviewer?url=n00000000000000000 00000000042508*

[11] Published by Stonewall Cymru as *Counted Out* (Robinson and Williams, 2003).

[12] My thanks go to Dr Paul Chaney for his collation of the equality commitments of the first and second assemblies. This was commissioned as part of the Welsh Assembly Government and DCLG 'Multi-Strand Project' (see Parken and Young, 2007, and Parken and Young, 2008).

References

Acker, J. (1990) 'Hierarchies, jobs, bodies: A theory of gendered organisations', *Gender and Society*, 4, 2, 139–58.

Adkins, L. (1995). *Gendered Work: Sexuality, Family and the Labour Market*, Milton Keynes: Open University Press.

— (2000). 'Mobile desire: aesthetics, sexuality and the "lesbian" at work', *Sexualities*, 3, 2, 201–18.

—— and C. Lury (1996). 'The cultural, the sexual, and the gendering of the labour market', in L. Adkins and V. Merchant (eds), *Sexualising the Social: Power and the Organization of Sexuality*, Basingstoke: Macmillan.

—— and D. Leonard (eds) (1996). *Sex in Question: French Materialist Feminism*, London: Taylor and Francis.

Allen, J. (1986). 'Lesbian economics', *Trivia*, winter, 37–53.

Arabsheibani, G. R., A. Marin and J. Wadsworth (2002). 'Gays' pay in the UK', paper presented to the Royal Economic Society conference, March.

—— (2003). 'In the pink: homosexual and heterosexual wage differentials in the UK', paper presented to the Applied Econometrics Association meeting, Brussels.

Badgett, M. V. Lee (1995). 'The wage effects of sexual orientation discrimination', *Industrial and Labour Relations Review*, 48, 4, 726–39.

—— and P. Hyman (1998). 'Introduction: towards lesbian, gay and bisexual perspectives', in 'Economics: why and how they make a difference', *Feminist Economics*, 4, 2, 49–54.

Bamforth, N. (1994). 'Sexual orientation and dismissal', *New Law Journal*, 14 October, 1403–19.

—— (1997). *Sexuality, Morality and Justice: A Theory of Lesbian and Gay Rights and Law*, London: Cassell.

Becker, G. S. (1981). *A Treatise on the Family*, Cambridge, MA: Harvard University Press.

Bellis, A. and M. Boyce (2005). *In or Out? Sexual Orientation and the Employability Agenda*, Brighton: SEQUAL Development Partnership, University of Sussex.

Breakwell, G. (1985). *Young Women in Gender Atypical Jobs: The Case of Trainee Technicians in the Engineering Industry*, London: Department of Employment.

Brown, C. L. (1998). 'Sexual orientation and labor economics', *Feminist Economics*, 4, 2, 49–54.

Caplan, P. (ed.) (1987). *The Cultural Construction of Sexuality*, London: Tavistock.

Chaney, P. and R. Fevre (2002). *An Absolute Duty: Equal Opportunities and the National Assembly for Wales*, Cardiff: Institute of Welsh Affairs with the Commission for Racial Equality, Disability Rights Commission and Equal Opportunities Commission.

Cockburn, C. (1985). *Machinery of Dominance: Women, Men and Technical Know-how*, London: Pluto.

—— (1991). *In the Way of Women: Men's Resistance to Sex Equality in Organizations*, Basingstoke: Macmillan.

Commission of the European Communities (1996). *Incorporating Equal Opportunities for Women and Men into all Community Policies and Activities*, communication from the Commission, COM(96) 67 (final), Luxembourg: Office for Official Publications of the European Communities.

Connolly, P. (1998). *Racisms, Gender Identities and Young Children*, London: Routledge.

Crenshaw, K. (1994). 'Mapping the margins: intersectionality, identity politics, and violence against women of colour', in M. A. Fineman and R. Mykitiuk (eds), *The Public Nature of Private Violence*, New York: Routledge, pp. 93–118.

Delphy, C. (1984). *Close To Home: A Materialist Analysis of Women's Oppression*, London: Hutchinson.

—— and D. Leonard (1992). *Familiar Exploitation: A New Analysis of Marriage in Contemporary Western Societies*, Cambridge: Polity Press.

Duncan, N. (ed.) (1996). *BodySpace: Destabilising Geographies of Gender and Sexuality*, London: Routledge.

Dunne, G. A. (1997). *Lesbian Lifestyles: Women's Work and the Politics of Sexuality*, Basingstoke, Macmillan.

—— (1999). 'A passion for "sameness"? Sexuality and gender accountability', in E. Silva and C. Smart (eds), *The 'New' Family*, London: Sage.

—— (2000). 'Lesbians as authentic workers? Institutional heterosexuality and the reproduction of gender inequalities', *Sexualities*, 3, 2, 133–48.

Department for Work and Pensions (2006). *Gender and Individual Incomes*, report for the Women and Equality Unit, *http://www.womenandequalityunit.gov.uk/indiv_incomes/report2006.pdf*.

Equal Opportunities Review (*EOR*) (2001). No. 95, January.

—— (2002). No. 101, January.

—— (2003). No. 113, January.

Estyn (2008). *Guidance for Inspection of Secondary Schools*, September, Cardiff: Estyn, *http://www.estyn.gov.uk/publications/secondary_handbook_2008.pdf*.

Fraser, N. (1997). *Justice Interruptus: Critical Reflections on the 'Postcolonialist' Condition*, New York: Routledge.

Gabb, J. (2002). 'Critical differentials: querying the incongruities among research on lesbian parent families', paper presented to the Parenting Under the Rainbow conference, Sheffield Hallam University, July.

Gheradi, S. (1995). *Gender, Symbolism and Organizational Culture*, London: Sage.

Giddings, L. A. (1998). 'Political economy and the construction of gender: the example of housework within same-sex households', *Feminist Economics*, 4, 2, 97–106.

Government Equalities Office (2008). *Equality Bill*, vol. I, clause 143, London: The Stationery Office.

Hall, M. (1989). 'Private experiences in the public domain: lesbians in organizations', in J. Hearn, D. L. Sheppard, P. Tancred Sheriff and G. Burrell (eds), *The Sexuality of Organization*, London: Sage.

Hamer, D. and C. Copeland (1999). 'The gay gene', in R. A. Nye (ed.), *Sexuality: A Reader*, Oxford: Oxford University Press, pp. 287–90.

Hawkes, G. (1996). *A Sociology of Sex and Sexuality*, Buckingham: Open University Press.

Himmelweit, S. (2002). 'Making visible the hidden economy: the case for gender-impact analysis of economic policy', *Feminist Economics*, 8, 1, 49–70.

Jackson, S. (1992). 'Towards an historical sociology of housework: a materialist feminist analysis', *Women's Studies International Forum*, 15, 2, 153–72.

—— (1995). 'Gender and heterosexuality: a materialist feminist analysis', in M. Maynard and J. Purvis (eds), *(Hetero)sexual Politics*, London: Taylor and Francis, pp. 11–26.

—— (1996). 'Heterosexuality and feminist theory', in D. Richardson (ed.), *Theorizing Heterosexuality*, Buckingham: Open University Press, pp. 21–38.

—— and S. Scott (1996). 'Sexual skirmishes and feminist factions: twenty-five years of debate on women and sexuality', in S. Jackson and S. Scott (eds), *Feminism and Sexuality*, Edinburgh: Edinburgh University Press, pp. 1–34.

John, S. and A. Patrick (1999). 'Poverty and social exclusion of lesbians and gay men in Glasgow', a report by Glasgow Women's Library, research funded by Glasgow City Council.

LeVay, S. (1999). 'The sexual brain', in R. A. Nye (ed.), *Sexuality: A Reader*, Oxford: Oxford University Press, pp. 290–3.

McDowell, L. (1997). *Capital Culture: Gender at Work in the 'City'*, Cambridge: Blackwell.

MacEwen Scott, A. (1994). 'Gender segregation in the retail industry', in A. MacEwen Scott (ed.), *Gender Segregation and Social Change*, Oxford: Oxford University Press.

McManus, S. (2003). *Sexual Orientation Research Phase1: A Review of Methodological Approaches*, Edinburgh: Scottish Executive.

Millar, J. and K. Gardiner (2004). *Low Pay, Household Resources and Poverty*, York: Joseph Rowntree Foundation/York Publishing Services.

Monaghan, K. (2002). 'Sex discrimination and pregnancy rights', paper submitted to TUC/ EOR Discrimination Law 2002 conference, 25 January.

National Assembly for Wales (NAW) (1999). Remit statement, Equality of Opportunity Committee (June 1999–April 2003), *http://www.assembly-wales.org/bus-home/bus-committees/bus-committees-first/bus-committees-first-eoc-home/bus-committees-first-eoc-committee.htm*.

—— (2001). *Communities First Guidance*, Cardiff: WAG.

—— (2003a). Draft forward work programme, Equality of Opportunity Committee, paper 1, *http://www.assemblywales.org/hom-pdfviewer?url=n00000000000000000000000000011599*.

—— (2003b). *Respecting Others: Anti-Bullying Guidance*, circular Number 23/2003, Cardiff: WAG.

—— (2004). *Report on Mainstreaming Equality in the Work of the Assembly*, Equality of Opportunity Committee report, EOC (2) 04–04, Cardiff: NAW, p. 6, annex A.

—— (2008). *Raising Awareness of the Needs and Rights of Lesbian, Gay and Bisexual (LGB) People When Accessing Healthcare Services in Wales*, Welsh health circular 031, issued 17 April 2008.

Nye, Robert A. (ed.) (1999). *Sexuality: A Reader*, London: Routledge.

Oudshoorn, N. (1999). 'Masculine and feminine hormones', in R. A. Nye (ed.), *Sexuality: A Reader*, Oxford: Oxford University Press, pp. 250–3.

Parken, A. (1998). 'Gender and sexuality at work: conflicts and compromises for lesbians', unpublished M.Sc. dissertation, University of Bristol.

—— (2003). 'Gender mainstreaming: "outing" heterosexism in the workplace', unpublished doctoral research, Cardiff University.

—— (2010). 'Mainstreaming across the equality dimensions: a multi-strand approach to mainstreaming equalities and human rights in policy-making', *Policy and Politics*, 38, 1, 79–99.

—— and H. Young (2007). *Integrating the Promotion of Equality and Human Rights for All*, research report for the Welsh Assembly Government and Equality and Human Rights Commission.

—— (2008). *Facilitating Cross-Strand Working*, Cardiff: WAG, *http://new.wales.gov.uk/topics/equality/research/facilitating/?lang=en*.

Pateman, C. (1988). *The Sexual Contract*, Cambridge Polity Press.

Plummer, K. (2000). 'Mapping the sociological gay: past, presents and futures of a sociology of same sex relations', in T. Sandfort., J. Schuyf, J. W. Dyvendak and J. Weeks (eds), *Lesbian and Gay Studies: An Introductory, Interdisciplinary Approach*, London: Sage, pp. 46–60.

Power, H. (1998). 'Rainbow's end: getting gay rights right', in *Making Rights Work*, Dartmouth Press.

Rahman, N. and S. Jackson (1997). 'Liberty, equality and sexuality: essentialism and the discourse of rights', *Journal of Gender Studies*, 6, 2, 117–29.

Rees, T. (1998). *Mainstreaming Equality in the European Union*, London: Routledge.

—— (2005). 'Reflections on the uneven development of gender mainstreaming in Europe', *International Journal of Feminist Politics*, 7, 4, 555–74.

Renold, E. (2001). '"Coming out": gender, (hetero)sexuality and the primary school', *Gender and Education*, 12, 3, 309–25.

Richardson, D. (2000). *Rethinking Sexuality*, London: Sage.

Robinson, A. L. and M. Williams (2003). *Counted Out: The First All Wales LGB Survey*, Cardiff: Stonewall Cymru.

Siltanen, J. (2002). 'Full wages and component wages', in S. Jackson and S. Scott (eds) *Gender: A Sociological Reader*, London: Routledge.

Simon, W. and J. H. Gagnon (1998). 'Homosexuality: the formulation of a sociological perspective', in P. M. Nardi and B. E. Schneider (eds), *Social Perspectives in Lesbian and Gay Studies*, London: Routledge, pp. 59–67.

Stonewall Cymru (2004). *Addressing the Needs of Wales' Forgotten Community of Interest*, Cardiff: Stonewall.

Taylor, S., and M. Tyler (2000). 'Emotional labour and sexual difference in the airline industry', *Work, Employment and Society*, 14, 1, 77–95.

Vance, C. S. (1992). 'Social construction theory: problems in the history of sexuality', in H. Crowley and S. Himmelweit (eds), *Knowing Women: Feminism and Knowledge*, Milton Keynes: Polity Press, pp. 132–45.

Verloo, M. (2006). 'Multiple inequalities, intersectionality and the European Union', *European Journal of Women's Studies*, 13, 3, 211–28.

Walby, S. (2005). 'Gender mainstreaming: productive tensions in theory and practice', *Social Politics* 12, 3, 312–43.

Welsh Assembly Government (WAG) (2002a). *Black, Minority Ethnic Housing Action Plan for Wales*, Cardiff: WAG.

WAG (2002b). *Creative Futures: Cymru Greadigol – A Culture Strategy for Wales*, Cardiff: WAG.

—— (2004a). *Making the Connections: Delivering Better Services for Wales – The WAG Vision for Public Services*, Cardiff: WAG.

—— (2004b). *The Wales Spatial Plan: People, Places, Futures*, Cardiff: WAG, *http://new.wales.gov.uk/dpsp/wsp/wsp-101104-pt1-e.pdf?lang=en* .

—— (2005a). *Designed for Life – Creating World Class Health and Social Care for Wales in the 21st Century*, Cardiff: WAG.

—— (2005b). *Health Care Standards for Wales: Making the Connections, Designed for Life*, Cardiff: WAG.

—— (2005c). *Delivering the Connections: From Vision to Action. Our 5-year Plan for Delivering Better Services for Wales*, Cardiff: WAG.

—— (2006a). *Rural Development Plan for Wales 2007–2013*, consultation draft, Cardiff: WAG.

—— (2006b). *The Learning Country 2: Delivering the Promise*, Cardiff: WAG.

—— (2006c). *Fulfilled Lives, Supportive Communities: A Strategy for Social Services in Wales Over the Next Decade*, Cardiff: WAG.

—— (2006d). *Evaluation of Anti-Bullying Policies in Schools in Wales*, Young and Inclusion Department, Cardiff: WAG.

—— (2007a). *The Carers' Strategy in Wales – Implementation Plan*, Cardiff: WAG.

—— (2007b). *One Wales: A Progressive Agenda for Wales*, an agreement between the Labour and Plaid Cymru groups in the National Assembly, 27 June, Cardiff: WAG.

—— (2008a). *Communities Next: Consultation on the Future of the Communities First Programme*, Cardiff: WAG.

—— (2008b). *Strategy for Older People in Wales, Living Longer, Living Better, 2008–2013*, Cardiff: WAG, *http://new.wales.gov.uk/strategy/strategies/2166490/olderpeopleII.pdf?lang=en.*

—— (2008c). *Single Equality Scheme: Consultation Document*, Cardiff: WAG.

Weeks, J. (1985). *Sexuality and its Discontents*, London: Routledge.

West, C. and D. Zimmerman (1987). 'The social construction of gender', *Gender and Society*, 1, 2, 125–51.

Williams, M. and A. L. Robinson (2003). *Counted Out: Findings from the Stonewall Cymru LGB Survey*, Cardiff: Stonewall Cymru.

—— (2007). *Counted In! The All Wales Survey of Lesbian, Gay and Bisexual People*, Cardiff: Stonewall Cymru.

Wilmot, A. (2007). 'In search of a question on sexual identity', paper presented at the 62nd annual conference of the American Association of Public Opinion Research, May, UK Office for National Statistics National Statistics Agency, *http://www.statistics.gov.uk/about/services/dcm/downloads/Sexual_Identity.pdf.*

Wintemute, R. (1994). 'Sexual orientation discrimination', in C. McCrudden and G. Chambers (eds), *Individual Rights and the Law in Britain*, Oxford: Oxford University Press.

Women's Gender Budget Group (WGBG) (2006). *Women's and Children's Poverty: Making the Links*, London: WGBG.

Yuval-Davies, N. (2006). 'Intersectionality and feminist politics', *European Journal of Women's Studies*, 13, 3, 193–210.

7

Making the World New? Education in Post-devolution Wales

SUE SANDERS

> They will not forgive us
> These girls
> Sitting in serried rows
> Hungry for attention
> Like shelves of unread books,
> If we do not
> Make the world new for them . . .

The title of the chapter is taken from Fiona Norris's 1985 poem 'Classroom Politics' in which she incites women to 'make the world new' through education. At that time the education systems of Wales and England were tightly associated, with policy for both emanating from Westminster (where at the peak in 1997 only 18 per cent of MPs were women) and enacted through local education authorities. Since the election of the first National Assembly for Wales in 1999, which saw 40 per cent of seats won by women, the policies have been disentangled and in aspects grown in different ways. This chapter will track the extent to which education in Wales can be seen to have been 'made different' *by* women. In order to do this it will look at the roles and number of women involved in education policymaking and implementation. It will also look for ways in which the policy serves women, in what ways education in Wales is made different *for* but not only for women. It will also take a broader perspective, more aligned with twenty-first-century concerns, and look at aspects of educational policy in Wales that tackle gendered issues.

In the years since devolution women have played key roles in policymaking in education and, of course, women have continued to be the larger proportion of the teaching workforce, responsible for enacting much of this policy. Weiner (2004) suggested that education feminists have tried to improve the educational conditions and life chances for girls and women so that they are equivalent (if not equal) to those of men. It would be wrong to suggest that all women in education would describe themselves as feminists, although many do, and additionally many would adhere to the social justice agenda which could be described as trying to improve the educational conditions and life chances for all regardless of factors such as ethnic background, social class, economic status and so on.

This chapter will consider three questions:

- Has there been and is there now a critical mass of women in positions of power/influence (as well as in the education workforce in general) who could effect change?
- What were the key aspects of post-devolution education policy for schools?
- What policy during this time has reflected consideration of gender specific issues or concerns about and for women?

It is not the intention to present a comparative study of education in Wales and education in England but aspects of the English education system will be used where they help to contextualize the Welsh situation.

Education in Wales

Under the Government of Wales Act of 1997, the National Assembly was given responsibility for education and training. This means that it has responsibility for all aspects of education in Wales other than that of teachers' pay and conditions. It sets the national priorities, strategic context and the overall level of funding for services. Education is led by a minister for education and lifelong learning. Her remit covers nearly all education and training matters, including:

- Sound foundations
- Comprehensive education and lifelong learning in Wales
- Learning and equality of opportunity
- Progress and practitioners

- Beyond compulsory education
- Access and the future of higher education

It should be noted that, as Rees points out, by the 1990s the Welsh Office had already 'accumulated major powers over most aspects of education and training, responsibilities which were delivered through the local education authorities and a number of quangos . . .' (Rees, 2007: 13). These powers had been acquired through what Jones calls 'creeping devolution' (G. E. Jones, 2006). So whilst pre-devolution policy was developed for 'England and Wales', the Welsh Office had the power to mediate this policy for Wales.

Local government also plays a key role, in some ways more so than in England, for in Wales local government has kept quite a significant degree of autonomy and flexibility. The majority of local government funding is not ring-fenced for any specific service area, which allows local authorities to respond to local needs and reflect local priorities. However, as there are twenty-two local authorities being run by 1,257 elected councillors, there is a potential for wide disparity. Each council has an elected executive. Those on the executive have a range of additional responsibilities over and above their duties as councillors, and education is one of these responsibilities. Local authorities are responsible for the allocation of a budget to their schools and have a scrutiny responsibility for the delivery of education within their region. This means that at a local level funding for aspects of education can vary. Such local differences need to be monitored and researched to ensure an equitable education system. It is Her Majesty's Inspectorate for Education and Training in Wales (Estyn) which carries out inspections to assess the effectiveness and efficiency of these local authorities.

The local authorities work with the Welsh Assembly Government Department for Children, Education, Lifelong Learning and Skills (DCELLS) to develop policies and strategies with the aim of supporting continuing improvement in education.

A critical mass of women?

Mackay (2001) argues that policy change is more likely if there is a critical mass of women in an organization. This section examines the extent to which there has been such a critical mass within aspects of the education system in Wales and looks at the number of women in key educational organizations. In this discussion, however, there is no quantification of critical mass. It is qualitative in nature, interpreted by those both within and without an organization. There is something organic in its nature, its power emerges from within, it is not given from without.

Positions of influence

There are key roles at a national level that not only have the power to influence policy and practice in education and to provide leadership for those working in the field but also to give signals to society at large about expectations. In post-devolution Wales two key roles, those of minister for education and chief inspector of schools, have both been held by women. Jane Davidson served as minister of education from 2000 until 2007. She had spent ten years as a Labour city councillor in Cardiff, was a former teacher and had worked with young people in the voluntary sector. She was seen by many as a feminist. Susan Lewis was educated in England and taught there for fifteen years, finally becoming an acting head teacher. In 1986 she came to Wales as Her Majesty's inspector (HMI) with responsibility for science and in 1995 she was promoted to staff inspector for secondary education. In 1997 she became the first female chief inspector in Wales and the first to be appointed by open competition. She was appointed for a second term of five years in 2002. She was proof that a woman could achieve a position at the top of their profession in Wales, just as Margaret Thatcher proved that a woman could be prime minister.

For post-devolution Wales, then, the face of education nationally has been female if not feminist. At the local political level, however, a very different position exists. At this level there are two key positions. First, there is the elected councillor who is given a portfolio or responsibility for education and, secondly, there is an officer, usually known as the director of education or as chief education officer, who is responsible for the day-to-day management of education provision. Within the twenty-two unitary authorities there are two women elected councillors with an education portfolio and only one female director of education. With the exception of Bridgend, which has a female leader and deputy leader of council as well as a female director of education and a female councillor as chair of the education scrutiny committee, the local management of schools in Wales is predominantly male. An examination of the more general workforce reveals differing pictures too.

Schools

It is within schools that we see the true impact of educational policy, where pupils and teachers meet potential role models and where policies regarding equity should be played out. The following section follows these through an examination of the teaching workforce.

Teachers

Teaching, particularly within the state sector, is a career that attracts a higher proportion of women than men. The gender of head teachers is considered in detail not only as a reflection of the success of aims relating to equality in both education and the workforce but for the potential as role models for female learners, the styles of management they may employ and the ethos they create in the school. As head teachers enact, interpret and, to an extent, prioritize the directives of central government, they are key players in the success of any policy or initiative. Whilst classroom teachers have been seen as subversive independent agents in their own classroom, the opportunity for this has diminished over the last twenty years through regular inspections, a national curriculum and in England (although to a lesser extent in Wales) guidance on how to teach.

Teaching was one of the professions to take gender equality, at least in terms of pay, seriously quite early on. Well before the Equal Pay Act of 1970, equal pay for teachers was in place, closely following the arrangements for civil servants between 1955 and 1961 (Oram, 1989). However, particularly since the demise of the single-sex school, the positions of power or leadership within schools have not reflected the gender ratio of the workforce. Attracting any teacher to apply for headships has been problematic for over a decade, as can be seen from the consecutive reports of the Select Committee on Education and Employment, but certainly traditionally men are more likely to apply and to apply earlier in their careers than women.

In the late 1980s an observer moving from a city in England with a high-profile equality agenda such as Birmingham to Wales would be struck by the low number of women head teachers of both primary and secondary schools. At the time of devolution there were 24,175 teachers in post in Wales; of these 16,477 (68 per cent) were female and 7,698 male (32 per cent). However, of the 1,860 head teachers, 981 (53 per cent) were male. Fewer than half as many men were teachers than women but they accounted for over half of the head teachers. Whilst there are, of course, far fewer secondary schools than primary schools in Wales, the number of teachers employed in each sector is not dissimilar. In 2000 there were 1,631 primary schools employing 12,001 teachers and 229 secondary schools employing 12,174 teachers. However, the gender ratios of each sector were markedly different. In 2000, 71 per cent of primary teachers and 52 per cent of secondary teachers were women.

The following section looks at the situation in primary and secondary schools separately and considers the shifts in this power/leadership balance over the following six years. It also looks to the future by examining whether those who might be considered 'women heads in waiting' constitute a critical mass.

Many arguments were propounded in the 1980s and 1990s as to why women did not apply for, or gain headships (for example, M. L. Jones, 1990). However, given the fact that entry requirements, training content and standards were set for both Wales and England and that there is movement of teachers between Wales and England, we might expect the situation in both territories to be similar. It can be argued that an examination of the situation in Wales compared to England will allow contextual/situation-based variables to emerge. As data from England is published as percentages this will be reported in the following sections for ease of comparison.

Primary schools

In 2000 there were 1,631 primary schools in Wales, with male teachers comprising 29 per cent of the workforce. We might expect, therefore, around 1,156 of primary head teachers to be female. In fact, 787 or nearly half of primary head teachers were male. In England 26 per cent of the total workforce were male. However, with a lower 40 per cent of head teachers being male it could be argued that the situation in England was slightly more equitable than that in Wales. These figures can be seen in tables 7.1 and 7.2. With the policies of the Assembly Government prioritizing equality we should expect an improvement in the ratio in Wales over time. If the improvement is greater than that in England over the same period of time we can argue that post-devolution policy and leadership have played a role.

In 2006, the date for which most recent figures are available, the situation in Wales is that 20 per cent of primary teachers are male with 43 per cent of head teachers being male. Over the six-year period there has been a 9 per cent drop in male primary school teachers and a 5 per cent drop in the number of male head teachers. On the face of it this does not reflect a successful policy of equality. However, before coming to this conclusion there are two factors to be explored: first, how the situation has changed in England and, secondly and importantly, what the situation is regarding the 'heads in waiting'. Are we at a point when women are poised to apply confidently and successfully for headships in Wales? To explore this aspect we will examine the statistics regarding deputy head teachers, the position from which normally a head teacher would be appointed.

In 2006 in England the proportion of male primary school teachers was still 16 per cent but the proportion of head teachers had dropped from 40 per cent to 33 per cent (table 7.2). These figures suggest that in England, whilst this is still twice as high as might be expected in an equitable world, women were making significant gains in positions of power and leadership.

In Wales in 2000 over 70 per cent of deputy head teachers were women. In 2006 there is a very similar proportion. In 2000 this reflected closely the proportion of women in the primary workforce (table 7.1). Consequently, in 2006 we might have expected there to be some 80 per cent female deputy head teachers of primary schools; however, the current figures represent a drop. In England the proportion of women deputy head teachers rose from 74 per cent to 78 per cent in the same time period not quite mirroring the rise in the proportion of women teachers but tracking it to some extent (table 7.2). Whilst the women 'heads in waiting' in Wales have not to date redressed the gender imbalance in headship, and nor have a similar proportion of women moved to become 'heads in waiting', they do represent a critical mass that could populate the heads' studies in years to come.

Secondary schools

As stated above, 55 per cent teachers in secondary schools in Wales in 2000 were women. However, only 15 per cent of secondary head teachers were women (table 7.3). This contrasts poorly with the situa-

Table 7.1: Distribution of full-time qualified teaching staff in maintained primary schools in Wales by sex

		2000/01		*2006/07*		*% +/–* *over period*
Head teacher	female	844	52%	870	57%	+5%
	male	786	48%	660	43%	
	total	1631		1530		
Deputy head teacher	female	854	71%	786	71%	nil
	male	351	29%	325	29%	
	total	1205		1111		
All teachers	female	9782	81%	11827	84%	+3%
	male	2219	19%	2237	16%	
	total	12001		14064		+17%

Source: Welsh Assembly Government, *Schools in Wales: General Statistics 2007*.

Table 7.2: Distribution of full-time qualified teaching staff in maintained primary schools in England by sex.

		2000	*2006*	*% +/–* *over period*
Head teacher	female	60%	67%	+7%
	male	40%	33%	
Deputy head teacher	female	74%	78%	+4%
	male	26%	22%	
All teachers	female	84%	84%	nil
	male	16%	16%	

Source: Department for Children, Schools and Families (DCSF) School Workforce in England 2007.

tion in primary schools (52 per cent from a base of 71 per cent of the workforce) and with the situation in England (29 per cent from a base of 54 per cent), suggesting that something structural or institutional within the secondary sector in Wales was discouraging women from seeking headship or stopping women from achieving headship. An efficacious equality policy should address this.

By 2006 the proportion of women secondary head teachers in Wales had risen to 21 per cent but the base had also risen from 55 per cent to 61 per cent (table 7.3). The 6 percentage point rise in the proportion of women head teachers exactly matches the 6 percentage

Table 7.3: Distribution of full-time qualified teaching staff in maintained secondary schools in Wales by sex

		2000/01		*2006/07*		*% +/–* *over period*
Head teacher	female	35	15%	46	21%	+6%
	male	194	85%	178	79%	
	total	229		224		
Deputy head teacher	female	108	29%	142	39%	+10%
	male	268	71%	222	61%	
	total	376		364		
All teachers	female	6695	55%	8156	61%	+6%
	male	5479	45%	5225	39%	
	total	12174		13381		+10%

Source: Welsh Assembly Government, *Schools in Wales: General Statistics 2007*.

Table 7.4: Distribution of full-time qualified teaching staff in maintained secondary schools in England by sex

		2000/01	*2006/07*	*% +/–* *over period*
Head teacher	female	29%	36%	+6%
	male	71%	64%	
Deputy head teacher	female	37%	44%	+7%
	male	63%	56%	
All teachers	female	54%	57%	+3%
	male	46%	43%	

Source: DCSF School Workforce in England 2007.

point rise in the proportion of women teachers. Whilst not representing progress at least we can say that the situation has not deteriorated. In England the picture is more encouraging; the proportion of women secondary school teachers has risen by a mere 3 percentage point whilst the proportion of head teachers has risen by 7 percentage point (table 7.4).

With some secondary schools having more than one deputy head and some with senior management teams, the identification of data for 'heads in waiting' is not as clear cut as in the primary sector. However, the reported deputy head figures are illustrative. In 2000, 29 per cent of secondary deputy head teachers in Wales were female and by 2006 this had risen to 39 per cent (a rise of 10 percentage point compared with the 6 percentage point rise in women teachers overall) (table 7.3). In England 37 per cent of deputy head teachers were women in 2000 and by 2006 this had risen by 7 percentage points to 44 per cent (against a rise of only 3 percentage points in women teachers) (table 7.4). Once again, England had a more impressive rise in female participation in leadership roles but the increase in the proportion of women 'heads in waiting' in Wales gives hope.

There is now a higher proportion of women than men in secondary teaching in Wales thus creating a larger mass from which 'heads in waiting' and hence head teachers can be drawn. The proportion of women 'heads in waiting' is encouraging, as it was in 2000. Why it has not translated itself into an increase in female head teachers, however, needs investigation.

Coleman (2005) identified regional differences in the proportion of female head teachers in England. These ranged from 43 per cent in London to 23 per cent in the north-west. I am not able to present such a regional breakdown for Wales but can report that Cardiff and Swansea, the two largest cities, have a low proportion of women head teachers compared with Pembrokeshire and Wrexham, more rural authorities, perhaps indicating that, as Coleman found in England, barriers to women becoming head teachers do appear to vary by region.

We can argue that, with supportive structures and appropriate professional development, we could see a more equitable situation in the leadership of our secondary schools.

Governors

All schools are overseen by a governing body, which plays an important role in the appointment of head teachers. Coleman (2005) found that head teachers' views of governors were that they often expressed doubts as to whether women would be tough enough as head teachers. One secondary head teacher reported being asked by male interviewers whether she 'had steel enough to do the job'. Head teachers perceived a stereotypical norm of masculine leadership held by governors (and parents) that led to men being appointed. Whilst Coleman (2005) identified underlying stereotypes of women head teachers as soft and caring and male leaders as tough and dominant, in reality this may not be the case. When asked to choose words to describe their management styles males and females chose the same words: open;

consultative; inclusive; collegiate; supportive; collaborative; demo-cratic; and coaching. However, there were also head teachers (both male and female) who described their style as decisive; determined; visionary; challenging; authoritative; and strategic. Coleman's research was carried out in England and anecdotal evidence suggests that the situation may be similar in Wales.

There are no detailed gender data available regarding chairs of governing bodies or of governing bodies themselves. Schools may choose to put this in the public domain but many do not. An opportu-nity sample of Welsh local education authority (LEA) governor support units found varying practice; for example, one received such information from schools on a voluntary basis, one did not have such information available and another was currently collecting this infor-mation. All units stressed the advice they gave to governors on the importance of appointment boards having the appropriate gender balance.

The inspectorate

Estyn is responsible for the inspection of schools and the education provision of local authorities. In terms of gender this organization is perhaps the most balanced of those examined in this chapter. Figures obtained through the Freedom of Information Act show that women have always been well represented at all levels within Estyn with the proportion of female inspectors rising from 45 per cent in 2003 when 69 per cent of teachers in Wales were women to 53 per cent in 2007 when 73 per cent of teachers were women. The board of Estyn, which was set up by Susan Lewis as part of the corporate plan for 2005–8, has eight members, seven of whom are women.

The learning country: educational policy in Wales 1999–2007

This section looks at the post-devolution policy at a time when the minister for education was a woman, Jane Davidson. It also looks at perceptions of education in Wales at a time when the inspection service in Wales was also led by a woman, Susan Lewis.

From the point of devolution to the 2007 election, education policy in Wales benefited from implementation against a stable and supportive background. Although there were many new initiatives and changes that had an impact on schools, teachers and pupils, there was by no means the sense of turmoil and loss of self-worth experienced by teachers in England at that time.

> We in Wales – and particularly governing bodies and practitioners – have much to be proud and confident about. (Davidson, 2001)

> There is much to celebrate. (Lewis, 2001)

There are three main reasons for this: the many statements of support for and valuing of teachers emanating from the National Assembly; no change of minister during that time; and the style of the incumbent chief inspector of schools, also in post for the whole period. Much was made of the stark contrast between the ethos of schools policy in Wales and England in the broadsheet media as well as in the educational press. Initially, this was predicated on the reported pronouncements of the outspoken and controversial then chief inspector of schools in England, Chris Woodhead.

> Chris Woodhead, the Chief Inspector of Schools in England, should adopt a less confrontational style, says a committee of MPs. But Mr Woodhead rejected the criticism, saying 'I am paid to challenge mediocrity, failure and complacency'.
>   Teachers' unions have long argued that many of Mr Woodhead's most trenchant criticisms of teachers – such as saying 15,000 teachers were incompetent – were not backed up with sufficient evidence. (BBC News, 1999)

Later, as policy about teaching methods in England became more and more prescriptive and secretaries of state for education came and went, often at times of political upheaval, the minister of education for Wales, Jane Davidson, was held up consistently as a role model, with contrasts made between Wales and England as regards the nature of policy and the style in which it was presented and implemented.

From 1999 to 2007 the schools inspectorate in England, known for much of that time as OFSTED (Office for Standards in Education), was led by five different chief inspectors: Chris Woodhead, Mike Tomlinson, David Bell, Maurice Smith and Christine Gilbert. Initially, the style was very confrontational, causing high levels of stress and anxiety in head teachers and their staff. In Wales too there were pressures associated with inspections, but the tone of annual reports, lack of sensational comment to the press and the adoption of the name Estyn, interpreted as 'to reach out', somehow kept a more measured relationship between the inspectors and the inspected.

Whilst some of the comparison between education in Wales and education in England was hyperbole and hype, there was enough substance for a substantial number of those working in Wales to feel differently about centrally determined policy from a large number of their counterparts in England.

> At the west end of the Severn Crossing it does not say 'Welcome to Wales: Leftwing Teachers' Utopia', but perhaps one day it will. As Estelle Morris, the education secretary in England, battles through arguments over staff shortages, 'two-tier' specialist schools and privatisation, in Wales the teaching profession is cooing. (Woodward, 2001)

Rees (2007) argues against the notion of this time as the new golden era of educational initiatives as promoted by the Welsh Assembly Government (WAG) and others. He sees these as continuations from pre-devolution Wales and attributes them to ideology and to the structures of Welsh society. Whether wholly due to the Welsh Assembly Government or not, the policy and structures described in this chapter are seated during this time.

By 2001 and during its first two years, the National Assembly had instituted a massive programme of support, development and change for training and education in Wales. This included the provision of nursery education from the age of three for all children whose parents wanted it, the reduction of the number of children in an infant (five to seven years) class to a maximum of thirty and the reintroduction of free school milk for pupils up to the age of seven.

With the publication of the paving document, *The Learning Country*, in 2001, WAG set out to consult on a number of key policy directions and also on the legislative proposals to give effect to them. This was the first comprehensive strategic statement on education and lifelong learning in Wales as well as being the first paving document for primary and secondary legislation in this field issued from the National Assembly. Published in September it had a consultation period during school time, thus allowing for discussion and debate between colleagues and teacher organizations. Similar policy in England would have consultancy times over the summer vacation with little opportunity for collaborative approaches to the consultation. These factors alone gave credence to notions of partnership between policymakers and practitioners in Wales. 'I do hope you will take advantage of the invitation to comment – and you will join with us to make Wales an unbeatable place in which to learn and prosper' (Davidson, 2001).

172

Although the legislation would be part of the forthcoming Education Bill to be introduced by the UK government, the document made clear that Wales was going to develop a distinctive approach to education policy.

> Some of the things that will feature in the forthcoming Education Bill will be of special interest to England alone. In so far as they are measures that do not fit with arrangements that work well and get good results in Wales, we intend that the Assembly will have the power not to proceed with them. (Davidson, 2001)

In setting out their strategic ten-year programme the Welsh Assembly Government set the goal for Wales to have 'one of the best education and lifelong learning systems in the world'. It was to realize sustainability, tackle social disadvantage, promote equality of opportunity, sustain an environment that celebrated diversity and make progress towards realizing the benefits of bilingualism. Underpinning policy were eleven axioms:

- High standards and expectations
- The interests of learners override all others
- Barriers to learning must be recognized and steadily overcome
- All learning pathways should have parity of esteem
- Inequalities in achievement must be narrowed in the interests of all
- Innovation must be supported
- The informed professional judgment of teachers, lecturers and trainers must be celebrated
- The basis for policy and programme development must be partnership
- Provision must reflect the wise use of money
- Policy must be evidence based
- The agenda for lifelong learning must be applied in ways that reflect the distinctive needs and circumstances of Wales.

In 2006 the Welsh Assembly Government revisited the strategic ten-year programme at its halfway point. It reviewed its progress and set out to provide a blueprint for completion of the exercise. During this time significant changes had taken place, often in direct juxtaposition with the rhetoric and strategies in England. In England the talk was of 'driving up standards' and there was much setting of targets.

Competitive league tables dominated work in schools. In Wales the statutory testing arrangements for pupils age seven, eleven and fourteen had been abolished. School league tables had been abolished. The Estyn inspection framework was revised to reflect a 'lighter touch'.

Amongst the seventeen identified challenges for the future in the 2006 document we find the first gendered observation: 'We must address the under-achievement of boys compared to girls' (WAG, 2006: 6).

Issues of gender

Whilst the education policy of Wales in the twenty-first century can be linked to social democracy (Paterson, 2003) with a strong drive for equality of opportunity and social justice, it is not obviously feminist and the underachievement of girls per se in any area of education remains undiscussed. Indeed, there is little specific mention of any gender issue other than boys' underachievement. The identification of this 'problem' and its choice for policy prioritization must be explored.

Identifying one sex as a deficit model is not new. However, it often emerges in educational policy at times of difficulty. In the 1980s concerns around engagement with science, mathematics and engineering allowed a climate in which the particular underachievement of girls in these areas was addressed. The United Kingdom needed more scientists and engineers. Girls were seen as a substantial, easily accessed untapped group of potential talent and so were identified for targeting. So, with the current concerns about disaffection and with an increasingly violent youth culture, associated with poor communication skills, low levels of literacy and poor social skills, this can be seen as the time for targeting boys for improvement in these areas. Such initiatives can be seen as 'of their time'.

On the other hand, such initiatives can be seen as a 'backlash' against the status quo. Mathematics and science are gateways to well-paid and respected jobs. Some commentators saw the pro-female initiatives of the 1980s as an invasion of male territory. Much has been written about the feminization of schooling over the last fifty years (Arnot and Mac an Ghaill, 2006). As the achievements of girls rise, boys' problems are explained as resulting from a school system that favours girls by remodelling the curriculum in line with girls' learning needs and using assessment procedures known to expose girls'

174

achievements (Stobart et al., 1992). Concerns are also expressed that boys' disaffection is directly linked to the dominance of women in teaching, particularly within the earlier years of education. There are, of course, other ways of explaining the lack of engagement and achievement such as looking at economic and societal changes. However, such was the persuasiveness of the female dominance argument that the recruitment of male teachers, particularly to primary education, has become a policy target in both Wales and England. This is discussed later in this chapter.

It is important that the current gender-specific concern is informed by the work with females and science in the 1980s. Of course, the actuality of underachievement is extremely complex with social class, economic status and ethnicity being key variables, often more so than gender. As Weiner notes, 'Lest we become over-optimistic, however, studies also show that even in richer western countries, these changes were not the same for all girls or all boys – white, middle-class girls were likely to benefit more than, for example, their black, working-class counterparts' (Weiner, 2004: 6). A statement such as 'the underachievement of boys', is too simplistic and should not be accepted by any educationalist. We should ask, which boys are underachieving and in what ways. A simple analysis by sex of statutory assessment outcomes and the results of public examinations is not a sufficient basis on which to build policy and strategies for change. Salisbury, Rees and Gorard (1999: foreword) found 'no convincing explanations of the phenomenon, and therefore little hope of an effective strategy to deal with it'. Just highlighting a 'problem' in such a general way is not helpful to schools or to teachers. It is to be hoped that appropriately funded, high quality research into underachievement with specific reference to Wales is being undertaken and that publicly funded research within Wales will examine the variable of gender. Any professional development or training provided to schools must be based on rigorous evidence and include carefully developed and tested strategies. Any setting of targets, however fuzzy, must be fine-tuned to take account of research evidence. A target such as 'improve boys' performance' is not helpful to schools, to LEAs or to Estyn.

Men into teaching

Both Wales and England have attempted to increase the number of men in primary teaching. This could be seen perhaps as a common sense approach to solving the identified underachievement of boys by providing role models who have achieved educationally (Thornton, 1999). There are also arguments for more male teachers, particularly during the formative years of primary education, because the rise in the number of children being raised by single mothers is assumed to result in their having no close male role model.

Research was commissioned to identify the reasons for the under-involvement of men in primary teaching in Wales (Edwards, 2003). Whilst no targets or time frame were set for improvements, initial teacher education and training institutions did receive some funding to assist with the recruitment of men. Each individual institution was able to use this money as it saw fit. The impact of this funding has not been evaluated at a national level.

There certainly seemed to be a will to change public perceptions. The 2003 General Teaching Council for Wales document on teacher recruitment in Wales was published with a photograph of a male teacher with a boy pupil on the cover. The need to increase the number of men entering teaching was emphasized by the specially commissioned report that was used as evidence for this document (White et al., 2003). To date in Wales the position has not improved. In 2003–4 there were 1,094 men working in primary schools, representing 19 per cent of the workforce. In 2006–7 there were 1,252 men, a small increase in actual numbers but as these now represented only 16 per cent of the workforce this is, in real terms, a decrease.

In England during the academic year 2007–8, a significant number of higher education institutions and LEAs were involved in running short courses specifically aimed at encouraging men to enter primary school teaching. The Training and Development Agency for Schools reported in a telephone conversation that there are no such courses available in Wales at the moment, 'probably because there is no need', but men from Wales could apply to attend the courses in England if they wished.

Currently there is no shortage of candidates for primary teaching in Wales; indeed, it is very over-subscribed and training targets have been substantially cut over the last few years. Unlike the past Labour policy of women-only short lists for parliamentary seats, no sub-targets of any type are set for teacher training, although it would be simple to argue for them in terms of a balanced teaching force, for example, by subject specialism and age. Of course, this can be interpreted as taking an equality approach and could be extrapolated to explain the lack of gendered policy around the female-specific issues highlighted earlier in this chapter. On the other hand, it could be seen as an example of Welsh society refusing to engage with gendered policy.

Will they forgive us?

Does education in post-devolution Wales have the potential to make the world better? First, in terms of women's representation in positions of power and leadership in schools, I believe the potential exists. The proportion of women deputy head teachers constitutes a critical mass for promotion. In 2005 the National Headship Development Programme introduced a mandatory qualification for new head teachers (National Professional Qualification for Headship – NPQH) in Wales. As of February 2008 1,196 teachers in Wales held this qualification and of these 60 per cent were women. Currently only 52 per cent of head teachers in Wales are women (women make up 73 per cent of the teaching workforce).

However, if the Welsh Assembly Government believes that women should play an equitable role it needs to develop strategies to encourage women to come forward. Coleman (2005) found that mentors played an important role in encouraging a teacher to apply for leadership roles. Three-quarters of all head teachers said that this had most likely come from their own head teacher or other members of the senior management team. Currently in secondary schools in Wales such a mentor is most likely to be male. In the primary sector the situation is more hopeful; most mentors would be female. Additionally Coleman (2005) found that encouragement from mentors is more important for secondary female heads. Yet at least half of all heads reported to her that they did not use special measures to develop female teachers. In contrast, in England positive steps are being taken to maximize female involvement in headship. Women into School Headship (WiSH) has been set up actively to encourage and prepare senior women in education for headship. It runs courses aimed at aspiring women seeking their first headship. Such initiatives appear valid, for Coleman (2005) found that mentoring and role models were particularly important for women and there was not much evidence of head teachers' giving special support to women in terms of career development. There would also be long-term gains through the development of supportive networks for women head teachers who can feel isolated.

However, to date we have no evidence of the effectiveness of such programmes.

Currently no such initiatives can be identified in Wales. Whether this is because there is satisfaction within Wales with the progress being made through existing programmes, such as NPQH, or because such programmes are under consideration awaiting outcomes in England is not clear. WiSH reported that it could make the course available in Wales and that any teacher in Wales would be able to attend a course in England

Secondly, is there evidence that education in Wales takes gender issues seriously? When researching this chapter, I was surprised that in 2007 very few easily available statistics regarding education were reported by sex. For example, in the important area of headship training none of the statistics provided were broken down by sex (Estyn, 2006). Many current documents do not have any gender-specific aspects. For example, in its advice to the Welsh Assembly Government on headship training Estyn made no mention of the need to monitor gender or ensure a reflection of the diversity of the work-force or learners in our schools. It did advise WAG to produce guidance aimed at helping appointing panels understand what constitutes good practice in fair selection. The data regarding women's involvement in the national headship scheme have not been reported in the Estyn reviews. The data appearing in this chapter were obtained from DCELLS through the Freedom of Information Act. It is to be hoped that the data have been available to those monitoring the national headship scheme. Whilst the numbers of women achieving this qualification is encouraging, it will not necessarily result in an increase in the number of women becoming head teachers. In 2007 Daugherty edited a themed edition of *The Welsh Journal of Education* focusing on education policy in Wales in the era of political devolution. No article was specifically about gender issues and no article discussed its subject from a gendered perspective.

Within education in Wales today there is little emphasis on the under-involvement or underachievement of girls; the major focus is on boys' problems and the dearth of men in teaching. However, we must note that the thrust of educational policy is social equity rather than female advancement and celebrate any ideological arguments for improvement in education.

Conclusions

This chapter has examined the extent to which education in Wales has been 'made different' *by* women and, in some limited ways, has 'made the world different' *for* women. It has not been possible to explore fully the position of female learners in Wales nor to examine curricular content from a feminist perspective. Neither has this chapter looked at the ways in which the education system reflects feminist ideology beyond noting that the non-competitive and non-confrontational ethos that typified educational policy in Wales, compared to that in England during this time, resonates with feminist ideology.

There is no doubt that two women, working at the highest level in education, were highly influential in both the setting of policy and the investigation of the impact of that policy. Within the key schools inspectorate women play a major role in significant numbers. However, at the point where policy impacts on practice the picture is somewhat different. Davies and Exell (2005) report that the two factors with the greatest impact on policy transmission to the local level are the attitudes and activities of the Local Education Authority and of the headteacher.

Within schools there is the potential for a more equitable situation regarding women in senior positions. A critical mass of women wait poised to take on headships and senior management roles. The numbers holding the prerequisite qualification is encouraging. WAG and the unitary authorities should develop strategies, with governors, to ensure equity of opportunity. On the other hand, we have no picture of the experiences of women in or aspiring to headship in Wales. Detailed research into the barriers to women's achieving or aspiring to headship should be a priority. A replication of Coleman's 2005 research in Wales would be beneficial and allow for evidence-based policy to be developed. There is excellent provision in Wales for the training of governors and this is supported by a dedicated centre for research. It should be possible for evidence to be made available and, if it is indicated as necessary, for training to be provided.

Within the local political and administrative arena women play a lesser role. Of the twenty-two directors of education in Wales only one is female. Of the twenty-two local councillors leading education only two are women. Unitary authorities need to be encouraged to examine the gender balance of those involved in education at all levels to seek to understand the causes of any imbalance in their own region and to develop strategies to address these.

The research for this chapter highlighted the fact that some key gendered aspects of education in Wales are invisible. Whilst gender-specific data regarding pupils, their performance and the teaching force are easily accessed, statistics regarding the gender of those following headship training are not reported and the composition of governing bodies is not collected. I have argued that it is through the increase of women in management roles and the equitable composition of governing bodies that the educational world could be made better *for* women.

Even when a gendered inequality, that of the lack of men in teaching, was identified, its profile diminished and it no longer appears to be a priority; indeed, the situation is worse than it was at the time of devolution and there appears to be no formal strategy to address the problem. My reading of educational policy in Wales over the last ten years is that it is to a very great extent couched in gender-neutral language and that the only two gender-specific policy issues have been allowed to fade. What reasons did WAG have for this? The words and phrases used in policy can 'frame' an issue in people's minds, often in ways which virtually predetermine their reaction to it.

Educational policy discourse now contains the idea that education can help to deliver social justice: 'Social Justice is about every one of us having the chances and opportunities to make the most of our lives and use our talents to the full'. (WAG, 2008). Rees (2007) identifies Welsh civil society as a key player in the forming of Welsh Assembly Government policy and it is arguable that WAG envisaged a more positive reaction from Welsh civil society to educational policies when the term 'social justice' was used than if gender inequality, in particular female inequality, were evoked. On the other hand, by telling us that educational policies aim for social justice for all, WAG allows any one of us to interpret them in a personal way – the policy will make improvements to *all* groups and hence to any group which we hold especially important.

So, whilst gender sits alongside many aspects such as economic standing, ethnicity, parental support in contributing to any individual's ability to access education, it no longer holds a special place in educational policy in Wales. Whether issues of poverty and social inclusion *are* more significant than those of gender or whether they sit more comfortably with Welsh civil society needs further investigation.

Of course, Wales is not alone in the UK in having shifted from discussing policy in terms of gender. Recent debates around the role of universities as engines of social justice demonstrate this. Whilst John Denham, universities secretary, claimed, 'Education is the most powerful tool we have in achieving social justice', he too couched this in gender-neutral terms: 'It must allow the most talented and hard working of our young people to achieve their full potential, irrespective of what kind of social background they came from, or the school they went to' (Denham, 2008).

In this chapter I have demonstrated that gender has not been central to the development of post-devolution education policy. However, ideas of social justice (not exclusively for women) have been. As WAG educational policy is now gender neutral, then it must be through the idea of social justice that a more equitable situation for both women and men will be achieved.

So did education policy in Wales make the world new? Yes, the competitive system of league tables and the stressful assessment procedures that WAG inherited were dismantled, but the change in the world of the school with its high proportion of women teachers but with mainly male management has not been so dramatic or positive. The world for the school pupil is different. It is a world with the potential for significant change, the potential to make the world new.

References

Arnot, M. and M. Mac an Ghaill (2006). '(Re) contextualising gender studies in education: schooling in late modernity', in M. Arnot and M. Mac an Ghaill (eds), *Reader in Gender and Education*, Abingdon: Routledge, pp. 1–14.

BBC News (1999). 'Woodhead: "I am paid to challenge mediocrity"', 14 June, *http://news.bbc.co.uk/1/hi/education/367060.stm*.

Coleman, M. (2005). *Gender and Headship in the 21st Century*, Nottingham: National Centre for School Leadership.

Davidson, J. (2001). 'Foreword', in *The Learning Country*, Cardiff: Welsh Assembly Government.

Davies, C. A. and N. Exell (2005). 'Summary of findings: Mass education, national identity and citizenship: policy development and transmission', unpublished executive summary for ESRC project RES-000-22-0555.

Daugherty, R. (ed.) (2007). 'Editorial', *The Welsh Journal of Education*, 14.

Denham J. (2008). *Telegraph.co.uk*, 12 September, *http://www.telegraph.co.uk/news/newstopics/politics/education/2798968/Universities-have-a-duty-to-promote-social-justice-says-John-Denham.html*.

Department for Children, Schools and Families (DCSF) (2007). *Teachers in Service, http://www.dfes.gov.uk/rsgateway/.*

Edwards, R. (2003). *The Recruitment of Men and Ethnic Minority Students to Primary PGCE Courses in England and Wales,* Cardiff: HEFCW.

Estyn (2002). *The Annual Report of Her Majesty's Chief Inspector of Education and Training in Wales 1999–2000,* Cardiff: HMSO.

—— (2006). *Impact of the Professional Headship Induction Programme,* Cardiff: Estyn.

General Teaching Council for Wales (2003). *Action Plan for Teacher Recruitment and Retention in Wales, http://gtcw.org.uk.*

Jones, G. E. (2006). 'Education and nationhood in Wales: an historiographical analysis', *Journal of Educational Administration and History,* 38, 3, 263–77.

Jones, M. L. (1990). 'The attitudes of men and women primary school teachers to promotion and education management', *Educational Management, Administration and Leadership,* 18, 3, 11–16.

Lewis, S. (2001). 'Foreword', in *The Annual Report of Her Majesty's Chief Inspector of Education and Training in Wales 1999–2000,* Cardiff: HMSO.

Mackay, F. (2001). *Love and Politics: Women Politicians and the Ethics of Care,* London: Continuum.

Norris, F. (1985). 'Classroom politics', in Raving Beauties (eds), *No Holds Barred,* London: The Women's Press.

Oram, A. (1989). 'A master should not serve under a mistress: women and men teachers 1900–1970', in S. Acker (ed.), *Teachers, Gender and Careers,* London: The Falmer Press, pp. 21–34.

Paterson, L. (2003). 'The three educational ideologies of the British Labour Party, 1997–2001', *Oxford Review of Education,* 29, 2, 165–86.

Rees, G. (2007). 'The impacts of parliamentary devolution on education policy in Wales', *The Welsh Journal of Education,* 14, 8–20.

Salisbury, J., G. Rees and S. Gorard (1999). 'Accounting for the differential attainment of boys and girls at school', *School Leadership and Management,* 19, 4, 403–26.

Stobart G., J. Elwood, M. Hayden and K. Mason (1992). 'Gender bias in examinations: how equal are the opportunities?' *British Educational Research Journal,* 18, 261–76.

Training and Development Agency for Schools (2008). *Taster Courses: Men into Primary Teaching, http://www.tda.gov.uk/.*

Thornton, M. (1999). 'Men into primary teaching', *Education, 3–13,* 27, 2, 50–6.

Weiner, G. (2004). 'Beyond access: pedagogic strategies for gender equality and quality basic education in schools', paper presented at invited seminar, 2–3 February, Nairobi, Kenya. *http://www.ioe.ac.uk/schools/efps/GenderEducDev/.*

Welsh Assembly Government (WAG) (2001). *The Learning Country*, Cardiff: WAG.

—— (2006). *The Learning Country 2: Delivering the Promise*, Cardiff: WAG.

—— (2007). *Schools in Wales: General Statistics 2007, http://new.wales. gov.uk/topics/statistics/publications/.*

—— (2008). *Topics: Social Justice, http://new.wales.gov.uk/topics/socialjustice/?lang=en.*

White, P., B. H. See, S. Gorard and K. Roberts (2003). *Review of Teacher Recruitment, Supply and Retention in Wales*, GTCW commissioned study, *www.gtcw.org.uk*.

Women into Secondary Headship (2008). *Wholehearted for Headship, http://www.dfes.gov.uk/rsgateway/* .

Woodward, W. (2001). 'Great Wales', *Guardian*, 2 October, *http://education.guardian.co.uk*.

8

Gendered Housing Policy: Women, Housing and Homelessness

SUSAN HUTSON AND TAMSIN STIRLING

This chapter outlines policies and legislation developed by the National Assembly for Wales around homelessness and housing over the last decade (see table 8.1). The focus is on the route into 'social housing', which is affordable rented accommodation provided by local authorities or housing associations. The chapter considers to what extent, and why, these policies can be seen as constituting a distinctive Welsh approach to housing. At the same time, it looks at gendered aspects of housing provision and their changing pattern over time.

In order to explore these issues, we interviewed a number of senior women working in the field of housing and this chapter is based, principally, on what they told us. These women worked in the statutory and voluntary sectors and one was a civil servant in the National Assembly. This gives an opportunity to trace the changing role of these different arenas of power in homelessness policies. We asked the interviewees to focus on the situation of women and children in their search for housing. They also spoke briefly of their own careers, making it possible to see the changing position of women both as managers and clients within the homelessness and housing system.

It is obvious that the situation of both the informants and the authors structure the findings. The two most senior women, amongst our informants, were a housing association chief executive and a senior official within the National Assembly. Two women were managers within local authority housing departments and four were directors in the voluntary sector. In addition, two women were working as independent housing consultants. Significantly, three of the women

Table 8.1: Homelessness under the Welsh Assembly Government

When	What	Further information
October 1998 – October 1999	Secondee worked on rough sleeping to advise Welsh Office/Assembly on effective strategies for assisting rough sleepers	Report as considered by Committee in December 1999, *http://www.assemblywales. org/bus-home/bus-committees/bus-committees-first/bus-committees-first-lge-home/bus-committees-first-lge-agendas.htm?ds=12%2F1999& submit=Submit*
2001	Homelessness Commission worked to advise Assembly on delivering its objectives to reduce homelessness	Final report as considered by Committee in October 2001 *http://www.assemblywales.org/ bus-home/bus-committees/bus-committees-first/bus-committees-first-lgh-home/bus-committees-first-lgh-agendas.htm?ds=10% 2F2001&submit=Submit*
February 2001	Secondary legislation to extend priority need groups – implementation 1st March 2001	*http://www.opsi.gov.uk/legislation/wales/wsi2001 /wsi_20010607_mi.pdf*
February 2002	Homelessness Act 2002 – required production of homelessness strategies by local authorities*	*http://www.opsi.gov.uk/acts/acts2002/pdf/ ukpga_20020007_en.pdf*
2002/03	Funding provided by the Assembly to support local authorities to review homelessness and develop homelessness strategies	
March 2003	First National Homelessness Strategy published by Assembly	
2004	Domestic Violence, Crime and Victims Act 2004*	*http://www.opsi.gov.uk/acts/acts2004/pdf/ ukpga_20040028_en.pdf*
2004/05 – 2006/07	Policy Agreements between Assembly and local government include targets on homelessness – linked to Performance Improvement Grant funding for local authorities	*http://new.wales.gov.uk/topics/localgovernment/ partnership/policyagreements/?lang=en*
March 2005	Domestic Abuse Strategy published by Assembly	*http://new.wales.gov.uk/dsjlg/publications/ commmunitysafety/domesticabusestrategy/ strategye?lang=en*
June 2005	Tarki report *Tackling Homelessness – key issues for local authorities* published emphasizing prevention agenda and providing homelessness MOT for local authorities	*http://new.wales.gov.uk/desh/publications/ housing/tacklehomelessness/guide.pdf?lang=en*

Table 8.1 continued

When	What	Further information
2005/06 and 2006/07	£1m prevention funding allocated to local authorities	
November 2005	Second National Homelessness Strategy covering period 2006–8 published by Assembly	*http://new.wales.gov.uk/desh/publications/ housing/homelessnessstrategy/strategye.pdf? lang=en*
March 2006	Secondary legislation to reduce use of bed and breakfast and improve quality of temporary accommodation – staged implementation April 2006, April 2007 and April 2008	*http://www.opsi.gov.uk/legislation/wales/wsi 2006/wsi_20060650_mi.pdf*
June 2007	*One Wales* commitment to developing a Ten Year Plan to confront homelessness	*http://new.wales.gov.uk/about/strategy/1wales/ ?lang=en*

* primary legislation passed at Westminster

interviewed had worked in Welsh Women's Aid, as volunteers, at the beginning of their careers. The two authors come from a similar generation to the women interviewed and have each researched on an all-Wales basis for twenty years – both within university departments and as freelancers.

Homelessness in the UK before the National Assembly was set up

As a starting point, it is important to understand the background to homelessness that the Assembly inherited in 1997. Homelessness hit the UK headlines in 1966 following the TV documentary film *Cathy Come Home*, which shocked the British public by showing the treatment of ordinary families who were homeless. Shelter, the campaigning organization for homeless people, was formed the following year. In 1977 the Housing (Homeless Person's) Act was passed. This was the first time that local authorities were given the duty to house certain categories of homeless people – namely those who were 'in priority need'. These were, principally, homeless women who had children or who were pregnant. (Duties towards people who are vulnerable as a result of fleeing domestic violence came later in 1996.) With only a few exceptions, the duty in 1977 did not extend to single homeless people. The intention of this original homelessness legislation was to provide a safety net primarily for homeless women with children. This split, between 'family' and 'single' homeless people structures homeless services to the present day.

By the late 1980s, young people were becoming visibly homeless and pictures of rough sleepers, particularly in London, were commonly featured in the press. This was an embarrassment to the government. Economic factors in Wales, such as the demise of mining, steel making and many traditional industries, accelerated youth unemployment and subsequently youth homelessness (Hutson and Jenkins, 1989; Hutson and Liddiard, 1994). On the basis of the 1977 act outlined above, the state had little responsibility to house these young people. However, in some areas of Wales, particularly in urban south-east Wales, the voluntary sector set up schemes to cater for their needs. Moreover, surveys (Randall, 1988; Hutson and Liddiard, 1991) were showing that young people leaving care at the age of sixteen were making up around a third of those using homelessness services. Overall the number of single people enquiring at housing departments as homeless rose from 29 per cent in 1987 to 44 per cent in 1996 (Hutson and Stirling, 2001).

Landmarks in homelessness in Wales

The first three years of the millennium saw the formalization of homelessness policies. A Homelessness Commission was set up to advise the National Assembly, with Shelter as a major lobbyist. In 2001, *Better Homes for People in Wales* was published, stating that: 'The homeless are the most socially excluded in our society' (WAG, 2001). In 2002, the local authorities were required to review homelessness and write strategies and in 2003 the first national homeless strategy was published. These measures reflected a concern with homelessness by the newly elected National Assembly. However, all these events were overshadowed by the passing of the Homeless Persons (Priority Need) (Wales) Order in 2001. This widened the categories which local authorities had a duty to house to include sixteen and seventeen year olds and prison-leavers. This significant change is considered in the next section.

A reading of the Assembly's official statements around homelessness, in acts and reports from 2001 to 2007, shows changes in the explanations of homelessness and its solution – from the early emphasis on eliminating rough sleeping, which reflected the concerns of Westminster, to concerns about the increasing cost of bed and breakfast as temporary accommodation and preventative measures to solve these, as outlined in detail in the 2005 Tarki report. The second national homelessness strategy, published in 2005, played down the role of National Assembly legislation in solving homelessness and emphasized the importance of local policy initiatives and 'joining up' services at a local level. The role of the private rented sector in providing housing was mentioned for the first time. It is in *One Wales*, published in 2007, that we get the first main focus on the acute shortage of housing, particularly for the first-time buyer (WAG, 2007b).

Table 8.1 sets out chronologically the main events in Welsh homelessness legislation but, in this chapter, we focus on the three landmarks which were most often mentioned by the women interviewees – namely, the passing of the Homeless Persons (Priority Need) (Wales) Order in 2001; the change to Supporting People funding from 2003; and the preventative agenda which covers a raft of measures passed by the National Assembly in 2005–6.

The Assembly extends the safety net – the 'new priorities' legislation

This secondary legislation in 2001 widened the categories which local authorities had a duty to house to include sixteen and seventeen year olds and homeless prison-leavers. (People homeless after leaving the armed forces were also included and the priority status of care-leavers and persons fleeing domestic violence were confirmed.) Significantly, prison-leavers and sixteen and seventeen year olds still do not have these rights in England.

This secondary legislation was announced on St David's Day, 1 March 2001. As one manager recounted, 'The politicians were excited about it'. It came in suddenly and the accompanying guidance was issued several weeks after the legislation. This act had a huge ideological impact and distinguishes Welsh homelessness policy from that of England. The ethos of this legislation links with a distinctive Welsh approach to politics, identified by Drakeford as 'an emphasis on collective effort and social solidarity' (2007: 172). Throughout this period, the Assembly's chief objective was to combat 'social exclusion'. The reasons for this are explained in Rhodri Morgan's words:

Inequality is the most insidious form of injustice because it prevents individuals from achieving their full potential. And every time inequality prevents any of our fellow citizens from exercising their talents, or accessing the services to which they are entitled, the total stock of freedom available to all of us is diminished. (Morgan, 2006)

Homelessness was linked into inequality in *Better Homes for People in Wales*, which stated that: 'The homeless are the most socially excluded in our society – in the most extreme case we have rough sleepers living a way of life which can cause irreparable harm to their health and well being' (WAG, 2001: section 13.2). This view, and the difference between Welsh and English policies, is echoed by one woman interviewee who felt that Wales has had a different experience of recent economic change and also a different response: 'We didn't embrace Thatcher's policies. We suffered from them. In Wales the watchword has been "collaboration and partnership" rather than "competition and choice" as it is in England.'

There is no doubt that the widening of priority categories was a key element in the increase in people reporting as homeless and that this was a greater increase than in England. The Tarki report stated that: 'In Wales, between 1997 and 2003, there was a 100% increase in homeless acceptances. This led to an increase in the use of temporary accommodation (215% rise) and, particularly bed and breakfast (500% rise)' (Tarki, 2005: 7). Local authorities, who were bound to provide this accommodation, expressed their concerns to the National Assembly but it was obvious that the legislation was not going to be altered. Interestingly, increasing demand led to more resources being diverted into homelessness services by some local authorities as new duties to the new priority groups, rising homelessness figures and, particularly, sharply increasing bed-and-breakfast budgets pushed homelessness into a prominent position within local authority executives. Two of our women local authority managers spoke of the greater recognition and expansion of their services. One homelessness manager said: 'We are assisted [now] by more resources which we got because of pressures.' It was clear that the 'new priorities' legislation drew local authorities, or the state, more directly into providing for single homeless people, many of whom were sixteen and seventeen year olds or prison-leavers. This work had previously been left to the voluntary sector because there had been no statutory duty to meet their needs.

Supporting People and support in tenancies

In the early 1990s there was a significant change in the UK in the way vulnerable people received support. A rundown of care in institutions for those with mental illness and learning difficulties was already well under way throughout the UK, meaning that more vulnerable people were living 'in the community'. Before 2003, support, in hostels such as homelessness hostels and schemes to resettle vulnerable people into independent housing, was provided through centrally funded housing benefit. In 2003 the 'support' element of housing benefit was taken away and placed, with other resources, into a Supporting People fund. In England, this fund was to be administered by the local authority. This funding covered elements of 'support' such as budgeting, support to maintain a tenancy and making links to training and employment opportunities.

Supporting People funding was crucial in several ways. First, vulnerable people were able to live independently in the community with the initial help of support workers. Secondly, the transition to the new funding regime led to a marked expansion of schemes. The third important aspect of Supporting People in Wales was that Edwina Hart, the then minister with responsibility for housing, retained most of this funding in the National Assembly rather than passing it down to the local authorities where there would be other demands on it. This undoubtedly led, later, to fewer cuts to the Supporting People funding in Wales than in England. As one voluntary sector director said: 'Supporting People played an enormous part [in homeless services]. The principles behind it made a shift in thinking. Rather than a Cinderella service it became a key one.' Another voluntary sector manager, when asked what were the main gains achieved in relation to housing and homelessness said: 'Commitment and Supporting People ... the human scale, the innovation. In England they are talking now of working holistically. We've been doing it for years.'

A preventative agenda

The emphasis on measures to prevent homelessness peaked in 2005 as the numbers of homeless people rose and the cost of temporary or bed-and-breakfast accommodation soared. The key to prevention lay in joint working and partnership between the housing department and other agencies such as social services (in relation to young people), drug and alcohol services as well as employment and health. Housing departments were required to work with the voluntary sector which already had expertise in providing hostel or specialized accommodation for certain groups such as young people or those with mental health issues. A 'preventative' approach to homelessness could involve housing departments' simply signposting people to appropriate services or providing direct services such as bonds to access private rented accommodation. In addition, housing departments were required to alter their internal policies, such as rent collection and eviction so that fewer people were evicted from social housing. They could even draw in support from Supporting People funds. The enlargement of support services with Supporting People was a key factor in this prevention agenda. Furniture schemes were established, in some local authorities, and 'mediation schemes', between sixteen and seventeen year olds and their parents, appeared particularly successful in reducing homelessness amongst this group. Small 'incentive' sums from the National Assembly were available or savings from bed-and-breakfast budgets were turned around into these preventative measures. It is likely that these preventative measures were successful in causing a drop in Welsh homelessness figures.

The Tarki report (2005) was important in setting out the preventative agenda. Tarki Technology Ltd, an independent consultancy which had been working with English local authorities to help reduce rising homeless figures, was commissioned by the Welsh Assembly Government to report on the situation in Wales. This report told local authorities to find the real reason for someone's presenting as homeless and to solve this through preventative measures and sources of help to avoid it. The aim was to accept fewer applicants whom they had a duty to house, or 'in priority need', by applying preventative measures more widely. The stance and clarity of this report, with action points outlined, changed practice. One homelessness manager felt that this report had 'turned around the whole way of working'. Another homelessness manager said: 'We don't have lower numbers coming through the door now but we screen them more. We don't just house them. We were doing that before. Now we don't assume that they have rights. We signpost them.' She went on to name the partnership agencies and services which now help her provide appropriate services for those presenting with housing problems: 'Now we have Gofal [an organization specializing in mental health], mediation, children's services, housing associations, Shelter Cymru, a credit union, tenancy support, and Supporting People.' In 2006 the National

Assembly strengthened its demands for prevention by passing secondary legislation to reduce the use of bed-and-breakfast accommodation and to improve the quality of temporary accommodation.

The main gains in housing/homelessness since 1997

There is no doubt that the first decade of devolved government in Wales saw a stronger awareness of homelessness as a problem and increased activity in the National Assembly and at the local authority level. A number of the women interviewed spoke about the expansion of services, in the statutory and the voluntary sector, but what they felt was most important was the recognition of their services which accompanied this expansion. One local authority homelessness manager said: 'It was that political acceptance of homelessness which has led to [more] resources and services.' The woman manager in another authority spoke of 'a recognition of homelessness services and what we offer because of the higher profile of homelessness in the Assembly and the explosion of numbers in 2002/3'. In similar vein, a woman in the voluntary sector spoke of 'the ability to get housing [the local authorities] to see the third [voluntary] sector as an example of good practice'. Supporting People funding was featured as an important gain by a number of women interviewed.

The Homelessness Act (2002) required local authorities to review homelessness in their area and produce homelessness strategies; the requirement that these strategies be produced was acknowledged as important: 'Our local authority would never have put together a homelessness strategy unless they had been required to do so.' Several acknowledged the preventative agenda as being important: 'Heading homelessness off at the pass . . . this is good because homelessness is a traumatic experience.'

Barriers in the housing market

Despite changes in the identification of who was recognized as 'homeless' and how they were to be processed, a serious problem was being created which was not really recognized until the *One Wales* report in 2007. This was the shortage of affordable housing and the impact this was to have throughout the housing market. First, there was an acute shortage of housing to buy for first-time buyers at the bottom of the market. Currently, there are numbers of young working households, including lower-paid key workers, who can afford to pay more than a social-sector rent but still cannot afford to buy at the very bottom of the housing market. This shortage affects social housing. As house prices increase, more people approach local authorities and housing associations for accommodation because they cannot afford to buy (Jones, 2006). At the same time, fewer people are moving out of the social rented sector because they cannot afford to buy. This means that the number of applicants registering on housing waiting lists rises and the number of households presenting as homeless increases. Significantly, women with children, particularly single mothers, are concentrated in social housing and this is connected with the lower incomes of women (National Statistics, 2000).

An additional factor, which is immediately significant for homeless people, is the declining number of social housing units. Right to buy legislation in 1981 led to a loss of over a third of council housing in Wales (Hutson and Stirling, 2001). Local authority building has been at a standstill due to funding restrictions and new build from housing associations has not compensated for this loss. One woman executive who was interviewed felt that there had been no gains in housing policy, particularly for women with children, because of the overall pressures on housing. This link between homelessness and the lack of affordable housing in Wales can be seen in rising waiting lists for social housing, young working families struggling to find somewhere to live and people forced to stay in temporary accommodation or with friends and relatives (Shelter Cymru, 2007).

There has been a current increase in joint ownership schemes with housing associations in Wales, particularly in rural areas. In addition, housing has been built through 'section 106' whereby new-build private developments over a certain size can be required to build a certain proportion of 'affordable housing', which usually means some type of shared ownership. Although some schemes have been successful, demand continues to outstrip supply so that they are not making significant inroads into overall demand. Moreover, a UK report (Burgess et al., 2007) queries whether negotiations between local authorities and developers are producing the type and tenure of housing needed for many of the people on their waiting and homelessness lists. What are needed are larger family houses and what are offered are small flats. There is a danger that, because the plight of the first-time buying working couple is more politically acceptable than homeless people seeking social housing, the problems of the former will overshadow the latter.

Homelessness statistics

What can official homelessness statistics tell us of the changes outlined above? The numbers (including those noted as enquirers and those accepted, in priority need or not) rose from 8,000 in 1999 to a peak of almost 17,000 in 2004. From there, numbers fell back to 11,000 in 2006 (see figure 8.1). The English homelessness figures, over the same period, saw a less sharp rise to a peak in 2003 and a sharper decline to figures below the 1997 level (Crisis, 2007). The introduction of the new priority categories in Wales undoubtedly led to this rise in those who were 'homeless and in priority need' as well as to an increase in homelessness enquiries. It is generally accepted that the recent fall in homeless figures is due to implementation of the prevention agenda (WAG, 2005).

A further breakdown of these statistics shows changing patterns in the make-up of homeless groups. Figure 8.1 shows that the total number of those in priority need has risen but that the percentage of pregnant women and women with children in this group has dropped. More single people are being accepted and housed.

The changes over time in Wales can be summed up by two snapshots:

- In 1999/2000, 3,652 households were accepted as unintentionally homeless and in priority need. These accepted households accounted for 30 per cent of all homelessness applicants. Of

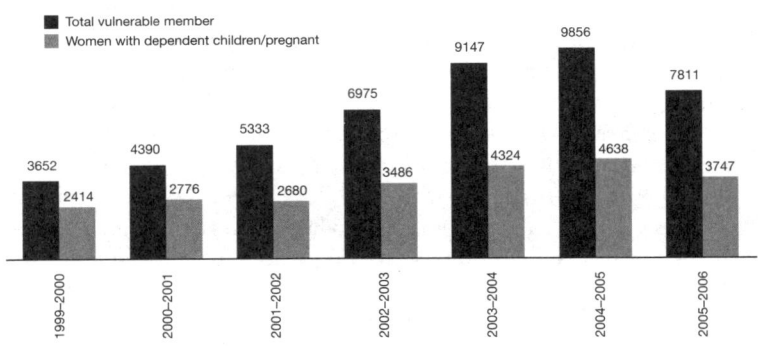

Figure 8.1: Women with dependent children compared with single households with a vulnerable member, 1999–2006
Source: Welsh Housing Statistics 2007

those households accepted, 66 per cent were women with dependent children or pregnant.

- In 2005/06, 7,811 households were accepted as unintentionally homeless and in priority need. These accepted households accounted for 42 per cent of all homelessness applicants. Of those households accepted, 48 per cent were women with dependent children or pregnant.

This shows that the number of households accepted as unintentionally homeless and in priority need more than doubled between the years indicated. Accepted households make up a higher percentage of all homeless applicants (a rise of 12 percentage points). Women with dependent children or pregnant make up a smaller percentage of these accepted households with a drop of 19 percentage points. It would appear that those single people who fell outside the priority categories of the 1977 Housing (Homelessness) Act are gradually being housed whilst the proportion of women with children being housed through the homeless route is dropping.

To summarize, the 'new priorities' legislation, in widening the duties of the state to homeless people, can be seen as a distinctly Welsh response to homelessness, resting on historical and social factors and reflecting the huge emphasis of the National Assembly on equality and social inclusion. The National Assembly further protected vulnerable people by retaining centrally some of Supporting People funding rather than devolving it to the local authorities. The preventative agenda, in part articulated by the Tarki report, 'turned around' local authority working to emphasize prevention. The general consensus is that services for homeless people have improved. However, the acute lack of affordable housing is already jeopardizing these gains. Housing statistics show an increase in demand from homeless people. A closer look at the statistics suggests that the number of single homeless people accepted by local authorities equals that of women with children. The decade of measures concerning homelessness has probably had most impact on single homeless people, who are disproportionately men, while the current and acute shortage of housing probably has had more effect on women with children, particularly those in social housing.

The voluntary sector, the National Assembly and the local authorities

The structure of homelessness provision hangs on legislation as illustrated by the Housing (Homeless Persons) Act 1977 and the 'new priorities' legislation. Behind the shape of homelessness services in Wales today lie three areas of power and organization – the National Assembly itself, the local authorities and the voluntary sector. The juxtaposition of these gives a particular kind of 'democracy'. The women interviewed, working themselves in these different sectors, gave us an interesting picture of this.

The voluntary sector

The voluntary sector was at the forefront of single homeless provision from the 1980s. It built up experience of delivering services to single homeless people. Local voluntary agencies, such as Adref and Swansea Young Single Homeless, were set up by concerned people, particularly in Cardiff, Swansea and in the Rhondda. Later, national charities set up projects, such as Barnardos and National Children's Homes. The Salvation Army, Wallich Clifford, the Cyrenians and Caerlas were already working with older single homeless people. Where housing was provided, these voluntary agencies formed partnerships with housing associations. These were benefiting from the funding for new-build from a Thatcher government whilst local authorities' new-build programme was effectively at a standstill. Special needs management allowance funding for support was available for housing associations in Wales, but not in England. Tai Cymru, the newly formed Welsh equivalent of the Housing Corporation, actively promoted supported accommodation for homeless and other vulnerable groups together with 'floating support' which was a new concept at the time. Local authorities were encouraged to commission services in the voluntary sector. Thus, at the beginning of the 1990s, most provision catering for the sharp increase in young single homelessness was in the hands of a dynamic voluntary sector, which was experimenting with new forms of housing and support.

When the Supporting People programme was announced, voluntary agencies were actively encouraged to set up new schemes. They were told, in advance, that when the period of transitional housing benefit ended in March 2003, all projects running would be funded.

This enabled those well-established voluntary agencies to expand and innovate. However, this further disadvantaged areas in west and north Wales where there were few voluntary agencies.

One woman interviewed, the director of a voluntary sector project working mostly with young homeless people, describes this expansion and details the way it was achieved:

> We were a small team. Now we deal with 720 young people a year; 15,000 cases of housing advice and 100 mediation cases ... We have used research, raised the profile of the project. We have tried new services, used assertive outreach, and proved that we get outcomes. We have developed a monitoring system ... We have listened to service users.

Another organization, run by an informant, was set up in 1989 as a housing association to house women coming from Welsh Women's Aid refuges in three counties. In 2007, it was working with other housing associations in eighteen local authority areas providing support to a range of vulnerable women.

As the 'new priorities' legislation increased the duties of local authorities towards vulnerable groups, including the homeless, they found that they could not fulfil these new duties – to sixteen and seventeen year olds and prison-leavers – without the help of the voluntary sector and housing associations. One woman, running a voluntary sector project for young people, said that, after the 'new priorities' legislation, one local authority said 'We'll cope with 16/17 year olds', but a year later came back and admitted that they could not cope with this client group.

Our informants drew sharp contrasts between voluntary agencies and local authorities. They pointed out that voluntary agencies are specialized, working in one area of work. Local authorities have to work across different, broad areas such as health, transport and social services. These different services compete for funds. Local authorities are accountable to the public, to the electorate, in all that they do. Public perceptions of single homelessness and vulnerable groups can be unfavourable and so services for them may not be a popular investment. Some voluntary agencies can get extra funding, from their national body or from trust funds. This means they can innovate, work at the cutting edge, and act quickly in response to need. A local authority cannot work like this.

The National Assembly

The National Assembly actively responded to the problem of home-lessness from 2001. The descriptions of the National Assembly by the women interviewed were interesting and overwhelmingly positive. The National Assembly was spoken of as 'humane' and a 'protector of vulnerable groups'. The National Assembly was 'ethical'. One woman said: 'The Welsh Assembly had a genuine concern to prevent home-lessness and get figures down . . . There were *political* reasons [for wanting this] but also *good* reasons.' All agreed that the National Assembly consulted, both with the voluntary sector and also with the local authorities. The passing of the 'new categories' legislation was seen as predominantly an action of the National Assembly. This legis-lation, together with the demands to reduce bed-and-breakfast accommodation, was fundamentally important in drawing the local authorities into a broader provision of homelessness services, not just focused on statutory duties. In speaking of the National Assembly, all saw Edwina Hart, the minister for social justice and regeneration between 2003 and 2007, as a champion for homeless people and vulnerable groups. Several women pointed out the obvious advantages of having the National Assembly rather than the old Welsh Office. One felt that, although teams in housing were larger and more special-ized in England, in Wales 'it was easier to see the whole picture'.

Local authorities

The local authorities had been housing women and children for decades, with an increasing number of single mothers as social changes were altering UK demography (Kiernan, 1989). Their involvement with other homeless people increased after the 'new priorities' legisla-tion. Political forces from Westminster were limiting funding for housing to local authorities whilst housing associations were expanding.

In the late 1990s, there was some evidence that the demand for council housing was dropping in both England and Wales. Empty properties in hard-to-let areas and a concentration of vulnerable households there were causing management problems. For example, in Penrhys, hundreds of houses were demolished. There was evidence that some families, fearing that they might be placed in such areas, preferred not to take the homelessness route into social housing. A high number of relets led some housing analysts to suggest that council housing was providing flexible short-term housing rather than tenure for life (Willcox, 1996). Some women and children undoubtedly profited from buying their council houses or moving into home ownership. Perhaps it was understandable, with these conditions in the housing market, that the problem of housing supply and the essential role of social rented housing were overlocked. The situation in 2007 had changed. A number of these hard-to-let areas had been redeveloped and waiting lists for them were growing. The number of relets had decreased significantly. It was harder to ex:t from social housing with higher house prices. Support policies were perhaps stabilizing some tenants and so reducing turnover.

Local authorities were drawn into providing for more single homeless people with the 'new priorities' legislation. One local authority manager spoke positively of this time: 'We wrote a 5 year plan to get out of the B&B overspends. It was accepted. There was a commitment at the members' level. . . The big B&B budget was turned around into other measures.' Expansion, partnership working, the Tarki report, Supporting People all changed the ways in which local authorities worked with homeless applicants.

Two main problems arise from relying on local authorities for the delivery of homelessness services. First, huge variations exist between local authorities in their commitment to and efficiency in providing for homeless people. Moreover, there are limits to which the National Assembly can require action within the local authority. Secondly, several women managers mentioned the difficulties of working across local authority boundaries. This is particularly important where a specialist service is needed for a small minority group.

To summarize, in the UK, welfare services are structured by legislation and also by the historical pattern of and relations between government, the local authorities and the voluntary sector. In homelessness, the lack of statutory duties towards single homeless people in 1977 led to an active voluntary sector, particularly in urban south Wales. Voluntary agencies had the advantage of being small, specialized and not dependent on public votes. Moreover, the National Assembly generally supported this sector. When local authorities were drawn in through the 'new priorities' legislation, they could meet their duties only through partnerships in the voluntary sector, which was already being encouraged by the Westminster government, anxious to bring down costs to the state. The danger of increased local authority responsibility in housing is the variation that exists between different local authorities in their concern for homelessness.

Housing and women

In the 1977 Housing (Homeless Persons) Act, women gain 'priority status' through their connection with children or pregnancy. They may or may not have a resident male partner although, if they or their partners are working, this may lessen their chances of qualifying for or wanting social housing. Many, but not all, women in social housing are single mothers. It is important to realize that, to qualify for social housing through the homeless route as opposed to just being on the waiting list, households must prove that they are 'homeless' by the act's definition: that they have not made themselves intentionally homeless and that they have a local connection of some kind as well as being in 'priority need'. Even if accepted, the household may have had to wait for a year or more in temporary accommodation. Even when they were rehoused, the only accommodation available might be a council house on a 'hard-to-let estate'. Thus having a legal right to accommodation has never ensured a smooth route into a suitable home for women with children (Smith, 1999).

Access to housing for women and children

Most of the women interviewed felt that access to housing for women with children had worsened. The main reason for this was the declining supply of affordable housing – either to rent or to buy. Rising housing prices affect women particularly, due to women's lower incomes. The economic restraints on homeless women are often combined with health or other issues and a lack of support networks. Women with children, particularly single mothers, are high users of temporary accommodation and social housing. They were likely to be disproportionately affected by the rising use of bed-and-breakfast accommodation in the early 1990s and the current shortage of social housing. Moreover, as a voluntary sector director pointed out, 'Things may be better in policies and strategies but women are still being turned down by workers on the ground'. She added that women may have easier access to housing today, 'but only if the woman presents with the backing of a support provider'.

Only three women felt that access to housing for women and children had improved over the decade and these were all based in the statutory sector. Two of these mentioned that estate regeneration, often with European money, had improved local authority housing stock thus giving women and children a better choice and better standards in housing. A homelessness manager felt that a number of women, who in the past might have presented as homeless, today were benefiting from the various preventative measures and neither becoming homeless nor even requiring social housing. She said:

> At the beginning of the decade, women and children would have been more likely to have been in B&B. There is more work going on in relation to advice and local authorities and others are less likely to evict for arrears so women and children are less likely to become homeless.

The demise of women's groups

Several informants provided a vivid picture of the dynamism of women's groups in the early 1980s when feminist ideas were impacting on Welsh society. One spoke of the building of new women's refuges through Tai Cymru: 'It was a time to fly; the golden days' [and perhaps even more crucial] 'I saw women who had rocked in their chairs in hospitals living in the community'. She spoke of how, working as a volunteer in Welsh Women's Aid, she had been empowered and women who had been abused had been similarly empowered and so been able to take staff posts. She pointed out that some of these women had gone on into Welsh politics.

One woman spoke of the self-help model in the women's refuges at that time: 'Self-help used to be women sitting down helping other women, like a collective. We asked women are you ready to talk to other women and we showed them how to do it. The best collective was in Carmarthen.' She contrasts this with the current professional model: 'Now it is not that collective model but support from the top. Now people aren't clear what they are doing. There is no challenging the system . . . Originally it was a safe place. Now it needs to be a more sophisticated model.'

There was a feeling, from these women, that things had changed and that there had been 'a slip in the feminist agenda'. Self-help amongst women does not sit easily with hierarchical management, budgets or partnership working. It was felt that Welsh Women's Aid had become mainstreamed and bureaucratized, that self-help was

outmoded. One woman said: 'Now it [self-help] seems old fashioned
... With mainstreaming there has been no one to shout for women.
With mainstreaming [of equalities issues], there is no one to be
radical.' However, one woman still involved with feminist networks
felt that

> A lot of good stuff is happening as a result of the legacy – little pockets
> of encouraging things – innovative ways of finding solutions to issues
> and bringing different organizations together – to meet unmet need –
> Jane Hutt has played a key role in enabling this to happen locally – more
> creative approach.

A focus on women as a priority group

A reading of the National Assembly reports and legislation shows
little consideration of women as a significant category. In Supporting
People plans, funding is divided up under categories such as 'learning
difficulties', 'elderly', 'ex-offenders' or 'drug and alcohol'. Whilst
'women fleeing domestic violence' can appear as a heading in these
publications, 'women' per se do not feature. One woman interviewed
explained that 'funding follows the label – "mental health", "drugs"
etc.', whereas women often do not fit into one label. She felt that
women, particularly, benefited from holistic support, pointing out
that this approach had been successful with young people.

The women interviewed were asked if there should be a refocus on
women in policy. Five felt that there should be a refocus on women,
one felt that this was not necessary and three were unsure. Several
agreed that the emphasis in the National Assembly on social exclusion
and anti-poverty had tended to override the particular problems of
women. Several people pointed out that Assembly members (AMs)
and also local authorities, needed to appeal to all the electorate and
that a 'feminist' campaign might not gain votes. One woman said that
the new 'equality' agenda had required the National Assembly to look
at their funding in terms of gender and also race and ethnicity. She
felt, however, that 'When we looked at things we found we were
usually aware of these issues anyway'. She strengthened her point of
view by suggesting that housing, and in fact most welfare services,
cater predominantly to women. She pointed out that the current
emphasis on services for the elderly and care and repair were services
where women are predominantly the consumers. However, another
interviewee pointed out that, although many women are now more

202

equal, there are still some who are not, concluding that: 'This equality suggests that things are OK but they are not.'

Three women, all with previous connection to Welsh Women's Aid, pointed out the importance of focusing on women and all-women services. One woman said: 'The women have the children. If you want a fair society you must work with women, invest in good parenting skills with women. This will help children to stand alone.' Another woman pointed out: 'There are women in mixed-sex services and hostels and this is not always a good thing. Some women are frightened of men.'

One woman called for a woman's commissioner. Another felt that the lead could come only from the National Assembly but pointed out that gender monitoring was difficult in housing where gender information is seldom collected.

One woman suggested that the guidance on relationship breakdown, which was issued by the Assembly in 2001 and apparently not widely used, could be revamped and form a basis for new guidance focusing on women and children. One suggested that 'a conference/event to bring things together is needed to generate enough enthusiasm to take things forward'.

Women as workers – the influence of women AMs

The women managers were asked: has the increased number of women AMs in the Assembly affected homelessness and housing? The majority view was that the number of women AMs had influenced the shape of homelessness policies. Interestingly, several women felt that the difference was in terms of an emphasis on support, the implementation of Supporting People in such a positive way, as well as more emphasis on services for children and young people. After all 'women are more caring' said one; 'more people people', said another. One felt that an increase in the number of women AMs had made the National Assembly seem 'more human, more supportive, more citizen based'. However, several commented that women AMs could be as tough and determined as men.

Women as workers – has being a woman affected your own career?

Everyone felt that being a woman had influenced their career – both in the choices they had made, their prospects and their ways of working.

Most felt that their gender had had a positive influence. Three mentioned the support, knowledge and empowerment they had gained through the women's movement. One woman had left school at the age of fifteen and gained an education through women's workshops, with free transport and a crèche. She spoke of this time: 'A group of women came together to achieve something for women.' Another woman felt that: 'My whole life I have been looking after women . . . I have worked in all-women services for 30 years.' Two women, both based in the local authorities, spoke of the encouragement they had had from progressive and female bosses. These women felt that women in the voluntary sector had 'showed me opportunities, they showed me how things could be changed'.

However, two women felt that they had succeeded despite being women. One said:

> You have to show that you are better . . . It was only a disadvantage being a woman. In meetings people thought I was the secretary. . . It is easier for women now but there is a glass ceiling and women have to decide whether they are prepared to sacrifice other things.

Another woman admitted: 'I cut my hair nicely when I got this job. It's difficult to be feminine and respected. Women are thought to be a bit more fluffy.'

To summarize, it must be remembered that the priority rights given to many women with children did and still do not ensure a smooth route into housing. Women managers in the local authorities felt that estate regeneration had improved the quality of housing for women with children and others had been kept out of homelessness through the recent preventative measures. Several women interviewed, with a background in Welsh Women's Aid, spoke of the demise of collective self-help methods and a bureaucratization which has stifled this. It was pointed out the concern with 'social inclusion' which dominated National Assembly action was a gender-free concept and one woman interviewed felt that gender equality had already been achieved. Others felt there was a need to recognize the specific needs of women, and suggested ways this could be done. Several felt that women AMs had been responsible for an emphasis on support and a more humane approach to homelessness. A majority felt that being a woman had been a positive factor in their own careers and mentioned the support they had had in work from women colleagues.

Conclusions

There is no doubt that the 'new priorities' legislation is a key landmark in housing policy and one which created a distinctive Welsh approach to homelessness. In addition, the way in which Supporting People and the preventative measures were interpreted in Wales was seen to be more supportive and collaborative than in England because of the emphasis on equality and social inclusion within the National Assembly. Several informants linked this 'human' approach directly to the number of women AMs.

The housing managers spoke of the National Assembly as 'ethical' and protective of vulnerable groups. The National Assembly also protected the voluntary sector because of its long experience in the field of single homelessness. The strength of the voluntary sector was seen to lie in its ability to specialize, to innovate and to work with groups who are less popular with the public. After the 'new priorities' legislation and the National Assembly's demand to reduce use of bed-and-breakfast accommodation, local authorities were drawn into homelessness. Increasing demand meant that they had to 'turn around' their approach and concentrate on prevention. Through this and wide partnership working with other agencies, some success was gained. However, one problem of relying on local authority action is the variation, from authority to authority, both in commitment to homelessness and in efficiency of working.

The 1977 Housing (Homelessness) Act formalized society's view about the vulnerability of women and children and the need to prioritize their access to social housing. Of course, priority in theory did not always guarantee ease of access or good quality housing. Nevertheless, homeless single men were left out in the cold. It appears that many of the National Assembly's policies around homelessness went some way to redress this balance for single homeless people, many of whom were men. This happened because of the growing demand from single homeless people; through the increase of measures to address rough sleeping; and the National Assembly's announcement of the new priority groups – of sixteen and seventeen year olds and prison-leavers. Perhaps, because of the National Assembly's humanitarian but gender-neutral policies as well as some decline in feminist ideas and challenge to the system, a renewed emphasis on women's position and particular needs in housing should be restated. This is particularly important as women are still economically worse off than men and so disproportionately dependent on affordable social housing.

Current problems in the broader housing market are likely to over-shadow some of the gains in homelessness policies. The current shortage of housing lies in the earlier policies of right to buy and the cessation of new-build in social housing – both of which originated from Westminster and come from earlier battles over the role of the state. It is important, however, that the situation of home ownership does not overshadow the need for affordable rented housing with good management. The considerable gains in support, which have come in through housing policies and which have enabled many people to gain control over their lives, must not be lost through lack of appropriate housing.

References

Burgess, G. and S. Monk with C. Whitehead (2007). *How Local Planning Authorities are Delivering Policies for Affordable Housing*, York: Joseph Rowntree Foundation, *http://www.jrf.org.uk*.

Crisis (2007). *Official Homeless Statistics, http://www.crisis.org.uk/policy-watch*.

Drakeford, M. (2007). 'Social justice in a devolved Wales', *Benefits*, 15, 2, 171–8.

Holmans, A. (2003). *Who's Counting: Demand for Homes in Wales 1998–2016*, London: Council of Mortgage Lenders.

Hutson, S. and R. Jenkins (1989). *Taking the Strain: Families, Unemployment and the Transition to Adulthood*, Milton Keynes: Open University Press.

Hutson, S. and M. Liddiard (1991). *Young and Homeless in Wales*, York: Joseph Rowntree Foundation.

—— (1994). *Youth Homelessness: The Construction of a Social Issue*, London: Macmillan.

Hutson, S., J. Pritchard, J. McNally and B. Kelly (2004). *Housing Histories of People Who Have Left Homelessness*, Cardiff: Welsh Assembly Government.

Hutson, S. and T. Stirling (2001). 'Access to social housing', in T. Stirling and W. Smith (eds), *Housing in Wales*, London: Chartered Housing, pp. 141–58.

Jones, M. (2006). *The Social Housing Cycle: Lettings and Homelessness in Wales 1980–2005*, Cambridge: Cambridge Centre for Housing and Planning Research.

Kiernan, K. (1989). 'The family: formation and fission', in H. Joshi (ed.), *The Changing Population of Britain*, Oxford: Blackwell, pp. 125–43.

Morgan, R. (2006). 'Twenty-first century socialism: a Welsh recipe', *http://www.compassonline.org.uk*.

National Statistics (2000). *Individual Incomes 1996/7–1998/9*, London: Cabinet Office.

Randall, G. (1988). *No Way Home: Homeless Young People in Central London*, London: Centrepoint Soho.

Shelter Cymru (2007). *An Unnatural Disaster*, *http://www.sheltercymru.org.uk*.

Smith, J. (1999). 'Gender and homelessness', in S. Hutson and D. Clapham (eds), *Public Policies and Private Troubles*, London: Cassells, pp. 108–32.

Tarki Technology Ltd (2005). *Tackling Homelessness: Key Issues for Consideration by Welsh Local Authorities*, Cardiff: Welsh Assembly Government.

Welsh Assembly Government (WAG) (2001). *Better Homes for People in Wales*, Cardiff: WAG.

—— (2007a). *Welsh Housing Statistics*, Cardiff: Statistical Directorate of the Welsh Assembly Government.

—— (2007b). *One Wales: A Progressive Agenda for the Government of Wales*, Cardiff: WAG.

Wilcox, S. (1996). *Housing Review 1996/7*, York: Joseph Rowntree Foundation.

9

The Material Resources of Older Women in Wales and Welsh Assembly Government Policy Responses

VANESSA BURHOLT

In Wales, over the next twenty years, demographic shifts will significantly change the age profile of the population and the proportion of people of current retirement ages in Wales will increase by 11 per cent (to 650,000) whilst the proportion of very old people (over eighty-five) in Wales is projected to increase by over a third (to 82,000) (WAG, 2003). In response to projected changes in the older population in Wales, in 2003 the Welsh Assembly Government launched the Strategy for Older People. The strategy presented a vision for ageing in Wales, underpinned by the United Nations Principles for Older People (independence, participation, care, self-fulfilment and dignity). In this chapter I look first at the benefits available to older people and the response of the Welsh Assembly Government to pensioner poverty. I then present findings from a study of the material resources of older people in Wales, paying particular attention to gender inequalities in access to these resources.

Tackling pensioner poverty

One of the key challenges identified by older people and organizations working on behalf of older people is the eradication of 'pensioner poverty'. People aged seventy-five and over rely more on benefits as a source of income and get a smaller proportion of their income from occupational pensions and investments than younger pensioners

(Office for National Statistics, 1999). It has been estimated that the level of income provided by the state is lower than that required to cover the costs of living (Natwest, 1999; Parker, 2000). In 2008–9, the full basic state pension was £90.70 a week for a single person and £145.05 a week for a couple. The pension credit scheme guarantees £124.05 for single pensioners, or £189.35 a week for people with partners. Additional pension credit amounts may be awarded where the older person has a disability or is a carer for someone with a disability. However, pension credit has to be applied for, and the proportion of older people claiming benefits consistently falls short of the proportion eligible for support (Bramley et al., 2000; Department of Social Security, 2001). In the UK in 2002–3 around 2.2 million older people lived in households below 60 per cent of median income (the most commonly used threshold of low income). This was over one-fifth of all pensioners (Palmer et al., 2003).

Age Concern Cymru have argued that the basic pension needs to be increased to £105 per week for a single person (Age Concern Cymru, 2004), which would raise many older people above the poverty line and ensure that they do not have to claim means-tested benefits. However, although Wales has a devolved government, it does not have tax-raising powers. Consequently, raising the state pension is beyond the powers of the devolved government and is controlled by central government.

The National Assembly for Wales and its executive body, the Welsh Assembly Government, have control over policy areas relating to social welfare, health and health services, housing, employment, education, local government and public administration. It is in these domains that the Welsh Assembly Government committed £13m (over a five-year period from April 2003 to 2008) to support the implementation of the strategy for older people in Wales. In the report *When I'm 64 . . . and More* (WAG, 2002) it was strongly recommended that the Welsh Assembly Government should combat poverty and poor housing among older people and promote greater uptake of benefits to ensure that older people are able to participate fully as citizens in every aspect of society.

In 2003 *The Strategy for Older People in Wales* spelt out the WAG response to the recommendations (WAG, 2003). Building on the premise that low benefit take-up may be due to the lack of specialist advice available to help people making claims from a complex benefits system (Age Concern Cymru, 2004), the government started to work on the local level through social inclusion programmes. These programmes aimed to improve access to and information on services for older people through the development of integrated 'one-stop' services centres that help maximize incomes and pensions and increase benefit take-up. In addition to the advice provided by the Pension Service, one-stop shops provided by the local authority and non-governmental organizations also aim to give advice to older people on issues ranging from pensions and benefits to health and housing, home helps, social care and residential homes.

If we look at Gwynedd we can see examples of these policies and programmes in action. At the time of the study discussed in this chapter, the Pension Service local service operated in the community providing benefit information to the most vulnerable and hard-to-reach people by offering a home visit or an appointment at an information point in places with which people were familiar. Weekly information points were held on partner premises, such as Siop Gwynedd, the Gwynedd Council one-stop shop in Blaenau Ffestiniog; council offices in Pwllheli; the Inland Revenue Office at Porthmadog; and Age Concern Gwynedd at Môn Offices in Caernarfon. They were open for eleven hours per week, and on average received thirty callers each week. Older people could call at the information points to obtain benefit advice, to resolve problems relating to their claim for benefit or to get help with form completion. The Pension Service local service offered a full benefit check for all people in face-to-face contact with them, and supported them through the myriad of claims processes. This helped reduce duplication for older people who may previously have been required to provide personal information repeatedly to a multitude of different service providers. In 2005–6 the Pension Service carried out 3,444 appointments and full benefit checks with people in the Gwynedd area and helped them complete 1,839 applications across the range of benefits including pension credit, attendance allowance, housing and council tax benefit. Older people were also referred to other departments or organizations where such action appeared appropriate, for example, to a complementary service such as Home Energy Efficiency Scheme in Wales.

In 2005 Link-Age in Wales was launched (Pension Service, 2005). This initiative aims to encourage the development of joined-up services and to provide a clear focus on the issue of maximizing income as one step towards tackling poverty. In Gwynedd, as a part of this programme a process was put into action whereby partner organizations such as the Gwynedd Council Older Persons Team, Welfare Rights, Age Concern, Housing Benefits Department, Care and Repair, Carers' Outreach and Soldiers, Sailors, Airmen and Families Association Forces Help (SSAFA) referred cases directly to local Pension Service staff in order promptly to identify entitlement and hasten the claims process. Citizens Advice Bureau Gwynedd a De Ynys Môn was authorized to act as an alternative office – their staff acting as 'nominated agents' having been trained and accredited to receive and verify claims for a number of different benefits on behalf of the Pension Service. Close working relationships were being developed with Gwynedd Council's Housing Benefit/Council Tax Benefit Department and the Welfare Rights Unit with a view to promoting benefit take-up. Through the Link-Age Wales initiative the Pension Service is developing joint working partnerships with local authorities and voluntary sector organizations to support benefit-related visiting teams delivered by other agencies.

Material resources and inequalities

Despite the Welsh Assembly Government's concern about pensioner poverty and its potential impact on the well-being of older people (Ferring et al., 2004) there is little indication that the policies up until 2008 took into account the relationship between material inequalities in later life and age (Social Security Committee, 2000), work status (Bardasi et al., 2002), marital status (Zaidi et al., 2001), health (Benzeval and Judge, 2001), living arrangements (Zaidi et al., 2001), ethnicity (Ginn and Arber, 2001) and location in terms of level of rurality (Cabinet Office, 2000), region (National Assembly for Wales, 2001) and level of deprivation in a neighbourhood (Phillipson and Scharf, 2004). Material resources are also related to gender (Bradshaw et al., 2003), which has not been addressed as a separate issue.

Women and Pensions: The Evidence (Department for Work and Pensions, 2005) and the Turner Report highlighted inequities in income between men and women, noting 'on average female pensioners are significantly poorer than male pensioners' (Turner, 2004: 260). Older women have been disadvantaged in the pension stakes in several ways: they are more likely than men to have worked part time, to have had lower average earnings and to have been employed in jobs where occupational pensions were not provided.

These factors have had a cumulative effect on the likelihood of the receipt of an occupational pension in later life. Consequently, twice as many women as men in Wales rely on means-tested benefits (Age Concern Cymru, 2004). The pension system is inequitable between men and women and for every pound that a man receives from a pension a woman will receive just 32p.

This chapter explores these inequalities by identifying the predictors of poverty in old age in Wales through an analysis of associations between age, location, ethnicity, household composition, education, health and social support, on the one hand, and material resources, on the other hand, for men and women in Wales. Although the Welsh Assembly Government is unable to change directly the level of state pension that an older man or women receives, it may be able to influence certain factors that contribute to material insecurity in later life.

The study

The project used data from Ageing Well: A European Study of Adult Well-Being (ESAW). ESAW was carried out between 2002 and 2003 in six European countries (Austria, Italy, Luxemburg, the Netherlands, Sweden and the United Kingdom). The UK data have been used to examine the material resources and well-being of older people across the UK and a thorough description of the methods involved in data collection can be found elsewhere (Burholt et al., 2007). This chapter draws on data for 468 people aged fifty and over living in Wales. The mean age of participants was sixty-five years (men 64 years; women 65.8 years). A majority (54 per cent) of participants were women.

In the analysis I consider the effect of age, gender, location (rural/urban, deprived neighbourhood), ethnicity, household composition, education, health and social support on the material resources of older people. The material resource measure captures elements of employment status and private investment, and is measured on a scale ranging from no more than basic material resources (for example, state pension only or below) to excellent material resources. A thorough description of the variables used in the analysis is available elsewhere (Burholt and Windle, 2006). In this chapter, predictors of material resources are identified using multiple regression. Using a stepwise regression procedure, the variables were entered and removed from the model. A nominal .05 significance level was used at each step. Where interval data are analysed the response rates in the samples were compared by an analysis of variance with post-hoc Tukey's HSD, which indicated whether there were significant differences in mean scores between groups.

Findings

Although women had fewer material resources than men in Wales, the difference was not statistically significant (mean score = 2.3 versus 2.5 respectively) (F(1/468) = 1.33, p<.25). Multiple regression was used to identify which factors were most useful in explaining gender differences in material resources.

For men living in Wales, the best fit was achieved with a main effects model[1] including health status, living in a deprived neighbourhood, marital status and level of education. The model was significantly better than would be expected by chance (p<.001) and accounted for 28 per cent of the variance in material resources (table 9.1). The analysis showed that good health correlated most strongly with greater levels of material resources. Older men who lived in a deprived area had lower material resources than those living elsewhere. Consistently with previous studies, older men who were married had higher levels of material resources compared to those who were not married. In addition, increases in education correlated with greater material resources. Analysis of variance showed that level of education differed significantly with respect to the rating of material

Table 9.1: Stepwise multiple linear regression model predicting material resources for men aged 50+ years in Wales

Predictor	B	SE	β
Constant	.814	.303	
Good health profile	.990	.172	.341[a]
Deprived neighbourhood	−.529	.183	−.184[a]
Married	.527	.185	.172[a]
Level of education	.234	.083	.175[a]

Model fit: R^2 0.29; adjusted R^2 0.28; f(4/213) = 21.61 (p<.001)
[a] p = <0.005

resources (F(3/212) = 8.57, p<.001). Men with primary education only had significantly lower resources than men educated beyond the primary level.

Having looked at the key factors affecting material resources for the older men in Wales, I examined any differences in the predictors of material resources for women. The regression model predicting the material resources of women was somewhat different to that for men. For older women the best fit was achieved with a main effects model including level of education, marital status, living in a deprived neighbourhood, age and health status. The model was significantly better than would be expected by chance (p<.001) and accounted for 35 per cent of the variance in material resources (table 9.2). The analysis for older women showed that level of education correlated most strongly with material resources: women with a higher level of education had greater material resources than others. As with the analysis of men, analysis of variance showed that level of education differs significantly with respect to the rating of material resources (F(3/249) = 14.76, p<.001). Women who finished secondary education had significantly greater levels of material resources than those who completed primary education only. In addition, women who had undertaken further education had higher levels of material resources than women educated to a lower level. As for men, women who were married and those who were in good health had greater levels of material resources than those who were not married or in poor health, whilst those living in deprived neighbourhoods had lower levels of material resources than those living elsewhere. For women, but not for men, age was also

Table 9.2: Stepwise multiple linear regression model predicting material resources for women aged 50+ years in Wales

Predictor	B	SE	β
Constant	7.962	.576	
Level of education	.440	.078	.303[a]
Married	.631	.160	.223[a]
Deprived neighbourhood	−.647	.154	−.225[a]
Age	.021	.007	−.173[a]
Good health profile	.442	.156	.150[a]

Model fit: R^2 0.37; adjusted R^2 0.35; f(5/250) = 28.26 (p<.001)
[a] p = <0.05

included in the model and was negatively correlated to material resources. In other words, for women only, increasing age was related to fewer material resources.

Discussion

Education

Level of education had the strongest association with material resources for women. The analysis showed that education had a differential effect on men and women. Whereas education further than primary level resulted in a greater level of material resources for men, for women the increase in material resources was significantly higher for those with secondary education rather than primary education only, and significantly higher again for women with higher education (for example, university education).

This trend for women with a lower education level to be materially disadvantaged in old age may well continue into the future. A study of five European countries (Belgium, West Germany, Italy, Spain and Sweden) showed that women with university-level education were more likely to return to work after childbearing in all countries with the exception of Sweden. In Sweden childcare provision enables graduates and non-graduates (including those whose lack of educational qualifications gives them low earnings potential) to work after childbearing (Gutiérrez-Domènech, 2005). This suggests that it is the availability of adequate and affordable childcare provision for all women (regardless of earning potential) that is key in ensuring that they can secure employment and contribute to a pension scheme. In the UK recent ESRC-funded research suggests that the growth of working parenthood, encouraged by the government's welfare-to-work and 'family friendly' employment policies, is experienced very differently by secure middle-class families and poor parents in low-paid jobs (Vincent et al., 2006). Consequently, black and ethnic minority and white working-class families are less likely to make use of childcare than middle-class white people because of a lack of accessibility, choice, quality and affordability in services (Focus Institute on Rights and Social Transformation, 2004). In the future, mothers without university education may be disadvantaged in terms of contributing to their own private or work-related pension scheme, and may be more likely to be reliant on a state pension in later life.

Overall, it is likely that the current population of older men and women in Wales with lower educational levels have had limited job opportunities and during their working lives were less able to access skilled jobs providing high salaries. This in turn has affected their ability to invest in private pensions, home ownership or savings (Bosma et al., 1999). In addition to affecting employment opportunities, education exerts an important influence on portfolio choice – that is, whether money is invested in pensions, shares and other assets. In general, households containing people with higher levels of education are more likely to hold diversified portfolios (King and Leape, 1998).

Location

The analysis indicated that both men and women living in deprived neighbourhoods had lower levels of material resources than people living elsewhere. This is not surprising, given that people with similar personal socio-economic characteristics (that is, low-skilled employment, low earning and investment history, low level of income) are less likely to be able to move away from disadvantaged communities whereas people with higher incomes and a different work-life history are more likely to be able to leave the area.

Marital status

The findings demonstrated that marital status is definitively related to levels of material resources. Men and women who were currently married were more likely to have higher levels of material resources than all other groups. Conversely, all unpartnered respondents had lower levels of material resources than married couples. These findings differ from those for the UK as a whole (Burholt and Windle, 2006).

It has been well documented that married older couples have higher incomes than others (Henrard, 1996). However, for the UK as a whole, the position of married older people in terms of their material resources is very similar to those who have never married (Burholt and Windle, 2006). Older people's financial situation in retirement is tied to engagement in the workforce throughout their life, which in turn affects pensions acquisition (state, occupational and private). Whereas married, widowed or divorced women are more likely than men to have been responsible for caring for children or partners, and thus have disrupted labour-market participation, this is not likely to be the case for never married women. In particular, other research suggests that never married women are the group of women most likely to have accrued an occupational pension, as they are most likely to have been engaged in employment throughout their working life (Arber, 2004). This is not the case in Wales. Although from this data I cannot establish why the group of women most likely to have been engaged in the workforce have not accrued pensions, life savings or other material resources that would contribute to their financial well-being in later life, I can refer to other work to suggest why this might be. Pensioner poverty in Wales is more of a problem than in other parts of the UK because lower levels of economic activity have prevented many people from developing and investing in pensions (Age Concern Cymru, 2004). In this respect never married older people are in a similar situation to those who have been divorced or widowed and demonstrate that in Wales (a married couple's) two pensions are required in order to meet financial need in later life.

The findings show that unpartnered older people have the lowest levels of material resources. These findings are troubling if one considers future marital trends in the UK. The most dramatic change is the 12 per cent increase in the proportion of the older population who are projected to be divorced by 2021 (Shaw, 1999). Given that the divorcees in this and other studies experienced low levels of material resources (see also Arber, 2004), this should be a cause for concern. As Arber notes,

> If the life course and societal mechanisms that have led to the material disadvantage of the current cohort of older divorcees continue over the next 20 years, there will be a very substantial sector of the older population of both men and women living in significantly disadvantaged material circumstances. (2004: 99–100)

Health

The findings showed that health was associated with material resources for men and women. Although I cannot use this cross-sectional data to look at cause and effect, there are many studies of health and material resources that take time into account (for a review of the literature see Benzeval and Judge, 2001). These studies have shown that income and health are causally related with the main

217

direction of causation running from income to health. In other words, income has an impact on health outcomes.

Some authors argue that material resources influence health directly (Denton and Walters, 1999; Department of Health, 1998; Gordon et al., 1999; Townsend et al., 1988; Walters et al., 1995) while others argue that the link is indirect. Material resources may influence individual behaviours such as smoking (Graham, 1993, 1994), drinking, eating and physical activity (Denton and Walters, 1999; Walters et al., 1995).

Some studies have found that the association between income and health is weaker for retired people than for those under retirement age (Benzeval et al., 2000). It is likely that this is because the measure used in these studies (income) does not reflect access to material resources accumulated over the lifetime (Benzeval and Judge, 2001). In this current study material resources included access to reserves, that is, private investment, relating to previous financial investments into an employment related pension, property, or other assets, such as savings accounts. The analysis would support other evidence that suggest that persistent poverty (represented in this case as an inability across the life-course to make investments and savings) is related to poor health and is cumulative over the life-course (Barker, 1992; Benzeval and Judge, 2001; Benzeval et al., 2001; Berney et al., 2001; Curtis et al., 2004; Davey-Smith et al., 1997; Kuh and Ben-Shlomo, 1997; Power and Matthews, 1997).

Age

The analysis showed that, for women only, increases in age correlated with decreases in material resources. However, there is limited evidence elsewhere to suggest that material resources decrease with age (Disney et al., 2002). I think it is unlikely that the lower levels of material resources for the oldest women in this study are due to decumulation over the life cycle, but are more likely to be a consequence of cohort effect. Cohort effect is the variation in characteristics (for example, material resources) of people of different ages that arise because they are born at different times and have experienced different factors as the environment and society change. Each birth cohort is exposed to a unique milieu that coincides with its lifespan.

Other research indicates that there have been substantial variations in material resources between age cohorts. Banks and Rohwedder (2001) suggest that there are three groups of retired and retiring households in the UK, which are differentiated by their lifetime experiences of saving and investment. However, this would suggest that a cohort affect would also be observed for men. As this was not the case, other explanations may be required. As noted above, older widows have lower levels of material resources than married couples. Elsewhere it has been found that widowhood has a major adverse effect on the material well-being of older women, but is not so great for men (Arber, 2004). As widowhood is more likely for women at advanced age, and is accompanied by a drop in income (Hungerford, 2001), it may be that the association between increased age and decreased material resources reflects these changes for the cohorts of oldest women in the study.

Conclusions

Ageing is predominantly a female experience. The majority of older people (aged sixty-five years and over) in the UK are women, with 113 women to every 100 males in the sixty-five to seventy-four age group. The ratio increases amongst the oldest old to 259 women to every 100 men aged eighty-five and over (National Statistics, 2004). Therefore, inequalities that financially disadvantage women in later life have an impact on a majority of the older population. Of particular importance to policymakers should be the greater reliance of women than men on state sources of pension. Recent analysis shows that fewer older women than older men receive a private pension (35 per cent versus 67 per cent) (Ginn, 2001), and in this study fewer women than men receive an occupational pension (57 per cent versus 71 per cent). Consequently, the decline in basic pension since 1980 is particularly pertinent to the material well-being of older women. This trend is likely to continue in the future with fewer women than men between the ages of twenty and fifty-nine with a private pension (38 per cent versus 64 per cent) (Ginn, 2001).

Overall, the findings suggest that differences in material resources in old age are generally determined by earlier life experiences, for example, engagement in the labour market and subsequent ability to save and invest. Whereas younger generations may move in and out of poverty, once older people move into material deprivation there is very little they can do about their position in later life (Rosenberg and Everitt, 2001). The cumulative impact of material disadvantage over the life-course is extremely important as it contributes to social exclusion (Phillipson and Scharf, 2004).

In this study older people with low levels of material resources (i) had a reduced consumption ability (that is the ability to purchase 'normal' goods and services), (ii) were less likely to have saved or accumulated assets in terms of a house, savings, private source of income, or accumulated an occupational or private pension; (iii) were less likely to be engaged in a paid occupation. These items represent three out of the five components that Burchardt et al., (1999) have identified as elements that contribute to social exclusion.

The findings indicate that social exclusion applies to particular groups of older people. These groups may be delineated by individual characteristics that are socially and structurally constructed, for example, gender (Estes, 2004), or by spatial segregation, for example, living in a deprived neighbourhood (Scharf et al., 2002). Older people with low levels of material resources were over-represented by those who are widowed (mainly women), divorced or separated, in poor health, with lower education and living in deprived neighbourhoods. These findings are supported by evidence from other studies which also show that being female and in the 'old-old' age cohorts rapidly increase the likelihood of living in poverty (Phillipson and Scharf, 2004; Rosenberg and Everitt, 2001). Of particular concern to policymakers should be:

1. the gendered dimension of material resources, which demonstrates lower levels of resources available to widowed women: 'Old age means something quite different – and more troubling – for women than for men' (The World Bank, 1994: 29, cited in Ginn, 2001);
2. the projected increase in the proportion of divorced older people, who currently appear to have fewer material resources than married couples;
3. the consistently low levels of material resources for people living in deprived areas versus those living in other areas;
4. the strong association between health and material resources;
5. the importance of education for future generations to have an equal chance of adequate material resources in later life.

The introduction of the strategy for older people in 2003 was a landmark in Wales and has received international recognition for its vision and scope. One of the objectives of the strategy for older people was to develop and promote policies and programmes to tackle poverty and social exclusion amongst older people (WAG, 2003). However, an interim report of progress over the first five years of the strategy indicated that of the twenty-two local authorities in Wales fewer than half stated in their annual plans that they would address this aim (eight authorities in 2004–5, eleven in 2005–6 and nine in 2006–7) (Porter et al., 2007).

The Welsh Assembly Government has committed itself to a ten-year strategy and *Living Longer, Living Better* outlines the key strategic objectives for the second five years from 2008 to 2013 (WAG, 2008). In the second phase of the strategy, the Welsh Assembly Government intends to implement a range of policies to 'increase income, encourage better financial management and stimulate wealth creation' (2008: 32). This includes increasing the take-up of housing benefit and council tax benefit, maximizing income (building on initiatives such as Link-Age Wales (Pension Service, 2005) and Better Health, Better Advice scheme), and ensuring that comprehensive benefit advice is available in *all* local authorities. However, experience across Wales to date suggests that one-stop shops providing the sort of information required by these government initiatives are usually located in larger towns (for example, Blaenau Ffestiniog and Tywyn in Gwynedd) and are not so easily accessible to older people living in more remote or deprived neighbourhoods. The location may particularly discriminate against older, rural-dwelling women. The latest statistics show that only around one-fifth of women aged seventy and over have a full driving licence compared to nearly two-thirds (64 per cent) of men (Department for Transport, 2001), rendering rural older women increasingly dependent on inadequate public or private transport (Windle and Burholt, 2003).

Many of the outcomes to be accomplished in the second phase of the strategy for older people in Wales will not be achieved (for example, participation in learning, sports and leisure activities) without improving the situation of particular groups of older people (especially women) who are excluded from participation because of limited financial resources. The Welsh Assembly Government acknowledges that 'more needs to be done to ensure older people fully take up benefit entitlement and have effective advice services' (WAG, 2008: 32). Previously, only small sums of money have been set aside to run this service. For example, the Age Concern one-stop shop in

Tywyn has been temporarily funded by an external grant source. Consequently, in Gwynedd there were only six members of staff – a partner liaison manager and five customer liaison managers – who serviced the information points and visited older people in their homes. Given the dispersed nature of rural communities within Gwynedd and the large geographical area that the county covers (2,548 square kilometres (Gwynedd Council, 2005)), staff spent a great deal of time travelling between different venues.

The Welsh Financial Inclusion Strategy has recently been under public scrutiny during a consultation phase (May 2009). The document states that 'the Welsh Assembly Government will work through the Financial Inclusion and Older People in Wales Strategies to build on existing initiatives such as Link-Age Wales. Older people will be regarded as a priority group with particular needs that merit specific attention' (WAG, 2009a: 61). The document suggests that the reduction of poverty in the older population will be supported by an additional £7m from the Welsh Assembly Government. However, a close inspection of the text and financial statements reveals that this is for the implementation of the second phase of the strategy for older people in Wales in its entirety. For example, the £4m allocation for 2009–10 includes funding for the commissioner for older people, the voluntary section and Assembly government programmes for older people. After employing the local authority strategy coordinators the remaining allocation for local authorities (£930,000) is distributed on the basis of the standard spending assessment formula for older people (WAG, 2009b). In fact, the Welsh Assembly Government has allocated only £1m per year for years 2008–11 to local authorities specifically to help increase the take-up of council tax benefit by older people *and* other vulnerable groups (WAG, 2009c). Clearly, it is crucial to monitor the progress of programmes that attempt to redress material inequalities in Wales, particularly for the groups (such as the oldest-old women) who are at the highest risk of material deprivation. It is intended that the Financial Inclusion Unit will establish baseline data in 2009 which will be used to evaluate which approaches and inventions (such as Link-Age Wales) are effective and which are not, and to identify benefits that arise for individuals or groups facing financial exclusion (WAG, 2009a). However, given the relatively small amount of investment in the services themselves, it remains to be seen whether the Welsh financial inclusion strategy provides a strong and sufficiently funded infrastructure to develop provision and extend assistance to those who require help in securing a decent income in later life and reducing gender inequalities in Wales.

Notes

[1] A main effects model used in regression analysis assumes that each of the independent variables has an independent effect on the dependent variable, that is, it assumes there is no interaction between the independent variables.

References

Age Concern Cymru (2004). *Budget Statement: Increase Basic State Pension to £105 a Week, says Age Concern Cymru*, News Release, Cardiff: Age Concern Cymru, retrieved on 23 October 2006 from: *http://www.accymru.org.uk/en/1417.htm*.

Arber, S. (2004). 'Gender, marital status, and ageing: linking material, health, and social resources', *Journal of Aging Studies*, 18, 91–108.

Banks, J. and S. Rohwedder (2001). 'Life-cycle saving patterns and pension arrangements in the UK', *Research in Economics*, 55, 83–107.

Bardasi, E., S. P. Jenkins and J. A. Rigg (2002). 'Retirement and the income of older people: a British perspective', *Ageing and Society*, 22, 131–59.

Barker, D. (1992). 'The fetal and infant origins of adult disease', London: British Medical Journal Publishing Group.

Benzeval, M., A. Dilnot, K. Judge and J. Taylor (2001). 'Income and health over the life course: evidence and policy implications', in H. Graham (ed.), *Understanding Health Inequalities*, Milton Keynes: Open University, pp. 96–112.

Benzeval, M. and K. Judge (2001). 'Income and health: the time dimension', *Social Science and Medicine*, 52, 1371–90.

Benzeval, M., J. Taylor and K. Judge (2000). 'Evidence on the relationship between low income and poor health: is the government doing enough?', *Fiscal Studies*, 21, 3, 375–99.

Berney, L., D. Blane, G. Davey-Smith and P. Holland (2001). 'Life course influences on health in early old age', in H. Graham, H. (ed.), *Understanding Health Inequalities,* Milton Keynes: Open University, pp. 79–95.

Bosma, H., C. Schrivers and P. Mackenbach (1999). 'Socioeconomic inequalities in mortality and importance of perceived control: cohort study', *British Medical Journal*, 319, 1469–70.

Bradshaw, J., N. Finch, P. A. Kemp, E. Mayhew and J. Williams (2003). *Gender and Poverty in Britain*, Working Paper Series no. 6, Manchester: Equal Opportunities Commission.

Bramley, G., S. Lancaster and D. Gordon (2000). 'Benefit take-up and the geography of poverty in Scotland', *Regional Studies*, 34, 6, 507–19.

Burchardt, T., J. Le Grand and D. Piachaud (1999). 'Social exclusion in Britain 1991–1995', *Social Policy and Administration*, 33, 3, 227–44.

Burholt, V. and G. Windle (2006). *The Material Resources and Well-being of Older People*, York: Joseph Rowntree Foundation.

Burholt, V., G. Windle, D. Ferring, C. Balducci, C. Fagerström, F. Thissen, G. Weber and G. C. Wenger (2007). 'Reliability and validity of the Older Americans Resources and Services (OARS) social resources scale in six European countries', *Journal of Gerontology B Social Sciences*, 62B(6), S371–S379.

Cabinet Office (2000). *Sharing the Nation's Prosperity: Economic, Social and Environmental Conditions in the Countryside,* London: Cabinet Office.

Curtis, S., H. Southall, P. Congdon and B. Dodgeon (2004). 'Area effects on health variation over the life-course: Analysis of the longitudinal study sample in England using new data on area of residence in childhood', *Social Science & Medicine*, 58, 59–74.

Davey-Smith, G., G. Hart, D. Blane, C. Gillis and V. Hawthorne (1997). 'Lifetime socioeconomic position and mortality: prospective observational study', *British Medical Journal*, 314, 547–52.

Denton, M. and V. Walters (1999). 'Gender differences in structural and behavioral determinants of health: an analysis of the social production of health', *Social Science & Medicine*, 48, 1221–35.

Department for Transport (2001). *Older Drivers: A Literature Review*, no. 25, London: Department for Transport.

Department of Health (1998). *Independent Inquiry into Inequalities in Health: Report*, London: The Stationery Office.

Department of Social Security (2001). *Income Related Benefits: Estimates of Take-up in 1999–2000*, London: The Stationery Office.

Department for Work and Pensions (2005). *Women and Pensions: The Evidence*, London: Department for Work and Pensions.

Disney, R., A. Henley and G. Stears (2002). 'Housing costs, house price shocks and savings behaviour among older households in Britain', *Regional Science and Urban Economics*, 32, 607–25.

Estes, C. L. (2004). 'Social security privatization and older women: a feminist political economy perspective', *Journal of Aging Studies*, 18, 9–26.

Ferring, D., C. Balducci, V. Burholt, C. Wenger, F. Thissen, G. Weber and I. Hallberg (2004). 'Life satisfaction of older people in six European countries: findings from the European Study on Adult Well-Being', *European Journal of Ageing*, 1, 1, 15–25.

Focus Institute on Rights and Social Transformation (2004). *Transforming the Child Care Sector: A Case for Multiculturising the State*, Trowbridge: Focus Institute on Rights and Social Transformation.

Ginn, J. (2001). *From Security to Risk: Pension Privatisation and Gender inequality*, London: Catalyst.

—— and S. Arber (2001). 'Pension prospects of minority ethnic groups: inequalities by gender and ethnicity', *British Journal of Sociology*, 52, 3, 519–39.

Gordon, D., M. Shaw, D. Dorling and G. Davey-Smith (1999). *Inequalities in Health: The Evidence Presented to the Independent Inquiry into Inequalities in Health, Chaired by Sir Donald Acheson*, Bristol: Policy Press.

Graham, H. (1993). *When Life's a Drag: Women, Smoking and Disadvantage*, London: HMSO.

—— (1994). 'Surviving by smoking', in S. Wilkinson and C. Kitzinger (eds), *Women and Health: Feminist Perspectives*, London: Taylor and Francis, pp. 102–23.

Gutiérrez-Domènech, M. (2005). 'Employment after motherhood: a European comparison', *Labour Economics*, 12, 1, 99–123.

Gwynedd Council (2005). *Gwynedd in Focus 2004/5*, Caernarfon, Gwynedd: Chief Executives Office, Gwynedd Council.

Henrard, J. C. (1996). 'Cultural problems of ageing especially regarding gender and intergenerational equity', *Social Science and Medicine*, 43, 5, 667–80.

Hungerford, T. L. (2001). 'The economic consequences of widowhood on elderly women in the United States and Germany', *Gerontologist*, 41, 1, 103–10.

King, M. A. and J. I. Leape (1998). 'Wealth and portfolio composition: theory and evidence', *Journal of Public Economics*, 69, 155–93.

Kuh, D. and Y. Ben-Shlomo (eds) (1997). *A Lifecourse Approach to Chronic Disease Epidemiology*, Oxford: Oxford University Press.

National Assembly for Wales (NAW) (2001). *Welsh House Condition Survey 1998*, Cardiff: NAW.

National Statistics (2004). 'Sex ratios among older people: by age, 1951 to 2001', *Social Trends*, 34, 3.

NatWest (1999). *NatWest Pensions Index*, vol. IV, Bristol: National Westminster Life Assurance Limited.

Office for National Statistics (1999). *Social Focus on Older People,* London: HMSO.

Palmer, G., J. North, J. Carr and P. Kenway (2003). *Monitoring Poverty and Social Exclusion 2003*, York: Joseph Rowntree Foundation.

Parker, H. (ed.) (2000). *Low Cost But Acceptable: A Minimum Income Standard for Households Aged 65–74 Years*, Bristol: Policy Press.

Pension Service (2005). *Link-Age in Wales: Joining up Services for Older People in Wales*, Cardiff: WAG.

Phillipson, C. and T. Scharf (2004). *The Impact of Government Policy on Social Exclusion Among Older People: A Review of the Literature for the Social Exclusion Unit in the Breaking the Cycle Series*, London: ODPM publications.

Porter, A., J. Peconi, A. Evans, D. Seddon, C. Robinson, J. Perry, G. Windle and G. Harper (2007). *Strategy for Older People in Wales: An Interim Review*, Swansea: All-Wales Alliance for Research and Development in Health and Social Care, Swansea University.

Power, C. and S. Matthews (1997). 'Origins of health inequalities in a national population sample', *Lancet*, 350, 1584–9.

Rosenberg, M. and J. Everitt (2001). 'Planning for aging populations: inside or outside the walls', *Planning in Progress*, 56, 3, 119–68.

Scharf, T., C. Phillipson and A. E. Smith (2002). *Growing Older in Socially Deprived Areas: Social Exclusion in Later Life*, London: Help the Aged.

Shaw, C. (1999). '1996-based population projections by legal marital status for England and Wales', *Population Trends*, 95, 23–32.

Social Security Committee (2000). *Pensioner Poverty: Response to the 7th Report of the Social Security Committee*, London: House of Commons.

The World Bank (1994). *Averting the Old Age Crisis*, New York: Oxford University Press.

Townsend, P., N. Davidson and M. Whitehead (1988). *Inequalities in Health*, London: Penguin Books.

Turner, A. (2004). *Pensions: Challenges and Choices: The First Report of the Pensions Commission*, London: The Pensions Commission, The Stationery Office.

Vincent, C., S. Ball and A. Braun (2006). 'Local childcare cultures: working class families and pre school childcare', paper presented at the American Education Research Association Annual Meeting, 7–11 April, San Francisco, USA.

Walters, V., R. Lenton and M. McKeary (1995). *Women's Health in the Context of Women's Lives*, Ottawa, Canada: Minister of Supply and Services.

Welsh Assembly Government (WAG) (2002). *When I'm 64 . . . and More. The Report from the Advisory Group on a Strategy for Older People in Wales*, Cardiff: WAG.

—— (2003). *The Strategy for Older People in Wales*, Cardiff: WAG.

—— (2008). *The Strategy for Older People in Wales, 2008–2013: Living Longer, Living Better*, Cardiff: WAG.

—— (2009a). *Financial Inclusion Strategy for Wales: Taking Everyone into Account*, Cardiff: WAG.

—— (2009b). *Strategy for Older People Budget Allocation for 2009/10*, retrieved from *http://wales.gov.uk/publications/accessinfo/drnew-homepage/peopledrs2/peopledrs2009/oldrpeoplsbudgt09–10/?lang=en* on 15 June 2009.

—— (2009c). *Increasing Incomes, Eradicating Exclusion: An Action Plan - Progress relating to the implementation of the Welsh Assembly Government's Financial Inclusion Strategy*, Cardiff: WAG.

Windle, G. and V. Burholt (2003). 'Older people in Wales, their transport and mobility: a literature review', *Quality in Ageing*, 4, 2, 28–35.

Zaidi, A., K. Rake and J. Falkingham (2001). *Income Mobility in Later Life*, SAGE Discussion Paper no. 3, London: The London School of Economics.

10

Devolution and Welsh Language Policy: A Gender Dimension?

CHARLOTTE AULL DAVIES

Although Welsh language policy is concerned with issues of equality and social justice for people in Wales, its particular relevance for women is not immediately apparent. However, a closer examination of existing policy and of the means established for its implementation reveals a number of areas in which their impact is gendered, although this gender dimension is implicit in these substantive areas rather than being explicitly acknowledged. In addition, the relationship between the Welsh language and other equalities agendas – for gender, as well as race and disability – has been controversial at times, and this chapter concludes with an examination of this relationship and of the implications of these cross-cutting agendas for the new Welsh language act currently being sought by many in the language movement.

Pre-devolution Welsh-language policy

From the Act of Union in 1536 until the middle decades of the twentieth century, the Welsh language had no official or legal status in Wales. The first legislation on the language was the 1942 Welsh Courts Act, which allowed Welsh speakers to give evidence in Welsh if they considered they would be at a disadvantage using English. The establishment of Cymdeithas yr Iaith Gymraeg (the Welsh Language Society) in 1962 heralded the start of more active campaigning on behalf of the language based on civil disobedience and non-violent direct action. The Welsh Language Act of 1967, which was in part a response to this more assertive approach, was based on the principle of equal validity for Welsh with English in public administration in Wales. However, while equal validity provided a strong basis for the language in theory, it was only applicable in strictly delineated areas and there was no mechanism to compel government agencies to adhere to it.

For the next twenty-five years, campaigns focused on trying to realize the promise of equal validity in a variety of contexts, for example, provision of bilingual road signs and official forms in Welsh and recognition of the right of individuals to correspond with public bodies in Welsh. As the act's shortcomings were made all too apparent, campaigners increasingly began to demand a new Welsh language act to remedy its faults, 'to secure, at the very least, the effective application of the principle of equal validity in public administration' (G. P. Davies, 1994: 48).

The new act that was eventually forthcoming, the 1993 Welsh Language Act, provided that Welsh and English should be treated 'on a basis of equality' in the judicial system and in public administration, although the meaning of this 'basis of equality' was not fully clarified and was subject to consideration of 'what is appropriate in the circumstances and reasonably practicable' (ibid.: 49). It is noteworthy that the act did not declare Welsh to be an official language in Wales despite the widespread support expressed for such a measure by both public bodies and civil society. However, the act did establish a mechanism to ensure that its provisions were carried out; this took the form of turning the non-statutory advisory Welsh Language Board into a statutory body. The new Welsh Language Board was expected to oversee and to approve the Welsh-language schemes that public bodies were required to develop to show their adherence to the principle that Welsh and English were treated on a basis of equality. In addition, the Welsh Language Board was given responsibility for administering most of the funding, formerly controlled by the Welsh Office, which provides for a range of programmes to support and promote the Welsh language.

Gender and pre-devolution Welsh language policy

The overlap between gender inequalities and inequalities experienced by speakers of a minority language, with one type of inequality reinforcing the other, has been explored elsewhere (for example, Morris and Williams, 1994) as have the parallels and contradictions in feminist and nationalist discourses (C. A. Davies, 1996). This relationship has meant that much of Welsh women's political activism has been absorbed by the broader nationalist movement in both its political and cultural manifestations. Women represented a high proportion of activists in the language campaigns of the 1970s and 1980s and toward the end of the period became increasingly prominent in leadership roles, notably as chairs of the Welsh Language Society. During the same period some Welsh women began to introduce a feminist perspective into the political nationalist movement, and by the end of the 1980s had transformed women's roles within Plaid Cymru (C. A. Davies, 1994). Welsh women have also been active campaigners in significant numbers in the numerous local campaigns for Welsh-medium schools in communities in all parts of Wales. This grass-roots movement has provided an arena for active public campaigning by women, often not themselves Welsh speaking, who wanted to ensure their children would become fluent in the language.

Thus, during the 1970s and 1980s, Welsh women were not generally engaged by feminist issues such as 'how women were represented and positioned linguistically in English', instead being 'more concerned with supporting *Cymdeithas yr Iaith*'s language campaigns, than fuelling public controversy about sexist language use in Welsh' (Awbery et al., 2002: 318). However, with the marked increase of the use of Welsh in public life that ensued with the enactment of the 1993 Welsh Language Act, the issue of discriminatory language, which had been proscribed in public spheres in English since the passage of the 1975 Sex Discrimination Act, took on a new relevance for the Welsh language. In particular, it became necessary to ensure that bilingual job advertisements, now mandated for public bodies by the Welsh Language Act, did not use inappropriately gendered language that could be discriminatory. In recognition of the lack of any public debate about the proper use of Welsh in circumstances that required gender neutrality, the Equal Opportunities Commission undertook to commission a study of the issues raised and to make specific recommendations regarding the language of job advertisements (Awbery, 1997). These recommendations covered the question of how to handle those job titles that are gender specific in Welsh, as well as other concerns such as the use of pronouns in the wording of advertisements. In formulating guidelines, which were agreed by both the Equal Opportunities Commission and the Welsh Language Board, care had to be taken to avoid introducing forms that could be perceived by the Welsh-speaking community as linguistic imperialism, that is, recommended forms had to be 'natural to the language . . . rather than trying to impose something unfamiliar which might be perceived as alien and English' (Awbery et al., 2002: 328). In the event, the guidelines were generally positively received, particularly by personnel officers, translators and others directly involved in drawing up job advertisements and specifications.

The public effect of this combination of policies (1975 Sex Discrimination Act and 1993 Welsh Language Act) has been a highly visible promotion of the status of the language, as it is commonly used in advertisements across the spectrum of public appointments, and also of the gender equality endorsed in the subtext by means of the non-sexist language used to name and describe these posts. The degree to which this has led to an improvement in employment prospects for women is, of course, difficult to assess. The Equal Opportunities Commission contracted a second study of gender and the Welsh language to assess the effect of the language and more specifically the 1993 Welsh Language Act on gender equality (Jones and Morris, 1997). This study concluded that one consequence of the act was to increase the demand for professional and administrative workers who could speak Welsh as organizations in the public sector developed their language schemes. In particular, increasing numbers of posts that entailed extensive face-to-face contact with the public had to have a Welsh-language requirement, and these positions, which are overwhelmingly for secretaries and receptionists, tended to be filled by women. On the other hand, the study expected that the smaller number of more senior positions expected to be created as a consequence of the act were more likely to be filled by men, given their existing advantageous position in the employment structures of local government and regional governmental agencies.

Thus although the 1993 act increased employment opportunities for Welsh-speaking women, it did not address their under-representation in more senior positions, nor did it mandate additional provision, in particular on-the-job training opportunities, to enable non-Welsh speakers, men and women, to acquire fluency in the language and thereby gain access to any new employment opportunities.

Welsh language policy since devolution

The Government of Wales Act 1998 stated that the National Assembly for Wales 'may do anything it considers appropriate . . . to support the Welsh language' (section 32) and it also established both Welsh and English as the working languages of the National Assembly (section 47). During its first term, the National Assembly carried out a comprehensive evaluation of language policy, in the process seeking input from a broad spectrum of individuals, public bodies and third-sector organizations. This review of existing policy provided the basis for the development of the Welsh Assembly Government's detailed Welsh language policy, *Iaith Pawb: A National Action Plan for a Bilingual Wales*, published toward the end of the first term in 2003. *Iaith Pawb* is by far the strongest commitment ever by government to supporting and strengthening the position of the Welsh language with the ultimate goal of creating 'a truly bilingual nation . . . where people can choose to live their lives through the medium of either Welsh or English and where the presence of the two languages is a visible and audible source of pride and strength to us all' (WAG, 2003: 11). Beyond the rhetoric, the policy sets out five key targets to be achieved by 2011, the most specific of which is a commitment to increase the proportion of Welsh speakers by 5 percentage points over the 2001 census level. Other targets are commitments to arrest the decline in the number of communities that are over 70 per cent Welsh-speaking, to increase the percentage of children receiving Welsh-medium preschool education, to increase the percentage of families in which Welsh is the principal home language and to increase Welsh-medium service delivery by public, private and voluntary organizations. All of these targets, and particularly those regarding the language of families and communities, have gender implications to which I return in the next section.

The very positive commitment to the Welsh language of *Iaith Pawb* and its ambitious set of targets was enthusiastically received by those concerned about the future of the language. However, serious reservations were expressed about the adequacy of its provision either of specific mechanisms or of additional resources to enable its implementation. Colin Williams (C. H. Williams, 2004) produced a thorough and wide-ranging review of *Iaith Pawb*, based on research interviews with civil servants and language activists as well as documentary analysis. He points to a number of fundamentally important areas in which such provision is lacking. For example, *Iaith Pawb* commits the National Assembly to mainstreaming the Welsh language in all its business – a commitment that it also has regarding gender equality – and to ensuring that such mainstreaming is carried out as well by local government. Yet the proportion of civil servants who can speak Welsh remains low, and the Welsh Assembly Government's Language Unit lacks the capacity to ensure adherence to the mainstreaming requirement outside those few departments with direct responsibility for Welsh-language issues, much less at local government level. Furthermore, there still remained no intention to seek legislation to extend the requirement for equal treatment for Welsh with English to the private sector (ibid.: 11–14). Besides mainstreaming the use of Welsh in government, *Iaith Pawb*'s commitment to increase the proportion of Welsh speakers in the next census by 5 percentage points would require a significantly enhanced and centrally led investment in Welsh-medium education at all levels, including establishing approximately one hundred new Welsh-medium primary schools (an increase of about 25 per cent over current numbers), which is not reflected in the current steady but less spectacular growth of this sector (ibid.: 16–18). Finally, although *Iaith Pawb* makes extensive reference to existing planning policy and other programmes to support local communities, its provision for housing and planning programmes and actions to improve the economies of Welsh-speaking areas, both fundamental to reversing the loss of Welsh-speaking communities, are generally judged to be unfocused and not likely to produce the targeted outcome (ibid.: 20–1).

In spite of serious misgivings about its efficacy, *Iaith Pawb* is nevertheless judged as filling an important role of expressing at an official level an evolving consensus in Wales, among Welsh speakers and non-Welsh speakers, regarding the valued place of the language in its national life. Whether it is also a means of improving the situation of the Welsh language in reality remains unclear, but Williams, one of its principal critics, sees some basis for optimism:

> For all its lacunae, *Iaith Pawb*'s declared act of political ambition in creating a bilingual Wales can serve as a binding promise to which we, as citizens, can hold government to account, as we strive to apply the more germane policies and press for the urgent systemic reforms whereby rhetoric is turned into reality. (ibid.: 24)

I turn now to a consideration of the degree to which activities of this nature may have a gender dimension.

Gender and post-devolution Welsh language policy

Turning first to the two key policy targets of increasing the percentage of families where Welsh is the principal language and increasing the numbers of preschool children receiving Welsh-medium education, *Iaith Pawb* suggested that these goals would be promoted primarily by continued Welsh Assembly Government support and increased funding for two existing programmes. The first of these programmes was Mudiad Ysgolion Meithrin, the Welsh nursery schools movement which has been active since the early 1970s. Women make up the vast majority of those active in this movement, as leaders of preschool playgroups, whether as paid employees, who are predominantly part-time, or as volunteers. Furthermore, this preponderance of women is also to be found throughout primary schooling, making women mainly responsible for the actual delivery of Welsh-medium education, both preschool and in the early school years. Clearly, this is an indication of the gender stereotyping of these positions and, more generally, of the work of caring for young children; it also underlines the centrality of women to the improvement of performance in this key target area.

The second programme noted in *Iaith Pawb* to facilitate attaining its target of more homes with Welsh as their principal language was Twf (meaning 'growth' in Welsh and standing for 'Transmission within families'). This is an innovative programme developed by the Welsh Language Board prior to the publication of the Welsh Assembly Government's Welsh language policy that was designed to promote the transmission of Welsh within families, particularly concentrating on families where only one parent speaks Welsh. There is a body of evidence that indicates women are central to language use in the family and in particular to its transmission to children. A recent ESRC-sponsored study designed to inform the Welsh Assembly Government's family language policy carried out in-depth case studies of twelve young children, their immediate families, kin and friendship networks and the community context in which they lived. The study concluded that 'Welsh-speaking mothers rather than fathers play a more significant role in the early Welsh language socialization of their children' (Jones and Morris, 2005: 10; also see Jones and Morris, 2007). This was primarily due to the fact that mothers are usually the principal care-givers especially for young children; in consequence they spend more time in one-to-one interaction with the child and this was found to be highly significant for Welsh-language acquisition in these early stages. In addition, the principal care-giver is more influential in selecting the child's other social contacts and activities. Although the authors of another study have claimed that they 'have not on the whole found that the language(s) the child speaks is related to whether it is the mother or the father who speaks that language' (Gathercole et al., 2007: 11), they qualified this result in relation to younger children, where gender did appear to be an influential factor. Another significant factor identified by Jones and Morris in Welsh-language acquisition by young children was the power relation between parents that determined who made language-related decisions for the household. In particular, they found that in the four cases where the children were deemed unlikely to learn Welsh within the family, the 'language-decision makers' were all English-speaking (Jones and Morris, 2007: 62).

Given these two factors of the key role of women both in provision of early Welsh-medium education and in affecting the likelihood of acquisition of Welsh by very young children through family practices, the apparent lack of mainstreaming of Welsh in the childcare policies developed by the Welsh Assembly Government (see Ball, 2006, and in this volume) seems to confirm the pessimistic assessment of the practical effects of *Iaith Pawb* discussed above (C. H. Williams, 2004).

Another key target set out in *Iaith Pawb* is a commitment to arrest the decline in the number of communities that are over 70 per cent Welsh-speaking. A recent review of the Twf scheme (Irvine et al., 2008) notes that it has so far concentrated on language transmission at the level of individuals and recommends that it give more consideration to how it 'could engage in more community activities' (p. 5). The study found that the level of Welsh-language use in local communities was an important indicator of the likelihood of its transmission in the home. This finding is consistent with the ethnographic study of Welsh-language transmission to young children discussed earlier, which noted, for example, that the 'density of Welsh-speakers in the community affects the language of day-to-day activities like going for a walk or going shopping', activities that were found to be very influential in language development (Jones and Morris, 2007: 66).

Clearly, there is a close relationship between the goals of Welsh-language transmission within the home and the retention of communities where Welsh is the main language of communication, that is, where the percentage of Welsh speakers is over 70 per cent.

Irvine et al.'s evaluative report on Twf suggests some ways in which the scheme could expand its activities to encourage greater community support for the Welsh language. They recommend that health visitors and midwives be more fully incorporated into the scheme, beyond their existing comparatively passive role of disseminating Twf information, as they are 'respected professionals within the community . . . [who] offer the potential to become credible agents of the Twf scheme' (Irvine et al., 2008: 4). Clearly, this suggestion, which targets positions that are primarily filled by women, points once again to the gendered nature of provisions to support the Welsh Assembly Government's Welsh language policy.

Another recommendation to increase the scheme's community engagement is that it should cooperate more closely with other programmes to support the Welsh language, such as Mudiad Ysgolion Meithrin, Welsh for Adults Centres, Mentrau Iaith and the Welsh Language Board's language action plans. Both of these latter two programmes were also put forward in *Iaith Pawb* as community initiatives for which the Welsh Assembly Government would provide additional support to facilitate meeting its target goal to stop the decline of Welsh-speaking communities. Mentrau Iaith are regionally based organizations that work to increase the use of Welsh in their areas by raising consciousness about the language and its use, creating new opportunities to socialize in Welsh, especially for children and young people, and providing advice and support to encourage the use of Welsh across all sectors (public, private and voluntary). Language action plans are of more recent vintage than Mentrau Iaith and are based on more restricted localities, particularly where the language is seen to be declining or under severe pressure. The language action plans, which have essentially the same goals as the Mentrau Iaith, are intended to act primarily as coordinators rather than organizers of Welsh-language activities in their local community. However, the line of demarcation of responsibilities and activities between the two organizations has sometimes been unclear (Gruffudd et al., 2004). The remit of both of these types of organizations, and particularly of the language action plans, suggests that their effectiveness may depend in large measure on how well connected they are within their localities. That is, they need to have access to the networks of families, kin and acquaintances that characterize the communities in which they work, as well as have good relationships with their 'partner' organizations within the area. Research that looked at family and kin relationships in Swansea over a forty-year period has found that women have been at the centre of these networks for the past half-century and remain so in spite of the major social changes that have occurred over this period, with greater geographic and social mobility and many more women in full-time employment. Thus, 'evidence . . . shows that at both formal and informal levels of community the work women do is crucially important to whether or not communities exist' (Charles and Davies, 2005: 688; see also Charles, Davies and Harris, 2008). The centrality of women to these community networks was implicitly acknowledged in an interview with an official from the Welsh Language Board, who described the ideal person to lead a language action plan as a middle-aged woman who has lived in the community all her life and knows everyone, especially whom to involve in activities and how to persuade them to participate. Clearly, the success of the programmes that the Welsh Assembly Government has proposed as the means to achieve *Iaith Pawb*'s key target goals is dependent on women's contributions across a range of activities.

Finally, *Iaith Pawb* made a target commitment to increase Welsh-medium service delivery by public, private and voluntary organizations. Again, because of the gendered nature of many service professions – the health visitors and midwives noted above being a case in point – this target goal appears to be likely to have a bigger impact on women workers and to be heavily dependent on women's activities. The main employment area selected for promoting the use of Welsh in the workplace by *Iaith Pawb* was the National Health Service, a recommendation that built upon existing provision, in particular the All Wales Task Group for Welsh Language Services. The development and implementation of the Welsh-language programme for all NHS Wales staff and students has a greater effect on women simply because of the employment profile of the health services, with its very high proportion of women employees.

Thus, as we have seen, Welsh language policy since devolution, as set out in *Iaith Pawb*, provides a positive and ambitious programme aiming to make Wales a genuinely bilingual nation and establishes a number of key target goals to achieve this aim. The most specific of these targets is that of increasing the proportion of Welsh speakers in Wales by 5 percentage points by the 2011 census. Other targets identify important problem areas for the language that need to be addressed, but they are vague about both the current situation and the targeted level for improvement – for example, the goal of increasing the number of families speaking Welsh at home does not attempt to define the current base level or to specify what percentage increase is to be sought over what period of time. Furthermore, there is very little new provision for implementation of this ambitious programme. The Welsh Assembly Government appears to be relying primarily on continued or somewhat enhanced support for existing Welsh-language programmes, mostly administered through the Welsh Language Board. In examining both the key target areas designated by *Iaith Pawb* and the programmes designed to achieve them, it is clear that their impact is gendered, although the gender dimension remains implicit and unacknowledged. It is likely that an explicit recognition and careful analysis of the differential impact on women and men of Welsh-language targets and programmes could lead to more effective implementation and improved results.

The Welsh language and equality issues

The position of the Welsh language and the rights of Welsh speakers have been affected by other equality issues, in particular those of race and gender. In the period prior to the 1993 Welsh Language Act, there developed a considerable amount of discomfort in the Welsh-speaking community about the impact of the 1976 Race Relations Act on Welsh-speaking areas. During the second half of the twentieth century, the large contiguous area of west and north-west Wales where Welsh was spoken by the majority of the population came under increasing pressure from comparatively large numbers of non-Welsh-speaking incomers. Their effect on Welsh-speaking communities was compounded by the economic weakness of these communities, which meant that local young people were forced to leave to find work and also that those who chose to remain found the local housing market being distorted by the greater financial resources of the incomers. The resulting spatial decline of the Welsh language in its heartland has been graphically documented using data from successive censuses (Aitchison and Carter, 1994). As noted above, the protection of these Welsh-speaking communities has been identified in *Iaith Pawb* as one of its key target goals. But, long prior to the establishment of the National Assembly for Wales, efforts were being made to protect the language in its heartland. These included special provision to teach Welsh to the children of incomers to allow primary schools to retain

Welsh as the language of education, along with the establishment of Welsh-medium secondary schools along the lines of those that had been set up in non-Welsh-speaking parts of Wales from the 1960s onwards. They also included attempts to ensure that public services could be provided in Welsh by making Welsh a requirement for some jobs and/or requiring that non-Welsh speakers obtaining public appointments undertake to learn the language. This latter effort was contested by non-Welsh speakers in several instances toward the end of the 1980s when they used the Race Relations Act to challenge the requirement that candidates be able to speak Welsh as a condition of employment for posts in these communities. Furthermore, the Commission for Racial Equality generally supported these legal challenges. As a result, there developed a belief among many Welsh speakers that 'the *Race Relations Act* was being wrongly used to deter public bodies from pursuing policies that would enable them to provide services to their people through the medium of Welsh, or bilingually' (G. P. Davies, 1994: 62).

This distrust between the Welsh-language community and the Commission for Racial Equality reached its zenith in the aftermath of a very widely publicized incident in 2001 when Seimon Glyn, a Gwynedd county councillor and member of Plaid Cymru, publicly suggested that the movement of non-Welsh speakers into Welsh-speaking areas was detrimental to the language and that it needed to be more carefully monitored. His remarks received quite wide and extremely negative publicity in the English-language press. Specifically the *Welsh Mirror* reported it under the headline 'Voice of Hate. "Racist" Plaid councillor's attack on the English' (18 January 2001). And, in a column in the *Independent on Sunday*, Janet Street-Porter expressed her hope that 'Mr Glyn is reported under the Race Relations Act' (21 January 2001). The response of the Welsh-language press was more complex. Prior to this incident most discussion of racism in the Welsh-language media revolved around an introspective questioning regarding the level of racism, with reference primarily to non-white ethnic minorities, within Welsh society generally and particularly within Welsh-speaking communities. Prompted to some degree by the creation of the National Assembly for Wales and the resulting prominence given to the concept of Welsh citizenship, arguments were put forward that Welsh speakers should examine more carefully their too easy assumption that Welsh-speaking society was not racist. However, following the attacks on Seimon Glyn, the discourse shifted to a consideration of the accusations of racism in the relationship between Welsh-speaking communities and English incomers. The early response is indicated by the February 2001 cover of *Barn*, a Welsh-language journal of current affairs and opinion, which reproduced the *Independent on Sunday* article with a superimposed headline '*Pwy sy'n hiliol?*' (Who is racist?). The editor claimed that one of the reasons Seimon Glyn's comments received such wide publicity was that the then head of the Commission for Racial Equality in Wales criticized him publicly following the report in the *Welsh Mirror* and noted that 'labelling as "racist" efforts to protect the last geographical strongholds of a fragile linguistic community . . . makes the Commission for Racial Equality' resemble Orwell's Ministry of Truth (Brooks, 2001: 6).[1]

From this low point, the Commission for Racial Equality began to improve its relationship with the Welsh-language community and has engaged in discussions with Cymuned, a movement to support Welsh-speaking communities that grew out of the Seimon Glyn controversy, and other organizations in the language movement (Jobbins, 2006). However, the claims of these two equalities strands can still clash. In a recent National Assembly for Wales committee hearing the representative from the Welsh Language Board took to task the representative from the Commission for Racial Equality for implying that other minority languages should be treated essentially the same as the Welsh language, reminding him that Welsh was statutorily mandated to be treated on a basis of equality with English.

The new Equality and Human Rights Commission, which has absorbed the Commission for Racial Equality as well as the Equal Opportunities Commission, may herald better relationships, although questions have been raised about the effectiveness of pursuing so many different and cross-cutting equalities strands within one organization. However, a recent study (Brooks, 2009) suggests that the pre-devolution discourse, both political and academic, that attempted to associate the Welsh language with racist ideologies has simply been transformed into a more subtle form since the establishment of the National Assembly for Wales. It documents how the concept of inclusivity has been used to portray the Welsh language as an agent of exclusion and Welsh-language activists as elitist, mainly by defining Welsh identities closely linked to language as 'ethnic' while implicitly associating 'civic' inclusion with the majority (unmarked) English language.

Relationships between the Welsh language and gender equalities strands have been less openly at variance. As discussed above, Welsh women were more active in language-related campaigns as opposed to women's equality in the pre-devolution period, but the 1993 Welsh Language Act did have the effect of stimulating some gender-based activities, especially the development of standards for non-sexist Welsh-language use in job advertisements. Equality for women has not been used as a weapon to discredit the efforts to protect Welsh-speaking communities or to undermine the will of Welsh speakers to defend these efforts as was the racial equalities agenda. One study (Charles and Davies, 1997) looked at the possible conflicts faced by workers in women's refuges who were helping to rehouse mainly non-Welsh-speaking women in Welsh-speaking communities. However, the research found that these workers, both Welsh and non-Welsh speakers, while keeping the interests of women seeking refuge as their first priority, still managed to balance this responsibility with their concern for, and in some cases active engagement with, the promotion of the Welsh language in their communities.

During the period immediately after the referendum to establish the National Assembly for Wales, a National Assembly advisory group was set up to make recommendations regarding the form the new body would take. A small coalition of 'powerful and highly influential "strategic" women' (Mackay 2004: 144) successfully lobbied this advisory group to ensure that the National Assembly for Wales would incorporate gender equality fundamentally in its working practices. It is significant that the advisory group recommended the creation of an equal opportunities committee with emphasis on gender, race and disability but omitted the Welsh language from this equalities agenda in the early stages. This has since been remedied but the impression remains that the position of the Welsh language in the various equalities agendas remains contested (see Chaney, this volume).

The future: a new Welsh language act?

The central campaign of the very broadly based Welsh-language movement at the present time is for a new Welsh Language Act. The existing 1993 Welsh Language Act is considered deficient in numerous respects, and the mechanism for its enforcement, the Welsh Language Board, has also been subject to a thorough critique (Williams and Morris, 2000). In addition, the 1993 act, as a product of the pre-devolution period, is considered no longer an appropriate basis for protecting and promoting the Welsh language at a time when Wales has its own devolved government with the capability of developing an integrated Welsh language policy. Debate is ongoing as to the content of a new act, but it seems clear that, whatever the detailed provisions, it is almost universally recommended that it establish Welsh as an official language in Wales and that it be based on the principle of the right of the individual to use Welsh, as opposed to the existing responsibility of public bodies to treat the language on a basis of equality with English (Lewis, 2008; C. H. Williams, 2007). This principle would necessitate that the rights of Welsh speakers to use their language would 'integrate Welsh as an essential part of the legislative agenda based on anti-discrimination . . . a strong principle recognised as fair by the majority – and so more likely to be accepted and implemented. Welsh would not be considered a "cause célèbre" or a fetish' (Williams, 2007: 220).[2] Such an approach would give the Welsh language a more central and less problematic position in the equalities agenda. This would also enable the creation of some form of regulatory body that would have the power 'to oversee the language legislation and implement it, exactly as with other responsibilities, such as race and disability' (ibid.: 224)[3] – and, it should be added, gender.

The relationship between the Welsh-language community and the main public body promoting gender equality, the Equal Opportunities Commission, has not had the same history of confrontation as that with the Commission for Racial Equality. This may be due in part to the greater overlap of personnel in these two campaigning areas, with women having been very prominent in Welsh-language activism for decades. However, the Welsh language was not initially included in the various equalities agenda of the National Assembly for Wales and its position vis-à-vis the newly established Equality and Human Right Commission remains unclear. A new language act that supported the language on the same individual rights agenda as gender, race and disability would help to establish the statutory rights of Welsh people, both to use the language and to be given support to learn it. Clearly, Welsh-language rights are a matter of social justice for both men and women, but as we have seen, their implementation in many areas has greater implications for women. Those who frame these policies as well as those who define the practices for carrying them out would almost certainly enhance their efficacy by acknowledging and accommodating the gendered nature of some of their provisions.

Notes

[1] 'Ond mae galw "hiliaeth" ar ymdrechion i warchod cadarnleoedd daearyddol olaf cymuned ieithyddol fregus yn drewi o gynllwyn, ac yn peri i'r Comisiwn Cydraddoldeb Hiliol ymddangos fel y *Ministry of Truth* yn nofel George Orwell, *1984*.'

[2] 'integreiddio'r Gymraeg fel rhan anhepgor o'r agenda deddfwriaethol ar sail gwrth-wahaniaethu . . . egwyddor gadarn, gydnabyddedig a theg i'r mwyafrif – ac felly yn fwy tebyg o gael ei derbyn a'i gweithredu. Fyddai'r Gymraeg ddim yn cael ei hystyried yn "cause célèbre" neu yn "fetish".'

[3] 'o oruchwylio'r deddfwriaeth ieithyddol a'i gweithredu, yn union fel y cyfrifoldebau eraill, megis hil ac anabledd.'

References

Aitchison, J. and H. Carter (1994). *A Geography of the Welsh Language 1961–1991*, Cardiff: University of Wales Press.

Awbery, G. (1997). *The Sex Discrimination Act and the Use of Welsh in the Workplace*, Cardiff: Equal Opportunities Commission.

——, K. Jones and D. Morris (2002). 'The politics of language and gender in Wales', in M. Hellinger and H. Bußmann (eds), *Gender Across Languages: The Linguistic Representation of Women and Men*, vol. 2, Amsterdam / Philadelphia: John Benjamins Publishing Company, pp. 313–30.

Ball, W. S. (2006). 'Making a difference, promoting gender equality?: transforming childcare policies for mothers, fathers and children in Wales', unpublished Ph.D. thesis, University of Wales Swansea.

Brooks, S. (2001). 'Golygyddol: Seimon Glyn', *Barn*, 457, Chwefror/February, 6–9.

—— (2009). 'The rhetoric of civic "inclusivity" and the Welsh language', *Contemporary Wales*, 22, 1, 1–15.

Charles, N. and C. A. Davies (1997). 'Contested communities: the refuge movement and cultural identities in Wales', *Sociological Review*, 45, 3, 416–36.

—— (2005). 'Studying the particular, illuminating the general: community studies and community in Wales', *Sociological Review*, 53, 4, 672–90.

—— and C. Harris (2008). *Families in Transition: Social Change, Family Formation and Kin Relationships*, Bristol: Policy Press.

Davies, C. A. (1994). 'Women, nationalism and feminism', in J. Aaron, T. Rees, S. Betts and M. Vincentelli (eds), *Our Sisters' Land: The Changing Identities of Women in Wales*, Cardiff: University of Wales Press, pp. 242–55.

—— (1996). 'Nationalism: discourse and practice', in N. Charles and F. Hughes-Freeland (eds), *Practising Feminism: Identity, Difference, Power*, London: Routledge, pp. 156–79.

Davies, G. P. (1994). 'Yr iaith Gymraeg a deddfwriaeth / the Welsh language and legislation', in R. H. Williams, H. Williams and E. Davies (eds), *Gwaith Cymdeithasol a'r Iaith Gymraeg / Social Work and the Welsh Language*, Caerdydd: Gwasg Prifysgol Cymru, pp. 242–55.

Gathercole, V. C. M., E. M. Thomas, E. Williams and M. Deuchar (2007). *Language Transmission in Bilingual Families in Wales*, Cardiff: Welsh Language Board.

Gruffudd, H., C. A. Davies and S. Morris (2004). *Cynlluniau Gweithredu Iaith: Gwerthusiad i Fwrdd yr Iaith Gymraeg* (Language Action Plans: Evaluation for the Welsh Language Board), Cardiff: Welsh Language Board.

Irvine, F., G. Roberts, Ll. Spencer, P. Jones and S. Tranter (2008). *Twf and Onwards: Impact Assessment and the Way Forward*, Cardiff: Welsh Language Board.

Jobbins, S. (2006). 'Beyond the pale', *Cambria*, May/June, 22–3 ff.

Jones, K. and D. Morris (1997). *Gender a'r Iaith Gymraeg: Arolwg Ymchwil* (Gender and the Welsh Language: Research Overview), Cardiff: Equal Opportunities Commission.

—— (2005). *End of Award Report: Welsh-language Socialization within the Family*, ESRC: RES 000–22–0611.

—— (2007). 'Welsh-language socialization within the family', *Contemporary Wales*, 20, 1, 52–70.

Lewis, G. (2008). *Hawl i'r Gymraeg*, Talybont, Ceredigion: Y Lolfa.

Mackay, F. (2004). 'Women's representation in Wales and Scotland', *Contemporary Wales*, 17, 1, 140–61.

Morris, D. and G. Williams (1994). 'Iaith ac ymarfer gwaith cymdeithasol: achos y Gymraeg / Language and social work practice: the Welsh case', in R. H. Williams, H. Williams and E. Davies (eds), *Gwaith Cymdeithasol a'r Iaith Gymraeg / Social Work and the Welsh Language*, Caerdydd: Gwasg Prifysgol Cymru, pp. 123–53.

Welsh Assembly Government (WAG) (2003). *Iaith Pawb: A National Plan for a Bilingual Wales / Iaith Pawb: Cynllun Gweithredu Cenedlaethol ar gyfer Cymru Ddwyieithog*, Cardiff: WAG.

Williams, C. H. (2004). '*Iaith Pawb*: the doctrine of plenary inclusion', *Contemporary Wales*, 17, 1, 1–27.

—— (2007). 'Deddfwriaeth newydd a'r Gymraeg' (New legislation and the Welsh language), *Contemporary Wales*, 19, 1, 217–33.

Williams, G. and D. Morris (2000). *Language Planning and Language Use: Welsh in a Global Age*, Cardiff: University of Wales Press.

III

CONCLUSION

11

The Future

NICKIE CHARLES AND CHARLOTTE AULL DAVIES

In this concluding chapter we address the relationship between devolution, gender and social justice. In so doing we bring together the discussions of different policy areas in the preceding chapters and consider what they can tell us about the relationship between gender and social justice in Wales. This enables us to evaluate the effect of the National Assembly's commitment to equality of opportunity on gender inequality and on the circumstances of women in Wales. In order to do this we look first at the relationship between descriptive and substantive representation as it is revealed in the different contributions to this volume. Despite a rhetoric of social justice and equality of opportunity and a commitment to gender mainstreaming, the contributors have shown that there are difficulties in translating this rhetoric into reality. We look at the problems that they identify and explore their relevance in the different policy areas. In the process we investigate the different ideas of social justice that prevail in these different policy areas and ask whether they are gendered. Finally, we turn our attention to the relationship between social justice and equalities, particularly gender equality, that is apparent in the different policy areas. Throughout, our attention is on gender and the impact of Welsh Assembly Government policies on women.

Descriptive and substantive representation

One of the dimensions of social justice that we discussed in the first chapter is that of political representation. It has been argued that it is unjust for men, or any other group, to monopolize political representation and that a socially just system of political representation would ensure that the distribution of different groups in the population would be reflected in the distribution of political representatives; this has come to be known as descriptive representation (Phillips, 1998). Our focus in this book has been on women and, in this regard, the gender parity of the National Assembly for Wales means that the proportion of women Assembly Members (AMs) reflects (more or less) the proportion of women in the population, although whether different groups of women are adequately represented is another question entirely. One of the issues that we have been addressing in this book, and one that exercises many commentators, is whether or not descriptive representation is translated into substantive representation, that is, whether policy development and policy outcomes are changed by the presence of women in political institutions.

It is clear from the first chapter that women's involvement in the devolution process and in political parties ensured, on the one hand, that gender parity in political representation was accepted as a legitimate goal and, on the other hand, that it has been all but achieved in the National Assembly in the years since devolution. It is also clear that strategic women contributed significantly to the existence of family-friendly working hours and the creation of the cross-party standing committee on equality and the equality duty. As a result, a commitment to equality of opportunity is institutionalized within the National Assembly for Wales and, as the contributors show, has provided an opportunity for the development of institutional mechanisms to further different aspects of the equalities agenda. This institutionalization is accompanied, as Chaney argues, by a rhetorical commitment to gender equality and gender mainstreaming which, while of symbolic significance and something that distinguishes the politics of the National Assembly from that of Westminster, has not yet resulted in substantive policy outcomes. The contributors provide different reasons for this which we attempt to bring together here.

In order to provide a framework within which to understand the different arguments about gender and social justice that have been presented in the book it is useful to return to the idea of there being a political and discursive opportunity structure. This directs us both to the institutional mechanisms which have been set in place to further the social justice and equalities agenda and to the ways in which debates and discussions about these issues are framed. Clearly, the establishment of a new political institution has created a differently gendered political opportunity structure which provides new

248

opportunities for political actors to influence policy (Charles, 2004). These political actors may be AMs and ministers, on the one hand, or social movement organizations, on the other, including a range of statutory and voluntary agencies between these two poles.

In their chapters, Chaney and Betts suggest that there are different ways of approaching both gender mainstreaming and the inclusion of previously marginalized groups in political processes. These can be characterized on the one hand as 'expert bureaucratic' and on the other as 'participative democratic'. Chaney argues that the approach to gender mainstreaming has been, in the main, expert bureaucratic. This has the effect of ceding power to the civil service and has, in his view, contributed to the delay in implementing gender mainstreaming and even, in some respects, undermined it (cf. Cockburn, 1990). This has meant that a considerable amount of energy has gone into providing equalities training for civil servants before the Welsh Assembly Government has been able to take the mainstreaming agenda forward and it is only relatively recently that effective policy tools have been put in place to ensure that the policy rhetoric becomes reality.

In contrast to this expert bureaucratic route, the Welsh Assembly Government has also adopted a participative democratic strategy by encouraging the involvement of civil society organizations in policy development and consultation processes and through establishing equality policy networks. The gender network, Wales Women's National Coalition, and the sexual orientation network, Stonewall Cymru, have been discussed in some detail in earlier chapters and can be seen as an attempt, on the part of the Welsh Assembly Government, to include previously marginalized groups in the policymaking process. The inclusion of civil society organizations, some of which are social movement organizations, also takes the form of the establishment of advisory groups, such as the Working Group on Domestic Abuse, which initially contributed to the development of policy and now over-sees its implementation. Members of the equality networks also participate in the equalities committee, and Assembly committees regularly call on civil society organizations to present expert evidence. The participative democratic strategy is also evident in the consultation processes in which the Welsh Assembly Government engages and the participation of civil society organizations in such exercises. Such measures can be seen as an attempt to create a more inclusive and participative democratic process; however, as Betts argues, inclusion on terms set by the Welsh Assembly Government may result in exclusion and continued marginalization. Her discussion, together with Ball's exploration of childcare policy since devolution, highlights the ways in which some of the consultation processes in which the Welsh Assembly Government engages have the effect of marginalizing groups and organizations which either lack the social capital and other resources needed to participate in the policymaking process or frame issues and arguments in ways that do not resonate with the dominant role equity discourse which is associated with liberal feminism. Both Betts and Ball argue that new opportunities have been created with the advent of devolved government, but that it is only certain groups and organizations that are able to take advantage of these. Betts suggests that these groups are those that possess bridging social capital, that is, they have links to the equality networks which, in turn, are able to represent their views to AMs and policymakers; in other words, they already operate within the same social networks as those they are seeking to influence. Ball argues that the organizations that are able to take advantage of these new opportunities are those that frame their arguments in ways that resonate with dominant discourses and, particularly, with liberal feminism. This means that those which do not already operate within those social networks and/or do not frame their arguments in ways that resonate with dominant discourses are in danger of continuing exclusion and marginalization. And, as Betts's chapter shows, it is particularly locally based groups which are excluded from these networks and which, while wishing to be incorporated into the policy process, are unable to make their voices heard. One of the problems with the mechanisms of inclusion which are being developed by the Welsh Assembly Government is that they are 'top down'. This means that, in relation to women and gender, they fail to engage organizations at local level, many of which, according to Sandra Betts, were not even aware of the existence of a gender policy network in the form of the Wales Women's National Coalition (WWNC). As we have seen, attempts are being made to remedy this, but it remains to be seen whether they will be successful.

What these two chapters point to is that the terms of inclusion are set by the Welsh Assembly Government in the form of the institutional mechanisms that have been put in place and of the discourses within which policy issues are framed. The new political and discursive opportunity structure has resulted in the incorporation of some groups and organizations into the policymaking process and the effect of this on both policy development and democratic participation should not be underestimated. A feminist and woman-centred agenda is clearly evident in developments such as the All-Wales Domestic Abuse Strategy and the explicit commitment of the National Assembly for Wales to gender mainstreaming; furthermore, feminist organizations, such as Welsh Women's Aid, have been incorporated into the policy-making process. In contrast, other groups and organizations which have not been incorporated in this way have not been heard at all; this is likely to be the situation of many locally based women's groups. Incorporation into the state can, however, result in a shift away from a more radical framing of issues towards one which sits more comfortably with liberalism and no longer poses such a serious challenge to the gender order (Charles, 2004; Ball and Charles, 2006). This is evident in the case of both childcare and domestic violence and several of the contributors remark that policy is increasingly framed in gender-neutral terms, which is consistent with a liberal feminist position. Indeed, the expansion of the equalities agenda, as Chaney points out, has resulted in a decreased visibility of gender and, despite the commitment to gender mainstreaming, there are some aspects of the mainstreaming agenda, such as gender budgeting, that are not included in the measures that have been proposed to take this agenda forward.

This evidence suggests that issues such as domestic violence, childcare and gender equality are framed within a discourse of liberal feminism. Liberal feminism is compatible with liberal individualism and the liberal welfare state and does not, at least on the surface, challenge the existing gender order. It also emphasizes sameness as the basis of gender equity and lends itself to ideas of gender neutrality; a major remedy for tackling gender inequality being simply the elimination of gender discrimination rather than recognition that women and men differ from each other and that these differences may need to be recognized and catered for in policy developments. In terms of this framework, difference is something that is seen as working against gender equity and relying on essentialist notions of masculinity and femininity. However, to counter this it has been argued that seeing equality as requiring equal treatment and emphasizing the 'sameness' of women and men effectively takes men as the norm (Fraser, 1997: 44). Some of the consequences of the liberal feminist agenda are brought out in the chapters by Ball and Parken. Ball argues that the liberal feminist agenda, which includes New Labour's policy commitment to ensuring that women are fully incorporated into the workforce, is more appropriate for some women than others and has a class basis; it also assumes a male model of paid work and devalues the unpaid caring usually carried out by women within the domestic sphere. Parken demonstrates that a policy based purely on the absence of discrimination fails to address the situation of marginalization and exclusion faced by lesbian, gay, bisexual and transexual individuals and its lack of attention to intersectionality means that gender and sexual orientation are not integrated in the development of policy. This shift away from a gendered discourse with women at the centre to a non-gender-specific or gender-neutral discourse courts the danger of making women invisible once more. This is something that is commented upon by several of the contributors.

There is some evidence that women make a difference to policy debates (see, for example, Chaney et al., 2007) and that they have different priorities from their male colleagues (Burrell, 1994; Norris, 1996; Stevens, 2007). However, it seems that, in order to bring about policy change, critical actors (or strategic women) are also important and the chapters in this volume lend credence to this view. Several of the contributors refer to the way in which strategic women are important to the development of policies in relation to gender and social justice. Thus, in the development of education policies, Jane Davidson, as minister of education and lifelong learning, and Susan Lewis, chief inspector of schools, are identified as key, while in the fields of housing, domestic violence and equalities policies Jane Hutt and Edwina Hart are singled out for mention. These women are seen as having contributed significantly to the ways in which policies have been developed. There is a weakness, however, in reliance on strategic women, especially in light of the widely held view that many gender-related issues have been prioritized because of the personal commitment of women ministers. There is a danger that when these women are no longer in such key positions the policies may no longer be pursued with such vigour. Indeed, in the 2007 elections the proportion of women AMs decreased slightly and the post of minister for social justice was, for the first time, held by a man rather than a strategic woman. Whether or not this will have an impact on policy development and implementation remains to be seen. What it means, however, is that there is no longer a strategic woman overseeing the domestic violence agenda. And recent developments in relation to the violence against women agenda are worrying in so far as, at the time of writing, a decision has been taken that Wales will not adopt the policy on violence against women that is being suggested by the Westminster government. This decision is being hotly contested by the WWNC, which is coordinating a campaign to ensure that it is reversed. The outcome of this will provide an indication of the ability of civil society organizations to influence Welsh Assembly Government policy.

The importance of strategic women in taking forward a woman-centred agenda and acting for women suggests that having gender parity in the National Assembly is not sufficient to ensure that policies that further gender equality and incorporate a gendered notion of social justice will be developed. Indeed, other research exploring the impact of femocrats on policy development has pointed to the importance of pressure for change coming not only from within a legislature but also from without (Charles, 2000; Flammang, 1987). This underlines, first, the need for femocrats to retain links with the women's movement in order to ensure that they do not become divorced from the movement's priorities and the claims that they are making and, secondly, that substantive change relates not only to there being a critical mass of women within legislatures but also to the existence of strategic policy actors both inside and outside legislative assemblies and an institutional framework which creates the possibility for a differently gendered way of working and doing politics (Jones, Charles and Davies, 2009).

National and local levels

There are clearly significant differences between national and local levels within Wales which emerge in several of the chapters. Charles and Jones suggest that differences between local and all-Wales domestic abuse strategies may relate to the scarcity of strategic women at local level and Sanders points out the lack of women in local education authorities, contrasting this with the situation both in schools and at the all-Wales level. Ball also notes that the policy actors she interviewed at national level display an understanding of gender equality that is premised on the desirability of women's entering the workforce on the same basis as men. The contrast between this view and that of the mothers she interviewed, who make decisions about the balance between paid work and unpaid caring on the basis of gendered moral rationalities and who, as a result, may decide that they want to spend time with their children rather than engaging in paid employment on a full-time basis, leads her to suggest that the New Labour agenda of full-time employment for parents combined with childcare provision is class based and meets the needs of middle-class, professional women. She also highlights the gap between policy actors at a national level and those at local level. At national level the conception of gender equality that prevails is one that conceptualizes it in masculine terms; thus, to achieve equality women need to engage in the work patterns that characterize male employment. At local level, in contrast, a different view of social justice prevails which is based on the elimination of poverty, deprivation and social exclusion; this view accepts existing gender divisions of paid work and caring and, therefore, does not address the gender dimension of social justice. Neither of these strategies, however, would integrate gender equity and social justice; the first because it pursues a male model (the universal bread-winner model) to which women are expected to conform, with care work being 'shifted from the market to the state' (Fraser, 1997: 56); the second because it is based on a gendered model whereby women engage in part-time paid work alongside care work but the cost to them of doing so is eliminated. Thus, care work is kept within the domestic sphere and is supported financially by the state (Fraser, 1997). Both these models can be found in different welfare states and neither has resulted in gender equity. A third way, according to Fraser, is a universal care-giver model; this model, she argues, would ensure equality of respect in contrast to the other models, neither of which is able to achieve this. The first because it 'holds women to the same standard as men, while constructing arrangements that prevent them from meeting it fully', the second because it 'sets up a double standard to accommodate gender difference, while institutionalising policies that fail to assure equivalent respect for "feminine" activities' (ibid.: 59–60). Furthermore, neither model 'asks men to change' (ibid.: 60). The first approach aims

> to make women more like men are now; the other [leaves] men and women pretty much unchanged, while aiming to make women's differ-ence costless. A third possibility is to *induce men to become more like most women are now*, namely, people who do primary carework. (Ibid.: 60, emphasis in original)

Ball argues that this respect for the care work that women undertake within the home is what is lacking in current childcare policies and that, in order for social justice for women to be achieved, this question needs to be addressed. What is significant, though, is that different models of gender equity and social justice are apparent at the local and national levels and that, at local level, gender equity is not seen as an integral part of social justice while, at national level, it is conceptualized in terms of equality and sameness with all the implications of this for difference-based conceptions of gender equity.

This distinction suggests that it is important to develop policies which speak to the needs and concerns of social actors at the local level, which, as we have seen, is not currently happening, and highlights the contrast between conceptions of gender equity and its relation to social justice which exist at National Assembly and local level. Having said that, however, it is also the case that there is an institutional and policy gap between the equalities machinery and that of social justice at national level. At local level, and within the National Assembly, social justice is seen as separate from gender equality and is conceptualized in class terms and in terms of redistribution rather than recognition. The difference between the levels is that, at national level, social justice and equalities are both seen as important while, at local level, an apparently ungendered view of social justice seems to prevail. We are not arguing here that the way in which social justice and gender equality are understood at national level is superior to the way in which it is understood at local level. There are clearly variations and the different understandings and how they are manifest in policy development and implementation depend upon the policy domain that is under discussion. Thus, in the context of anti-bullying policies in schools, Parken suggests that the ways in which such policies are being implemented locally demonstrate an understanding of intersectionality which is superior to the understanding enshrined in sexual orientation and gender equality policy at national and international levels.

Social justice

The political culture of Wales is characterized by a commitment to redistributive social justice which, as we saw in chapter 1, has a long tradition and is linked to the labour movement, socialism and class-based politics. Superimposed on this is a model of social justice which relates to ideas of equality and equity which, at least in relation to gender, emerged from the women's liberation movement of the 1960s and 1970s and which, our contributors suggest, is more apparent at national than local level. So, although it has been suggested that traditional social justice concerns were linked, as a result of devolution, with the gender (and other) equalities agendas (Chaney et al., 2007), their integration into policy development and implementation has yet to be fully realized. The individual chapters show that the idea of redistributive justice is widely recognized and, in many cases, drives policy. Thus education and housing policy, policy for older people and child poverty policy are all explicitly concerned with reducing poverty and class-based inequalities. In contrast, they do not explicitly address gender, often adopting a consciously gender-neutral position. Education policy provides a partial exception, but here gender becomes apparent only in the concern with boys' underachievement and the lack of male role models at primary level. The Welsh language policy, which derives from a recognition model of social justice, is similarly gender neutral despite the obvious centrality of women to its implementation and to the vitality of Welsh speaking. Even in policy areas which are clearly gendered, such as childcare and domestic violence, and where concerns about gender equality are central to policy development and implementation, recognition of and respect for '"feminine" activities and life patterns' are not in evidence (Fraser, 1997: 60). Thus care work within the domestic sphere is afforded neither recognition nor respect as a valued and socially necessary activity, and the same is true of the gendered nature and experience of domestic violence. Moreover, these and other policy areas, because of the predominance of views which equate gender equity with equality and sameness, are characterized by gender-neutral language and policies which are in danger of reinforcing, rather than eliminating, gender-based inequalities.

The social justice agenda, in particular policy areas such as housing, education, sexual orientation and older people, is, therefore, not gendered in the sense that gender equality is not seen as an integral part of social justice. And, in other policy areas, the equation of equality with sameness is in danger of rendering invisible the important gender differences that give rise to social injustice. So, despite the fact that the political and discursive opportunity structures are open to claims framed in terms of equality and/or social justice and, as we saw in chapter 1, there is an institutional basis within National Assembly for Wales for social justice and equalities, they remain separate. This institutional and rhetorical separation makes it difficult to

256

integrate claims for recognition and redistribution and this lack of integration is apparent in the different policy areas and in the contrast between political culture at local and national level (see also Charles, Davies and Jones, 2008).

There is also a lack of integration of the different equality strands which is particularly highlighted by Parken and Davies. Indeed, there have been serious conflicts between different equality agendas which are particularly evident in relation to language and which are still apparent in the lack of integration of language into the mainstreaming agenda and, in particular, its absence from the new policy tools which have been developed to ensure the compliance of policies with the equalities agenda. In addition to this the gender mainstreaming agenda does not include gender budgeting, and our contributors have highlighted areas where statistics are not disaggregated by gender; this is commented upon in relation to education and housing. Both gender budgeting and gender-disaggregated statistics are central parts of gender mainstreaming and their omission from gender mainstreaming by the National Assembly gives cause for concern. Is it the case, as Chaney suggests, that with the development of many equalities strands and the very important recognition of intersectionality, gender is in danger of slipping down the equalities agenda and becoming invisible?

What we have argued here, and what the individual chapters show, is that the model of social justice that prevails in Wales is class based. Furthermore, it takes different forms at local and national level, which have different implications for gender equity (Fraser, 1997). Superimposed on this is a commitment to gender equality but this has not yet been integrated into policy development and, even where it is central, a language of gender neutrality has been adopted. This is associated with a failure to develop a concept of social justice that fully recognizes its gender dimensions.

The future?

The establishment of the National Assembly for Wales, along with the achievement, virtually from its inception, of a gender balance in its elected membership, has clearly made a positive difference for women in Wales. The election of women in equal numbers to men – and, possibly of more importance, the election of a significant number of women whose prior experience made them aware of feminist concerns – has meant that issues such as domestic violence and childcare occupy a prominent position on the National Assembly and Welsh Assembly Government agendas. The priority given to such issues cannot be seen simply as a product of the gender balance among AMs, however, as it also relates to the political complexion of the Welsh Assembly Government. In the first two terms this was, like the Westminster government, Labour and, since 2007, has been a Labour-Plaid Cymru coalition. A concern with these policy areas also characterizes the New Labour government in Westminster so, in this sense, the priorities of the Welsh Assembly Government have not differed significantly from those of the UK government. Over and above this, however, the fact that the National Assembly for Wales has a statutory duty to consider gender equality across all its business, a duty established in the 1998 Government of Wales Act and reiterated in the 2006 Act, differentiates it from the Westminster government. Furthermore, the equality duty, as well as being symbolically important, has provided an opportunity to argue for the inclusion of gender equality considerations in all policy areas thereby creating a political and discursive opportunity structure which has been open to arguments framed in terms of equalities.

As the chapters in this book show, however, considerations of gender equality and the gender impact of different policies have not yet been fully integrated into the policymaking process. Most of the positive outcomes of Welsh Assembly Government policies for women have come less from the gender mainstreaming duty of the National Assembly for Wales and more from the reflection in its policy concerns of the long-standing commitment in Welsh political culture to redistributive social justice. Thus policies intended to foster social inclusion, alleviate child poverty, improve educational opportunities and give assistance to older people do not explicitly address gender but clearly improve conditions for women; indeed, they probably improve them more for women than men, given that women are more likely to be affected by these social injustices. A greater percentage of women than men live in poverty; child poverty is very closely linked to women's circumstances, in particular their access to paid employment; and there is a higher proportion of women among the older population. In another area of significant policy activity, that of domestic violence, although there have been positive outcomes for different groups of women, the Welsh Assembly Government may actually be in danger of undermining some of them by advocating a gender-neutral approach which fails to recognize that domestic violence is gendered.

The evidence presented in this book strongly suggests that what is needed is an integration of the largely redistributive social justice agenda with the various equalities agendas. This is clearly a complex undertaking which requires not only bringing the different equalities agendas into the entire range of policy considerations but also addressing how they interact with one another. As Chaney shows in his chapter, and as Parken demonstrates, beginnings have already been made but there is still a long way to go. And embracing an ambitious and inclusive equalities agenda courts the danger, not only of gender slipping down the agenda, but of the task becoming so challenging that it is difficult to ensure that it has an impact on policy development, implementation and outcomes. It is far from easy to predict whether such an intersectional approach will be effective, although the impact of the recently established Equality and Human Rights Commission in Wales and its ability to bring together the various equalities strands may eventually provide some indication, as will the further development of the Welsh Assembly Government equalities agenda. The gendering of redistributive social justice which would result from such an integration needs to be accompanied by a recognition of the value of the unpaid work that is carried out by women, largely within the domestic sphere, and a revaluing of waged work so that the balance between them shifts and both become 'valued components of a good life for everyone' (Fraser, 2009: 116). There is little sign of this happening at the moment, however, given the current emphasis on participation in paid employment for all and the male model of equity that this implies.

The ability of the Welsh Assembly Government to further a social justice agenda is, of course, dependent on its ability to develop and implement policy and a major constraint on this is the relatively limited powers of the National Assembly. For example, although the Welsh Assembly Government is able to develop policies relating to housing, education, childcare and health, Westminster controls the policy agenda both in relation to domestic violence (and criminal justice more widely) and to benefits for older people. And, as we have seen, this limits the policy initiatives that the Welsh Assembly Government is able to take. Indeed, in relation to gender equality, it is largely New Labour's liberal feminist agenda that has been implemented within Wales. This, together with the dominant, class-based conception of social justice that predominates, has, as we have seen, resulted in policies which have improved girls' and women's circumstances. These developments have been possible because the political complexions of the Welsh Assembly Government – initially Labour and now a Labour-Plaid Cymru coalition – and the Labour government in London have been similar. Even in these circumstances, however, there are considerable tensions between them, especially when the devolution of real power is on the agenda. Indeed, if a Conservative government were elected to Westminster, there is likely to be much more significant divergence between Welsh Assembly Government policies and those developed by central government. Given the Conservatives' record, and the continuing powers of the Westminster government over critical policy areas, this is likely to create serious tensions between the National Assembly and Westminster, which may have a negative effect on the ability of the Welsh Assembly Government to develop an integrated equalities and social justice agenda. The new Government of Wales Act 2006 has provisions for the National Assembly to expand the policy areas for which it can legislate through a complex process of petitioning the government in Westminster. This is only now being tested and it is unclear how effective at gaining National Assembly for Wales control over significant policy areas these mechanisms will prove to be. And it remains to be seen how effective it would be in maintaining a distinctively Welsh social justice agenda in Wales with a government of a different political hue at Westminster.

References

Ball, W. and N. Charles (2006). 'Feminist social movements and policy change: devolution, childcare and domestic violence policies in Wales', *Women's Studies International Forum*, 29, 172–83.

Burrell, B. C. (1994). *A Woman's Place is in the House*, Ann Arbor, MI: Unversity of Michigan Press.

Chaney, P., F. Mackay and L. McAllister (2007). *Women, Politics and Constitutional Change: The First Years of the National Assembly for Wales*, Cardiff: University of Wales Press.

Charles, N. (2000). *Feminism, the State and Social Policy*, Basingstoke: Macmillan.

—— (2004). 'Feminist politics and devolution: a preliminary analysis', *Social Politics*, 11, 2, 297–311.

——, C. A. Davies and S. Jones (2008). 'Women in local and devolved government', paper presented to the Government Equalities Office seminar, 27 November.

Cockburn, C. (1990). *In the Way of Women*, Basingstoke: Macmillan.

Flammang, J. A. (1987). 'Women made a difference: comparable worth in San Jose', in M. F. Katzenstein and C. M. Mueller (eds), *The Women's Movements of the United States and Western Europe: Consciousness, Political Opportunity, and Public Policy*, Philadelphia: Temple University Press.

Fraser, N. (1997). 'After the family wage: a postindustrial thought experiment', in Fraser, *Justice Interruptus*, London and New York: Routledge.

—— (2009). 'Feminism, capitalism and the cunning of history', *New Left Review* 56, 97–117.

Jones, S., N. Charles and C. A. Davies (2009). 'Transforming masculinist political cultures? Doing politics in new political institutions', *Sociological Research Online*, 14, 2/3, *http://www.socresonline.org.uk/14/2/1.html*.

Norris, P. (1996). 'Women politicians: transforming Westminster?', in J. Lovenduski and P. Norris (eds), *Women in Politics*, Oxford: Oxford University Press.

Phillips, A. (1998). 'Democracy and representation: or, why should it matter who our representatives are?', in A. Phillips (ed.), *Feminism and Politics*, Oxford: Oxford University Press.

Stevens, A. (2007). *Women in Politics*, Basingstoke: Palgrave Macmillan.

Index

263

'Johnnie was disarmingly honest, funny and unafraid to bare his soul. Tiggy tells their story with such love and tenderness – an endearing tribute to a remarkable man we'll never hear the like of again.'

Peter Kay

'Tiggy Walker's marriage to radio star Johnnie Walker has inspired her to write a beguiling story of mutual support, humour in adversity and old-fashioned resilience: a triumph of true love and a loving memoir of one of the best DJs ever.'

Mark Knopfler

'This is a hugely impressive book telling the story of a very special relationship. Touching and highly moving, it recounts the highs and lows of two lives bound together by the most profound love. Tiggy doesn't flinch from detailing the very toughest times of her and Johnnie's marriage but also conveys the great heights of happiness they found in each other. It's the kind of book that once you start, you'll find yourself reading right through to the very end. A truly inspirational story of loving and caring.'

Ken Bruce

'It's a beautiful memoir, a beautiful tribute to love – in its glorious beginnings, its many complications and its loss. Tiggy writes with wit, searing honesty (of course she does!) and irrepressible spirit about her private love for a man who was known by a nation. Funny, painful and always life affirming, this is a must-read for anyone who is interested in good music, an honest conversation, Johnnie Walker, and what it really means to be a carer. Which is pretty much all of us.'

Rachel Joyce

'Honest, unflinching, hilarious, profound and deeply personal, Tiggy has given us a true love story in every sense. The meeting of soul mates, the pressures of living in a public arena and dealing with the private triumphs and tribulations we can all relate to and the heartbreak of seeing the one we love slowly succumb to illness and then leave us behind. This book gives us not only an invitation into the extraordinary life of a broadcasting legend but also the journey his wife, lover, best friend, carer and most important person in that life has been on. We can all learn something from this story, and Tiggy, I bloody love you for sharing Johnnie with us.'

Michael Ball

'*Both Sides Now* is a simple story of love and care. Beautifully written and searingly honest about the brutal reality of caring for someone you love. Tiggy shares her life with a radio DJ legend – flaws and all! Carers will read this and weep as the reality of their day-to-day challenges, exhaustion and breaking points leap off the page with unexpected familiarity. Caring is indiscriminate, it touches all our lives and Johnnie and Tiggy exemplified that – caring for one another pretty much throughout their marriage. Their passion to do everything they could as patrons of Carers UK to make life better for carers shines through in this quite extraordinary story written with raw emotion, humour and love.'

Helen Walker, Chief Executive Carers UK

TIGGY WALKER

BOTH
SIDES NOW

Laughter, Grief and
Everything in Between with
Johnnie Walker

HarperCollins*Publishers*

HarperCollins*Publishers*
1 London Bridge Street
London SE1 9GF

www.harpercollins.co.uk

HarperCollins*Publishers*
Macken House, 39/40 Mayor Street Upper
Dublin 1, D01 C9W8, Ireland

First published by HarperCollins*Publishers* 2025

1 3 5 7 9 10 8 6 4 2

'Loving You Makes Me a Better Man', words and music by Rodney Crowell
© 2001. Reproduced by permission of Sony/ATV Tunes LLC/Sony Music
Publishing Ltd, London N1C 4DJ.

Images supplied by the author, apart from those kindly provided by the following:
page 2 top left © Bella West; page 2 top right © Carly Cook; page 2 bottom
© Rodney Wayman; page 3 top right, page 6 middle and page 8 bottom
© Melanie Aldridge; page 4 bottom © Tommy King; page 6 bottom
© Paul Thomas; page 8 top © Jane Treays.

A catalogue record of this book is
available from the British Library

ISBN 978-0-00-877003-7

Printed and bound in the UK using 100%
renewable electricity at CPI Group (UK) Ltd

To Johnnie,
with all my love.

'Darlin', I'll wait for you,
and should I fall behind,
wait for me'

Bruce Springsteen

FOREWORD

By Johnnie

Well, I guess you could say I've been a wild one all right. A typical Aries. When I met Tiggy I'd recently left rehab, so I was as clean as a whistle. It was a bit of a con, really, because you never lose that wild streak. It's part of your DNA, your energy, your drive. For years I called Tiggy 'a straight', which she was, not because she was dull – far from it; she lights up every room she enters – but because she was so sensible, with her feet firmly on the ground, unlike mine. I guess something in me recognised that stability in her and I thought, *I'll have some of that.* I need some of that. Of course, I really fancied her too. Her laugh, her energy, her blue eyes, her curves …

I've got a favourite record called 'The Joker' by Steve Miller Band, which includes the lines 'I really love your peaches/Wanna shake your tree'. And I did shake Tiggy's tree in more ways than one. I credit myself with opening her up to a more spiritual and less religious outlook on life. One of the first ideas I ever shared with her was that we are spirits on a human journey. I believe that we select the life we want to experience, getting a preview of all its joys and pitfalls before we make the final decision to take on the human form. Each human journey teaches us new lessons, until one day your soul has learned all it needs to from the human experience.

Tiggy chose a tough life, marrying me. Not only was I wild to her straight, which took some adjustment for us both, but I presented her with one health challenge after another. She's done far more caring of me than I would have wanted. She deserved so much more, and I genuinely wish I'd bought her more fun and less stress.

I've always admitted that apart from working hard on the radio, I can be pretty lazy. I act when I need to, but only then. Many is the time that I turned up five minutes before a show, giving my producers a high degree of stress, because I knew I could get away with it and I liked the energy from being on the edge. It's the same in my marriage. Tiggy is a producer and has the skills to run everything brilliantly. So, I've let her. As she says, I only work when there's a gun to my head or a mic in front of my mouth. Got to say, I've been bloody lucky – although I do think I've worn her out, which I feel bad about. She'll have a good rest when I'm gone.

I wish I'd earned more too. I would have loved to treat her to lavish holidays and amazing restaurants, both of which she would have adored. I've been terrible with money all my life, and it's thanks to her that we live in a house that we own and have had all the exciting trips we have. Just not on a luxury level. Not once has she ever been dissatisfied, though. As long as we were connected, she was happy.

I've been a radio man – one of a dying breed (literally) of jocks who went into this medium because we wanted to share the thing we were most passionate and excited about: music. It was never about fame or money. I know that Tiggy wouldn't have been attracted to me if it had been. She loves honest, real people. I know she's always respected me the most when she's watched me at work. I don't know why. A radio studio is just where I've always belonged, and so I guess working the desk and talking on mic became second nature to me. Over the years my music knowledge has earned me some brownie points too. She always reminded me how blessed I was to fall into the right job at such a young age. I was twenty-one. There is, however, a downside to being a radio man – which she also reminds me about. We're in the driving seat, often alone, with no one talking back to us. She is the opposite. A real people person who cares about those in her life. She's incredibly loved because she gives love. She's found it hard that I've lacked such qualities. Outspoken as she always has been with me, she said to me at our very final party at home, when I DJ'd live for the last time, 'Just because you're fucking dying doesn't mean you can be rude to everyone!'

I have been ill a lot and an introverted, insular DJ – with a wild streak. What did she do to deserve me? Well, as I tell her whenever she gets upset, 'Darlin' – you chose this life!'

I think we've learned a lot from each other. Marriage isn't easy, and somehow we've made it to the end, largely thanks to her forgiveness of my stupidities and failings. I do wonder where and when she and I will meet again. Will we live another life together, and if so, what will the relationship be? I pretty much know it will be her turn to lean on me. That is, if she ever needs to come back again.

I will end, as I always do, with a song, and if there's one I'd like to dedicate to her it would be Hal Ketchum's 'Loving You Makes Me a Better Man'. Because she has.

Loving you makes me a better man
These things I don't know how to do
You make me think I can

I've got a long way to go
But I know what I know like the back of my hand
Loving you makes me a better man

I've been wrong more than I cared to say
Time after time I've been lost
Just couldn't find my way

You shed a light on the path through the night
Leading right to the side where I stand
Loving you makes me a better man

I made mistakes, didn't have what it takes
Just to walk out, leave it alone
I've got a long lot of heartaches that follow me home

Time goes on, I watch it disappear
I've got a mind of my own
Now that I have you near

You came to me and it's easy to see
There's a line that I've crossed in the sand
Loving you makes me a better man
Loving you makes me a better man

Johnnie Walker, October 2024

THEN

LET THE MUSIC BEGIN

Ours is a love story. But it's so much more than that. It's a story of mistakes, challenges, changes, caring and an occasional sprinkling of stardust.

I had no inkling that you were to be a part of my life. I used to listen to you on Tuesday lunchtimes at Alton Convent doing the Radio 1 Chart Show when I was thirteen and you were twenty-nine. But after that I lost all knowledge of you. When Gordon, my songwriter 'Summer of 2001' fling, asked if I wanted to meet you, I was surprised. I thought you must be dead, having not heard your name in twenty-seven years. I declined the offer.

Monday nights were my sacrosanct yoga nights in Primrose Hill, but who was it who called me that evening so that it was too late for me to go? I've no idea. What I do know is, that call changed everything. Resigned to an evening at home, I made my sitting room a candlelit haven to do my own practice. I was deep into my asanas when the phone went again. It was Gordon. He'd already met up with you, yet you wanted to meet me too — because secretly you'd had a psychic inkling that I'd be important to you. It all seemed rather tiresome to have to shower, reapply make-up, get dressed and go back to Soho for the second time that day. I told Gordon I would meet you at The Union, my club in Greek Street. I wasn't fast getting there. I knew this was just Gordon's way of showing off that he had a girlfriend fifteen years younger than him. Men ... I couldn't see him anywhere in the club. I was about to leave when suddenly before me there was Gordon, sat back on a sofa, grinning, and you were walking towards me with your hands outstretched. What an extraordinary sensation. I knew you. I recognised you. Not your face, but your being. Your soul, in fact. Here you were, my oldest friend who I had not seen for so long. And certainly not in this life. You kissed my cheek, sat me down next to you and we talked as if we were carrying on our conversation from our last life together. The connection was instant and total. It felt that there was so much we didn't need to say. So much we agreed on. And Gordon did not.

It cannot be denied that the timing of our meeting was strange. On a personal level and a global one. That day you had ended a long-running on/off relationship with your then girlfriend. Even though it had been a mutual decision, you were still in shock. To meet me on the same day did not allow you much recovery time – a fact that would bite us both very firmly on our backsides before long. The global situation almost felt pre-empted by us. We spoke of how spiritually bereft people in the West are. How materialistic. 'Something big has to happen to make people reassess their lives,' I suggested. The next day two planes flew into the Twin Towers.

I knew I would see you again. So did Gordon. Within ten days he ended it. While he never mentioned your name as the reason, I knew he was making space for you. He recognised that he was a stepping stone in my life. In other words, he wasn't going to get in our way. His reward for being so sensitive was being played on your Radio 2 *Drivetime* radio show, the song making the Radio 2 playlist, him getting a record deal and earning proper money for the first time in decades. He was very nearly the Christmas Number One. 'How Wonderful You Are' is a song I listen to with fondness, remembering the late, idiosyncratic, beautifully bonkers Gordon Haskell.

For you and me, a future lay ahead we could never have imagined.

I guess nothing about us as a couple was that normal. For a start, our deeper contact began when I sent a message to your Radio 2 *Drivetime* show about 9/11 – two days after we had met. I forwarded a fascinating email from an artist friend in Chicago with her reaction at the USA being attacked. While I didn't know what your show covered as I had never listened to Radio 2, I thought it might be interesting. But mainly it was a great excuse to contact you. I included my mobile number. On Friday afternoon I was in Dorset, where I owned a gorgeous cottage in the village of Ashmore. This was my weekend decompression place away from the bustle of Soho. I had grown up a country girl in

Hampshire, but at the age of sixteen announced that my future life would be in Dorset, following a one-day trip to Brownsea Island, compounded by a love of Thomas Hardy. As soon as I could afford to, I bought a property there. I was shopping in the local town of Shaftesbury when you called asking me out to dinner in London that night. I explained that I couldn't. You asked what I was up to. I blushed as I told you that I was just going into the florist as I was doing the church flowers that weekend. I had never done them before and indeed haven't since, but St Nicholas's Church in Ashmore had become a part of my life. I felt great comfort in the services each Sunday. In a village the church is also about community, and I was gently becoming part of Ashmore's, albeit on a weekend-only basis. I could hear the shock in your voice. Church flowers? Who is this woman? I felt so very un-rock 'n' roll and thought I'd probably blown it. Desperately back-peddling, I spluttered out that my sister Fiona was coming for the weekend to help me, because I couldn't do a flower arrangement to save my life. Happily, the utterly upper-middle-class-establishment image I'd managed to paint of myself in those two words, 'church flowers', did not put you off and we spent the weekend texting each other. Our first date was on the Monday evening – just one week after we met. It was a yoga class: my sacrosanct Monday night. You had told me when we met that you also did yoga. (Men!) So, taking you at your word, I booked us both into my regular class. You were already waiting for me in the light, airy reception area in

Primrose Hill when I arrived. You took my breath away. You were dressed head to toe in white, looking like a yoga guru. It was the first time I realised how attractive you were. It wasn't long into the class, as I looked back at you between my legs in Downward Dog, that I saw you were in total confusion. Limbs everywhere. I realised you had *never* done yoga. I cursed myself for messing up our first date. I'd made you look an idiot. Yet again, I thought I'd blown it. At the end of the longest ninety minutes, I rushed back to you and said, 'I'm so sorry, Johnnie.'

'What do you mean?' you said. 'I had all that time to admire your arse.'

After a quick supper at Manna vegetarian restaurant, when, to your annoyance, Simon the yoga teacher joined us, you drove me home in your old Saab. Before you set off you picked up a CD and put on a song: John Prine's 'All the Way With You'. I wondered if this was just a track you especially liked or if you were trying to tell me something. And if you were, was that something that you wanted to have sex with me, or spend your life with me? The latter seemed too far-fetched to contemplate. You stopped several times more on the short trip to Marylebone, putting on other songs. Were all your journeys so musically punctuated?

I asked you in for coffee (since you didn't drink in those days, still glowing in the goodness of rehab). You hated my flat. It was so neat, so Heal's, like a hotel. But as I tried to explain, my home and heart were in Dorset. We sat on opposite ends of the taupe suede sofa, longing to hold each other. We agreed that a hug was permissible and wouldn't be disloyal to Gordon, but the attraction was too great.

Our first kiss happened an hour later as you were about to leave. You leaned down to wish me goodnight and our lips met. If there was one moment in my life I could relive, it would be that. It felt as if we floated, and that a beautiful throng of angels flew silently around us, lifting us towards heaven. It was an out-of-body, out-of-this-world experience. We both felt it. Afterwards we looked into each other's eyes with a sense of wonder.

'Did I dream that we kissed last night?' I texted you in the morning.

'We did. And it was dreamy,' you assured me. I believe that what we experienced was pure love, and at that moment our two souls entwined and made a vow that whatever should come to pass, they would keep us together. And what two brave souls we have, for it seems that we were to be given one test after another, but they would not let us go. Even though at times I tried.

Next morning at Blink, the commercials production company where I was a producer, as everyone shared what they had done the night before, I casually mentioned I'd had a date with Johnnie Walker. There was a flurry of excitement from the production managers. James, the boss – a huge music fan – stayed silent at his desk, but seconds later Bachman–Turner Overdrive blasted out from his laptop: 'B-b-b-b-baby, you just ain't seen nothin' yet!' Everyone dissolved in laughter, including me.

I loved working at Blink. It was the best production company for commercials in Soho. I felt it was my reward after years in the business. Ten years before, I had opened my own production company, Wowhaus, in London, making commercials for Germany. I'd spent a year working at a production company in Munich, where I'd produced the commercials for visiting English and American directors, but generally, they were not that happy working in Germany – so I represented them for Germany, but based in London, where they could continue to use their familiar crews. The exchange rate was in our favour, it was a new concept and a great idea, except that potential clients were nervous of going with a new company in another country. We were a risk. After a year of selling hard in Frankfurt, Hamburg, Munich and Düsseldorf advertising agencies, renting out my flat to sofa surf and living on air, I felt the idea had failed. 'How many weeks can you hold on before the bank shuts you down?' asked my accountant, GT. The answer was three. 'Hold on!' he insisted. I did – and in came a Grundig TV commercial, and after that I never looked back. I sold the company after seven years, and when Blink asked me to join them I felt I had arrived at my natural home.

My first visit to your flat was a shock. At the opposite end of Marylebone High Street to mine, you rented a tiny, two-bedroom scruffy flat above Giraffe restaurant. Advertising was a world where we portrayed style, perfection and neatness. In my naivety I assumed that's how a successful BBC presenter would live. Far from it. Your furniture looked to be out of a charity shop. The flat was cramped, the bathroom grim, the kitchen in need of ripping out – everywhere was grubby because each surface was covered with stuff, and worst of all, thousands of CDs created chimney-like piles on every available bit of floor space. These weren't CDs you loved. These were ones you had been sent by the music pluggers who wanted nothing more than for Johnnie Walker to feature them on his show. Your reputation as a music influencer was still intact from your early pirate radio and Radio 1 days, when you had discovered many an act or artist. The strange thing for me was that, seeing all this music begging to be heard, my interest in new music got immediately crushed. Just by visiting your flat. Rather than a new CD being something exciting that I deliberately sought out, suddenly CDs represented pressure and untidiness. It was just too overwhelming to see them all begging to be heard. How could you differentiate between which ones would be good and which not? It was like huge amounts of homework. And honestly, you listened to so few of them. How could you do otherwise? There were so many. (Of course, as the years passed and everything became digital, that issue evaporated. Maybe you were sent masses of download links instead, which you could ignore. I didn't see them. Ironically, today, I still want to buy CDs rather than relying on streaming services. I prefer the physical to the digital.)

Your flat and mine: already it was clear we were very different people, and yet we continued to fall head over heels in love. Especially when you made it down to my Dorset cottage – the Clock House in Ashmore. I'm not sure you'd ever done country living. An AGA, a scrubbed white-painted table, an open fire, a well-stocked wine rack – it was all too much temptation, and after you had a mind coach called Tony Buzan as a guest on your *Drivetime* show, who told you that you were not alcoholic, you took the bold decision to share a bottle of red with me in front of the roaring fire. As it happens, Tony was right. While you would always prove yourself to have addictive traits, you were not an alcoholic, and I will always be grateful to Mr Buzan for telling you that. Sharing delicious bottles of red and white Burgundy has been one of our joys, and let's face it, we were both a bit freer when we'd had a glass or four.

My bedroom at the cottage had windows on two sides. You credit that and my Simon Horn sleigh bed with its amazing mattress as the reason for the best night's sleep you've ever had. I was so happy that you felt content there – until I went off riding my horse, Wicked Willy, when you did get a bit fractious and bored. No shop. No pub. Nothing. Ashmore has a dew pond, a church, a village hall, great walks and not a lot else. Not very rock 'n' roll.

There was much to learn about you. The radio stations, the two previous marriages, your two children, Sam and Beth (both in their twenties), your recent time in rehab and the reason you went there. The story that you were most ashamed about: that you had been sucked in by the 'fake sheikh' from the *News of the World*. He had met you to discuss a supposed radio show for somewhere in the Middle East. During this pretend negotiation he had said how hard it was to find good cocaine in London, and after much persuasion convinced you to chop out two lines of the white powder. You snorted yours but he declined his – which was when you smelled a rat. The hidden camera that took your photo meant you were on the front of the Sunday 'red top' paper. You had been 'stung'. (This front-page news is one thing you never showed me.) You were fired from Radio 2, went to rehab and had to fight in court to clear your name from the accusations as best you could. It would have been the end of your career had your ardent fans not saved you. The effects on you were enormous, not least financially, as you were left with enormous legal debts. Crikey – you certainly weren't the average date. Getting to know you was a mixture of heady excitement and deep alarm. One thing I could see early on: you were never going to be boring.

It wasn't long into our dating that you told me you would take me away for a weekend on your Harley-Davidson Fat Boy. Me on a motorbike – whatever next? Along with your biker friend Snapper we set off to Tintagel from my cottage. 'You're going to freeze,' you told me as I appeared in jeans and a Barbour jacket. You were right. It was a godforsaken challenge – uncomfortable, cold, mind-numbingly dull and lonely. We rocked up at the worst hotel I've ever seen. 'Isn't this fantastic?' you exclaimed. It reminded me of the first meal you took me to: a Thai in a scruffy café at the end of the King's Road, which during the day was an egg, chips and tea venue. A far cry from The Union, the Ivy and Quaglino's where I hung out in those days. Oh, Johnnie – how different our reference points were back then. The one notable moment of that trip was on a rock together on a north-Cornish beach. You asked me what my dreams were. 'To make a film called *ANTONIA* …' I said, and I told you the story of how my father had given me a beaten-up red book called *Antonia* by Naomi Jacob when I was sixteen. I was just departing for Umbria to stay with a distant family friend. It was my first solo trip and my first time to Italy. He told me to read it there because it was about an amazing Italian woman. He then added that it would make a great film. Deep within me, he had sown a seed, and the very first tender shoots were now eager to appear.

I returned the question and your reply was simply, 'To spend the rest of my life with you.' And coming home on a dark Sunday night, at a brightly lit petrol station where I bought a life-saving fleece, you looked into my eyes and I just knew you were nanoseconds away from proposing. Even then I knew you so well. But I think you also knew me, and that a service station under cruel strip lighting would not be the right setting for the story I would want to tell for the rest of my life.

Gigs after your *Drivetime* show soon became a part of our life: Ryan Adams, REM, Bruce Springsteen, Billy Joel, David Bowie, Brian Wilson, Elton John, Fleetwood Mac, Simon & Garfunkel, the Dixie Chicks, The Who, Neil

Diamond, The Rolling Stones, Eagles, Carly Simon, Crosby, Stills & Nash, mavericks like John Otway and many more, at London venues that ranged from Wembley Stadium, the Royal Albert Hall and the O2 to the smaller scale La Scala and Bush Hall. Our first gig together was James Taylor at the Hammersmith Apollo. I'd never listened to him before, which is extraordinary as he writes exactly the sort of music I enjoy – mellow and meaningful. It was my first experience of going backstage afterwards. How normal it all was. The large, badly lit room was quite un-special. James was relaxed and warm, greeting you like a cherished friend.

As we left and walked back to your car a punter shouted, 'Hi, Johnnie. Is that Sally Traffic with you?' and for the first time I revealed to you a spark of my fire as I responded to said punter:

'No, I'm bloody well not. I'm a lot younger than her.' How you laughed. Sally was your on-air bounce whom you had brought into the station to do the traffic news. You had great broadcast chemistry, but it was at times a feisty-sounding relationship.

I loved the Ryan Adams concert. I had never heard of him until I met you, and his album *Gold* was quickly one of my favourites. Watching him sing 'La Cienega Just Smiled', with you holding me from behind … It was bliss. And I must admit to some vanity. Many in the audience knew who you were. You were such a respected music man, and being the woman held by you made me feel a few inches taller – which at my height is a fabulous feeling.

A new motorbike made its entrance into your life: a BMW Road King. You announced that it was to be called Earl. You would be the Duke of Earl. At which we started singing, 'Duke, Duke, Duke, Duke of Earl, Earl, Earl …' You looked at me and said that made me your duchess. Thus, from the very early days of being together I called you Duke, and you called me Duchess, or usually Duch. Being someone with a recognisable voice, this proved to be very handy in public, as it must have reduced the JW sightings considerably as I never called you by your name.

The euphoria we experienced together in those first months was like nothing I have ever felt for its intensity and joy. We were nuts for each other. We were literally high on love.

When at the start of December I had to fly to Australia to shoot a Volvo car commercial, you rushed into the reception at Blink thirty minutes before you were due on air for the *Drivetime* show. 'What are you doing here? You should be at the studio!' I panicked.

You, cool as ever about time, handed me a package. 'Open it on the plane.' I did, some five hours later as the jumbo taxied along the runway. Inside was a MiniDisc player with a disc for me to listen to. And a Wright & Teague silver ring with the words 'Dedicated to the one I love'. It was the first song on your playlist. I cried so much that the air hostess came to check I was OK. It hurt me so much to be taking off and flying away from the man I loved so deeply.

We were only a few months into our relationship, but already you were dominating my every waking moment. You filled my heart. You were my reason to be. So when on the first day of filming the Volvo car ad in a New South Wales rainforest I got a text from your biker friend Snapper warning me that your ex was getting her claws back in, the earth crumbled beneath me. My director, Laszlo, was asking me what on earth had happened. My entire demeanour had changed, and the biggest day of car photography of my life was a total blur. I had no idea what awaited me on my return to England. But I knew it wasn't going to be good, and I dreaded it.

I landed back in England on Christmas Eve. As I pushed my trolley through the arrivals hall at Heathrow, looking for a driver holding a sign with my name on it, I noticed instead that the waiting crowd were enjoying a gorilla playing a guitar. All I could muster was a brief smile. Behind the gorilla stood a pantomime cow. Some reunion, I thought. It was only when I realised the gorilla was singing Gordon's new single 'How Wonderful You Are' that I turned around for a double-take. In a blur, the gorilla started laughing and the cow took its head off. Suddenly I was in your arms. You were laughing nervously. I was in shock.

A few hours later you, me, Gordon, Snapper (the unsung back of the cow) were in my kitchen in Dorset. Gordon – still our friend despite our break-up – always smoked, but suddenly for the first time ever I saw you light up a cigarette. But you had quit in rehab on Antigua – that relatively recent chapter of your life after the *News of the World* sting – what were you doing? I HATE smoking on a deep, pathological level. I could see you were on edge. I couldn't wait for the others to go. We needed to talk.

I was sitting on my white-painted kitchen table with you on the bench in front of me. I looked down into your eyes. 'What's been going on, Johnnie?' With alarming honesty, you confessed to visiting your recent ex and her child – who was not yours but to whom you had become an unofficial godfather (psychologically explained by you trying to make up for the lack of time you spent with your own daughter, Beth, when she was a young child) – and that she had done a big seduction number on you – candles, see-through negligee and cheap perfume. You tried to push her off, but that dark side of yours that finds temptation just too exciting ultimately could not resist. I know you didn't do the whole deed, but in my heart I felt you had betrayed me.

The bubble of our heady love had burst. I couldn't believe I could be stabbed so deep by an external act. It was two days before my forty-first birthday. I never had a period again. Years later, a consultant gynaecologist would tell me that shock can start the menopause. That act, that weakness of yours, that desperation of hers, I believe stopped us from ever having a child, and for you it was the start of an emotionally traumatic time that you always claimed was the cause of your cancer, which ultimately changed your health forever. You referred back to your regret of that slip for the next twenty years.

It wasn't the easiest Christmas. It was my first experience of your actions breaking a bit of me – just over three months after getting together. Defensively, you criticised me for living in the perfect world of advertising, of not knowing what hardship meant, of being a 'straight' (Me? A straight? I was far from that in my friends' eyes, always being a bit of a fun-loving party girl.) I fought back, telling you I had to sofa surf for a year when I started my own production company, working like crazy to get it going. You didn't want to hear that.

You got into such a state of feeling utterly guilty, confused and pulled between two women (for the record, I NEVER pulled – it's not the way I behave) that you ended everything, and for a few weeks I licked my wounds and built a protective zone around me. I loved my Dorset life. My horse, my cottage, my antidote to making commercials in the week. I never expected to hear from you again, but then on a Saturday evening in late January, when I was in my candle-lit bedroom meditating, you called. You were on Win Green – a mile away. You asked to come round, and in many ways that was my *Sliding Doors* moment. If I had told you to get lost and leave me alone, I would have gone on with my career and my stable, successful life. I would have been in control of my destiny and avoided a whole load of pain. But as it was, I felt sorry for you because it was cold and dark, and your voice – well, let's face it, you know how to use that voice. Around you came. As I have always said, you were my destiny – whether I wanted it or not.

In the three weeks of your absence I had done two things. I had told Blink I needed to leave and take a sabbatical. I was honestly so thrown by the emotion of the previous few months that I knew I wasn't performing as well as I should. My second act was thanks to my dear granny, who had left me £5,000 in her will. I decided to spend it on a month's Italian course in Florence, going out at the end of March. My E.M. Forster tribute trip to nurse my broken heart was starting on your fifty-seventh birthday. You asked if you could come out for that weekend. I was too weak to say no and start my adventure alone, even though it was supposed to be my time to heal. For those two nights I booked a hotel on the River Arno that I'd always fancied, the Hotel Lungarno.

It was here we experienced our first bit of magic together. An Italian plugger in the music business arranged for us to have an upgrade to the biggest suite. It was a huge room overlooking the Arno, with the crispest white sheets, white sofas, a bottle of bubbly on ice and white flowers on the enormous coffee table. It was as perfect as an advertising set. The next day a chauffeur arrived to drive us around Tuscany. He took us to medieval villages and Siena – one of my favourite Italian towns. I couldn't believe it. What a start to my month.

On Sunday we were free to walk the wonderful streets of Florence. Is it the olive skin of the men, or their beautiful dark hair? Whatever it was, the male inhabitants of the city unnerved you. At a bar on one side of the famous Ponte Vecchio you ordered a brandy, which you knocked back in one gulp. We walked to the centre of the bridge and watched the brown water flow slowly beneath us. You picked something off the ground and faced me. 'Tiggy, would you do me the greatest honour of becoming my wife?' I was stunned. 'Are you sure, Johnnie?' I kept repeating it. 'Are you sure?' I already had the measure of you. You had proved yourself to be an emotional, hot-headed decision maker, and also a touch possessive. It was fairly obvious that you did not want a Florentine man taking me away from you, so you were literally ring-fencing me for my four-week sojourn. You insisted you were sure, and put a Coca-Cola ring pull on my wedding finger.

At the hotel we drank the champagne. When you left early the next morning I was in a heightened state. You had convinced me that your intentions were true. We were getting married. And you wanted to do it in July. It was unbelievable. Only a couple of months before this you had ended it all. It seemed too amazing to be true, but of course I *wanted* it to be true, so I let it overtake my being. In my Italian conversation practice for the next four weeks, I could talk about only one thing: *mi sposo*.

While in Florence I went to Salvatore Ferragamo and bought the most expensive outfit I've ever purchased. Wide-legged trousers and a flouncy top in lilac, along with a pair of subtle-pink, high-heeled suede sandals. It was altered to fit me perfectly. This was my wedding outfit for July.

On my return home, speaking Italian a little better but still very much lacking, we went to the Larmer Tree Gardens

– home of the now-defunct Larmer Tree Festival – to talk about the wedding. We had missed meeting each other there by minutes when I was going out with Gordon. You saw he was one of the acts at the festival and had a Tannoy announcement put out for him, but we had left just five minutes before. Both of us love those gardens, which is why we chose them for our wedding venue. As a huge favour to us they squeezed an extra day into their schedule when they were due to be closed. We were shown where the ceremony could take place. There's a little round temple on the main lawn where we could do the honours. I was only joking when I called it the Temple of Doom, but as it happens that joke backfired on me.

Five weeks before the ceremony I collected the invitations from the printer, which were a postcard of the 'Temple of Doom' with the date on the back. I spent the weekend addressing the invitation envelopes. Alone. You had gone to visit your 'godchild' and ex for the weekend. This was something you had done about once a month, and while it made me feel uneasy, I would never have stopped you as you felt an emotional obligation towards the child. This particular weekend you didn't contact me once. Not even a text. By Monday my nerves were on edge. *Here we go*, I thought, *the next blow*. While I didn't need to call you to know what you were thinking, because already we were telepathically connected, I did just to be certain. I was right. You wanted to cancel the wedding. A right hook to my solar plexus. But it wasn't just the massive blow to my gut and heart. I had friends and family flying in from Australia, Italy and Germany, all so happy that I'd found the man of my dreams. I had to tell them, and everyone who had saved the date, that it was off. Oh, the humiliation. The indignity. The heartache. Made all the worse by the fact that you were bloody famous. I wrote a lame poem that you 'weren't quite ready to get wed at the end of July'. I was so brave. You didn't have to do a thing. You just went back to London to broadcast your *Drivetime* show. I couldn't listen that evening. The Salvatore Ferragamo outfit was put away, never to be worn. I've never spent so much on an outfit since.

Looking back at how accommodating and accepting I was that day, I believe I can only attribute it to our entwined souls. The belief, the knowing, that you were my destiny whether I wanted it or not. No matter how hard it would be. I could see your dilemma and suffering. The ex played on your incredibly susceptible guilt strings – something she knew how to do. And it was something that would be your Achilles' heel for several years to come. I'm proud that over our time together you would shed that coat of guilt, learning to believe in your inherent goodness rather than your weakness. That said, the scar of that day never completely healed in me. And the regret of it stayed with you to your grave.

You asked what I would do about the honeymoon that I'd booked at La Residencia in Deià, Mallorca. I told you that I was still going but would leave two days earlier so I wasn't around for what would have been the wedding day. You said you wanted to come too, since apparently the relationship wasn't over, just the ceremony. God, you had some gall. But oh, the immense amusement that I felt when we arrived and they said, 'Welcome Mr and Mrs Gatfield. Congratulations!' The hotel hadn't got the memo. And as I had booked it, they used my then surname – that of my previous husband, which I still used. Something competitive in me felt that you didn't hold all the cards after all. It was like a sharp slap for your poor behaviour. The bed was covered in red rose petals and a bottle of champagne on ice awaited us. We never opened it out of shame. I swept the petals away. I also slipped the silver ring 'Dedicated to the one I love' I was wearing on my wedding finger.

You always said that it was on our 'not the honeymoon' that you really fell in love with me. My instinct on the Ponte Vecchio had been utterly correct. But seeing how I behaved may have taught you something that you hadn't seen in me before, or indeed in any woman that you'd dated. Strength. Principles. Independence. You allowed yourself to let go, and one night as we sat naked together under a star-encrusted sky, making love in a jacuzzi, something in you connected – to me. You had never stayed anywhere quite so beautiful and luxurious. It made you feel better about yourself. Yes, you were worth this. You allowed your true self to be seen. You weren't the man ashamed of his *News of the World* drug sting, the man who had felt such paranoia and guilt. You were a man staying at one of the world's most gorgeous hotels with a woman you had fallen for but were afraid to commit to. You began to recognise that you and I were equals, destined to help each other. Both our souls were longing for you to realise that. We had an amazing nine days. On returning, you were determined to right the huge wrong and marry me. You compared us to Native Americans – a culture you always loved. You told me that they honeymoon before the wedding. If they return together the ceremony occurs; if apart, nothing happens and nothing is said. We returned together.

Our actual ceremony – to which we invited almost no one, as I was understandably petrified of another last-minute cancellation – took place in St Nicholas's Church, Ashmore, on Saturday, 21 December 2002. The Bishop of Salisbury had given us (both divorcees) dispensation to marry in church. In retrospect it was definitely worth waiting. We needed all of God's help to get us through the years ahead. As part of the ceremony you asked our friend Paul Venables to read out a piece you had chosen – 'The Invitation' by Oriah Mountain Dreamer. 'It doesn't interest me who you know – I want to know if you will stand in the centre of the fire with me and not shrink back ...' Soon followed by 'Come on Baby Light My Fire' by The Doors as we walked down the aisle (played on the organ!).

A wedding lunch for my parents, all of our siblings, your dear son Sam, who was your best man, and our very closest friends (including Gordon) was held at the Museum Inn in Farnham, Dorset. Then we took a blustery drive down to the Dorset coast to the Anchor Inn at Seatown, as you wanted to wake by the sea. On the way there you received a text from your ex on news of the wedding: 'May God forgive you.' It was like a curse.

OUR TOP TEN MEANINGFUL SONGS

John Prine
ALL THE WAY WITH YOU
The first song you played me.

Hal Ketchum
LOVING YOU MAKES ME A BETTER MAN
You honestly felt that was true.

The Mamas & the Papas
DEDICATED TO THE ONE I LOVE
The ring I still wear.

Richard Hawley
BABY YOU'RE MY LIGHT
The first single you gave me.

The Doors
LIGHT MY FIRE

We came down the aisle to it – played on the organ!

Cyndi Lauper
TIME AFTER TIME

Played by Terry Wogan for you, from me,
when you were diagnosed with cancer.

Simon & Garfunkel
BRIDGE OVER TROUBLED WATER

You played this when you announced your cancer;
I cannot hear it without thinking of that moment.

Bruce Springsteen
IF I SHOULD FALL BEHIND

Encapsulates our caring for each other.

Judy Collins
AMAZING GRACE

Your final song on-air and at your funeral.

Joni Mitchell
BOTH SIDES NOW

Though you didn't know it when you were 'down there',
your coffin would come in to this.

NOW

GOODBYE, WOGAN HOUSE

I know I like everything neat, but it really is something to fall terribly ill on New Year's Day. It's made measuring time so easy.

Christmas 2023 is such a quiet one for us. We just have to make sure you don't catch anything. We avoid parties, and go out just one night to the Grosvenor Arms in Hindon. We sit at your favourite corner table, where you can hide your portable oxygen machine and wear your nose cannula without being too visible. We order pizzas, salad, red wine. We know how to date well together. Isn't it a great evening, just you and me bantering and quaffing away? 'You should live in Hindon when I'm gone, Duch. It would really suit you,' you say, glowing from the wine and the ambient warmth of the pub. Thank goodness it is such a gorgeous evening, for neither of us know it will be our last night out together.

On New Year's Eve you are doing your first live show at Radio 2 since the end of September. We both know you have declined since then, announcing as you did in early December that this would be your last Christmas on earth.

For six weeks you were muttering your concern about doing the show live. It will be your seventh live one of the year. Pre-records at home in your den have become a necessity due to your health. But New Year's Eve is an important day and all the shows are live that day – unusual for a Sunday. I keep saying that if you aren't up for it then Bob Harris would happily cover for you. Of course, you won't hear of that. It's one thing to have cover when you're away on holiday, but when you're in the country, no! Good old DJ paranoia. Seeing how worked up you are getting about it, I realise it will definitely be the very last live one, so it is laden with significance.

It doesn't help that we couldn't go to our flat in London the night before. You've long ceased to be able to get up the stairs, even though it's only on the first floor. That part of our lives has already been taken from you. From us. It means that we drive up from Shaftesbury in the morning. You drive. You love driving. You're the best driver I know. Fast, confident, yet safe. You love your Lexus. Such a work-horse of a car that has done you proud for fourteen years, taking you up and down to London. We arrive so early that we have time to drive up to Primrose Hill so I can go into the flat to collect the post and check it. You stay in the car. You want to follow your usual routine of driving past Pret a Manger on Great Portland Street and getting lunch. It's closed. I feel your heart sink. Although it is unspoken between us, we both know this will be your last live show. It's sad that your normal pattern is curtailed. No matter – a new Gail's has opened right opposite and in there I blow an eyewatering £28 on a couple of loaves, a sandwich for you and two small salads. It's our opening conversation in the studio with Paul Thomas, your executive producer – the expensiveness of Gail's. We sound like two country yokels experiencing the high costs of the big city for the first time. In fact, Paul and Jamie, the studio manager (SM), wholeheartedly agree.

You are on fire as you broadcast. The text machine goes nuts. Hundreds of messages pour in for two hours. Johnnie is live! Let's get him. I sit opposite you, sorting requests into piles – Bruce, Eagles, Bowie, Rod, Elton, Steely Dan, Stevie Wonder ... All through the show the music choices are free-forming according to requests. You get your jingle and sound-effects package going. Car horns abound. You may be wearing a nose cannula so you can get enough oxygen, but who would know? Your adrenalin is pumping.

Tony Blackburn comes in for an impromptu on-air chat. The two of you are hilarious together. You give him such a hard time, basically telling him he's obsessed with himself and his own fame. Tony wittily responds, saying he signs autographs to himself. It's bloody funny. I know there's a one-off show between the two of you in the can to be broadcast in March, but honestly everyone missed a trick not putting you two together more often. Off-air, he asks why you're on oxygen. You lie, saying that you have a bit of a cold. I am quite certain that Tony is not fooled by that lame excuse.

As the two hours draw to a close you start making mistakes. I know you aren't getting enough oxygen to your brain. When I tell you that my dearest friend Jacquie is listening in the Seychelles with Gail, you give a name-check to Jacquie and Claire. 'Awks,' texts Jacquie on hearing it. 'Who is Claire?' Gail asks.

It's emotional for me, saying goodbye to Wogan House. For almost eighteen years you've been broadcasting from here. I take photos of everything – the studio, the mic, the control room, Elton's piano, the coffee machine. You are too far gone to be emotional. Being the gentleman you are, you spend some moments with Clement the doorman, who himself is a gentleman. It's all very poignant, walking away from a building that has been your longest-lasting broadcast home. All that history in there. The memories of so many guests and presenters soaked into the walls. The end of a big era.

We both know I will drive us home. I take us up Marylebone High Street with its Christmas lights. We pass Nottingham Street, which is where we lived for the first few years of our marriage, in the spacious, wonderful flat that I wish we'd never sold. As we go down the Marylebone Road towards the Westway to leave London the tears fall quietly down my face. I instinctively know that you will never come to London again and that over twenty-two years of fantastic fun that we have had here together has ended.

It's New Year's Eve. Across the country people are preparing parties and getting changed. We are tonking down the

M3 and A303. We are rewarded with the occasional burst of fireworks. You tell me I drive well – a compliment I always love because of your own skill. Your Lexus is the largest horse in our stable of three. It's like taking out a thoroughbred that's just a little too big and strong for me – but fun to ride.

As we approach home we weigh up our options. We can't drop in at a pub or restaurant because a) they will be fully booked and b) I think you will fall asleep. So we head home. I light candles, put out a cheese board and one of the Gail's loaves and open a bottle of very expensive red Burgundy, which must have been a gift from our close friend Charles. I do not realise the heavy symbolism of my choice. Bread and wine. The Last Supper.

We watch a few minutes of the New Year's Eve concert on the BBC. Slightly blurred from the wine, I go to my bathroom. I turn on the radio as I always do when I enter any room alone. Sat on the loo, I hear the midnight bells from Big Ben chime. I roar with laughter. This strikes me as the funniest way to see in the New Year. Loo flushed, I go to find you to share the hilarity. I find you in your bathroom, also on the loo. We both see in 2024 on the John …

New Year's Day, 1 January 2024 – the day our lives turn upside down. If it wasn't for the fact that we are due to spend it with Jane and Charles, you would have stayed in bed. They, d'Arcy, Gary and us – the gang of six – have so often spent NYE together. Once till 4.30 a.m. as you once bragged about on air. But because of your show yesterday, it has to be a New Year's Day lunch this time. You do look a little grey as we get in the car. I can see your energy is low. Once again I drive, neither of us realising that you have driven your last. Such a loss for you – you, who might have been a racing driver if not a DJ. You were training at Jim Russell's racing school in 1966 when you got a job on the pirate station Swinging Radio England, later jumping ship to Radio Caroline. DJing has certainly provided greater longevity than racing would have. Your destiny was to play tracks, not drive on them.

At Jane and Charles's, in front of their roaring log fire, you sit with your coat on, shivering. You look white. You cannot drink. You don't eat. You just shake. Getting covered in more and more rugs. When you go to the loo you make such a noise that Charles stands like a sentry waiting for you to come out in one piece. When you do, all you can do is cry on my shoulder and ask, 'Duch, what's happening to me?'

I left the key in the car. Somehow it runs down the battery. The Lexus won't start. What a day. Now dark. Jane drives us all home. Happily, she has drunk very little of Charles's fine wines. Sadly, so have I. You go straight to bed. I stay up and feel annoyed with myself that I agreed to a lunch today. I should have known that you'd need a complete day of rest after a show. What a start to 2024.

THEN

FALL AND I'LL CATCH YOU

You were standing in for Terry Wogan on the *Radio 2 Breakfast Show* for the two weeks after the wedding. We were high on love. In bed at every possible moment. It meant that our actual honeymoon had to be delayed until Terry returned. We chose Kerala in India, and I can only say it was the worst holiday of my life. I already had 'honeymoon cystitis', and somehow we just didn't take to India the way so many do. While the food was sensational, and the Ayurvedic treatments fabulous, there were many negatives. The mosquitoes were appalling – I was covered in bites even before we did the dreaded backwater cruise. In a small boat with a small crew, where it got dark at 6 p.m. because the sun sets so early and there was just one fading battery-run lamp, where we had no wine and had to huddle under mosquito nets, we endured what you always referred to as the worst night of your life. You wanted to jump off the boat and swim to shore, you were getting bitten so badly. While we had booked two nights on the boat, we begged to be taken back to shore in the morning. The dear crew couldn't understand why we weren't loving it. I almost had blood poisoning from the bites. Meanwhile you were going into yourself. You became more and more distant, telling me you weren't joining me for supper. You claimed to be feeling ill. I thought you were being tricky. I felt certain that you were regretting getting married. My abiding memory is sitting alone at dinner with my half-bottle of white wine. (There were only two wines in India in 2003 – one white; one red; both awful. The same brand wherever you went.) The entertainment provided was a young Indian man with a guitar singing 'Tequila Sunrise' by Eagles. The whole trip was so ghastly that I cannot abide that song, and I have never returned to India. I doubt I ever will.

The Delhi Belly you returned with continued for months. You finally agreed that you should see a doctor. However, you did not have a tropical disease as I thought. In fact, you had a growing obstruction in your bowel. While you said nothing to me, this had been your fear. It was with such guilt that you held my hands outside the private clinic only metres from our Marylebone flat and said, 'Tigs, I'm so sorry. I have cancer.' This was even worse to take on board than the cancelled wedding. *Oh my God*, I thought, *he's going to die*. Nothing had or has shocked me as much in my life. It was a Friday and so we were going down to my cottage in Ashmore for the weekend. Even though it was you who had been given the diagnosis, I was the one who fell apart. We had gone through so much turmoil to marry, just for you to then die? I couldn't fathom it at all. You drove the whole journey while I wept. It took all weekend for my shock to pass. On this occasion you were the strong one, calling your children, Sam and Beth, to let them know the terrible news.

You were a public figure on a massive weekday radio show – this was not something you could hide. Having told Radio 2 management the news, you made the announcement on air, playing Simon & Garfunkel's 'Bridge Over Troubled Water' for all those suffering with cancer. You stepped away from your show, and we spent the first year of our marriage together fighting the non-Hodgkin lymphoma in your bowel. It was such a rapid gear change to everything in our lives. If there had been any semblance of a honeymoon period lingering after India, it ended sharpish.

We hadn't lived together before we married, so this was a baptism of fire. We had recently done up and moved into a fabulous mansion-block flat in Marylebone. While I thought the flat would be a wonderful, positive fresh start to married life, it became a place of fear, stress and illness. You were so sick. Chemo knocked you about in a way I've never seen since. You were hospitalised between each cycle of the poisonous drug combination known as CHOP. I stopped doing any commercials. I existed for one thing only – to help you survive. I became cut off from family, friends and work. Later I would learn through our work with Carers UK that this is the norm. Carers become isolated. It's partly because you are caring, and partly because you just don't want to share your story. It's too hard for people to hear. Too hard to share. And feels almost disloyal if you do. You became my work: taking you to Barts Hospital at all times of the day and night; answering to your every need. I was slowly going inward, getting lost, getting nothing in return. If I thought I knew you when we married, I soon realised I didn't at all. You were so consumed with a fear of death that you became difficult and closed. On occasion, cruel. Indeed, more than once I thought I'd made a terrible mistake and married a total bastard. The more needy I became for reassurance, affection or gratitude, the more insular you became. It was hell.

During a few days at my Dorset cottage seven months into your treatment, you were rushed to Salisbury District Hospital. 'Call a fucking ambulance!' you shrieked in excruciating pain. After an afternoon on a ward when your life was slipping from you, you were diagnosed as having peritonitis. Your bowel had been perforated by the chemo. You were given lifesaving surgery in the middle of the night. You were on life support for the next few days. Visiting you when you were conscious again was the greatest relief of my life; you asked me to get on the bed with you, and your dedicated nurse left the room so we could hold each other in complete privacy. You always say that was the most overwhelming moment of love in your life. I wasn't as relaxed. I was terrified of pulling out one of the many tubes coming out of your body that were keeping you alive. It would have been ironic if I'd accidentally undone all the doctor's good work.

The surgeon, Nick Carty, said to me as you started to pull through that you were far from safe. He also added that you should never, ever smoke again. It was the worst thing you could do to your body. I took this message very much to heart.

After a month of recovery in hospital, when your huge, fourteen-inch-long, extremely deep stomach incision had to heal up, you had to learn to walk again. When you were released you returned to a new cottage in Farnham, Dorset, as I had moved home in your absence. You wanted a cottage with a garage for your motorbikes. I sold my beloved Clock House for you – one of several property moves I would later regret.

You named the thatched house 'Marky's Cottage' after a man in the village who had been born there and lived in the village all his life. His only absence had been during the First World War, which he'd fought in under-age. This was a promise you made to him in the pub one night – where you were instructed to have a Guinness a day to build you up. You'd had a few red wines too. So while you were a tad inebriated when you made your grand declaration, it was a lovely gesture and immortalised a true Dorset character and a part of the village's history.

You credit that cottage, its woodburning stove (which you sat next to daily), our new working cocker spaniel Fergus and the Museum Inn as your route to healing. Ultimately, all the chemo, surgery and care had worked. The following spring you returned to your *Drivetime* show, much to the delight of all. You had been off-air for just under a year. Meanwhile, in a parallel of our life, in the script I was writing, *ANTONIA*, I had the groom fall ill on honeymoon. I've never explained that to anyone, it's just my nod to the shocking start to our marriage that we endured.

You went on to have many more operations and illnesses. It's as if the cancer took your health and immune system down a big notch, because other problems crept in. I must confess that having given my all to you during your cancer year, my heart would sink when something else went wrong. *Oh, not again*, I would think, and sometimes say. I remember one stint in Salisbury District Hospital when I told the registrar that you had to be released because you were on-air at the weekend. He looked at me askance. 'But he has pneumonia. He's very sick.' Again, when you had been taken to hospital in an ambulance, I was beyond shocked to hear from the cardiac nurse who called the next morning that not only had you just had a heart attack, but that you needed a triple heart bypass. 'Can he do his show this Sunday?' I asked (I was by this point your agent and manager). Again, I was told, 'Your husband is very ill. He'll be off work for six weeks at the very least.' Over the years I visited you so often in hospital, taking you your specific requests from home: sweeties, food, tissues, clothing, batteries, radios, magazines, toiletries, DVD players ... You saved your mischievous requests for others. As you waited for a date for your heart bypass, you persuaded a friend to bring you in a bottle of red wine. Goodness knows what others brought you. Fags? Jack Daniel's? Oh, how you enjoyed being a monkey.

The result of so much medical intervention is that you ended up with scars going all the way up your body, from your ankle to the top of your chest, as if you could be entirely unzipped. I've always joked that very little remains of the man I married, as it's all been removed, replaced or enhanced.

The one illness that did not leave an outward physical scar was the one that finally got you. Months after your triple heart bypass, which entailed them opening up your sternum and wiring you back together again, you kept complaining that they had retied you too tightly. You felt a heaviness across your chest and still found breathing difficult. You wanted to be opened up again for them to redo it. Instead, the heart team referred you to the respiratory team. You were made to do breath tests on and off treadmills, you had scans, and then, in August 2019, we went to meet Dr Rohan Mehta from the respiratory department. He told us that you had idiopathic pulmonary fibrosis (IPF). In layman's terms, this meant that your lungs were inflaming, scaring and then being rendered useless. Idiopathic means that the cause of this was unknown. We learned that it was incurable and that while steroids and certain extremely expensive drugs could slow the progress, nothing could reverse it. You were given a prognosis of two to five years. I asked about a lung transplant but was told that would be plan D. Reading between the lines, you were probably already too old and too ill to receive such an enormously invasive operation. We sat in Dr Mehta's room, trying to quantify this amount of time. You were seventy-four. I was calculating how many more holidays we had left; you were wondering if you'd make it to eighty. Happily, you did qualify for the extremely expensive drugs that could stem the progression, but sadly you were one of the 50 per cent of patients who reacted extremely badly. Dr Mehta agreed that £10,000 a year of NHS money was not well spent if it gave you constant diarrhoea.

You bought a portable oxygen concentrator. A box the size of a cereal packet would hang over your shoulder on a strap, and a plastic cannula would provide good-quality oxygen through your nose. You could turn it up or down as needed, and you went everywhere with it, including Radio 2. You wore it during shows, and you soon wore it all night, which led to us parting to separate bedrooms. Later it would be replaced by a far larger and noisier machine that became your lifeline in the final year of your life. Life was about oxygen levels and heart rate. Steadily, you could do less and less, and I had to do more and more.

It wasn't just you who suffered sickness in our marriage. Ten years after your cancer interlude and five years before your heart attack and IPF diagnosis, it was my turn to call in the caring favour ...

Of all the rollercoaster moments of our life, the one I will always consider the hardest is the one that I believe caused my breast cancer. I always bragged to you that I would never get the disease because I let everything out, but when something occurred that I could not discuss with a soul, I felt the tumour in me starting to grow. I will never forget the morning. It was a Saturday, and I had just returned from an early-morning walk up to Shaftesbury with our latest working cocker spaniel, Darcey. You were still in bed in our room at the Old Fox and Hounds. You said, as you did whenever some shit had hit the fan, 'Tiggy, I need to discuss something with you.' The tone of your voice and your use of my name gave away that there was menace behind the discussion. It normally took you days to summon up your courage to broach difficult subjects, but a gun was pointing at your head. The Jimmy Savile saga has put a slur on all DJs of your generation, but it also opened the floodgates for women to make accusations, and you were an obvious target. An anonymous woman in Manchester went to the police saying that you had sexually abused her in the 1970s backstage at a gig. She alleged that you had ripped her tights and groped her breasts. Somehow, the head of HR at the BBC and the latest controller of Radio 2, then Bob Shennan, had been informed, presumably by the police. By 11 a.m. that Saturday we were on a call with Bob, who said he needed to take you off-air. All I could see was your well-earned, incredible reputation – plus our life – falling from beneath us. Everything. Our entire identity. Destroyed. In one fell swoop. You didn't deserve such injustice. And despite that occasional little dark streak of yours, I know that fundamentally you always have been a very good, decent man – with a few character flaws. We discussed with Bob that if he took you off-air, it pretty much sent out a signal that you were guilty. The anonymous woman would have won before any evidence had even been heard. Bob, in his fairness, finally agreed. You could stay on-air, and the whole issue went to the Crown Prosecution Service (CPS).

You were interviewed within weeks, but when you heard the evidence you immediately smelled a rat. You were described as having buck teeth and curly hair, and reeking of whisky. Since you'd never had buck teeth, and curly hair was a brief post-chemo phenomenon much later in your fifties, and it was a well-documented fact that you detested Scottish whisky, the evidence was utterly flawed. What was correct was that you were at the said club the night she claimed, as you were the compere, but so, too, was a band, which included one member with buck teeth, curly hair and a taste for whisky, who has since been done for abuse against women. That didn't stop you being under investigation for months by the CPS. There was no case, the police who interviewed you immediately realised that, and the wait was intolerable. It was unfair, unnecessary, unjust. I felt the stress of this situation every second of my waking life. I held it, this ghastly threat. I believed completely in your innocence, but was utterly powerless. I felt my life force diminish. I discovered the lump two months into the waiting game.

My main memory of chemo, which I hated with such a force that I ended up needing talking therapy to get me through it, was me lying in the guest bedroom feeling utterly sick, my head pounding, with me crying my heart out, yelling, 'That fucking woman!' and you crying that you were so sorry that you had caused this. Fame – why do people want it? I felt so sorry for you. You always had an over-developed sense of guilt, and here I was, suffering deeply because of something you were falsely accused of. It really upset you.

I believe right down to the depths of my soul that the mistaken allegation of that woman caused my cancer and thus also destroyed my future health, for you never completely get over the threat of cancer returning. That fear is always lurking at the back of your mind. I was so angry with her that I fantasised – a lot at the time – about going to find her and confronting her. She hadn't hurt you; she had hurt another woman, an innocent sister. You were strong. You knew you were innocent and all would ulti-mately be fine. But I was not used to the machinations of being in the public eye. Never before had I felt the down-side of fame with such overwhelming force, and never before or since have I had to keep such an awful event in our marriage a secret. You've always had a favoured expres-sion: 'No amount of worrying ever changed tomorrow.' It's been a guiding light for you, that saying, and it has kept you grounded in your life of fame. I wish I had embraced that belief myself back in 2013. I have since reflected on the anonymous woman. I'm truly sorry she suffered sexual abuse. I too suffered from some in my youth, so I know the effects. I always chose to do nothing about it – it's all so long ago and would achieve little but pain for the remaining family of the man. But I do know this – time plays havoc with our memories and it is a deep sadness for me that she remembers the incident but not the perpetrator. I hope she has found some peace.

For the record, while you felt enormous guilt about my sickness, you really should not. The system failed us. The CPS was cruel and slow. You, my darling, were a steadfast and devoted carer. You took me to over seventy appointments, you waited, and you discussed at length all my fears. You held me as I sobbed with chemo sickness. You shaved my head when my hair started falling out. And for the only time in our marriage you put me before radio. Friends of yours could see your abject fear of losing me, but you never did open up to anyone. You just absorbed it, occasionally crying with me. Throughout that horrible eighteen months of operations, chemo, radiotherapy and Herceptin, you were my rock. I couldn't have got through that time without you. And should it ever reappear I don't think I could face it without you.

It was during this period that we became the co-patrons for Carers UK, a charity supporting unpaid carers. If only I'd known about them when I was caring for you; I would have coped so much better. Being a part of the charity gave meaning and purpose to our illnesses. Together we would go to events up and down the country, raising money and awareness of the need for support for the charity. We even took a group of friends to walk a section of the Great Wall of China – the wild section with uneven rubble, and no steps or barriers to stop you falling off. You struggled to get up there and I discovered I had vertigo, but an unforgettable week with the best views I've ever seen led to some deeply forged friendships and our group raising over £65,000 (a lot of which came from your friend, the comedian Peter Kay, who is a very generous man). I will always be proud of how devoted you became to the charity and all the good you did for them. Not just the Great Wall of China fundraising trip, but your willingness to attend all the events they held, being the star turn, giving talks, encouraging donations, meeting other carers, supporting the poetry events, talking about the charity on-air and being the catalyst to Radio 2 getting behind Carers Week. OK, I was the person motivating you and coordinating all these things, but you always said yes to everything the charity and I asked of you, and you really deserve recognition for that.

Everything really does happen for a reason and our health issues have meant that we gained such an understanding of what so many others also go through. You said to me from the start that you believe we are spirits on a human journey. The tougher it is, the more our spirits learn. Sickness and caring are two of the fastest ways to do that. So I guess it was worth it for our spiritual growth, as well as helping Carers UK.

MY TOP TEN
SONGS YOU SHARED WITH ME

Ryan Adams
LA CIENEGA JUST SMILED

Jackson Browne
FOR A DANCER

Avett Brothers
I AND LOVE AND YOU

Buffalo Springfield
FOR WHAT IT'S WORTH

Johnny Cash
HURT

Robert Plant & Alison Krauss
PLEASE READ THE LETTER

Lucinda Williams
RIGHTEOUSLY

Sixto Rodriguez
I WONDER

Josh Ritter
HOMECOMING

Nathaniel Rateliff & the Night Sweats
S.O.B.

NOW

FOR BETTER, FOR WORSE

We meet the palliative care nurse for North Dorset in November 2023, after a Zoom consultation with a doctor who said that it was time to get the ball rolling on end-of-life care. It was one of those throw-away comments that doctors can make without realising they've just blindsided you. End-of-life care … It's a medical catchphrase. You're asked, 'Is your husband receiving end-of-life care?' I don't know. Is he? Talk about a label.

Caroline Gullis is an angel in a smart grey suit and sensible flats. She has authority, wisdom, strength and empathy. I call her on 2 January 2024 and ask if I should be worried. And as it happens, she says that I should be. The days that follow are a blur of activity and change. She comes. She arranges others to come – district nurses, occupational therapist nurses, respiratory nurses, nurses I've never heard of, the GP. Your health has collapsed. Your lungs haven't collapsed but have taken a huge walloping. We are told that doing that live show was too much stress for your already very sick body, that you have no resilience and now can never come up to the level that you were on a few days ago. Your instincts had been right. You weren't strong enough for a live show. You now need huge levels of support and have been labelled a Gold Star patient. While it sounds like you've been promised a life of club-class flights, it means that because you are so vulnerable you now go to the top of the queue – for appointments, ambulances and any medical needs. These are your perks. Your priority status. Not that you wanted them.

A lot happens in six weeks. A lot. The fabulous local NHS set you up for your new disabled and nearing-end-of-life status. An occupational nurse comes to see what equipment you need. Grab rails? NO! Reclining seat? NO! Commode? NO! Stool for the shower? Well, OK. As it turns out, that seat is little used. Showering has suddenly become a hugely stressful event for you. Even though I'm there with you, holding the shower hose while you sit on your NHS white stool, with your nose cannula in, the steam makes you panic. You can't breathe. You take some of the many drugs you have been given to manage stress, but these don't touch the sides when it comes to the shower. It becomes an issue we choose to ignore: the fact that you are living life unwashed. It strikes me as letting go. A giving-up of the human spirit. We try you kneeling beside the bath while I wash your hair, but we end up at the kitchen sink.

The district nurses come in thick and fast – what a resource they are. When you are concerned about a new development I call them and they come round. Emma is your favourite. She has a wonderful manner with you. She plonks herself down on your bedroom floor and chats. She is calm, reassuring; she doesn't wind you up. It helps a lot that she used to be on a respiratory ward. Your greatest fear is that you are going to 'drown' from lack of oxygen and your lungs seizing up. She assures you that your body will just get more and more tired, that you will end up spending more time in bed, you will sleep more, and one day you just won't wake up because your organs are not getting enough oxygen. You take that. We both do. A gentle exit while you're in the land of nod is what we both hope for. Doesn't everyone? When, where, how? The moment of our death is surely the mystery event that we all think about, and in our sleep is definitely the favoured route.

The biggest issues are your oxygen and controlling the balance of your drugs. You've been given Oramorph – a liquid morphine – which helps calm you and so you breathe more easily. At first, I am terrified of you getting addicted to it, and I have grounds for my fears. I realise that every evening at around 6 p.m., instead of asking for a G&T, you are taking a slug of the new drug. The Oramorph Cocktail Hour. I suggest that it isn't recreational. You are defensive. Actually, you are rude. When I hide the bottle so you don't abuse it, saying I will give it to you when you need it, you go ballistic. We have a terrible scene. One evening when I'm already in bed you stagger into my room. 'Give me my bloody Oramorph.' Your desperation for it is deep. Your verbal abuse shocks me. I give you the bottle. Indeed, I throw it forcefully at the sofa next to where you're standing. I shout at you that my bedroom is my safe space, my alone space, that you must never come in there again. The huge sadness is that you almost never enter my room again. That was our last row. After that you are in charge of your Oramorph. I have to recalibrate. Stop being so worried. Your body, your stress, your survival method. We both have to get used to our new norm.

A week later the respiratory nurses arrive and assess your failing lungs. At this point you are still able to walk – not far, not fast – but their tests reveal the rapid rate of your decline. I am so alarmed by this that I say to them privately, 'He doesn't have long, does he?' They say, as does everyone whom we quiz on the length of time left, 'We cannot say. You just never know.' And they don't.

Two new large, loud oxygen concentrator machines arrive, with huge four-metre-long clear plastic tubes attached to them so you can move around relatively freely; long white tanks of oxygen that we rename the milk bottles; masks; cannulas … truly you are spoilt. Almost immediately you are on oxygen 24/7. The tubes become something I trip over – a health-and-safety hazard if ever there was one. One Sunday lunch in the future a tube will cause me to trip and drop a roast chicken on the floor as I bring it to the table. We still eat it – though the plate doesn't survive.

Despite your depleted state, you continue to make your radio shows. I let your executive producer Paul Thomas know what has happened. He is deeply sensitive, telling me

I must keep him in the picture because no one wants to push you too hard. They are remote, so they cannot judge when you should stop. That is being left to me. Liz Barnes, your incredibly patient producer, becomes even more patient. Of course, you want to go on broadcasting, but the shows start taking a lot longer to record. You get yourself to your den, I bring coffee and a Berocca, you print out all your notes, Liz appears on FaceTime and slowly you record the links. You lift your voice, digging deep. The links cannot be too long as you get breathless. 'Take your time, Johnnie,' Liz will say over and again. Some days the time you need to take is two days. You will do hour one on the first day, hour two on the next. It wipes you out, but you know that you have to keep going because if you stop, it's like saying you've given up, that the game of both broadcasting and life is over. This is one of those times when you reveal to me your inordinate strength of character.

Your voice is your livelihood. You know how you should sound, and you know that you don't sound like a robust Johnnie Walker anymore. The breathlessness cannot be completely hidden. That said, Paul gives your voice recordings a huge level of treatment before they are broadcast. These include a de-reverb plug to remove the room reflections from your den, a very heavy dose of AI noise reduction to reduce the wind sound from the oxygen concentrator, a 'soothe' plug to reduce any whistle from your teeth, some standard compression and 'limiting' to make sure your voice has broadcast energy, and finally a good bit of equalisation (EQ) to remove some of the 'mud' and put some air into the top end. You are now processed. Ultra-processed Walker. You are incredibly impressed by and grateful for Paul's extraordinary 'geekery'.

Radio 2 want to do a special retrospective show about you. Paul was going to come in December. If only he had; it would have been so much easier for you both. He and I get a date in the diary for as soon as we can in January. There is a sense of urgency between him and me to get it done as soon as possible. Just in case … I collect him from Gillingham train station. He is with us for the whole day, interviewing you in chunks so that you can have a breather in between. He is moved by seeing you in such a state. He last saw you in the studio on NYE when you were still able to strut – almost. You must seem so declined to him, and in just a few weeks. Paul has thought deeply about the songs you might choose. He almost nails it. He's done his research thoroughly and I can see he truly cares about you and the programme he's making. He's clearly very good at interviewing you, as he goes on to make a great tribute show. The end of that show makes me cry when I hear the final edit before transmission. While the three of us have lunch together you ask bluntly, 'Is this for when I'm dead or before?' The answer is 'both'. As it happens the reaction when it does play out at Easter is huge – and probably will be again when you're *brown bread*.

Paul is the first of many guests that start arriving. I find myself doing a lot of catering, worrying about what people will eat, trying to find time to get out and shop. I am suddenly time poor. You have gone from helping out here and there with the dishwasher and running the cars to being rendered totally useless domestically. What is more, I'm suddenly doing so much extra for you — early-morning tea and oatcake, two stages of breakfast, dressing you, emptying the pee bottle, making your bed, running around turning oxygen machines on and off as you move around, a lot more laundry as the new drugs affect your insides, juggling medical appointments and equipment arriving, washing your feet and your hair, organising and administering your pills, undressing you before bed, tucking you in, wishing you goodnight while wondering if it is the final time I'm wishing you goodnight.

The change to both our lives is dramatic, sudden and all encompassing. In the first six weeks of our new regime, I think you are going to die very soon. I certainly do not think you will make your birthday at the end of March. I cry every day. I am overwhelmed. I am struggling to cope. Fortunately, at this point very few people know you are unwell so contact from the outside world is as yet containable.

The thing I realise after some weeks is that part of my emotional breakdown is that I am grieving for our life together. It's anticipatory grief. We are never, ever going to go out anywhere ever again. I live for holidays, films and theatre, and going to restaurants — it's all I want to do. To go and do these things with you. And while, yes, you are still here with me at home, we won't ever do any of those fun things together. Ever again. It's unimaginable to think that our pizza together at the Grosvenor Arms in Hindon was our last date.

Jane, of the gang of six and my closest girlfriend in Dorset, is full of concern and wants me to go to the doctor to get an antidepressant. I think that would make me a failure. I am not depressed, I'm just not coping because I am overwhelmed. I resist for weeks. As it happens it is the greatest gift she has ever given me. I start them on 1 March and while the first four days are grim, by week two they start to make a difference. I am myself again. The Tiggy I used to be before I even met you. I feel like a survivor, not a victim. It's a huge step forward. I may never stop taking them! I am also offered counselling. I'm touched that there is such a level of care for the carer now. It wasn't like that twenty-one years ago when you had cancer. Nonetheless, I respond that I am fine. 'I am not depressed,' I stress, hoping that will be written in my notes. 'I am simply exhausted and overwhelmed.' I really couldn't pile having to talk about myself for an hour a week on top of everything else I have to do. Besides, I really don't want to leave you alone any more than I have to.

To get up and down the corridor from your room to the sitting room is getting so hard for you. You have to sit down after ten feet to regain your breath. It's painful to watch. You have been assessed and told you can have a wheelchair, but there's a wait. We have a mobility shop nearby in

Ludwell – Freedom Mobility. I go in there and find a treasure trove of items for the elderly and infirm, from wide slippers with Velcro fastenings to mobility vehicles. They have a wheelchair they rent out for £5 a day. A new form of car hire for us. I take a photo and share it with you. You agree it's a good idea, though I can see there's resistance in you. It's a step, isn't it? A step towards being less able, less of the virile man you have always been. It would just be there for back-up, I suggest.

I pick it up just after I collect your Australian grandson James (son of Sam) and his girlfriend, Holly, from the train station on 7 February. They have come to London for two weeks to stay in our Primrose Hill flat while we still have it. James was a teenager when we last saw him five years ago; now he's a young handsome hunk of a man. He brings in glamorous Holly and the black wheelchair as he arrives. You greet James warmly and within seconds jump into your new chariot – and that's it. Never again will you walk anywhere. The difference it makes to your life is massive. And how different our home looks as I roll up all the rugs decorating our wooden floors.

Something wonderful happens with James's visit. Your daughter Beth, James's aunt, wants to see him too. Because we can only cope with James and Holly staying one night as you're feeling so bad, Beth and her partner, Rachael, come to supper at ours that night. I do a traditional roast chicken and all the trimmings. We have a great dinner. You, unbelievably, pull yourself up the way you do for a show, regaling everyone with great showbiz stories, delighting James and Holly, and amusing us all. There is laughter, joy and love. Oh, the power of good food and wine! It is a night many of us will remember. The final time your family break bread together around our table, and probably the final time you will hold court with such aplomb. I'm so happy you gave James that memory of you.

The wheelchair is a blessing for you, a curse for me. You need to be pushed everywhere. I am well and truly house-bound with you in case you need an urgent trip to the loo. I feel the tension rising in me. I am dressing you, nursing you, pushing you. I feel stress quite keenly. I am on edge most of the time. One afternoon I need to pop to Boots for a prescription – thirty minutes, tops. I return to a sitting room in chaos. 'What's happened?' I ask, bemused. You needed to pee. You tried unsuccessfully to move yourself in the wheelchair. The result was a car crash, an accidental repositioning of furniture and you having to use your water bottle as a receptacle. After that we order a new pee bottle and I try to get the ball rolling on an electric wheelchair.

What a difference the electric wheelchair, 'Quickie', makes – to both of us. Because you love driving, you turn circles and go up and down the corridor. We both feel a sense of freedom. How you love to nip down to your den to do prep on your radio shows, or nip over to your table to get a box of tissues. You nip a lot. I just have to swap over your oxygen machines if you go from one end of our long house to the other. Each time I get the full blast of the piercing, hateful *BEEEEEP* as the new oxygen machine offensively and loudly switches on. And then the constant drone of the motor. Conversely, when I switch the machine off it shudders and comes to a blissful, silent halt.

Your boss Helen Thomas wants to visit. You are the reason she's at Radio 2 as you brought her in from Radio 4 to be your *Drivetime* producer. Your connection goes deep, especially for her. She loves all her presenters, but without doubt she has a soft spot for you as you were her first at Radio 2. She's always credited you with increasing her music knowledge. I have a new routine of collecting visitors from Gillingham station, bringing them back and making lunch while they chat with you. The car is a great place for Helen and me to have an honest conversation. We like and respect each other a lot, but we don't always agree. I say to her that you don't really have an ego. She snorts with laughter, saying you so do – that all her presenters do. They wouldn't be presenters without it. Well, maybe that's true, but I do think yours is under control and is one of the reasons you are so loved. I reflect on a recent conversation with Bob Harris, who called to see how I'm doing. He's been put on standby in case you stop broadcasting. 'When Johnnie stops are you getting the gig, Bob?' I ask, being nosey and territorial.

'Oh, I think so, don't you?' Now that, to me, is a healthy presenter's ego. You wouldn't say that. You wouldn't even think it. You have humility running through your veins.

Helen's visit is lovely. From the moment she comes through the door she brings in her fantastic energy and I see you respond. I realise that what you love to do now is reminisce, and you two have so many stories and laughs to share.

Before she leaves I ask if she wants a photo of the two of you together. She is thrilled. She's also incredibly photogenic. Of the many visitors we are to receive over the coming months, Helen's visit stays with me as one of the most special because, after me, she probably knows the real you as well as anyone else, and has been so instrumental and supportive in our lives. In the car going back to the station I touch her arm. 'Are you OK?' I ask, concerned. I'm glad I took that photo. It's hard for people saying goodbye to you. You've been a truly significant person in her life. I know that when I return home you will be exhausted, but relieved and happy to have seen her. I am right.

A commode. Your mother died on one, and recently your sister fell off hers and subsequently died. There's no two ways about it, you are damned resistant to having one in your room at night, but after an accident, as you can no longer rush to the loo, I suggest the time is right. You are deaf to my suggestion. Then one day, when a district nurse is visiting, I come into your room to find her sitting on your bed talking very sensitively to you. She looks up at me and smiles, telling me you have agreed to one.

I feel a sense of embarrassment when it's delivered. To the man dropping it off it's all part of the norm. For me, it is a sign of further decline. A nudge closer to the end. He shows me the locks on the wheels. The bucket underneath the plastic removable seat I discover for myself, which – I will later learn to my cost – needs to be pushed very firmly all the way in to protect the carpet beneath. You deny its existence and will not let it in your room. For some reason I park it in the guest bedroom, which also acts as my study. I have to avoid Zoom calls in there.

Its arrival is shortly before I go away on a recce to Sardinia for my film. I have to go and see the Mamuthones festival, as I've written it into my script without having experienced it. I have no choice but to go now.

Have I ever cried as much as when I leave you? I cannot speak the word 'goodbye' as I am sobbing too much. I am convinced I will never see you again. The pain is so great, the fear so deep, that I cry for over an hour in the taxi. The poor driver.

I have created a full schedule of the people who will care for you while I am gone. Our friend Claire, former godmother of Darcey Dog, has offered to do the overnights. She arrives each evening to find that a different set of friends has been round to bring you dinner and get you pissed. It's party time every night I'm gone, and Claire picks up the pieces. But she also does something else rather magical: she brings the commode into your room at night. She takes the fear and shame away. Together, you rename it 'the Alien'.

Reading the papers every day on your iPad as you do, you furnish me with all sorts of news that I don't get time to discover while I'm away. There is one piece of news that delights you. There's almost a sense of pride behind it. 'Do you know what you have done?' you ask me. 'You have put Vinted into profit for the first time.' This is a fact you share gleefully with every guest who comes round over the next few weeks.

It's true. Since you only wear jogging pants and incredibly casual wear these days, it struck me that some of your formal clothes clogging up both your and my wardrobes were surplus to requirement. You said you'd never wear them again, so they should go. And thus, my market stall began. It started with your dressing-up gear – the ghastly Seventies-style shirt and waistcoat that you wore at the Goodwood Revival festival when they recreated a radio studio in which you DJed. They go quickly. I move on to any lace-up trainers, since you can't do laces any more. Many of these are unworn and lucky men around the country are suddenly wearing almost-new HOFF trainers for a fraction of their original cost.

As you lie in bed I stand by your wardrobe pulling out individual items. 'Keep!' or 'Go!' are your commands. You are very certain in your choices. The goers are removed to my study and hung up on my stall. I photograph them, upload them to the app, put in the relevant info and off they go.

Offers come in. 'Duke, someone wants to offer £20 on the cowboy boots.' You are part of the process. You give a yay or nay to offers, and we find this hilarious. When we get to the really flash items you get more interested: the tailor-made three-piece country suit; the Barbour jackets; the Paul

Smith linen suit. Some I find hard to part with as I wrap them in tissue. None more so than your Richard James teal corduroy velvet suit. I think it is the best item you have ever bought. Richard James himself sold it to you in his Savile Row shop. My description reads: 'OK, peacocks – this is the best suit I've ever seen my husband in. Just style and gorgeousness in abundance.' I put it on for £140 – a big price on Vinted. Several men are in touch for exact measurements, sad that they are just too big, short or fat for it. It finally sells for the asking price to a man who sadly gives no feedback. Maybe he's a dealer and sold it on to someone else for considerably more. I hope wherever that beautiful bit of schmutter ended up, it is loved. I still miss it.

When my stall is empty I return to your wardrobe. 'You'll never wear this again,' I say, holding up a brown Gant cord jacket. You agree and make other suggestions. You suggest things that I'd have given to the charity shop, like a Stone Roses T-shirt – and you are right. You have a great sense of what has value.

Part of this is amusement, part of it is lightening our load so we feel less encumbered with 'stuff', but for me it is getting things done and sorted before I am grieving, when I won't see any joy in Vinted. In a way it's me preparing my path forward. If I sort this stuff now, I will have more time to grieve. When you become an experienced market trader on Vinted you quickly learn several things: get the price right; photography is key; women don't buy, they just like. Men are fantastic decisive buyers; sell to them at weekends

– they're bored. Package nicely. Despatch immediately. Putting in a note always goes down well. Labels sell. Non-labels are much harder to shift.

One weekend I make over £500. It brings us enormous amusement. In a pretty small life where you cannot leave your own four walls, this connection with the outside world seems fun. I keep telling you that we're sharing the love of all the beautiful, stylish clothes you have bought over the years. For, yes, my Duke, you have always been considered by my friends a snappy dresser and a darned good clothes horse.

In two months I take £1,327 – 90 per cent of which comes from your clothes. It's the start of the booze fund at your wake – a fund you consider very important, as you really want our friends and family to enjoy your send-off.

I've earned a night out. It's mid-April and I'm starting to suffer from cabin fever. The perfect excuse is needing to write a column for *Dorset Magazine*, and for that I simply HAVE to attend a talk by food writer Angela Clutton at nearby café Sorelle. I invite my friend Annabel to come with me. 'Stay out as long as you want,' you assure me. I prepare your supper and leave it out for you. I am possibly the most excited person at the event – I am OUT! – but the talk is over by 8 p.m. I'm crestfallen, so I suggest to Annabel a drink at the Grosvenor Arms. I let you know, and not only are you delighted that I want to stay out, but you ask if I can bring you back a margarita. This is the oddest request, but I'm used to odd requests from you. The bar girl, wanting to make you happy, asks her manager, but sadly they are not allowed to sell take-away alcohol. You look at me appalled when I return home empty-handed. I notice your untouched supper. 'Where's my pizza?' you ask, disconsolate. Never before have I twigged that a margarita/ margherita can be both drunk and eaten. It wasn't such an odd request after all, but you are disappointed, which I make worse by finding the misunderstanding incredibly funny. You do not at all. I make a note that you need a take-away pizza – soon.

THEN

HERE COMES
THE WEEKEND

I feel I met you too late. Of course, I met you when I should, but it came right at the end of your radio peak. I knew you for just your final couple of years on *Drivetime* (and you were off for almost a year of that). It was an incredible show, exactly what the BBC should broadcast. It had intelligence, warmth, entertainment, good music and a fabulous magazine approach with business news, sports, traffic and a daily guest. People would say how they would sit in their car in their driveway to hear the end of your interviews because they were so good. If an author came on, by the end of the evening their book was number one on Amazon. The influence and effect you had on your 7 million listeners was amazing. I loved watching you at work. You were a master in the studio, in total control, fully under-standing what the listener wanted, what questions you should ask, what to play next, and of course all the knobs and faders. Masterful.

While I know it was hard on your energy after the cancer, with you staying in bed until the afternoon before going into the studio, you were still doing great shows on what had been your slot for seven years. When you drove down to our Dorset cottage one Friday evening in 2005 to tell me you were being taken off *Drivetime* you were devastated. Completely and utterly. It was just about the worst bit of news you received in our time together, second only to the cancer diagnosis. Not only did you love that show and your connection with the listeners, but you knew your peak was over. The controller, Lesley Douglas, needed you to make way for Chris Evans. Chris is a very clever, creative, energetic broadcaster. But he wasn't you. And ironically, you told me it was the second time in your career you were being fired to make way for him. It felt like Chris was your nemesis, and you found it hard to feel anything but blatant annoyance towards him. (No wonder I was uncharacteristically icy with him when we met a year after he had taken over *Drivetime*. I was actually told by Bob Shennan, the new controller, to go easy on Chris, that it wasn't his fault. I was quite amused at the thought of such a huge presenter being affected by me, the loyal wife!) Your dream, if you don't mind me sharing, was that you would get the *Breakfast Show* when Terry Wogan stopped. You did three months a year as cover, and you LOVED it. How you enjoyed giving people a positive start to their day. You would get all the team to stand at the window just before 7 a.m., open your arms and make a daily affirmation: 'We open our arms to all the abundances the universe has to offer ...' and off you would go with a brilliant show. What we didn't know was that Chris had been brought in to Radio 2 specifically to take over that show when Terry stopped. A double whammy. You were collateral damage of management decisions.

Without a doubt, for you, me and millions of listeners, it was the first of many decisions Radio 2 took that upset its traditional, and extremely loyal, older audience. You always said, the glory days of the network were when Terry got people to work, you got them home, and in between Ken Bruce, Jeremy Vine and Steve Wright did fabulous shows. But times move on, and the management direction has been to attract younger listeners and be inclusive of female presenters.

It took you at least five years to get over the upset of losing your beloved show. You were moved to Sundays – the worst day of the week as you can't enjoy Saturday evenings, and so the concept of the weekend is pretty much taken from you. And business still takes place Monday to Friday – pluggers, requests for appearances and dedications, plus interviews for the show – so it feels like there's never a break or a down day. When at the start of 2019 you were given the *Rock Show* on Saturday nights it really was curtains for any sort of normal social life.

I would come up to the London flat with you to keep you company (having shifted our life to Dorset after you came off *Drivetime*). I remember the evening you struggled into the flat after 10 p.m., leaning on the big retro radiator as if you couldn't manage any more steps into the flat, saying this was no way for a man in his seventies to live. You were exhausted.

While Sundays started with a lame attempt at a spiritual show, in 2006 it became *Sounds of the 70s*. It was sad that your old friend and Cockney Rebel frontman Steve Harley lost that gig to you, but as he was always indebted to you for launching his music career, he bore no ill will and your friendship continued until his untimely death. It was a great decade for you to do, even though you had always hankered after the Sixties show (Bob Shennan astutely asked me if it was the decade you wanted or the time slot – Saturday morning). It upset you that you weren't playing new music, but as one of your former producers, Paul Rodgers, said, it was new music to the younger generation. It played to your strengths and knowledge, but with it something died in you – that desire to find new music that you could share on-air. You'd always been so proud of that – and so respected and known for that.

It wasn't long after you lost *Drivetime* that an envelope arrived from Number 10. 'If it's an invitation from Tony Blair, we're not bloody going.' It was, in fact, an invitation to receive an MBE. You didn't have to think about it. You knew your parents would have been proud, and mine still could be. And they were. It's very special to go to Buckingham Palace to receive this honour. Sam, Beth and I all attended with you. The then Prince Charles shook your hand and said, 'I suppose you're all going out for a jolly good lunch?' And he was right – we had a great one at Elena's L'Etoile in Charlotte Street. To my recollection that's the only time the four of us had a 'family' event together, as not long afterwards Sam and his wife, Jules, moved to Singapore. This was such a sad loss for you. Not only were you losing your 'son and heir', as you liked to call him, but your grandson, sweet baby James, too.

We took a major decision about our lifestyle at this time. You were finding London too noisy and busy, and suggested we move to a big house in the country. 'Are you sure, Johnnie?' That question again. I said how we could never afford to return to such an amazing apartment in London again if we left. You were sure. Absolutely certain. Yet when we sold that beautiful flat in Marylebone and bought a much smaller pied-à-terre near the BBC, *and* a bloody great farmhouse in Dorset, you weren't sure. You spent as much time as you could at the new London flat, agreeing to interviews any day of the week to have an excuse to be up there. I, meanwhile, was floating around a large – and haunted – five-bedroom house, wondering what the hell I was doing there and feeling very at sea. Once, as you were about to drive back to London, I even ran down the drive and lay across it so you couldn't leave. What did you do? You stopped the car, laughed your head off and took a photo of me.

It was while I was at that house, alone, that your biography came out in 2007. It was possibly because I was unhappy or because the ghost, 'Old Sod' (a name we learned from the previous owners), was giving me a hard time, banging doors at night, that I fell ill. I got flu – real flu – and was bedridden for two weeks. When I felt strong enough I opened the copy you had dedicated to me and started reading. Oh my God, Johnnie, I was horrified. Your life consisted of one situation after another when you trashed it. That reel-to-reel recorder you spent months saving for when you were a teenager and then threw it out of the window. Your rebellious nature at work; walking out of amazing jobs because of the music policy; living in a car with Sam when he was a little boy because you had no money. By the time I got to the part when you met me, I just thought, *WHAT have I done?* If I'd read that book first, I would not have married you!

You were unable to come home and look after me while I had flu, as there were important people to interview, but you were concerned enough to arrange for your friend Angela Donovan to come down with her husband and another friend, supposedly to give me a healing. I couldn't understand why it would take three people to get rid of my flu, and when they arrived, Angela walked into the room with an extraordinary hunched gait, like the Hunchback of Notre-Dame. I couldn't think what was up with her, but it turned out she was channelling Old Sod, the ghost! Within minutes I found myself sitting with you and those three, taking part in an exorcism of our house! Really, as events go, this was up there with the most extraordinary. I was totally freaked out, and then you all said you had to go. 'Johnnie,' I begged, 'please don't leave me. PLEASE.' You said you had to, you had an important dinner in London, so you lit a fire in my snug, told me to wait in there and promised me you'd be home by 2 a.m. You all left and, disconsolate, I went into my snug. The window was shut, the fire was lit – and there on my desk was a huge black crow, crowing. I have never been so scared. There was no way on God's earth I was staying in that house – we sold it six months later.

Next, we moved to a beautiful converted granary surrounded by fields. However, it was east of Salisbury, far from our patch in Dorset where all our friends were. The big lesson we learned there was that friends (and good pubs) really do make a home. We were like fish out of water. There was one upside – apart from getting our puppy, Darcey, and meeting Sarah, who became our right-hand woman – we were much nearer to Radio Solent, the local BBC radio station for Hampshire, Dorset and the Isle of Wight.

You asked me to call the controller there to see if you could have a look around. Part of you hoped that you might be able to do some of your Sunday shows from there to save driving up to London so often. So I called the managing editor Mia Costello, who seemed only too delighted for you to visit. We had a great chat on the phone, and she asked if I would come too. We were duly shown around their studios, and given the full guest-of-honour treatment. Just as we were about to leave Mia leaned over to me and said, 'You have a great voice for radio. I knew it when we spoke on the phone. It's why I wanted you to come.' Instantly, she offered us a two-hander weekly show! You were delighted, and I was flattered. When I put this to the then controller of Radio 2, Lewis Carnie, his response was immediate:

'Johnnie is a radio legend. He is NOT doing local radio.' You were annoyed, of course, but Mia took the news on the chin, and instead offered to train me up.

The Radio Solent *Breakfast Show* presenter Julian Clegg was given the task of showing me how to run a desk and speak into the mic, and before long I was doing stand-in on the *Early Breakfast* shows. It was fabulous to have the opportunity, but oh, how AWFUL it was to get up at 3.30 a.m. to be ready to take the station on-air at 5 a.m. How do people do that every day? I would get many texts from you, of course, giving me your expert tips. 'Put your fader up! Speak louder! Come out of the song now!' It was such a rock to have you there. The other thing you taught me was 'doors to manual'. For you, there had to be a way to get out of the set programmed music and put on a CD of your own choosing. You made sure I knew how to do that. I learned then that you and I have one big similarity – we are both obstinate about our music choices. After all, why do it if it's not for sharing the music you love? In the end I did twenty-five shows, both in the week and on Saturdays, which were later and involved a newspaper review, which was much more fun. Honestly, we were always so grateful to Mia for giving me the opportunity, and very sad when she moved on some months later, as the new man in charge certainly did not want Johnnie Walker's 'missus' doing any shows on his watch.

Our next move in 2009 was to Shaftesbury, back in our beloved Dorset, back near our friends and favourite pubs.

And there we stayed, doing up one house after another. By this stage you were used to your weekend working. You had found your new rhythm and had finally got over the upset of coming off *Drivetime* and not getting *Breakfast*.

A number of years later, in 2018, I made another foray into radio, and when it came to my voice behind a mic you were nothing but complimentary. You loved it. So when I told you I'd got myself a weekly radio show at community radio station Abbey 104 in Sherborne, you were delighted, and when it went out you were actually impressed. I've always liked a magazine-style show, as you had on *Drivetime*. I played great music because I could play whatever I wanted. (Not being cocky, but you always loved my taste in music. It was slightly different to yours – a bit younger, certainly – but good enough for you to pick my brains each week for ideas for your own show.) My magazine features included a weekly arts round-up of TV and film, a guest interview – you and Leo Sayer being my top two bookings – and 'Tiggy's Kitchen'. I really believe in spreading the word about home-cooked, healthy food, so each week I would cook a dish at home and then get you to try it, recording as I went. While you weren't exactly Stanley Tucci in your praise, you did generally react well to my efforts, though a few months in, when I created an okra sensation, you just went 'Yuk!' on tasting it. How we laughed! It was great radio.

I loved doing that show. I had listeners around the world (thanks to being your wife), and the great thing is, they stayed with me for the entire year that I did it. The show was called *Afternoon Delight* and, yes, my opening jingle was the corny song of the same name.

A year later, in 2019, one thing that could happen because of your weekend shift was the *Sounds of the 70s Live* tour. This consisted of you talking about the decade, interspersed with live renditions of some of your favourite songs of the decade. Leo Green was the musical director, and Damien Edwards the lead singer. It was a great show, and the audience loved it, but your health was fading by then, having already been diagnosed with IPF. You had been on intravenous steroids for a week to give you strength, but all it had done was bloat you (and led to me cheekily re-naming you Bloaty McBoatface). The band also did Tony Blackburn's *Sounds of the 60s* tour. We would hear that Tony was dancing every night and doing combat rolls on stage. Really?! It was all you could do to sit on a stool and make it to the end of the evening. After the sixth show you lay on the sofa in your dressing room. 'Please tell me that was the last one.' I had to break the news that there were sixteen more. It was too much for you. Your sister Maureen came to that show, and in her firm, big-sisterly way she said to me, 'He's not well. He needs to take care and slow down, or else …'

In the background, fans from Scotland and the North were complaining that you had no dates up there. You felt bad about it, but you just weren't well enough to do such long journeys and return for your weekend shows. This was not something we could say publicly because everyone in showbiz has to keep up the impression that they are fit, well and ready to broadcast.

You had various well-respected agents during our time together, but none of them brought you any extra work. You were never comfortable with TV as you were afraid of the camera lens seeing into you, plus, by your own admission, you were bloody lazy. So they didn't have much to work with. The result was that, as my commercials producing career had ended, I could support you and became your agent and manager. I was free, and though I say so myself, I am an amazing scheduler and full of ideas. On the one hand this was a brilliant solution. On the other, it wasn't. My life became focused around you, your career and trying to keep you healthy. At meals we would talk shop. Our life became the business of you and your diary: you being on-air, you doing interviews, you doing talks on a Saga cruise, you attending this or that, you doing tours and shows.

Without any doubt, the successful career girl I once was had taken a step back. I was now the main support for the Johnnie Walker show. And while I enjoyed learning about the radio world (and doing some myself), my own creative and financial needs were not met. Where once I had earned more than you ever did, now I took a small stipend from the business. Of course, you always said, 'Pay yourself more, Duch,' but you never were great at financial realities. No longer did I buy designer clothes or go to fancy restaurants – but in all fairness, nor did I need to. What I missed was the excitement of a new creative project and working with my production team and crews, feeling I could make a real contribution in my own right, not just as the back-up crew to you.

My father would reassure me that I was doing the most important job that I could. 'Behind every great man stands an even greater woman' and similar platitudes would flow from him whenever I complained to him privately about my lack of fulfilment. To my father you had an enormously important role in society, making millions of people happy. As he saw it, it was a greater use of my time and skills to keep you going than making commercials to sell things people didn't want or need. He was a wise man who believed in duty. 'What can we do for others?' seemed to be our family motto.

My mother, too, was always concerned that I was looking after you. When once I said I was going to New York for the weekend she simply replied, 'But what about Johnnie? Who's going to look after him?' It was incomprehensible to her that you could survive alone for four days. Indeed, she herself took this responsibility to heart. Where once I had been the central character and driving force in my family, I was gradually pushed away. No longer did my mother want shopping days with me or a day out to an art gallery. She'd always say, 'But, darling – you're SO busy,' and without me even realising it, a huge separation was occurring. I was so conditioned to be a good wife, to put my needs last. Indeed – to have NO needs. I feel I was the last of a generation of women who did not demand their own rights to a career or freedom. I admire and almost envy the women of the generation after me. I mean, I didn't even have kids, I just had you! But somehow a life in the public ear and eye is demanding. And you had already been so ill. Alone, you weren't great at coping. We both knew that. Just think back to how you lived in that terrible flat when I met you. As I always say, you were my destiny, and I know I kept you broadcasting for many more years than you would have done without me. This gives me comfort and an understanding of my decisions. That said, I will never marry again. I'm just no good at it. I mean, I am good for the man. I'm brilliant! But I get lost at my own expense, and I never, ever want to do that again.

I ran every element of our lives, business and domestic. You just had to do the shows. (And even then, you'd ask me for song suggestions!) You were as happy as Larry. You didn't have any stress. I did. When we had an almighty six-year fight with HMRC about IR35 (the off-payroll working rules) I spent much of my nervous energy dealing with our accountants, lawyers and the BBC to get it resolved. It was only in 2023 when I sent my accountant a letter stating that you were now under palliative care, which he shared with HMRC, that they finally backed down. After many thousands of pounds of fees, and a lot of time and effort, that particular nightmare was over, but the fact is, I have done a lot of fighting for you. A lot.

So, for balance, let's remember something particularly wonderful about being involved with your career:

lockdown. The most magical few months of our marriage. Not only did it give me the perfect reason to cancel the remains of the *Sounds of the 70s Live* tour, but also this time most certainly extended your life, as you no longer had the exhaustion of schlepping up and down to London each week. Everyone over seventy was banished from BBC Studios as a safety measure, so you now had to do your show from the garden room of our beautiful Georgian farmhouse that we'd renovated in St James, Shaftesbury. You called your friend Rodney Wayman, who lives locally and had a business in recording equipment – Solid State Sound. He ran to your rescue, getting a RØDECaster mini production studio and mics set up.

Coincidentally, you also fell terribly ill at that time. You had already been diagnosed with IPF the previous summer of 2019, but you were so ill that, with the sense of medical panic across the country, it was assumed you had the dreaded Covid already – which in those first weeks was considered a death sentence. The GP told me to call your respiratory consultant, Rohan Mehta, and ask if you would be put on a ventilator if you went into Salisbury District Hospital. At that point a ventilator was considered the only hope for Covid survival. While he was hugely sympathetic about you being so ill, he was honest, which I will always be grateful for. He said you would not be put on a ventilator. My guess is that younger and healthier patients would be put on them long before someone in your already weak predicament. You would be put on a CPAP machine on a small ward, and I would almost certainly never see you again. I was gulping down uncontrollable tears.

I called the GP again. This time I spoke to Dr Perkins. 'Look, what if it's a chest infection?' I argued. 'Why don't we just stuff him with antibiotics just in case?' She agreed completely and within the hour a volunteer was at our front door with the drugs. When I took these to you I spoke in no uncertain terms: 'Johnnie, there's two lots of antibiotics here and you are going to take them all, no questions, because right now you are fighting for your life. Understood?' You nodded compliantly and opened your mouth. As it happens, Dr Perkins and I were right.

However, you were too knackered and ill to do your show alone. Knowing that you had successfully thrust me in front of a mic on the *Radio 2 Breakfast Show* a couple of times, and that I'd done my summer of *Early Breakfast* fill-ins on Radio Solent, as well as my own weekly afternoon radio show at Abbey 104 for the previous year, you felt safe with me sharing the airwaves with you. You asked Lee Thompson, your then producer, if it would be OK to use me on this one show. Lee said it would be fine. Good man! No one asked Helen Thomas, who was now the controller of Radio 2, because you knew she would say no, so you just did it – you and Lee, dicing with the management. After the show went out you called Lee to ask about the reaction. He was amazed. There were even more emails than usual – everyone had loved me being on with you! So we did it again, and again. You loved it. Lee loved it. The listeners loved it. And I loved it. But one person did not. Helen. We were given the impression that she hated it. You say it was because you never asked her; she says it was because the format of the *Sounds of ...* shows is a single presenter. It was the one big stand-off you and she had, but it could not be argued; at this extraordinary time, we were replicating the locked-down lives of so many people around the country. You claim I made you speak in a different way – I was your bounce, as Sally Traffic had once been – and it is no exaggeration to say that you adored having me on the show. We recorded the links on a Tuesday, and I gave up each of those days, helping you select songs, requests and subject matters. I would prep the room with blankets and cushions to soak up the sound, which would later be treated by executive producer Paul Thomas with his computer 'add-ons' to improve the quality of your voice. Lee was brilliant with me; he gave me the reins but didn't let me slip up. And you, Johnnie – nothing was ever better than doing radio with you, the master. I was like Darcey Dog looking up to you with awe and respect. You were the top dog, and I was next to you, wagging my tail. Happy, happy days.

However, the fact that Helen wasn't happy meant that all was not well. A phone call with her had me in tears. 'I love you, Tigs, but this is *Sounds of the 70s* and you don't belong on this show ...' she told me. So after five months, during which I had worked for absolutely nothing yet felt I had made a big contribution to lockdown, I stood down.

You were very upset that I stopped, feeling that the show lacked something without me, and you really disliked going back to pre-records alone. If it wasn't this show, you really wanted to do another one with me – as Mia Costello had suggested years before. 'They spend their lives trying to create on-air chemistry with presenters – and failing – yet we have it in spades,' you said. Oh, you were angry. We did a few specials together for Boom Radio, but the prize you were after was the BBC. We both knew it would never happen, so I say, let's be grateful for those five months. To this day I have people telling me how they loved it and how much it improved their lockdowns. And that, for me, is *almost* gratitude enough.

One great result of doing these shows was that I was contacted by Helen Stiles, the editor of *Dorset Magazine*. She said she liked my 'voice', by which she meant the things I said, not my diction, so this was when she asked if I'd be interested in writing a monthly column for her magazine – 'I can't pay much but I'm lovely to work with.' After the first column about us doing the show together, Helen gave me the lead columnist's position, just inside the back cover. She will never know what a boost that was for me – not only me finding my voice again, but just having something to focus on outside of you. Calling my column 'Life's for Living', I now had an excuse to experience all sorts of things in Dorset and write about them, but more than anything, my relationship with Helen became one of great importance to me. It was a lifeline outside of 'us', and she was absolutely right: she has always been lovely to work with.

Our radio stint also led to us doing a series of podcasts together. Northern Irish producer John Daly said he'd love to do something with the two of us. The best idea we could all come up with was that we as a couple should interview other couples, and as I have naturally developed quite an obsession with the person behind other thrones, I loved the idea. John came up with the fabulous title, *Consciously Coupling*, and Hotel Chocolat agreed to sponsor the show to promote their Velvetiser hot chocolate makers. Then we just had to find the right couples. These days everyone with a name is asked to be on every podcast, or so it seems. Usually there is no fee, but Hotel Chocolat, being the decent, ethical company that it is, sent every couple a Velvetiser and a selection of their hot chocolate sachets. Not a bad sweetener!

The interviews mainly happened during the second and third lockdowns, by which time we'd all accepted the quality of Zoom interviews. For us, it was fabulous just to commune with other couples, as we were all so starved of socialising. I was really pleased with the cross-section of guests we had – such a variety of relationships. Clare Balding and Alice Arnold were our first couple; they were delightful, warm, natural and so obviously meant to be together. Plus, Alice had been Clare's carer through cancer, so we had mutual empathy about that. Recording in the early evening, it felt as if we should all have a huge G&T in our hands. I really wanted to meet up with them afterwards and felt I could easily slump down on their sofa for an evening.

Hairy Biker Dave Myers and his wife Lili was a totally different story. She was strong, almost critical of him, while he simpered, amused by her power and soft insults. You asked if she had been afraid of the *Strictly* curse when he had such a memorable time with his dance partner, Karen. Lili looked at you askance: 'Have you seen him in Lycra?' Dave clearly adored her, but I would say she wore the biker trousers.

Damon and Georgie Hill were lovely together, so honest and warm, navigating a life where he was well past his Formula 1 driving years and now presenting. It felt they had come through a lot together – like Georgie's fear of him crashing – and got to a place of calm and deep support for each other. Anton Du Beke was as we expected: hilarious, an entertainer, scarred by his childhood but finding solace in showbiz. The story of him meeting gorgeous Hannah was hilarious, and she laughed delightfully and supportively most of the time. Fellow radio man Ken Bruce with his wife, Kerith, were emotionally the closest to us. I think only you radio men know what it's like to go in day after day and perform no matter your mood or circumstance. They talked openly about caring for their special-needs son, and their warmth and love for him and the family was wonderful. They were very natural, good, honest people, and I felt we got a rare glimpse into Ken's true self. We did twelve really different couples in total, and were often asked which was our favourite episode. It's fair to say we liked them all. Just like parents with their children.

These podcasts scratched your itch, but I would say without doubt that apart from not being asked to do *Desert Island Discs* on Radio 4 and not getting the *Radio 2 Breakfast Show*, your major radio disappointment was that we never had an official radio show together. You knew that we would be great. You knew that we both loved the banter and that we had great chemistry together on-air. It would have been fantastic, and I know we would have made people happy, as we did on the few Boom Radio shows we did together, but it wasn't to be.

After lockdown, when you were allowed access to BBC Studios again, you returned to Wogan House quite a few times. One notable stint was when Tony Blackburn was ill and you agreed to stand in for his *Sounds of the 60s* shows early on Saturday mornings. Very early. I came with you to each one to give my support and hated that alarm going off at 4 a.m., but you were a pro and just got on with it. You really enjoyed doing these shows. You love Sixties music, and the sense that your day was done by 8 a.m. was invigorating. You also appreciated the energy in Wogan House on a Saturday morning. You saw your old mucker Sally Traffic each week and Dermot O'Leary would pop in for a chinwag. So different to a Sunday afternoon, when often the shows either side of yours were pre-recorded so no one else would be in.

It was on one of these Saturdays that you inadvertently took a black sweet out of your mouth and left it on the side of the faders, as you suddenly had to speak. You were always fastidious about leaving a studio spick and span – all rubbish thrown away, cables neat, chair in place – no one more so at the station, I would imagine. So when I heard Michael Ball the next morning, shocked and appalled that someone – a presenter – had left a black Jakemans sweet on the fader, all hell broke loose. He was naming all the possible culprits – Zoe Ball, Rylan Clark, Liza Tarbuck. The one person he said it would not be was Johnnie Walker, because he was far too professional. Presenters called in to plead their innocence, and the mystery for Michael was intense. On hearing this, I went into you, still in bed. 'Duke, is there any chance that you left a Jakemans on the fader yesterday morning?' Your hand went straight to cover your mouth. Your eyes widened. Ashamed, you realised that yes you had. You immediately texted Michael, who received the message while still on-air. To his great shock, *you* – the only one he was sure was innocent – were the guilty party. 'Jakemansgate', which lasted almost an entire show, was solved. Later, when you went to the studio for your *Sounds of the 70s* show, you bumped into Michael holding a bag of Jakemans. His face in that photo was priceless. You just looked like a naughty boy, laughing. Walker, you were caught!

Once Tony was better, your executive producer Paul Thomas shared an idea: to record a show with both you and Tony. A musical face-off: the Sixties versus the Seventies. Everyone liked the idea, and later in 2023 it was recorded. You each took turns to drive the desk, and obviously whoever was driving had the power. I came in for the final half-hour of the recording; you were in the driving seat, and I couldn't believe the stick you were giving Tony, who in return was firing back reposts. 'Oh my God, he's being so rude,' I said to Johnny Kalifornia, who was producing.

'That's nothing. It's been fireworks for two hours,' replied Johnny. I was inwardly concerned that you had been too vicious, and I think you worried about the same, admitting that you gave Tony quite a hard time – I did not envy Johnny having to edit that one. The result was 'Clash of the Pirates', and it was without doubt the funniest radio show I have ever heard on Radio 2. I've no idea if it got any awards, but it truly deserved them – for you, Tony and poor Johnny K, who had to make it broadcastable.

It's a shame that you and Tony didn't do more shows together. Two true radio legends, two pirates – so different in style, but the affection, shared history and respect between you both has always been palpable.

GOING PUBLIC

You seem to have plateaued again. You go down a notch and you stay there until something pushes you down to the next level. During these plateaus we get accustomed to our new normal and adjust our actions and expectations accordingly. I feel safe enough to make a suggestion: I want to interview you. I want to capture this time while I can. You're a radio man, and your voice is your greatest form of communication. I feel deeply that you have things that need to be said, which cannot be said in a Seventies or rock show. That you have thoughts, wisdom, experiences, beliefs that should be shared. I think your listeners would be interested in knowing you better. You agree.

I have a first stab at interviewing you in your den, but you're a bit tetchy. You are an instinctive and brilliant interviewer, and because you find it so easy, you tend to be critical of my interviewing style. 'That is TWO questions. Why are you LOOKING at me like that? What are you trying to ask?' Crikey, you can be tough. On the second attempt I get better answers, but you do seem a tad breathless. I wonder if you are finding this stressful. It's only after twenty minutes that I realise I have failed to switch on your oxygen machine as we came down the corridor to your den. You contain your annoyance at my dreadful nursing, but it doesn't stop me feeling very bad about it.

I dwell on the recordings and realise it's going to be quite a tough edit, especially as the best bits are so breathless. Nevertheless, I am sure there is something usable and interesting there. I call John Daly from OJO Productions, who made our podcast series, and share my hunch that you should be recorded talking about this time. Something tells me it could be of interest, because you are now counting down your weeks and months. It's a profound time and, being the spiritual man that you are, it is surely a poignant and reflective time. I ask if my interview could go up on our podcast site and if it would cost anything. 'It would cost you nothing,' he says in his charming Northern Irish lilt. 'And what is more, if you'd like me to come over [from Belfast] and interview you both, I will. If it would be helpful.' It is such an instinctive, immediate, heartfelt offer. You agree with me that it's a lovely idea. We've only ever known John on Zoom, so just from a purely social aspect it would be great.

I collect John from Gillingham station on 11 April 2024. We chew the cud together first and then set up in your den around a small table. I've no idea what we will talk about, except that I know caring should be part of the discussion, though by no means exclusively. I am alarmed when you start proceedings with a question for me: 'Can I ask you something? … As soon as we returned from honeymoon in India I was diagnosed with cancer, so the vows of in sickness and in health were immediately tested. Now, here we are at the end of my life, when you're having to care for me all over again. You definitely saved my life when I went through cancer – I'm positive I couldn't have made it without you – your love was just so sustaining and gave me so much to look forward to, and your caring for me now makes my days so much better than they would be without you. Do you feel life's been a bit unfair to you, that you've been landed with this person who's required so much care?' My answer is immediate: 'It's been a long journey of caring. I think that's made me wiser, more compassionate, more patient. I think it's been one huge great learning curve.'

I've never been interviewed by you before, but I rather like it. You get straight in there, disarmingly so, demanding an honest response. John sits beside us, quietly listening. He interjects with small questions, gently guiding us down a path. He and I both make sure you don't talk too much, as you quickly run out of puff. He stays the night at a local B&B, not wanting to impose on us. He is a remarkably sensitive and kind man. The next day we record more, and you go off on quite an obscure spiritual angle. The difference between me and John is stark: I say, 'What the hell are you talking about that for?' while he says, 'That's great,

Johnnie. That's great,' knowing full well he won't cut it into the finished programme – he's keeping you positive and engaged. He knows how to handle talent.

We are exhausted after John goes but pleased we did it. He leaves with hours of material, and I feel very glad that he is editing it and not me. I wouldn't know where to start or end, as it was such a broad conversation. When he sends us his first cut a couple of weeks later we are amazed by what he has done. We only mention one thing we would take out. He then drops in music that Fergus Thirlwell composed for our podcast series. It sits in there so well, providing wonderful, delicate punctuation points.

Together we agree that the perfect time to put this on our podcast platform is at the start of Carers Week, on 10 June, but first I suggest that I send it to Helen Thomas at Radio 2, in case she'd like it for BBC Sounds. You say she'll never go for it, and I agree, but John and I both think there's no harm in asking. You are a much-loved member of the Radio 2 family, after all. Helen is a busy woman; the WeTransfer link runs out and I assume nothing will happen, but then, as she goes to a D-Day celebration on a train, she asks for a new link. She listens, and within twenty-four hours not only has she heard it, but so have all the management team at the network. They would love to mark Carers Week and put it on BBC Sounds, with Jeremy Vine topping and tailing it and three songs you spoke about dropped in. They don't want to change a word. They all think it's amazing. I get emails from all the station bigwigs saying how incredible it is. We are most of all thrilled for John and his OJO production company. He gave all his effort, time and travel for free. Now this was being rewarded by having a far larger exposure than our podcast platform would achieve. Over the ten podcasts, we had around 160,000 listens; the scope on BBC Sounds would be so much greater. On top of that, Radio 2 get behind Carers Week wholeheartedly. The entire thing seems to have been blessed with fairy dust, like nothing else I've touched before. A lot of people hear it (the BBC don't release podcast figures, but we are told it was 'a lot', and honestly, everyone we ever meet subsequently seems to have heard it). The social-media posts about it certainly get more likes than I knew possible. Even if we don't quite understand why, people have found it moving.

'HELLO?' I say unwelcomingly, even angrily, down the receiver of the house phone. It says *Anonymous* on the screen. I don't want to speak to them and it's a very bad moment to call, but I feel I have to answer.

It's a bad moment because a very old pirate radio friend of yours has been calling all week. Whenever I've picked up the phone to him he's announced himself with such self-congratulatory confidence that it sounds like he's going to tell me I've just won £5 million on the lottery. 'Hey, Tiggy! It's Keith ...' I cannot handle him, not right now, which is why I've ignored the constantly ringing phone all day. Lisa, my hairdresser, has just arrived – she's doing you a favour, coming in after work to cut your locks. You're being slow and truculent in your room, struggling to put on a T-shirt. 'I will not be hurried!' you yell at me. We are both so frayed at the edges.

Yesterday I was on the Jeremy Vine show at Radio 2. Being the loyal co-patrons of Carers UK as we are, we both agreed that letting the world know about your IPF in Carers Week would help highlight the plight of other unpaid carers. While you've secretly had the disease for almost five years now, these past six months have been on a different level, and we feel that something needs to be said, to explain your ever-shortening links on a show if nothing else.

I was so calm when I walked into the new Radio 2 studio. I love a radio studio for its quiet, still, cut-off-from-the-world space. The way the heavy door closes with a gentle whoosh, shutting out any outside noise, sealing you in, safe. Jeremy was so warm, his hug full of love and concern. The headphones on, the microphone almost at my lips – I felt I could speak gently. I don't really know what I said to him. It just came out, from my heart. He got you on the line, and I pictured you in your wheelchair, your oxygen on Level 9 – it's highest. You sounded dreadful – panting, hoarse, struggling. I am so used to your voice, but hearing it coming down the line into the studio where I was and you should have been got to me, and I started to cry quietly. As Bruce Springsteen sang 'If I Should Fall Behind' (the live MTV Unplugged version) you cried too, as did many listeners. Jeremy came to sit next to me, and Ryan the producer brought in tissues. We continued the conversation, and you were completely on point regarding Carers Week. So very you – not wanting to be the focus, thinking of others, embracing the caring brief and ignoring Jeremy's more personal questions. Nonetheless, Jeremy had a moment of epiphany when he realised you will never come to the station again and that he will never see you again. I could see it hit him.

Messages started coming in immediately to my phone from friends who had no idea how ill you were. I answered them all the way home on the train and have been all day today as well. I balked when Radio 2 sent me the Instagram post they had done. I was filmed and had no idea. Thousands like it. I wish I'd worn more make-up, but I'm pleased I wore my blue linen jacket. The things we see that others don't.

When we sit and make these grand decisions to speak out we forget about the fallout, how overwhelmed by attention we will be. It's as if our energy is stolen from us. All I could do on my return was lie on the sofa. It was a Monday night, but we had red wine with some cheese for supper. I couldn't cook. Not last night. I was spent ...

You are just coming into the kitchen, your T-shirt finally on, heading to the sink so I can wash your hair before Lisa starts cutting. My sleeves are rolled up, the big white jug full of warm water. I know it's difficult for you having a hair wash because you have to stand for over a minute – you have to work yourself up to it – but your hair is so filthy, and Lisa is still quietly waiting.

The phone rings at just the wrong time, but what if it's something important? I am always warm when I answer. Today I am not. I am stressed. I am exhausted.

'HELLO?' I say, my voice telling the caller to fuck off because they are a nuisance and have chosen the worse second of the day to call.

At the other end a calm, kind voice responds: 'Hi, Tiggy. It's *Elton* ...'

I bluster. Try to apologise. Get my knickers in a twist and give up. I hand you the phone and you and Elton John chat away like the two friends of old that you are. Your lives have gone down very separate paths, but Elton wants to make sure he thanks you for all you did for him (like help get his first number one with Kiki Dee – 'Don't Go Breaking My Heart'). You in turn thank him for a truly beautiful deed he did for my brother Simon. Simon was one of the leading goldsmiths in the country, working for Theo Fennell. He made masses of jewellery for Elton, and when he was dying of cancer you asked if Elton would send him a message. You meant a short text. Instead, a video arrived of Elton telling Simon how talented he was and how grateful he was for all the treasured items he had made for him. In truth, Simon saw this on the last conscious day of his life. You upped the ante somewhat and told Elton he saw it in his last hours. Well, it was close enough. And for Simon it was one of the greatest accolades he could have received at the end of his extraordinary career. Elton is a good, kind man, and how typical that you felt you had to give him thanks rather than receiving it.

None of us is perfect, but I am a complete house snob – I don't mind admitting it. I grew up in a beautiful timber-framed farmhouse in Hampshire (which my parents bought for £15,000 in 1966). To me, it was the norm to live in houses with character and draughts. Throughout our marriage I've done up a number of places and I have loved doing it, every house demanding a different approach. Our previous house was a beautiful, small Georgian farmhouse on the edge of Shaftesbury. I remember the day I first drove down St James Street and noticed it. I nearly crashed it was so beautiful. Instantly I knew I wanted to live there, and about eight years later, after an enormous and expensive renovation, we did. I loved that house. I was proud of it. It was our forever home. With the help of my interior designer nephew Mark Lewis, we did a great job – it was even featured in two house magazines. It's also where we did our five months of *Sounds of the 70s* together. Fond memories ...

However, it is also the house where you first fell ill with your lungs. Was it the house? The damp patch that appeared above your bed? The porous nature of stone? Or just bad timing? Whatever it was, it became increasingly difficult for you to walk upstairs. You had to sit in our bedroom chair to recover each time. Your den was on the top floor of the house, and you never went there as it was such an effort.

I realised with a sinking heart in the summer of 2020 that we were going to have to move again – just five years after moving into our 'forever' home – this time to a house with a downstairs bedroom and bathroom. I scoured Rightmove and noticed a development of three one-storey houses being built down the road in Hartgrove. At our first viewing it had a roof and breeze-block walls, but that was all. Taking a huge plunge, we put in an offer and put our house on the market. In December, we swapped Georgian character over three floors for characterless modernity over one floor. It is the greatest gesture of love I have ever shown you. And for you it was the perfect house to move into. Warm, well insulated, and not one step to be found. I would joke with you that if you ever needed a wheelchair, you'd be fine. Your health instantly improved, much to the amazement of your respiratory consultant.

While the house has an impressively huge open-plan main room with vaulted ceilings and incredible views across the rolling Dorset hills up to Shaftesbury, it just is not a pretty house. If I drove past it – which I wouldn't, as it is so tucked away and private – I would almost certainly say I never want to live there. But you love it. You've never been happier in any of our homes. While I have always felt that the house I live in is a reflection of me and part of the definition of who I am, for you it is more functional. In fact, I will go as far as to say I felt ashamed of it when inviting people round. Yes, I AM a house snob. Hands up. Guilty.

So it is the greatest irony of my life that we have never

had more visitors to any house than we have had to this one. And I have never felt as ashamed as the day our friends John and Steph Illsley came over. Their house on the Solent is one of the most amazing homes I have ever been in. It epitomises everything I might once have hoped for: large, relaxed, full of art, homely yet stylish, amazing jaw-dropping views over the water. You can feel the years of family living that have happened there; happiness and contentment drip off the walls. But then John is the bass player of one of the most successful bands ever – Dire Straits – and not a BBC DJ.

As they arrive one Friday afternoon in April, I hear myself apologising for our gaff. I want to hide I feel so ashamed of our modern rabbit hutch. I wish they were visiting our stunning Georgian farmhouse, but that reveals such an insecurity in me. They agree it is the perfect house for you, and they are fabulous guests. Steph arrives with such beautiful goodies: flowers from her garden, a yellow glass vase, sensational homemade cheese biscuits from her mother, Daylesford biscuits … All such thoughtful and perfectly selected offerings. What I love about their visit is that John sits close to you and gets right in there, asking how you are. He is so caring. Why shouldn't a rock star be like that? I am just very touched by how gentle and kind he is with you. And Steph is so warm with me. This visit goes deep into my heart. Steph later writes that they loved their visit and would love to pop over again. It's a lesson for me. Maybe I am not defined by the house I live in.

I have had a policy for the past couple of months that if you want to come and see us for supper, you bring it. Jane and Charles, our besties, came last night, but she too is caring for her ninety-six-year-old mother and just didn't have the time or the culinary joy to make supper, so I suggested fish and chips, which I know they enjoy. We had never had fish and chips at home. You thought it was a great solution, and I was ecstatic when I collected them – £46 to feed four of us, and all I had to do was drive into Shaftesbury. It was an adventure. Despite our limitations, there are still new experiences to be had. Charles brought two bottles of Chablis Premier Cru because he knows it's my favourite white, and because he is a very generous man. Always.

This takeaway experience will not be repeated – our delicate stomachs cannot take it. How glad I am that I persuaded you that 'the Alien' (your commode) should be parked next to your bed last night, stomach-churning though it is for me to deal with this morning. But sadly, it's part of the caring story. Your pee bottle is easy to handle; the commode bucket less so. It makes me retch. But I love you. And I know you feel embarrassed. Possibly ashamed. You mustn't.

Shall we talk about sleep? The fact that as you get more, I get less. You're on about fifteen hours a day to my five. Bedtime is two hours earlier than it used to be, but the summer sun rises early. It's not just the light that wakes me; it's also the wildlife from living in such a rural setting – magpies, a distant cow that wants milking, a cockerel. To add to nature's disturbance, you seem to need more early-morning visits to the loo. You have a thing about the Alien – your mother dying on hers goes deep – so you'd rather climb into your wheelchair and go to the bathroom. You yourself are quiet, but the *beep-beep* and *whir* of your vehicle drives me to distraction. And because you enjoy a bit of precision driving, you go backwards and forwards, backwards and forwards, often getting tied up with your oxygen tube. Tomorrow I will tell you that you HAVE to sleep with the Alien in your room again. *Every night.* We have slipped back from Claire's great triumph in February. You love to get your way, and not sleeping next to it is your only request each bedtime. Now it's no longer negotiable. I'd rather deal with cleaning it than be woken by the noise of you in the corridor. While I respect your neurosis about commodes, I'm afraid I'm playing hardball on this one.

There's something about sleep deprivation: it turns you into a grumpy, self-pitying victim. Oh, you're dying, are you? Well, what about the fact that I've not slept for days? What about me? I'm not a jealous person, but your ability to sleep is beyond enviable.

In my desperation for a proper kip I take a sleeping pill, temazepam, illegally given to me by a friend. I wake eleven and a half hours later. I don't know when I last felt such bliss. I could have slept even longer, but it's a big day. I've actually slept past the call telling me that your hospital bed will arrive in an hour. I have to get you up. I tear the bedding off your small double bed. As I manhandle the mattress and divan into the corridor, a sadness hits me that you will never sleep in a normal bed again. *Another last*, I think. I replace this sadness with a self-congratulatory pride that I managed such a physical job alone and even have time to hoover.

It has been quite a campaign from the nurses for you to get this bed. They think you will find it easier. It has a wonderful selection of controls: you can raise the whole thing up and down, tilt up your back, raise your legs or do both of those at the same time and turn yourself into a sandwich. The mattress is plastic, but I put a padded cover over it so you don't even realise when you get in it. I fear a reaction from you, but you seem pleased. Indeed, you go back to bed as soon as you've recorded your *Rock Show*. It's a licence to rest all day, and you can, you know. Tilt up, tilt down, sleep – eat your heart out. I've ordered a table so you can eat in bed with greater comfort, and so the hospitalisation of our home continues.

I've followed many a diet during our marriage. My propensity is to curve; I'm a juicy pit pony of a girl and have had very few moments in my life where my body was looking good, despite exercising and always eating healthily. One of the things I love about this period is that we are on the 'Keep Johnnie Happy Diet'. I'm pathologically unable to cook unhealthy food, but I have been allowing carbs and I'm trying to cook foods you actually enjoy rather than feel you should eat. I mean, when I went Paleo I did feel for you. The most exciting life ever got was a sweet potato wedge with your white fish and greens.

I am loving this freedom, and the strange thing is that I have lost some weight – but that is probably because I am running around more, or because of the sertraline antidepressant I'm taking. Or perhaps it's the new breakfast regime. You are eating so much less, but I seem incapable of serving you tiny portions. I know that eating and breathing together is hard, but let's be honest, your appetite has shrunk. You eat so slowly, and you look at most dishes I serve you for about thirty seconds before starting, as if you're thinking, *How the hell am I going to attack this?* I sit opposite you feeling guilty for asking you to eat something when it's so hard, even though I have cooked from scratch and with love. Food can heal, but not in your case. You leave a good portion of your plate, and because I grew up in a family of eight where nothing was ever left, I save all your leftovers for my breakfast. Today I am having one spinach falafel, with tahini and crudités (from yesterday's lunch), plus a helping of a courgette and butter bean dish that was last night's supper. An odd combination to kickstart the day.

Today is Wednesday. A great day in my week as Mariana, our cleaner, now comes for an extra couple of hours so I can have a guilt-free morning off. Today, tennis, and meeting a friend called Jan who lost her husband to motor neurone disease last November. She cries every day still. I cannot imagine how awful that must be. I absorb this with dread. As you note over lunch, 'Well, you won't cry every day.'

'You're right,' I agree, 'I won't,' and we both laugh. The truth is, I've no idea how many tears lie within me, or for how long they will flow, but I really couldn't keep it up for that long. Poor Jan. I'm glad she has her sons to comfort her. I wish I had some children who would comfort me when the time comes.

When Claire Allfree from *The Telegraph* interviewed us last week for Saturday's paper I joked with her about post arriving addressed to Johnnie Walker DJ Extraordinaire, Dorset. 'Please don't write that,' I asked. 'We'll be inundated.' She did write it, and now we are being inundated. The pile builds up for you to open. Credit HAS to be given to the wonderful postal service of Dorset – they never make a fuss about it, they just deliver. They read the messages such as, 'Please, please, lovely post people, deliver this to our National Treasure. Thank you.' The British are so polite. And they send such beautiful wishes. You mean SO much to your listeners.

Another thing Claire wrote is still smarting with me: that we sleep in separate rooms. Yes, we do, but I read it as if we are romantically separated, when in fact it's because you sleep with an oxygen machine that is so sodding noisy that no one knows how you sleep next to it – but then you are partially deaf. I sometimes try to cajole you into my bed for the night just so we can hug, but you like your room, and close proximity to your machine. I miss the skin-on-skin touch. The closest I get is when I bathe you, gently letting you down into the water on your bath lift, but only my hands touch you, lathering you up and rinsing you down.

The fallout from an intense week of publicity is with us. Whether you have been exhausted by it or just feel relieved that your truth is out there, you have gone off into one of your distant, dark places. You are and always have been 90 per cent light, but your 10 per cent of dark will sometimes rear its head, as it has this week. You close yourself off, go into your computer world, shopping for things you don't need, going down rat runs of conspiracy theories and goodness knows what. You shut me out. Your hearing is getting worse – that doesn't help. This week we've been two ships on different routes. We've not even passed in the night. The culmination of you being lost is always that you smoke. You struggle not to, because I am so against it for your health. Unfortunately for you I can always smell it when I come back home. You feel guilty, I get upset, you become defensive. We both know it's indicative of how down you are. It's your smoke signal that you're unhappy.

Smoking has been the reason why I have thrown my wedding ring at you more than once. I've even gone away for days. I just cannot understand why you would do that to your body when so many people have fought to help you live – not least me. You know it punishes me, and maybe that's why you do it, but more than that, I know it's your 'fuck it' action. You just don't care. You want to be drawn to the dark and not the light.

It was only Angel Caroline, your palliative nurse, who made me truly understand that you are an addict, and I can never change you. I now accept that I cannot. It doesn't, however, mean I accept that smoking is a good idea, given the state of your lungs.

As I've been lost, exhausted and angry this week, I have withheld my full-on caring powers. I've only done the perfunctory jobs for you, like meals. For two days your pee bottle has not been emptied, your bed has not been made, or breakfast delivered to your bed. I have not spoken to you except when necessary. You know you've hurt me, and because I am tired of caring, tired of being tied to these four walls, tired of putting you before my career, tired of carrying the whole damn show all the time and never having any fun, I feel used. This is my protest. While I do it to show I'm hurt, I wonder if it's also an oblique form of punishment.

I remember a medium called Jean who I spoke to last year. When I ask for another reading, the first words she says are 'housebound' and 'France'. My father appears. He is adamant that I need a break, that I am being taken for granted and not being given anything in return (he's changed his tune in heaven!). Jean says I *must* take a holiday at the end of July, that you should go into a home and I must not feel guilty. I believe Jean is right. It has given me the freedom and permission to think for myself for once. I mean, I had thought that you would be long gone by now, and yet you keep going. Jean says your body is weak, but your soul is strong. She's not kidding. She says your soul is stronger than mine – yup – but she cannot tell me when you will go, even though I ask. She would have to talk to your soul, and she is not allowed to do that. All she will say is that they're preparing a lovely garden for you up there. Keep up the digging, I say. I share with her my fear that you will outlive me, that I will keel over from exhaustion or get cancer again. She says that I must tell my soul that cannot happen. It's a warning that I take seriously.

Afterwards, I listen to a message from my friend Camilla. Would I like to join her and her mother at a house she's been lent in Saint-Hippolyte-du-Fort in the South of France at the end of July? It's uncanny. My flight is booked within hours and now we just have to work out what to do with you.

When I tell Angel Caroline she agrees it is a very good thing for me to do. Respite: I need it – her words, not mine. We discuss what to do with you. I mention that you've been smoking, and it is the first time I hear this calm, controlled woman sound horrified. 'Not in the house?' she asks, alarmed. I don't know because you do it when I'm not here. 'He mustn't. There is so much oxygen in your house he would explode. He must be off his oxygen for at least forty minutes and he must be outside.' She really is afraid of you self-combusting. I mean, there is a funny side to this. A cartoonish end. A headline if ever there was one: 'Johnnie Walker DJ Explodes!' Departing as a human firework – you never do things by halves. Just try not to take the house out with you.

I hope that the thought of a break from you will give me the strength to get through the next five weeks before my trip. I'm starting to pack my washbag already I'm so excited. Freedom, travel, planes, stimulation, friendship, laughter, baguettes, local wines. No caring duties at all. Never has the word 'respite' sounded so sweet.

We need to really make sure that whatever time we have left together is loving. I think a break from you will help that from my side, and I hope from your side too. I mean, it probably isn't normal or right for a wife to ask her husband if he is ever actually going to die, as I did this week. It was cruel of me, but it comes from you being cold and me being terrified that you will outlive me because I am so exhausted. I get paranoid about chest pains. I feel trapped. I can't go on like this forever; I do need my own chapter to start. I cannot stress enough: I was certain you'd be gone by now, but like the Duracell Bunny, you just don't stop. I ask myself – I ask you – 'What are you holding on for?' You seem to be inde-structible. Great for your listeners, not great for me. Do I strike you as unloving? Or just very angry that you now take so much and give so little? You have an excuse now, but it's always been a bit like that. Unconsciously, I signed up for that when I met you, but right now, the balance has tipped even further, and we're in a place that is hard for me to stomach. I think and hope that this is because I am just overtired. The break cannot come soon enough.

You lie on the sofa and ask me to sit by you. You take my hand and tell me it's getting harder. You suggest that the game may soon be up. I am wary. I tell you that you have told me that before and then pulled back up. It leaves me on an emotional roller-coaster, and I ask that you bear that in mind, but maybe you are sharing your fear. I do understand that. Without doubt we are grappling with not knowing the when or how. The mystery of death is hard to contend with – in my case because I cannot plan; in your case because you must be wondering just what the hell is going to happen. My fear is that I am being too practical. I do the Waitrose online order and wonder if I should get you more digestive biscuits and cornflakes knowing I don't touch them, and if you should suddenly go, they'll go to waste.

Every single morning I go into your room and check to see if you're breathing. I often delay going in, in case you are not. What will I do? Who will I call? Will I just want you to myself for a final few hours first, before all the drama and bollocks start? The next chapter in our show. Will I regret the final words I say to you? Or will I need to tell you then, too late, how you have been the biggest, most extraordinary thing to have happened in my life? Too often I tell you how many sacrifices I have made to keep you on the road. Have I told you enough what you have brought to my life? The excitement, the fun, the amazing companionship, the love, the incredible lessons you have taught me about strength, chutzpah and belief. Have I told myself that? Or will I only realise when it's too late?

MARTHA AND THE VAN DWELLERS

I know that if anyone asked you what you loved best about being married to me, it wouldn't be sex, drugs and rock 'n' roll. It might be our homes, the stability and the laughter, but I suggest it would be that I got you travelling in a way that you had not before. Yes, you'd had plenty of motorbike trips in France and America with your mates, which fed your wanderlust, but for you it was the journey, not the destination. I flipped that around, broadening your horizons, getting you to enjoy the places we stayed in. And you loved it.

Honestly, for someone in showbiz you really had not tasted much of the good life. Wild, yes, but not what I considered good. Radio, I soon learned, is the poor relation of the media.

After you were so ill with your cancer, I booked us three weeks in a friend's hotel in Negril, Jamaica. You arrived skinny, pale and bald; you left so much stronger, with colour and more hair. It was transformational. You loved Ras Roddy outside on the West End Road, who sold street food – and more. You loved the Jamaican vibe, the plantain, the fish, the callaloo, jerk prawn and, of course, behind my back, the ganja.

On a future visit to another hotel on Negril Beach you visited Ras Roddy again. 'Johnnie, my man! Johnnie be goooood!' He gave you a chocolate brownie. 'Be careful. Share it with your friends, Johnnie!' A few days later, shortly before sunset when we'd have cocktails in the hot tub, I had a huge thirst for a cup of tea. 'We have that cake in the fridge!' I reminded him. How good it tasted – we ate it all, and soon followed it with a rum punch. The following twenty-four hours were some of the worst in my life. You found it funny that your straight, non-drug-taking wife had 'pulled a whitey', but you also had to take extreme care of me, as I became deeply paranoid and stoned for over a day. I hated every moment of it, but you were remarkably concerned and caring.

Winter sun became part of our annual agenda – it was the health tonic you needed to keep you strong. I would save through the year towards our holiday fund. Antigua, Saint Lucia, Grenada, Mauritius, Koh Samui and Australia were our winter destinations, as well as many more visits to Jamaica.

Australia was a destination that suited us both, as my brother Graham and your son Sam live in Sydney with their respective families. What joy we had with both of them. Their way of life was so enviable: sunshine, pools, decks, outdoor cooking, great beaches, fabulous food and wine. Byron Bay was a particular favourite. We loved the Indian Pacific train that took us from Perth across the enormous empty arid Nullarbor Plain (literally meaning 'no trees') to Sydney: three days of calm. We also had wine-maker friends Steve Webber and Leanne DeBortoli there, with whom we shared bottles of Pinot straight off the bottling plant followed by many of their repertoire of wines. They took us on tours of cellar doors in the Yarra Valley and the Mornington Peninsula, and shared good food, excellent wine and laughter like we've never known. Do you remember the plastic chicken you bought in a gift shop on Phillip Island? The evening became a hilarious celebration of Johnnie's Big Cock with their neighbours 'down the lane'. Steve and Leanne gave us lasting memo-ries, and gave me a belief that when I return, if I return, I want to be a winemaker.

We didn't just enjoy long haul, though. Short haul led us to the island of Paxos in Greece – an island that has given and given to us. Our first trip there was due to a photo of the small fishing village of Loggos on the Simpson Travel website. We loved its simplicity. Then I met someone at a local Dorset yoga class who had a house there. Frank Musker (coincidentally a songwriter for Chaka Khan, Aerosmith and Queen among others) and his wife, Rozzi, were people we were destined to meet. Time and again they would invite us to stay in their *spitáki*, so for years we loved going there in September. Thanks to Frank and Rozzi – known affectionately as 'the King and Queen of Paxos' – it was unbelievably social. It seems everyone went there: one night I sat next to the Rolling Stones' manager, and several other times we met up with leading rock musicians also on holiday there.

Island life is beautiful, small and simple; it gets under your skin. The other island we embraced was Tresco in the Isles of Scilly. You had always wanted to live by the sea, maybe because of all that time you spent on board the MV *Mi Amigo* when you were on Radio Caroline, and on Tresco we could own a week by the sea each year with their 'Islandshare' scheme. Our week in May in beautiful Seagrass overlooking the azure-blue sea towards St Martin's has been like a home from home and, happily, is very close to the gorgeous Ruin Beach Café, which to you meant black Americanos/croissant/pizza/wine/crab linguine and catch of the day. You loved that café so much, even more than the subtropical gardens, the beaches, the walks or the other islands. The Ruin was your ruin. That said, I did get you out for some walks before you became too limited. We loved to wander round to Gimble Porth and sit on a bench dedicated to Charles Baines. On it was the charming inscription, 'Let us sit together and watch for seals,' which we would do quietly, soaking up the beauty of the sea, land and rocky outcrops around us.

What you loved about me, and I about you, was that, while we adored an occasional taste of luxury, it didn't always have to be that way. We both enjoyed extremes – just not the in between. So when in 2008 you bought a white Auto-Trail

Cheyenne motorhome so that we could go on travel adventures together, I embraced the idea. You named her Martha, and we were the Van Dwellers – you, me and Darcey Dog. A motorhome, I discovered, can have many layouts. Martha had two bench sofas at the back with a table in between where we ate and played backgammon. At night you transformed this space into a double bed, the sofa cushions becoming mattresses. Martha had a tiny kitchenette complete with fridge, tiny sink, a loo and shower room. A wardrobe and head-height cupboards all round her gave storage for our clothes, books, DVDs and your vast selection of maps. She was the perfect size for two and a small dog. Plus, you got her an awning so that when we set up home in a campsite we could lay out a picnic table and chairs. It couldn't have been further away from a rock 'n' roll lifestyle.

How we loved getting Martha ready for trips. You would plan the journeys while I would organise food, bedding and backgammon. Our first trip was down the west coast of France. From Mont Saint-Michel to Santander in Spain. She was loaded with beautiful Emma Bridgewater colourful melamine plates, bowls and stripey cutlery and our two bicycles were attached at the back. Your bike to this day probably still sits in the Îsle de Ré bike shop, for it is there you fell for an electric bike, buying it for 1,000 euros and telling the man you'd be back to collect your own bike later. How you laughed as we drove out of town leaving it behind. You never were one for physical exertion, and you've always enjoyed an engine.

You had stayed in masses of campsites on biking trips, but as I had never camped, you were more than a little concerned about how I would deal with the shower blocks. How funny you found it to watch me waddling over to them with my towel and washbag. Fearing I would react badly, you gave me your assurance that I just had to say the word 'chateau' and we would be in one. I timed that word perfectly. When we arrived in Saint-Émilion the word slipped out of my mouth, we found an amazing chateau in the middle of the beautiful medieval town and got the final suite available. (Martha remained incognito in the town car park.) At reception they asked if we would like to dine there. You told them we'd think about it, and their eyebrows rose very discreetly. Only when we got to the room did I discover that it was at that time one of the top-fifty restaurants in the world. We took the last remaining table, and the food was magnificent.

With my fiftieth birthday under two years off, we decided to purchase the wine for my party there. Every spare crevice in Martha was stacked with bottles of fine Saint-Émilion Grand Cru, which still needed to be left a couple of years before drinking. By chance, the next night we met up with some friends who were also camping in France, and who were also bon vivants. Tom was then the general manager of Le Manoir aux Quat'Saisons – one of the finest hotels and restaurants in England. We parked up next to each other and after supper you suggested serving a rather fine wine. No one objected. Then Tom served a rather fine wine, and so it went on. What a night we had – £80 bottles being demolished in plastic camping wine glasses. We became so loud that other campers started to complain, and we were threatened with eviction from the site. Ha – two such upstanding Englishmen! The next day, with my future birthday wine stash seriously depleted, you drove away, quite illegally, given that I was still prostrate on the bed trying to sleep off my terrible hangover. Thank goodness for the onboard loo. I was kneeling in front of it as we made our way to Biarritz. It's a sad leftover of that night that I still cannot face Saint-Émilion wine, and at my fiftieth drank almost none of it, focusing on the champagne instead.

A Pembrokeshire coast trip allowed Darcey Dog to come with us. How she loved an adventure as much as you – new walks, beaches, sleeping tucked up next to me (where she thought you couldn't see her). How we loved the crashing seas and the characterful harbour villages. And on this trip we went one better: we towed my Fiat 500 behind us, so once we'd set up home on a campsite, we had freedom to travel.

Missing my production life so much, I did a few freelance producing jobs to keep my hand in, and you and Martha came on a couple of them. I'm not sure that the film crew could believe that Johnnie Walker was doing the craft services, but you were very good at it. Tea, coffee, snacks – you even got up at dawn to give the director and the cameraman a fry-up halfway up Snowdon on a Visit Wales commercial. In the Highlands of Scotland, where I was shooting a promo for the band Police Dog Hogan's track 'Fraserburgh Train', the budget was so small that Martha was the catering hub, production office, toilet facilities and wardrobe truck. Darcey came with us too on that job, and so beguiled was the director by her that she ended up being in it – running slow-mo across a mountain ridge, her black ears flying in the wind. Our girl immortalised! Your legs also featured, dressed in plus fours. Although we shot your whole body, you hit the cutting-room floor. Oh, the cruel rejection of an edit suite.

Martha was a fabulous asset to our lives. She was the perfect thing for festivals like Glastonbury, but the festival she's best remembered for was the Larmer Tree Festival on the Dorset–Wiltshire border, where not only did we entertain band Police Dog Hogan after their set, but later we managed to have an on-board disco with some friends, truly testing her suspension. It's ridiculous to love a vehicle, but we got everything down pat with her. Then one day, you went alone to a motorhome show in Birmingham, and thanks to your burning need to spend, and never being quite satisfied with what you've got, you traded her in. For £12,000 *more* you bought a smaller, vastly inferior grey Fiat van, and it's fair to say that I never forgave you. You tried to reason it by saying that Martha was too big for you to park these days. Realising that was unconvincing logic and that you'd made a stupid mistake, you tried to change your decision as soon as you got home, but dealers are bastards and you had to pay a huge premium if you wanted her back. It was the end of our camping days, for the grey thing was never liked by either Darcey or me. It was smaller, astonishingly uncomfortable and, frankly, we both missed the luxury and soul of dear Martha.

Our final holiday was in September 2023, in Greece, at a new hotel called the Mar-Bella Elix on the mainland. I was too nervous for us to stay on Paxos in case you fell ill. You were now struggling so badly with your lungs, just walking along the corridor to our room was hard for you; you had to stop several times to catch your breath and hold your chest. I lived in fear of you having a heart attack. You couldn't cope with the beach, for while there was a funicular to take us down to it – the very reason I chose the hotel – there were then over twenty steps to go right down to the beach, and you just couldn't do it. You remained by the pool, and each morning I would pop down alone for my daily sea swim.

The irony of the location was that the hotel looked out directly onto Paxos. Every day my heart ached to be on our special island where we had friends, cafés and beaches we loved, and the boats to Antipaxos, the small island just off Paxos, which we adored visiting. It got too much for me. I went to ask the hotel tour desk how we could pop over for the day to see friends for coffee. The only option was the weekly tourist boat trip to Paxos, which stopped in the main town of Gaios for forty-five minutes. It cost 240 euros for both of us. There was no choice. I booked it and we were met at the harbour by Frank and Rozzi, plus our other island friends James and Catherine. Frank looked at me sipping my cappuccino and just said, 'You are Paxos people.' How I knew it. The boat trip went on to Antipaxos and into the caves on the west of the island, and because you love boats it was a good day, even though you weren't fit enough to jump into the sea for a swim with me. Back at the hotel the girl at the tour desk asked if we'd seen our friends OK. I said we had. 'Good, because that was the most expensive coffee you'll ever have.' She wasn't wrong, but how happy I was that you got to see our beloved Greek island just one more time.

The thought of you not being my travelling companion one day fills me with huge sadness. We really have been brilliant together, and honestly, they have been our best times.

OUR TEN BEST ADVENTURES

Tensing Pen, Negril, Jamaica – our first time to the Caribbean and where you truly healed from your cancer treatment.

Venice – we went three times in November or March. You loved the boat taxi from the airport to the hotel as you felt like James Bond. The best was when we returned on the Orient Express.

La Residencia in Deià – our 'not the honeymoon' where you say you truly fell in love with me.

Taking Martha the Motorhome on her inaugural trip down the west coast of France, bringing back St-Émilion wine and an early electric bike.

Taking the Indian Pacific train across Australia from Perth to Sydney.

Visiting Steve and Leanne Webber of De Bortoli Wines on the Mornington Peninsula. When you mix a magical setting with great hosts, fine wine, amazing food, hilarious company and visits to cellar doors at niche vineyards, life doesn't get much better.

All our holidays on Paxos.

The first time I took you to Tresco. You loved it, as I knew you would. Having always wanted a house by the sea, you could fulfil that dream by getting an Islandshare house there – a beautiful coastal pad just for one week of the year.

Your niece Trudi's wedding to Todd in Vancouver, which we followed with a drive to the stunning Emerald Lake, and a train ride from Vancouver to Seattle.

The Great Wall of China. Truly extraordinary to be taken along the wild wall section by the expert William Lindesay. After one week of utterly basic living we took our Carers UK fundraising group of friends to the Chinese Embassy in Beijing to have the poshest tea surrounded by fine art, thanks to our friend Dame Barbara Woodward who was then the UK's Ambassador to China.

NOW

IF I WERE A RICH MAN

'I wish we were rich.' Where did that come from? Money has a loud voice, but it doesn't have soul. You have soul, Johnnie Walker – that's far more important. Besides, what can you possibly do with money now? (Except pay for some carers so I can have time out. I know they're expensive.)

You've just been texting with John Illsley (of Dire Straits), who told you about the party they have just thrown in a big marquee in the garden of their spectacular home. I guess we would have been there in healthier times. You start imagining how amazing it would have been, with wonderful guests, catering and decoration. You don't mention music, but I can only assume that was pretty good too.

You and money were never destined to go together. It was not in your stars. I know it's galling that because you are a big radio name people assume you are wealthy, but they don't realise that radio really is the poor relation of the BBC. 'I'm not a star like Wogan and Graham Norton,' you always said. You are right; you are just a jock and have always been paid as such. If you wanted to be rich, you would have taken that offer from Smooth Radio all those years ago, or done a Ken Bruce and gone to Greatest Hits, but we both know that the BBC is your home. You get fabulous production, you've always enjoyed great guests, you get incredible support – especially now – and you are the grandfather of the Radio 2 family. Plus, there are no ads.

When we met you were in a rented flat and you had huge debts due to the legal fees of fighting the *News of the World* sting. And let's face it, you are profligate with money. My accountant, GT, became *our* accountant. 'Walker pisses money up against the wall,' was his quickly formed, astute observation. Buying has been one of your addictions, but look where you are now? In a house that you like and I still shop at Waitrose. Just. I remind you how lucky we are. How we have everything we need. How we are better off than most. I guess it's just that we have spent quite a bit of time with people far richer than ourselves and you compare yourself with them. We are so often the poor guests who keep our heads held high because you are Johnnie Walker. I am proud of that and what you have achieved. I know you are too, but you seem bemused as to why it hasn't resulted in a healthier bank balance.

This desire of yours to be rich goes back a long way. 'Why aren't you wealthy like Noel Edmonds?' your mother would goad you when you were at Radio 1 in the 1970s. I see that went deep. You saw failure in her eyes, as she was just judging you by financial success. I remind you, yet again, that what you have now – love, respect and a Radio 2 show

– still, at the age of seventy-nine, is way beyond what Noel Edmonds could dream of having. I'm sure he'd cash in every helicopter he's ever owned to be in the position you are now. Do not measure yourself in financial terms. Look at your longevity and the legacy you will leave. As I always tell you, you should be so proud, because the love for you will live on. I promise. You only half hear this.

It is a credit to your ego that you have no idea just how important you are and have been in radio, to thousands of listeners, but you have been. You have a very special voice that touches souls – I'd almost say your voice heals. And when you go you will be irreplaceable. When you look down on your life from above that is what you will see, and you will realise that it was a life well lived (with a few blips). There is no money in heaven. Indeed, the rich have a hard time getting in according to the Bible. You are rich, Johnnie, just not in the obvious bank-balance way – and you cannot take that with you. You are rich in love from your listeners. Just look at the emails and cards that flow in day after day telling you how great you are and how missed you will be. That love you most certainly will take with you. It is the greatest currency.

It's 26 June 2024, my half-birthday, which as a child I always celebrated because Boxing Day is arguably the worst day of the year for an actual birthday. It remains special to me to this day, although I don't shout about it. You mark it – bless you. I wake at our little London flat in Primrose Hill

— the one that Darcey Dog selected for us. As a puppy she couldn't cope with the pavements near the BBC so a walk on Primrose Hill had her tail wagging furiously. We saw this flat with her and, while we were looking at the bedroom, she was busy taking a house plant out of its pot in the sitting room, spreading soil all over the cream carpet. She literally marked the place — so we swapped the flat near the BBC for this one. I came up last night to see my niece Brigitte, who has flown in from Sydney with her husband and girls. It is so good to see them, to sit in the Riding House Café drinking cocktails and red wine, catching up after five years when we have lost her amazing mother, Kim, and two of my brothers, Simon and Emlyn. I guess you are next.

I sleep so well in Primrose Hill. It is much quieter these days; since Covid no one goes out till the small hours. It's certainly quieter than the middle of nowhere where we live — no cockerels, cows or magpies fighting. It is bliss! I feel as if I have come on holiday. Just one night away from our open prison of a home is such a relief — as good as going to a Caribbean island. I feel so free. I see the matinee of *A View from the Bridge* with Dominic West; it's excellent. The audience love it, and I am part of something bigger than being your carer. I am carried completely by Arthur Miller's gripping story. I even find an actor for my film — a birthday present to myself. Our friends Rodney and Mariana have got you covered during the day, and your daughter Beth stays with you overnight. Thank you to them for this twenty-four hours of freedom.

I return home on a crowded, hot train. I collect wood-fired pizzas from the Grosvenor Arms and rush them back to you, waiting for me with a card, flowers and a new tennis skirt. Separation is so healthy. I babble with excitement, tell you the plot of the play, drink red wine, eat too much pizza. I am just so happy. It's one of my best ever half-birthdays. And doubtless my last one with you. You are genuinely pleased to see me sparkle again. It's been too long.

You soon have something important to discuss with me, though. I pretty much know what is coming. I can see it hasn't worked for you – its ability to move up and down does nothing for you; it brings you no comfort; the duvet falls off every night: you hate the mattress. You don't have enough space to lay out your iPad and phone. You look too big for it. So yes, I will move the hospital bed out and bring back in your much-loved four-foot divan bed from where it sits, lonely, in the garage. Thank heavens I didn't give it away. You just have to wait until I can get some help. It was quite an undertaking doing the swap in the first place.

I move you and your concentrator to my room. I thought you'd slept in this bed for the last time, but here you are, back in the marital bed! Mariana and I strip the offending NHS bed and then realise we can't even get it through the door. It is so heavy we can't possibly lift it. I call the district nurse's office and they say I mustn't attempt to disassemble it. You stay in my bed all day, sleeping like a baby, possibly relieved to be on a beautiful mattress again. You stay there for the night but insist on using your bathroom. I go in the guest room but continue to use my en-suite bathroom. I lie in bed with criss-cross images in my head. It's all wrong. The feng shui is not working. Neither of us sleep well, both discombobulated by the wrongness of the set-up.

Sarah, who had been our cleaner and support mechanism for so many years of our marriage before she retired, is coming to see us. We agree that if anyone can sort this, Sarah can. Especially if we ask our neighbour John to help out. He's a helicopter pilot; he can do anything. Together they work out how to take the bed apart. I don't care if we shouldn't. I just want you to be back in the safe haven of your room. They carry it to the garage and bring back your beloved bed. I never thought Sarah would be making up a bed for us again, but in she went, duvet and cover in hand, hospital corners for the bottom sheet. You are so happy in that bed I can't get you out of it until suppertime.

'What's on the menu tonight?' you ask at about 6 p.m., as you do each evening as you decide whether to have a G&T, a glass of wine or just water with your bowl of Kettle crisps.

'Friday night is Dirty Burger Night.' You are delighted. Dirty Burger Night happens as a treat about once a month. For you, it's a Linda McCartney vegetarian one; for me, it's Waitrose rose veal. You always ask, 'Why is it a "dirty" burger?' and I always tell you that it's because Suzi Perry calls it that, as do many. We had been at a carers' awards do, and we'd invited a few names to sit at our table – Michael Ball, Tony Blackburn, Anneka Rice and Suzi Perry. Once all the wonderful carers had been acknowledged for their self-less work, and the dinner had been cleared, you and Suzi still had a glint in your eye. Loving to be led astray, you readily agreed when she suggested we go on for a drink. We went on for several in the end, and at some point in the early hours Suzi announced that we needed a dirty burger. She knew the bar of a hotel near Park Lane. I am always impressed by people who know where to go at any time of the day or night to eat or drink. I was also impressed that she didn't eat her bun – but then she works on TV, and I don't; I needed the blotting paper. It was the first and last time that we took a cab back home as the sun was coming up. We giggled at the naughtiness of it, and fell into bed for a long, deep sleep.

Tonight's effort isn't my best dirty burger ever – the beef tomato was sliced a bit too thick, and I added a lettuce leaf too many – and you struggle to eat yours. But then you have started to mention more and more how hard it is to eat and breathe. You go very slowly. You remove most of the salad.

As a dinner conversation you talk about IPF symptoms towards the end of life. Not the best meal-time discussion, but it's the one time of the day when we really look into each other's eyes. You've been doing more research, and hearing from listeners who have lost a family member to it. It has always been a risk that you would pick up an infection and drop like a stone, but you've got through the winter. (You seem to be impervious to infections. You are the only person I know who never got Covid.) So it seems that the slowing down and sleeping more is your natural path to the end. That said, after supper you say that you're bored of this now. 'Dirty burgers?' I ask. No, the fighting to breathe and everything being such an almighty effort. It is Friday, 28 June. I wonder if your soul will hear you, for I feel you will determine when you go. What is money when life has actually become too much effort to live? Some things money cannot buy, and one of those is health.

LOVE ME, LOVE MY DOG

If I were to give thanks for just one thing in our marriage, it would be Darcey Dog. It cannot be understated just what a special creature she was. Unable as we were to have children together, she was our surrogate child. You, me and her: that was our family.

You initiated her arrival, hearing about a litter of working cocker spaniels in the New Forest. We'd already had one working cocker – dear Fergus – who, while we loved him hugely, was a tad too wild for us as you recovered from cancer. Fergus was adopted by Madonna's estate manager, Willy. As Martin Shankleman, your former business correspondent on *Drivetime*, observed, 'Fergus just used you, Johnnie, to get up the showbiz ladder.' I believe that to this day Guy Ritchie still has Fergus's offspring at Ashcombe.

When we met Darcey's litter the extrovert ones bounded over to me, but the quiet, rather insecure and bullied runt came and sat at your feet. She looked up at you with her pleading eyes. 'Hello,' you said, picking her up. Darcey chose you. She recognised something in you, and weeks later home she came. Her confidence grew, and living as we did then in the Granary, on the edge of a farm with a pheasant shoot, she had a great youth chasing pheasants and deer. How that girl could run.

At puppy class we realised she pretty much disliked most other dogs, but she adored humans – she could get her way with them. Our mad theory was always that she was Lady Diana reincarnated, because she shared those same eyes looking up pleadingly from under her fringe. Plus, she truly was the people's pooch. She was loved wherever she went, which sometimes included your interviews in London. She was a hit with Patti Smith and met more rockstars than I ever did.

Her traits were delightful. When she was excited she'd cock her body round in a curve, wagging that docked tail with vigour, and she tried to talk. Of course, she could bark, but she had more in her vocabulary. She really tried to convey her emotions with a call-cum-squeal that revealed her mood. There was intonation in her voice, and we would stand before her, asking, 'What are you saying, Darcey?' and she'd honestly appreciate our efforts to understand. She considered herself just as human as us.

She adapted between her Dorset and Primrose Hill life with delight. She loved the contrast: pheasants in the country; squirrels in London. She didn't care what she chased. She never caught anything, but oh, the challenge of trying. Her stumpy tail would wag furiously as she hysterically squealed with excitement. That dog loved life, loved people, loved us. She also loved to be good. Her favourite compliment was, 'You're such a good girl, Darcey.' She really appreciated that acknowledgement. She was a wonderful example to us all, and her spirit touched all who she met. As such, she had a wonderful social life, went for walks with many of her human friends and knew more people in Shaftesbury than we ever did.

She only ever went to a kennel for two nights of her life. There were too many people offering to have her to stay. Her first godmother was Sarah, our right-hand woman for many years, and then when we moved to Shaftesbury her new godparents were our friends Jonathan and Claire. It didn't matter what mischief she got up to, they all adored her. She could do no wrong, just entertain.

She was going blind and deaf and becoming arthritic by the time she was fourteen, but that didn't stop her having the best week of her life when we took her to Tresco in November on a 'doggie break' – the only occasion Tresco allows people to bring their dogs to the island. After the plane and boat ride, she knew when she got there that the place was special. She ran around ecstatically – it was quite extraordinary how she reacted. Finally, she was joining us in one of our favourite places and it was as if she knew that. She and I walked every inch of the island's paths and beaches together. She didn't want to leave, but whoever does?

Four months later in 2022 was Storm Eunice. As I explained to Darcey, the BBC said we weren't to go out walking because of the danger. It was the only day of her life this had happened, and it was not well received. Later that night, after she'd happily polished off the remains of your supper, we had a power cut. We decided to go to bed early, so you let her out for her final pee. What you didn't tell me was that she'd turned right and not left into the fenced in part of the garden. After a while I commented that she'd been a long time. We both took turns looking in the garden with a torch, but she wasn't there. She had clearly taken herself off for a hooley. We called our neighbours in case she was in their gardens. Mark across the drive from us got out his truck, and in the pitch black we went searching the local roads. There was no sign of her. It was a bitterly cold night. Back home, empty-handed, I put up a post on the Nextdoor app. During her life she'd torn off on quite a few occasions, but she was always found. This time I had a very different feeling in the pit of my stomach.

Even though I felt it was hopeless I was up early the next morning scouring fields. So were many people in the area. Our home became Rescue HQ, with people descending on us and conducting their own search parties or using drones. I would stop strangers to ask them to look out for her, only to discover that they were already out looking for her. Hundreds of people searched for that little dog.

After three days my only way to deal with it was to sit in bed and write. I never wanted to forget a single detail of her last precious day:

Is Celeriac Poisonous for Dogs? Darcey's Final Day.

I sat on the stool by the grey sofa watching her sleep. She looked so content, her legs stretched out, her head comfortably resting on two blue linen cushions. As if she'd finally mastered human pillow habits. She stood up and wagged her stump of a tail, shoving her nose close to mine. On this day she was particularly happy and bouncy. She tore around the kitchen, skidding on the wooden floor and crashing into chairs. I drew the long grey linen curtains to open the bifold door to the garden. Out she tore. Throwing herself on the lawn and arching her back as she rolled in this blissful daily wake-up manoeuvre, her tail wagging throughout. She returned, leaping back across the threshold of the door, bringing in the smallest smudge of mud across her head.

By lunchtime Storm Eunice had kicked off. Our bins had all gone flying, recycling spreading itself across the lawn and newspapers splatting against our fence before crossing to our neighbour's garden and then into the field beyond. As Johnnie tried to grab what he could, Darcey joined him, cantering around, her head towards the considerable wind, her ears flying back and up.

This storm had changed the daily pattern. I lay back on the grey sofa against the two blue linen cushions with a post-yoga cup of tea. Such novelty appealed to Darcey, who came up for a cuddle. I pointed out that the mud was still on her topknot and she needed a bath. This fell on unwilling ears, and she sloped off in case I meant 'now'.

It was a simple supper for the humans that evening. Sea bass, spinach and celeriac purée. The latter was remarkably sharp. Making it with zero-fat quark did it no favours. Johnnie didn't finish his. Darcey was in luck. Sea bass skin, and his rejected celeriac, was going spare. She wolfed it all down.

The power cut happened soon after 9 p.m. There was nothing to do but go to bed. It was customary for her to spend about five minutes outside at night, having a good sniff around all the corners of the garden. But when we looked outside she was nowhere. We searched the local roads, but went to bed feeling sick.

The next morning I was up early searching the cow shed up the lane, going to speak to neighbours and walking her favourite fields. For two days stacks of friends and people we've never met were out, many taking dogs.

At some point Johnnie joked, 'I think it was your celeriac purée.' And tonight, three days since she left us, I found myself googling 'Is celeriac poisonous for dogs?' I am happy to discover it is not and is full of nutrients.

I'm glad she had a little extra in her tummy when she left. I hope it kept her warm on what was a blisteringly cold night. I hope desperately that she departed this world in a moment of euphoria, giddy on the wildness of the night. She has been such a very special dog her entire life, bringing joy and love to so many, that she deserved nothing less. For me, my heart has to hold on to that image because any thought of her suffering is too heart-breaking to bear.

I shall never forget Darcey. I shall never forget Storm Eunice. I shall always blame the power cut. And I will never eat celeriac again.

22/2/22

I remember your phone call as I was driving back from town five days after she'd gone. 'Where are you, Duch?' You had never, ever called me to ask where I was, so I knew it was about Darcey. As I got out of the car I said, 'She's home, isn't she?' You nodded, told me she was in the garden. Mark, our neighbour, was a local farmer and had found her and brought her back. I just wasn't expecting to see her little body wrapped tightly in a blue blanket. I could see the rigid shape of her frame, her legs, her nose. I let out a scream so deep that I had no idea I was capable of such a sound. It was my primal scream. You had been in the middle of recording your *Sounds of the 70s* show when she was brought back. You had to record the second half of the show having just discovered that our 'daughter' had drowned in a local pond on what had been the coldest night of the year.

I called Jonathan and Claire. Within minutes they were round with Jake, their son. The two men dug Darcey's grave and, after both you and Jonathan had bravely groomed her, you wrapped her up once more and laid her in it. All we could do was hold each other in our grief.

My wonderful dog-loving editor Helen Stiles at *Dorset Magazine* read my tribute to Darcey and said that not only could it be my next month's column but that she'd give me three pages. She paid Darcey the highest compliment, saying she'd have put the photo of her smiling on Tresco on the cover of the magazine if it had been taken in Dorset.

Weeks later we had a funeral for her. About thirty of her friends, godparents and family attended. Even my mother came. You gave a brief eulogy, and our friend and old mucker, the psychic, Tarot-reading Big Pete, recited a poem he had written for her, with us all gathered around. Afterwards we had lunch. It was a beautiful day and send-off to the most amazing dog anyone there had ever known.

Darcey chose you. And while I did all the walking and feeding and scheduling of her diary (yes, she had a diary!), she looked up to you as the master of our pack. In the last photo of the three of us together she lies across me, but looks up to you with such devotion and love. There is no doubt that for both of us the first encounter we both look forward to in heaven is with Darcey Dog, her black body cocking round in a curve, her stumpy tail wagging and her delightful doggy voice welcoming us.

Friends asked about getting another dog, but how could we replace such a special creature? Not only would it feel disloyal, but almost certainly it would be a disappointment after the one and only Darcey Walker. She was sent to us by divine providence, and one day maybe another will be sent to me. If so, I think it will be a miniature sausage dog ... called Sizzle.

NOW

THEY SHOOT HORSES, DON'T THEY?

It's 1 July 2024, six months since your health crashed and both our lives changed. Last night I had an unusual dream for me – it was incredibly clear. I was on a train pulling into Tisbury station and there you were in your beautiful cord jacket you bought in Venice (now sold on Vinted). You were tall, strong, handsome – and you were standing. You have always loved meeting me at the station – the joy of reconnection and being one again. It was so beautiful to see you like that. Whoever knew that your husband standing on a train platform could be a thing of such profound joy. We learn too late, don't we?

Six months in: a point I never imagined you would make, but there you are, soul intact, *Rock Show* recorded for today and waiting to watch your crush Emma Raducanu play at Wimbledon. While you seem perfectly fine given your basic level of existence, I have never felt so deeply and profoundly exhausted. I've a column to finish for *Dorset Magazine* and for the first time ever, I have no energy or inspiration to write it. A first-time writer's block. I put it down to fatigue.

I spoke with an old friend, Karin, earlier. We shared a room when we both worked in Paris in 1980. She has taken a spiritual and coaching route through life. I tell her my deep-rooted fear that you will outlive me as I am going to get overcome with exhaustion and fall ill. She impresses upon me that I must change my thinking. She is a great believer in the 'law of attraction', whereby if you think a thing too much it will become reality. I must change my mindset. But you are so sodding strong and I see no sign of you letting go. 'I've carried him and his life for twenty-two years. I don't know how much longer I can go on,' I tell her. She understands. All my friendship group know I keep our show on the road. How I have ever since we got married. Today I am longing to know when it can be a solo show. Not because I don't love you – I do so deeply and will miss you incredibly – but I just want to curl up in a ball and sleep for days without letting you down. I want to be off the hook, to go to the cinema and be free to stay out all day. Indeed, I really want to go and see Kevin Costner's *Horizon* at the Everyman in Salisbury tomorrow, but I've not found the right moment to tell you, for I know that it will fill me with guilt. Carer's guilt. How long will this go on? Will six months become twelve? You're going to finish me off if we're not careful.

Another show day. It's Wednesday, so today is *Sounds of the 70s*. Every pre-recorded show is checked by someone in management before it airs. You say you've never been so censored in what you can say or play as a result. You love telling people that you cannot play 'Hong Kong Garden' or the Goons' 'The Ying Tong Song' because they are deemed racist. Pre-records have kept your career going, but I know it frustrates you. If a guest ever mentions having a spliff or any drugs in the Seventies, it is cut out before it airs. Only last week, when you interviewed music PR Alan Edwards, the story about him being backstage in someone's dressing room with a Hells Angel who got him to play Russian Roulette with a loaded pistol was removed. It's always the best stories that are taken out. How you love a live interview and show – no one can censor you then. You can just apologise.

I take you your black coffee and Berocca Boost as usual. I turn your oxygen down to Level 5 so the mic doesn't pick up the sound. You and Liz talk about the show, and then I hear your voice do a total gear change as you start to record. How do you do it? You project, you sound strong, you are humorous. I tell you, your listeners don't know how lucky they are. They get the very best of you – the last remaining strands of the old Johnnie. You showman, you. Doctor Showbiz doing his bit.

I'm left with an exhausted husk who I put to bed early after I've undressed him. Tonight, you cry at bedtime. We're side by side on your bed as you hold my arm. 'I'm sorry I'm going to leave you,' you sob. You talk about what a hard time we have been put through during our marriage – the illnesses, the challenges. How strong we have had to be to keep going, how incredible it is that we have. Especially me. You apologise that you have let me down at times, that you have not loved me with the strength and goodness with which I have loved you. You tell me that my pure heart has taught you so much. Honestly, darl, I may be as loyal as they come, but I'm really not *that* special a person, yet you truly believe I am, and I love that about you. You make me feel special, though really I'm just well brought up by two very moral, good, loving, intelligent human beings. I was taught to put others before myself. To recognise those worse off than me, and not to envy those who have it better. To you, that makes me a saint.

To be honest, I've cried today too, but only because I am so depleted of energy. It frightens me when I am like this, as I know from experience that it means my immune system is getting low. I am known for being positive – which of course I am still in public, but even that is getting more taxing.

Johnnie, I miss our life together so very much. You have been my playmate for almost twenty-three years; now you are my charge who I must care for. I know I am lucky to have this transitional time with you, but honestly, the grieving has not only started already; it has well and truly taken hold.

I'm slightly concerned that my final words to you will be, 'I'm bloody knackered.'

I notice how much you tell me you love me when I say goodnight. When I walked into my room tonight you texted me too, just for good measure: 'Tiggy, I love you SO much.' Are you trying to tell me something? You will be there in the morning, won't you? Am I reading too much into a text because a deeply hidden part of my subconscious is hoping it is nearly over?

As you know, I am the Queen of the Diary. I adore scheduling – an important production skill – and have always spent hours on it so that our life flows as well and efficiently as it possibly can. It started when Terry Wogan was alive and you filled in for three months of his *Radio 2 Breakfast Show* each year. That was the backbone of our year's planning. Everything else, such as holidays and events, would come on the back of Terry and Helen's plans. Since then, it has been based around your shows, which of course, until lockdown, were always live. At the start of each year I have worked with your producers, giving them twelve months of dates. This year in January I put your show dates in the diary, and I thought I was being overly optimistic putting them in till the end of June. Now that date has passed. How long should I enter them for? You said yesterday you're getting worse, but I think we both know that the shows are your lifeline. They give you a purpose, a reason to get up. When you stop them, you will probably soon stop yourself. I have put them in till the end of July. Four more weeks. I think I am being very cautious.

This was an issue most of all in January and February when you sounded worse than you do now. I'd ask if you wanted a break for a week; you said you'd never have the strength to return. Some shows took two days to record you were so puffed and exhausted. Since you 'came out' about your illness you seem to have got a new lease of life, ironically. You seem to feel freer and laugh on-air, calling yourself Puffing Billy – turning adversity into advantage.

Now, as I look back at the earlier months of this year, it makes me reflect on something you kept saying back then. You were fretting about a couple outside Wogan House on NYE. I wanted to do a video of you to put up on the socials before the show, so we went down to the entrance. The couple were waiting to see Michael Ball when he came out, so I let them know they were at the wrong studio, as he was coming from Maida Vale. I continued talking to you, suggesting where you should stand. 'Oh, are you famous?' they asked. I shared a laugh with you. Are you, Johnnie?! A penny dropped very slowly. The man asked if you were *that* Johnnie Walker? It seems you were. And while you weren't the prize they were after, they did remember you from your Radio 1 days (ha ha!) and wanted a photo with you as a consolation. You politely agreed and they snuck in close to you, grinning broadly. At least they had something to show the kids, even though it was clearly an enormous step down from Michael. We don't always get what we want.

Producer Paul has always protected you when you come to the studio. That day he wouldn't let the BA (broadcast assistant) come into the show, as she had a cold. You were exposed to just him and studio manager Jamie – both fighting fit. So the question that has stayed with you since is: did one of the mystery couple have Covid or a virus, and was that the blow that struck you down at New Year? Because without doubt you are stronger, healthier and less coldy now than you were back in January and February – the months when I thought you really would go any day.

Paul is in constant touch with me, telling me that it has to come from us, the decision to stop. And here we are in July. I do check with you most weeks if you're OK still doing the show, and yes, you are. Over the past two weeks your shows have been particularly good, and that gives you confidence. Indeed, since coming clean about your illness you are enjoying them more, which in turn feeds you. You always were contrary – 'I'm dying. Oh no I'm not!'

Our friend Dave Holmes arrives from the Isle of Wight. 'Just popping in to see how you are.' He asks the two nurses who are here doing a routine visit, 'Has he told you who I am?' He has not. 'I'm his undertaker!' They think it's a joke, but actually it's true. Dave told you years ago he'd do it for you. Once the nurses have left, you hit him with questions. What car will I be driven away in? What will be over me? What will I be wearing as I leave the house? Will I go in the fridge? Can Tigs visit me? Can I have Bruce Springsteen's 'Born to Run' blasting from speakers in the hearse? Is it OK for me to go to the crematorium in Salisbury alone while the wake happens? Dave answers everything with his usual reassuring calmness.

GT, our accountant is coming to check that we have everything in order, and he wants to see you. You start proceedings. 'How will Tigs survive?' GT and I go back decades. I was one of his first clients when he opened his own accountancy firm and I opened my production company Wowhaus. We were brave newbies together.

GT looks at you and tells you not to worry. I am resourceful, a survivor. He turns to me and tells me I need to work again – music to my ears. He tells us both I need to sell the Primrose Hill flat. It's not necessarily my ideal decision – I crave more culture – but as GT says, I don't need to own an expensive asset to spend under fifty nights a year in the Big Smoke. I need to simplify my life. He is, and always will be, my voice of reason.

He looks over your will. He asks about your assets. We all laugh – there are none. The property is in my name, and your pension is tiny. You never were good with money. Fantastic at spending it; less good at holding on to it. I have always squirrelled money away to pay for our holidays. I am squirrelling now to keep us going should you need to stop working. In a way I've secretly admired your carefree attitude, though I couldn't remotely be like that myself. Life – it's all a big board game, isn't it? And we all have different ways of playing it.

This time has become a marathon and I am a sprinter. This endurance race is depleting all my reserves and shows no sign of stopping. That is the dilemma of this period. I love you, I want to care for you, but it is exhausting me. Not so much the physical side; I can bathe and dress you, empty pee bottles and commodes, and grab oxygen tubes on top of cooking, cleaning, gardening, doing the bins, shopping, making beds, running the home and our lives as well as anyone. I have realised with the guidance of my longstanding homeopath, Carole, that my tiredness is mainly emotional and spiritual. In essence, I feel trapped. I'm not free to go away, to plan my life, to find my power. My focus is almost exclusively on your needs. I want to be in control and, thus, the greatest gift I could be given would be for someone to tell me when this will end, because then I could adjust my mental thinking accordingly. This is a marathon now, but is it actually a double marathon? Will you outlive me? Not that old chestnut again.

We discuss why you are holding on. I quote a friend who said quite matter-of-factly, 'Of course he's holding on, because you look after him so well. He's fed, washed, cared for, forgiven and thousands of people are sending him love. Who wouldn't hold on for that?'

Who isn't fed by love? Your listeners idolise you. Some idolise *us*, saying what an amazing inspirational couple we are. Us? WHY? I'd say we're as flawed as the next couple.

Apart from giving me a remedy and telling me to keep off coffee for three days, Carole's advice is that I have to live in the NOW. She fears that all the time I'm planning my future – be it where I'll live, my film or how to keep going financially – I am affecting your soul. Maybe you aren't letting go because I'm not at peace. She tells me to let go, to stop fretting about your end date and just embrace each day. She knows I'll be heartbroken, but she recognises more the fatigue. I must change my mantra, stop saying how tired I am, and just appreciate the good moments we have left.

I am more relaxed by the time I'm home from seeing her. I try to lasso you with your oxygen pipe. I hide the cuckoo bell you use to summon me in my top so my stomach appears to call like a bird when you press the button. I avoid any negatives. I make a chicken pie. You see I'm trying my new 'live in the moment' mantra, and in return hold my hand tightly at bedtime. You look small. It's such a struggle, you remind me.

Despite my determination to change for the better, my resolve to stay positive lasts thirty-two hours before I break down. My throat is swollen, I'm exhausted after a sleepless, fretful night and I haven't stopped all day. I feel like a servant, and you are, as ever, within your bubble. I force a flare-up and remind you that it cannot go on like this. I need help. But, of course, neither of us knows just what or how or who that help should be. I cry that I don't want our last months together to be miserable because I am so spent. I don't want to be angry that I have to do so much while you seem to be having a great time in bed or on your blue chair. I want us to have a good end. Not just you. Us. I deserve that after the sacrifices I've made. For the first time in my life I wish I had a child of my own who would come and help me, take the pressure off, give me time out or make me a cup of tea. I am hungry to be looked after for a while. Your son Sam would be here in a heartbeat if he didn't live in Australia. My mother has sent me a sheet of handwritten prayers, but right now I need something more tangible.

One of the things that really gets to me is that you never leave the house – you've hardly left it on your own since lockdown. And every married woman I know likes time alone in her home. I become a different person when you're not here. I listen to music you hate. I dance around. I make everything look beautiful. Just so. There's no farting, or empty coffee cups to pick up. But I cannot be alone in my home until you go. I have to leave the building to relax – which is really not what I always want at all. Of course, when you do next leave me alone in the house it will be in perpetuity, which isn't what I want either. I've always enjoyed you coming home.

You have had a lot of medical challenges during our marriage. Cancer, peritonitis, having much of your gut removed, stoma reversal op, tinnitus clinic (in Estonian!), stents, hospitalisation for various complaints, including pneumonia at least twice, heart attack, triple heart bypass, new knee, eyes lasered, eye lenses replaced and a lot of dental stuff. It has been fairly ongoing, and within these events I have faced the prospect of you dying more than once. Indeed, when you had an emergency operation for the peritonitis you stopped living three times on the operating table, but you came back, showing me early on in our time together that you are Captain Scarlet – indestructible. You've often talked about the film *They Shoot Horses, Don't They?* Well, I think you and I are one of the last couples on that dance floor, clinging to each other, still moving – just.

THEN

THE GOOD, THE BAD AND THE FAMOUS

Fame is an odd thing if you've never been exposed to it. The fabulous thing about you is that you never considered yourself famous. You were a radio jock, not a television presenter. You had the perfect situation. You had the influence of fame without the day-to-day recognition.

By and large fame was beneficial to us, though not at the start when I felt hopelessly out of my depth. I soon realised that you are all in a fame club (no matter what you are famous for) and some in that club are wary of outsiders. Do you remember the time you introduced me to Sharon Osbourne at the Elton John tribute? I told her she looked lovely, and she looked me up and down like a piece of shit, her face saying, 'How dare you address me directly.' Then I spoke to Billy Connolly; his silent look said the same. When you introduced me to Jeremy Clarkson at the Goodwood Festival of Speed it was a similar reaction. Just because you're famous does not mean you have manners – though of course you always did. On the few occasions you were noticed when you didn't want to be, for example because you were just about to eat fish and chips in a pub, you'd just turn to the person – chips on fork – and say, 'I'm off-duty, mate.' They always respected that.

There's no doubt that fame opens doors: to theatre and film openings, to festivals and of course to concerts. I mean, the list of musicians I've met with you is pretty starry: Elton John, Jackson Browne, Roger Daltrey, Robert Plant, Bonnie Raitt, the Dixie Chicks (all three), Mick Fleetwood, Neil Finn, James Taylor, Charles Esten, old timers Frankie Valli and Andy Williams, Christine McVie, Lulu and so many more. But nothing and no one will ever beat the time you introduced me to my hero, David Bowie. I've been crazy about him since the age of twelve, so I could never have imagined that event occurring. It was a Radio 2 gig (God bless that station) at Maida Vale. We swept up on your yellow Fatboy Harley-Davidson (which, for me, was quite a wild entrance). After the gig for around a hundred people, you talked your way backstage, where we were absolutely not invited – that privilege was for the Alan Yentobs of this world, but you got us back there – and as Bowie stepped out of the meet-and-greet with the great and the good of the BBC, you stepped forward, introduced yourself and quickly passed his attention to me. I said, overawed, 'I don't know what to say.' And Bowie, mirroring me, said, 'Neither do I' as if he too was overawed to meet me. I spoke about his set list. I loved that he'd played 'The Bewlay Brothers'. He seemed pleased. We probably only spoke for two minutes, but in those two minutes there was no one else that mattered in his life – or mine. He was fully present with me. Nothing else existed and it made me feel extraordinary. Had he always had that talent or did he learn it? It made him feel as powerful as I imagine Jesus Christ was. It's an awful thing to say to you, that it was almost the greatest moment of my life. The only moment to beat it was our first kiss. Those two events have in common that they were not mere earthly occurrences. Something other happened. Something spiritual and outside my body. They were both touched by God.

We have since talked often about Bowie and his power, not just as a musician, but as a man so visionary that I question whether he was man – or alien. To this day I know we have not seen the last of him. Whether as a hologram, or something not yet invented, I know he will come again. That suggests I'm saying he was Jesus Christ, and I don't think that. But he was beyond human.

One of my prouder starlit moments with you was when you introduced Bruce Springsteen on stage at St Luke's Church in the East End of London when he was doing that fabulous Seeger Sessions tour in 2006. It was being recorded for Radio 2 (again). The venue was small (again), and I sat with my former boss, James Studholme, in the side balcony. I was scared that you would falter in your duty; James reassured me that you would be fine. You did your bit, and I could hear in your voice the enormity of the event. Even though you've interviewed him several times, this was your musical hero, an artist you had lauded for years, and you were in front of an audience. Before you knew it, you'd delivered your intro and your hero was coming on stage with his guitar, saying, 'Thank you, Johnnie,' before he shouted out, 'One, two, three, four ...!' and the band burst into song. Jeepers, what a moment. Talk about a proud wife.

Then there was backstage at the Round House when Elton did a Radio 2 gig. There was backstage, where all the bigwigs went, and then there was the real backstage – the inner sanctum of Elton's space. That's where we went – the only two invited in, as Elton wanted to see you. You, he and Ray Cooper (percussionist extraordinaire) sat on an L-shaped sofa. You told Elton he now had more hair than you these days, and Elton responded that he should do for the money it cost. The three of you reminisced and laughed. On the other side of the room was David Furnish and his friends. He totally ignored me. So there I was, standing in the middle of this room, feeling a total misfit. I didn't know where to put myself. Was I supposed to laugh at you three on the sofa? I smiled politely a lot until, happily, you'd had enough. In fairness, you were hugely apologetic that I'd stood there feeling like an idiot, though you didn't think I looked like one.

Your favourite story by far, and the one you told on your *Sounds of the 70s* show with huge amusement, was my faux pas at the Who concert at the Royal Albert Hall in aid of the Teenage Cancer Trust. Roger Daltrey had invited you/ us to be in his box with his wife and some other friends. As we sat there waiting for the gig to start I became aware of two men talking behind us. One was clearly a close friend of Mick Jagger as he mentioned him many times. The man with him had the most fabulous mane of hair. It's possibly a fault of mine, but I do pay people compliments (unless they are Sharon Osbourne), so I said to him how I loved his hair and that it gave him a look of power and strength. He really had something about him. He seemed pleased. After I turned back to you, I overheard him telling Mick Jagger's friend that he had never played at the Royal Albert Hall. It seemed rather cocky to me, but of course I was intrigued. I turned back again, 'Are you in a band?' He was. I asked which one, hoping like mad I would have heard of it. 'U2,' was his response. 'Fuck!' was mine. It was Adam Clayton, the bass player. Now, in fairness, he said that no one recognised him with the hair, which he had grown over lockdown, and he was loving being able to travel on the Tube. You didn't recognise him either, and it certainly gave the folks at Radio 2 a titter. It reminded me of the American tourist walking through the Scottish Highlands who bumped into our late, great monarch and asked her if she had ever met the queen. She said she had not but that her companion had. He asked her to take a photo of him with her companion. The queen never let on a word about who she was.

If there's one story I will tell as an old lady, it will be about the musician we met who hadn't yet found fame – although he was still trying in his late sixties. One day you turned to me and said, 'I want to go to a pub in Glastonbury on Thursday evening to see a band.' A pub? It clearly wasn't anyone big. You had read in the music press – *MOJO*, I think – someone raving about the greatest undiscovered rocker out there: Willie Nile. Willie was known by all the musicians – The Who, Bruce, Bono, etc. – but while they had all made the BIG time, Willie was playing pubs and working men's clubs. Having read the article about him, you looked up his UK tour dates to find out he was playing near us in two days' time.

We packed up Martha the Motorhome, deciding to go on to Putsborough Sands the next day, and off we set in time to have supper at the pub. As we sat in the back bar you nudged me – 'There's the band.' It wasn't that astute of you. I mean, they were five guys dressed top to toe in black with New York accents. They were having their pre-gig meal. Once they had finished eating you walked over. 'I'm sorry to bother you, I just wanted to say hello. My name's Johnnie Walker.' The older guy with the jet-black quiff of hair looked at you, saying, 'You're shitting me.' You said you were not shitting him. 'You can't be ...' Willie continued. After several attempts, you assured him that you were indeed called Johnnie Walker and that you were a radio DJ on BBC Radio 2. You said it with assurance. Willie looked to his UK tour manager, Mickie, then back at you. He was utterly stunned. That VERY morning when he'd got up he'd said to Mickie, 'There's one person in this country I need to get my music to. Johnnie Walker.' Mickie had responded that this was not an easy ask. At all. And yet ten hours later, there you stood, waiting to hear Willie play.

Without doubt it was the most magical of meetings, and from then on we became not just firm friends; you two were soul brothers. On future UK tours the whole band would come and stay with us for a night. I remember the night I had to do dinner for them – the head count was about twelve including Janice, their driver, and our friend Big Pete. I asked if there were any intolerances. Just a few – dairy, gluten, seafood, red meat, mushrooms, garlic, nuts, rice and spices. Ay ay ay! Willie apologised. A highly individualised antipasto plate per person was followed by a simple lemon chicken, pomme dauphinoise made with stock instead of cream, and a gluten-free cake with berries. And still Willie's Italian partner, Cristina, had to raid the fridge to satisfy her needs, bringing a pack of Prosciutto ham and a whole avocado to the table. Thank goodness the red wine flowed.

Willie has a spirit the like of which I've never known. He writes, he performs, he tours. His life is music. He's never made the big time, but he assures me he doesn't want that. Bruce Springsteen plays with him and the band at least once a year for a charity gig at Asbury Park, New Jersey. The Who had him as their support act at a gig last year. He just lives the dream without the trappings. He has a band of ardent fans who follow him round the world, and I would include ourselves in that. Be it the 100 Club in London or a gig in Milan, we've been there to see him. Once we drove down to Montepulciano in Tuscany to see him play in a particularly smart vineyard. What a trip! We christened our new white Fiat Spider Bianca to get there, me quaking in the passenger seat on the terrifyingly narrow motorways as I was way too close to the crash barrier for my liking. Cristina, a cool Italian rock photographer, shrugged. 'Sure, we all drive like crazy. It's in our DNA.' She wasn't wrong.

When you were due to take a sabbatical month from Radio 2 I had one of my best ideas to date: Willie should do your *Rock Show*. I threw the idea to him. It was such an outside chance, but taking the bull by the horns, Willie recorded an hour-long demo show. With my hand on my heart, I can say it was the best hour of radio never broadcast. It was funny, with stories from 'the Village' where Willie lives in New York. I loved the one about him bumping into Patti Smith at the launderette some years past. He just said, off-hand, 'All her clothes were black. What other colour is there?' It was brilliant, personal, full of great music and stories about musicians, because he knew them all. It didn't cut the mustard for Radio 2 controller Helen Thomas, but if I had a radio station, Willie Nile would most certainly be my *Rock Show* host.

You and Willie always recognised the spirit and strength in each other, united, of course, by music. And while I don't imagine he will ever get fame in the traditional rockstar sense, to me he walks with the heart of someone who could handle it. And not many can.

OUR TOP TEN GIGS TOGETHER

James Taylor at the Hammersmith Odeon

My first backstage experience and the night a punter shouted over to ask if I was Sally Traffic, and I responded that I bloody wasn't!

David Bowie at Radio 2

The afternoon I met my hero. A highlight of my life.

Bruce Springsteen at St Luke's Church in East London

My most nervous moment ever as you introduced The Boss on stage.

Neil Young and Bruce Springsteen from the side of the Pyramid Stage at Glastonbury

Despite being thrown off several times by the US roadcrew, I still got there. An unparalleled privilege.

Elton John at the Round House

We were invited backstage – and then into the inner sanctum, where I met Elton.

Simon & Garfunkel at Hyde Park

Just wow. We'd argued beforehand and didn't talk throughout. But still. Just wow.

REM at St James's Church, Piccadilly

Just extraordinary to see them at the top of their game
in a small church.

Eagles at Wembley

Shared with our friends Anna and Steve from Tresco. A bold dresser,
I told Anna not to let me down. She wore a loud yellow suit.

The Peter Green Tribute Concert at the Palladium

The most star-studded line-up of guitarists ever at this hottest
of gigs just before lockdown.

Bruce Springsteen in Dublin

We thought it was his goodbye tour, but as it happens it was your
goodbye concert, not his. Never to be forgotten.

NOW

THE BEGINNING
OF THE END

Last night a photo popped up on my phone of us having dinner at the Gurnard's Head in Cornwall. It was 21 December 2022. Our twentieth wedding anniversary. I looked fit and slim in my black cord boiler suit. You looked suitably tasty in jeans and my favourite navy-blue linen shirt. We had the table by the fire and enjoyed a good meal and a glass too many of wine. We were demob happy. In all your decades of work you'd never had a sabbatical, so I'd asked Radio 2 if you could take a month unpaid leave in January. They agreed readily. This was the first night of our time out. The night before going to our beloved Tresco for Christmas.

You've always preferred getting there by helicopter rather than plane – altogether more rock star. Six of us got into the chopper at Penzance Heliport. You were already on nightly oxygen so your freedom pass to go anywhere was your portable oxygen concentrator. You were asked to carry it on board because of the battery. We were so excited as we saw the first of the islands that make up the Isles of Scilly. I was quite anxious about it flying on time as I had an important Zoom meeting at 5 p.m. I told you that whatever happened I needed to be on that call, as I was meeting an important actress to talk about the lead role in my film.

We landed smoothly and on time. What happened next I remember in slow-motion. I got off the chopper first. I wanted to wait for you and hold your arm as you got off, but I was called forward because of the rotating blades. I just remember turning round to check that you were OK. As you stepped down I could see something wasn't too stable. You were clutching your oxygen machine hanging on your shoulder. It cost a lot (thousands!) and you couldn't survive without it. The step was small, and the poor guy who should have been helping you was getting a walking stick out of the hold for another customer who looked more unstable than you. It was a bad decision that the poor man has to live with.

'Oh, Johnnie,' I whimpered as I watched you fall to the ground below like a tree being felled. You were stiff and upright as you clung to the machine, trying to protect that rather than your head, which landed first and hard against the plastic honeycombed-shaped flooring below. You lay still. I'm not the only one who thought you were dead. The ground staff rushed towards you. A wheelchair appeared. Blood gushed from your forehead in a honeycomb shape. 'Oh, Johnnie,' I kept repeating. I still had to wait where I was because of the blades. To this day I question myself about this. I am so law abiding and well behaved – you might have been about to pass away, but I didn't move to be by your side, as I was told not to. Pussy.

We may have landed on an island with only 150 residents, but the rescue procedure could not be faulted. Within minutes a first responder was looking at your wound. The cut went down to the bone. He apologised but you would have to go to the main island of St Mary's where there is a cottage hospital. A Noddy-car ambulance drove us to the quay. As we waited for the boat our dear friend Anna appeared. 'Johnnie, that's a corker!' She clutched my hand. I was in deep shock; she saw that and said I had to stick with you, take our luggage and very possibly accept that we'd be in Truro hospital later. Our Christmas break had lasted all of ten minutes. Never did I think it would involve both a boat and land ambulance.

You know, Johnnie, you have brought a lot of drama to my life. A lot. And not always good drama. But you have also shown me how luck has been sprinkled across your life. You were very lucky that you were still alive. You were even more lucky that the nurse on duty had recently relocated to the island of St Mary's and was a trauma specialist. She had the ability to sew up very nasty wounds like yours. When we were told that the final boat back to Tresco was at 4.45 p.m. she sped up her sewing.

There were no taxis to be had. It was 22 December and they'd all broken up for Christmas. So the hospital staff bundled us and all our luggage back into the ambulance and rushed us down to St Mary's quay. We staggered down the steps to the last boat, you looking like a survivor from the First World War.

As the boat crashed across the waves I clung to my laptop and tried calling my casting director. Could she delay the actress meeting? No. The actress had family Christmas commitments. So producer Jayne-Ann had to start the meeting without me.

What a sight we were as we arrived at the New Inn pub where we were staying: you bandaged around your head and me gasping to get into our room to join the meeting. I was fifteen minutes late, and switched from desperate wife to film writer and director. The actress was charming and intelligent, with an innate strength. I shall never forget the day I met her.

The word on Tresco spread like wildfire – Johnnie Walker had thrown himself out of the helicopter head-first. Some asked, 'Why didn't he wait for it to land?' – I love the humour of those islanders. In truth, it meant that you lay in bed for much of the five-day break. I had huge stomping walks alone, and Christmas lunch for me was spent with thirty strangers – the other residents of the pub – while you slept in bed.

Without doubt, that accident was the start of your decline. As part of your sabbatical, we were next heading for three weeks in Grenada. As we arrived at reception you were coughing constantly and in a bad way. I asked if there was a nurses' station at the hotel. Mercifully there was and yet again we were put in a buggy to a medical facility the minute we arrived. Your pulse was 28bpm. I asked the nurse to use another machine as it was clearly faulty. She kindly obliged, but that too read 28bpm. I muttered that I didn't have the nerves left to go away with you again. An hour of heavy-duty oxygen and your pulse increased. We were taken to our room and instead of going out for dinner as I had dreamt about, I ate a room-service meal while you slept.

You were notable at the two resorts where we stayed in Grenada – you were the only person on the beach staggering around with a walking stick. It had become your much-needed prop since the fall. You couldn't get in the sea or walk very far. Of course, you were still the naughtiest resident at the hotel. As you were the almost-final guest in the pool bar late one evening, the smiling night staff had to take you in a buggy back to our room and help you to the door. While many, like me, would be embarrassed by this, you thought it was brilliant when I reminded you about it in the morning. I can see that look of pride in your eye. 'I may be seventy-seven but rock 'n' roll is alive and well, and I'm still one of its ambassadors. Despite the stick!' You are and will be a monkey till the day you die. It's one of the things everyone loves about you. Including me – most of the time.

That photo of us at the Gurnard's Head will always be precious to me. Though neither of us knew it, it was your last night of being a strutting, virile man. After that fall you started to become an old and frail one. It's been downhill ever since, and I so miss the man I last saw on the night of our twentieth wedding anniversary, and the life of fun we shared together.

An afterthought on dates. I have realised that everything dramatic you've done has been on significant dates, as if the stars were double aligned. You first fell ill on our honeymoon. You fell out of a helicopter the day after our big wedding anniversary, and this year you neatly deteriorated on 1 January. Subconsciously, you always choose significant dates. So that has got me wondering, will you decide to let go on a date that will give added dramatic impact? I rather think you might. So I've been racking my brains for the next days of import. If I were a bookie I would be giving short odds on your demise on the following dates:

14 August – the fifty-seventh anniversary of the Marine, Broadcasting (Offences) Act 1967, when you continued to broadcast on Radio Caroline, making you a criminal and a radio legend in one move.

20 August – five years to the day when your respiratory consultant, Rohan Mehta, said you had two to five years left.

7 September – to make sure you are the headline news at the Radio 2 in the Park weekend in Preston.

21 December – our twenty-second wedding anniversary.

25 December – just so I will always hate Christmas.

26 December – just so I will always hate my birthday even more than I already do.

1 January 2025 – just to make it a neat year since your
   final decline.

26 January 2025 – the final *Sounds of the 70s* show in
   your contract.

30 March 2025 – your eightieth birthday.

For verification, these dates are being predicted on 11 July
2024!

THEN

STARDUST

You so often apologised to me for being so ill/such a lot of work to keep afloat/so dominating in my life. Mainly when I got down about it. It wasn't your fault you were ill. It's just the way the dice rolled. Yes, you have dominated my life, but that's because that soul of mine that intertwined with yours when we first kissed accepted that I was going to play second fiddle to you and your career. I didn't consciously recognise it at the time, otherwise I would have run! But I am certain that's what happened. That said, I have often bitched about being lost and out of my power, which is why it's so important that, as you get weaker and the final curtain gets closer, we look back at the sprinklings of stardust that have peppered our marriage, at the many things that only happened because you are you. Let's pretend we're sitting across our dining-room table from each other. You have laid the table, lit the candles and opened a bottle of Chablis, while I have cooked us a healthy supper of trout fillet, cavolo nero (or 'hedge' as you call anything green) and sweet potato wedges – a fairly usual meal for us. As the first glass slips down, cool and delicious, our day floats away and our minds turn to some of our highlights together.

I'll start with the first Radio 2 Presenters' Christmas Dinner at the Reform Club in 2001. What a fabulous grand Pall Mall setting – back in the days before the budgets were slashed. Jim Moir was the controller. He was old school, with a fantastic touch for what and who worked well on the station. 'Evolution, not revolution' was always his mantra. At that dinner, so new into our relationship, you introduced me to Terry Wogan, who was charm itself. 'You're far too good for him,' he joshed with me as we walked up the grand staircase together. Then he added, 'The trouble with Johnnie is that he doesn't know how good *he* is.' How right. I sat next to Jeremy Vine at dinner. He was about to start on the station in the old Jimmy Young slot. I spoke to him, bemused that he would leave *Newsnight* – then the bastion of intelligent BBC journalism – to go to Radio 2. Why was he dumbing down? His answer was that he wanted his name on a show, and how right he proved to be.

I would never have gone to Glastonbury without you. It wasn't, as with many, a rite of passage I needed to go through before middle age. I just thought, *Why not?* The first time was magical as we stayed in a tipi in the Healing Fields. That area sits above the site and was a spiritual haven from the scrum below. We were with your old biking mate Snapper – a wild West Countryman if ever there was one. I woke the first morning to him squatting down next to me. 'Morning, Duchess. I've bought you a cuppa.' I opened my eyes to see that he was stark bollock naked. His pendulous manhood remains my dominant memory of that weekend. I couldn't face the tea. We returned a couple more times with Martha in the three years we had her. How good it was being AAA – access all areas. Being short, I struggle with big crowds and honestly refer to the festival as a war zone, but if you get to stand at the side of the Pyramid Stage watching the bands, that is a major dollop of privilege. I can go one further. You used to DJ on that stage between sets. You shared it with a local DJ, Chris Bull, who still does it to this day. When we went in 2012, we went to see Chris. For some reason you and he both asked me to put on a song, so I did: Oasis, 'Wonderwall'. What happened was beyond my belief. The thousands of people sitting on the grass in front of the stage got up and sang. I stared in amazement. So did you and Chris. 'How do we follow that?' you asked. It was the first time in my life, possibly the only, when I could see the power of music. I felt like a megalomaniac for the rest of the afternoon.

The Boat That Rocked film premiere in Leicester Square was pretty memorable too. Because you were the only pirate DJ there we were papped endlessly as we went down the red carpet. That was a new experience. I kept thinking, *Breathe in, weight on the back leg, smile.* While the film was a shocking representation of what it was actually like on Radio Caroline, it did bring that important piece of social history to the awareness of people around the world. At the end of the film, Philip Seymour Hoffman says, 'I realised we've just lived the best days of our lives.' You told director Richard Curtis you wished you'd thought of saying that when Radio Caroline actually did end. He graciously said he'd had forty-five years to come up with the line. The after-party was amazing. It's the only time I've stood just behind Paul McCartney, and I unashamedly shook Bill Nighy's hand just by the chocolate fountain.

Goodwood has over the years given us heaps of enjoyment at the Festival of Speed, the Revival, the Members' Meeting, Goodwood Racing and, one year, the Vintage Festival. Charles, then Lord March and now the Duke of Richmond, has to be one of the hardest-working, most stylish and dignified people in the world. And Janet, his wife, is a pure, down-to-earth delight – and a real duchess! (One of only twenty-four, excluding the royals.) As for their guest list, it has to be the best in Britain, if not the world. You never knew who you would be sat next to at dinner: racing drivers, actors, musicians or leading businessmen. The balls they throw are out of this world. One year the theme was Venice and they actually built a miniature Rialto Bridge to enter the enormous ballroom (located in a marquee). On a couple of occasions we were put up in Goodwood House itself, where for you the major attraction was not the incredible art collection, but the butler, Monty, and his impressive butler's table of drinks. How you would love to sink into one of the divine red velvet sofas in the drawing room at the end of an evening with a tipple. The first time we stayed was for the one-off Vintage Festival, at which you were broadcasting your *Sounds of the 70s* show live. The house got a bit overrun with guests, partly because some did not want to leave. I remember the actor Matt Smith being there with an entourage and them all demolishing the breakfast buffet. But the really memorable time was when we were put in the Queen's Room. Goodness. This was where Her Majesty would stay. The next day I said to Charles how honoured I felt that we had been put in the best room. 'I don't want to disappoint you, Tiggy, but there is a King's Room too, which is even better.' We were both amused.

Because it was known that you loved Formula 1, that led to a few great invites. For you, the best was Monaco and being shown round the pits before the race – that, and an amazing dinner on board an incredibly smart boat the night before. Privileges you cannot buy. I preferred our last time at Silverstone when we did the famous grid walk. Oh, the noise and power! I bumped into the *Strictly Come Dancing* professionals Janette Manrara and her sparkly husband Aljaž Škorjanec. He was as excited as me to be there. 'Just look where dancing has got you,' I observed. 'You're right,' he responded, as if I was some sort of sage.

There have been some incredible dinners. Your friend Mitch Tonks invited us to a special one at his restaurant the Seahorse in Dartmouth (our favourite eatery in the UK). The extraordinary and legendary butcher-cum-chef from Tuscany called Dario Cecchini was cooking with his team. What a night. We were sat with Robin and Judy Hutson who owned the Pig hotels (our favourite accommodations in the UK), and much hilarity was enjoyed by all. There is no doubt that the people who party best are chefs and hoteliers. There is a camaraderie between them, an understanding of what a tough business it is, and how much fun there is to be had when they take time out. The next morning Mitch took us in his boat from the Dart Marina Hotel to his Rockfish restaurant in Brixham. Eight of us had a memorable breakfast of brandy, white wine and John Dory.

As a result of that night Robin and Judy invited us to a couple of their Smoked and Uncut music festivals at their Pig hotels, the best moment being when you and actor Hugh Bonneville came to dinner wearing the same shirt.

As John and Steph Illsley were also there that night, a couple of months later we all had lunch at their stunning house on the Solent. I was sitting next to Mark Knopfler, lead singer of Dire Straits, who I love. What heart and soul he has. As we left that day he said to me he would do anything for you. That really touched my heart. My mother, on the other hand, has never been impressed by any of your showbiz trappings – except the Queen's Room at Goodwood – and meeting 'Lord Grantham', who I swear she has a bit of a crush on. I told Hugh Bonneville that he has a unique ability to make a ninety-two-year-old, highly respectable, deeply Christian woman somewhat fluttery. He looked at me with a totally straight face and said, 'It's why I went into showbiz.'

The Peter Green Tribute Show at the London Palladium on 25 February 2020 has to go down as one of the most body-tingling, star-studded rock gigs we ever went to. Tickets were like gold dust, and it was only thanks to having Mick Fleetwood on your show a couple of days previously that we managed to secure tickets. What a privilege. The line-up of artists included Billy Gibbons ('Is that beard for real?' I whispered in your ear), David Gilmour, Christine McVie, Jonny Lang, Kirk Hammett, Andy Fairweather Low, John Mayall, Zak Starkey, Steven Tyler, Bill Wyman, Mick Fleetwood, of course, who had pulled it together, and last but not least, Neil Finn, who came to find us afterwards – the last time you saw him. I have to admit that it was the only time in my life that I transcended out of my seat as Kirk Hammett from Metallica played with Billy Gibbons and Steve Tyler on his guitar, which had once belonged to Peter Green. It was simply sublime. Pulling all those artists together on the same night took huge amounts of planning and preparation. And as luck would have it, it happened just a few weeks before the world locked down for Covid.

All the special events that happened after the lockdowns had so much more weight to them, as we all felt so very grateful to be doing anything outside the house. Our final bit of glamour was the night you were asked to DJ at the Palace of Versailles near Paris in July 2023. To be honest, I was truly nervous to accept the gig for you. At this stage you could no longer get health insurance, and I was terrified that the pressure of performing in public would be too much for you. However, it was for Sir Jim Ratcliffe, who was throwing a party for his staff, and I knew you respected his business chutzpah. Plus, his brother, Bob, had been one of your motorbike gang in the past. Clearly the budget was not an issue. I was so chuffed that you were asked to do a one-hour set that I just said yes without even negotiating or telling them your health was dodgy. I wanted us both to experience the thrill of going to Versailles for what I knew would be your final public appearance. What a place to bow out! I would have paid *them*.

Beforehand we had heated rows about what should be on the set list, me feeling that, at sixteen years younger, I was a bit more in touch with what people would want to dance to. You insisted that 'Hi Ho Silver Lining' was always a hit on the dance floor. I told you that if you played that, the night would be a disaster. I hadn't heard it since my primary school days, and even then I thought it was pretty dubious. We brought one of your producers, Johnny Kalifornia, with us for technical back-up, insurance in case you should feel ill and for another opinion on songs. It was late by the time you did your set. Michael McIntyre had amused the guests between courses, a musical firework display reflecting in the formal Versailles ponds had given us all a thrill, Jools Holland and his band had played, and then finally it was your turn. As ever, I had that manager/wife set of nerves about whether people would like your choices. I slipped into the party to watch you. At the bar I met the most amazing woman called Fran Millar, who is the CEO of Belstaff. She couldn't believe I was your wife – I imagine because I was younger than you. I know she'd had a good evening, but still I'm not sure if I've ever felt as flattered as I did when this good-looking, fit, beautifully dressed and incredibly successful woman looked down at me and said, 'Tiggy, you are the woman I want to be one day.' Was it simply that I was sober? As she and I spoke, I heard the dreaded opening chords of 'Hi Ho Silver Lining'. I spun round and looked up at you. And you, my Johnnie, looked defiantly back with that 'I know what I'm fucking doing, baby' look that you saved for those times you were right and I was clearly wrong. For the dance floor not only filled with many dancers, but they started doing a form of the conga. Oh, how that thrilled you. I just had to laugh and acknowledge your DJing superiority.

I don't think stardust is dependent on fame, privilege, power or indeed palaces. We've had stardust in so many ways. Bobbing on a boat off Tresco with Steve and Anna who live on the island. Or driving Bianca to Ringstead Bay on the Dorset coast for a swim (me, not you!). Staying in a beach hut with Darcey Dog at Mudeford Sandbank. Having a Campari and soda at Roxi Bar in Loggos as the sun sets. Or dancing together in our kitchen to John Prine's 'All the Way With You'. We have been blessed.

The bottle of Chablis is empty, and you suggest a glass of red and a bit of cheese, plus a couple of batons of Hotel Chocolat 70 per cent. We've always known how to have a great evening together. Good food, good wine, good memories, laughter. What extraordinary companions we have been to each other.

You add, 'If there's one email I wish I'd kept, it's the one from the man who named you Tiggy Stardust. Why didn't we ever think of that name for you?'

Because, my darling Duke, we're not the kind of people to call ourselves 'Stardust'. While it was delightful that he did, we're just a couple who enjoy the sparkle on those few occasions it's been sprinkled on us. We just possibly had more than our fair share.

TEN SONGS I'D LIKE TO PLAY FOR YOU

You always loved it when I had a song-playing session for you. You really enjoyed hearing my choices. These are selected for you, now you're on high.

Tom Baxter
THIS BOY

For you knew how to stand up after falling down.

Neil Diamond
MAN OF GOD

You were.

Glen Campbell
THESE DAYS
*Such a beautiful rendition of this Jackson Browne song,
and captures the gentle decline of a music man.*

Jackson Browne
THE LOAD OUT
*A wonderful song about the end of a show as it's
all packed away ...*

Pink Floyd
GREAT GIG IN THE SKY
I bet that's what you're having up there.

Emmylou Harris
GOODBYE
*Because I never said those words at the end.
I called an ambulance instead.*

Bruce Springsteen
WILD HORSES
*You were chasing 'wild horses', especially as a young man.
We loved his film Western Stars with his profound,
soulful voiceovers.*

Joan as Police Woman
ETERNAL FLAME
Fantastic song, and my flame for you is eternal.

Elton John and Brandi Carlile
DO YOU BELIEVE IN ANGELS?

This is the one song since you died that I know you would have loved. Their voices together are sublime. I really want you to hear it. I saw them perform it together at The Palladium thanks to your dear boss Helen.

Mark Knopfler
GOING HOME: THEME OF THE LOCAL HERO

Because it's one of the best ever tracks to end a film and it will fill you full of hope that one day we'll be together again. Just like in the movies ...

NOW
YOU'VE GOT A FRIEND
(OR TWO)

After some days of emotion (mine, not yours), just possibly the homeopathy is working its magic. That or having a day off has done it. I've been to London – for lunch with girlfriends, one of whom is over from Seattle. We eat at Spring in Somerset House, a delightfully light and airy restaurant with delicious food. I look around at the clientele and think, *This is more like it*. An urban fix, girlfriends, honest chat and Chablis. It is absolutely what I need. I return so brimming with life and excitement that you don't recognise me from yesterday. I bring good energy back to the house, while you have two messages you want to share. Daniel Cainer has written you a song using your mantra, 'No amount of worrying ever changed tomorrow.' And Peter Kay has left you an amazing voice note about our podcast and your shows. He tells you that *Sounds of the 70s* is your purpose and that you must go on doing it, and he asks how I am. He says it must be tough for me. Bless him for thinking of me, and caring. I've never met him, but he's always been so kind to you.

The thing about having so many guests these days is that we're not getting that much time just for us to be together. This is our time. A profound, special, limited time. But others want a piece of that. Of course they do. They want to see you, tell you nice things, say goodbye. In these six months we have seen more people at our home than we have in our entire marriage. This week no fewer than nineteen people are visiting. It is the main thing that is robbing me of my strength. It's a lot of tea, coffee, wine, biscuits, cakes, soups and salads to prep. Plus I have to tidy the house every time, make sure you're up and dressed, and occasionally bathed like today. And when you don't feel like talking, I have to. Often you fall asleep in front of them. I lose hours and hours of my life making small talk when I should be doing stuff. The garden is suffering from neglect.

Of course, friends are so valuable. And to you, they are the only thing that significantly changes your world from one day to the next. They bring news and gossip, energy, ideas, memories, laughs. I feel they are important for you. It is wonderful that so many people care.

I have had a rule for a couple of months that if you want to come for supper, you cook it. We have our 'gang of six' – d'Arcy, Gary, Jane and Charles – and the only way we can meet up together is for everyone to come to ours. D'Arcy does a three-course meal that we all devour. There's much chatter and hilarity around the table, but you reverse in your wheelchair away from the table. You can't quite cope with it all. Later I find you outside having a fag with your

At the Hotel Splendido, September 2003. Oh what a night!

My moment of megalomania – DJ'ing on the Pyramid Stage at Glastonbury, 2012.

Me and Johnnie during my
chemo months, 2014.

A full circle moment with our friend Carly
Cook — she edited Johnnie's biography
and is now my agent.

Fundraising with
our Dorset friends
for Carers UK.
Sunrise on the
Great Wall of
China, October
2017.

Recording *Sounds
of the 70s* together
from home during
lockdown one.

Darcey's doggy holiday on Tresco, November 2021. Her finest week.

Our last photo with Darcey in 2021. I may be holding her but it's Johnnie who she looks up to with adoration.

ABOVE: What are the chances? Johnnie and Hugh Bonneville turn up to The Pig Hotel Smoked & Uncut festival in the same shirt.

RIGHT: The F1 Gridwalk at Silverstone, July 2021. It was THE place to be in the world at that moment and a true privilege.

Our 20th Wedding Anniversary at The Gurnard's Head, Cornwall, December 2022. The last time Johnnie was strutting. His downfall started the next day when he fell out of a helicopter.

Delighted to see his old 'bounce' Sally Traffic while standing in on *Sounds of the 60s*, April 2023.

The mystery of 'Jakemansgate' is solved. Johnnie repentant with Michael Ball outside Wogan House.

LEFT: Last gig together . . . Bruce Springsteen at the RDS in Dublin, May 2023.

DJ'ing at Versailles Palace, July 2023,
in his final public appearance.

Johnnie and Tony Blackburn fighting
it out at Radio 2 after recording
'Clash of The Pirates', 2023.

Johnnie's son, Sam, visits from Australia, November 2023.
Sunday lunch at The Grosvenor Arms, Hindon.

Johnnie's final live show at Radio 2, New Year's Eve 2023.

ABOVE: Kitchen Disco, August 2024, with Johnnie's boss Helen Thomas and fellow DJ Mark Goodier.

RIGHT: Johnnie and me recording his last *Sounds of the 70s* show in his den at home, October 2024.

ABOVE: Retired with time to read all the many 'thank you' cards he was sent.

ABOVE: The day Michael and Emily Eavis came for tea — in the drive.

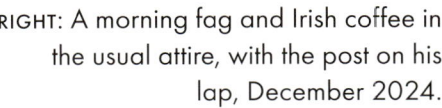

RIGHT: A morning fag and Irish coffee in the usual attire, with the post on his lap, December 2024.

My 64th birthday, December 2024. But whose cake is it? The last ever photo of Johnnie taken by our friend, Jane Treays. He died five days later.

Outside Johnnie's funeral at St Peters Church, Shaftesbury, January 2025.
He was taken away with 'Born to Run' blaring from the hearse.

cannula blowing oxygen up your nose. You don't care. I'm really shocked. It is the only time in twenty-two and a half years that you have blatantly smoked in front of me. It's a real 'fuck it' statement. You retire to bed, our guests leave and at midnight, when I finish tidying up, I fall asleep fully clothed on my bed. The open smoking feels like a deliberate slap in the face to me. I just keel over. I wake in the morning in a crumpled new Toast shirt with mascara down my face. That, I feel, should be our last supper event. I'm not saying that to protect you, but myself.

Next day your friend Mike comes to lunch. His jumper is on the sofa, but he is not. I ask where he is. You have sent this poor man from London, who has no satnav or Google Maps, to go and buy you a pack of cigarettes, as no one else will. Poor Mike is gone for over thirty minutes, totally lost in deepest rural Dorset. You're on another planet if you think I don't care anymore about you smoking. I tell you that's fine if you want to smoke, but I don't have the strength to care for someone I don't respect. I make an appointment at the local care home, which I am going to check out the week after next. This shocks you and elates me. I'm finally acting on what the medium Jean said – that you would be better off in a home. I suddenly realise that you can be a part of my life without me being trapped by the caring. I can sell this house. Go somewhere I love. Not be constantly knackered and frustrated. I see light at the end of the very long, dark tunnel I am in. You tell me you hate the idea, that you want to keep doing your show. That really is your trump card. I can hardly put you in a home with half your room taken up with a studio set-up. But the thought of being free … it gives me the hugest sense of hope. And a bit of a thrill to be honest. I have not become a total bitch. I am at the end of my tether. I know I am no fun to be with. I go through the motions of daily life, but I'm not engaging in it or enjoying myself. I am sure a break from me would be as healthy for you as it would for me.

I am getting more sluggish by the day. I told my fitness instructor this morning that in the past four weeks I've gained 5kg. FIVE KILOS! How? I exercise six days a week. I don't think my habits have changed. But then you just have to remember what goes with guests: cake, wine, gin, crisps … She says the perfect thing to me: that I cannot worry about my weight right now. I'll have plenty of time to get myself back together, and I know she will be only too happy to be part of that betterment of Tig. I am surrounded by some wonderful women who are all there, ready to catch me.

I am not alone in my depletion, though. You are wrung out too. At bedtime you tell me you've had enough. It is all such an enormous effort for you. When I help take off your jogging pants as you lie on your bed, you need a minute's break to regain your breath before I put on your pyjamas. Your oxygen goes down to 62; 90 is the lowest it should be. Every night, and indeed many times during the day, you test your oxygen level with your oximeter. It's the best physical indicator of how much your body is struggling. At bedtime we always wait for you to recover to at least 80 before turning the oxygen concentrator down a few notches for the night. Most of the day it's on maximum, as the smallest physical effort now slaughters you. The question arises, why are you taking so many pills to keep you going? Steroids, statins, blood thinners … Plus I load you up with vitamins and minerals to keep you strong. Perhaps we should cut some back. We agree we will talk to Angel Caroline about all this and what you can safely drop.

A friend contacts me after a visit. They are worried about me, and honestly, I'm a little worried about me. I am not coping too well. I'm feeling a bit unhinged. Worrying more about me than you. And my dreams are insane.

I recognise the similar symptoms to when I went through chemo – not knowing when it would end, not being able to plan and drive things forward, not travelling, having no control, feeling trapped by the situation. I was offered counselling when I was prescribed my antidepressants in March. At the time I laughed. I don't need that! I just need to stop crying and regain some energy. But now I think I do need counselling. It's not a weakness. The weakness would be if I crumbled altogether. Then what use am I to either of us?

I am lucky. The GP surgery answers my online request for help quickly. Within a day I'm talking to a counsellor on the phone, and she offers me six weeks of free sessions starting next week. She realises I just need to be heard, to vent. I do.

It's great timing as ten minutes later I'm talking to Fi Glover for Times Radio. Just the knowledge that I'm getting some help gives me strength. She asks if you're still rock 'n' roll. I tell her that you've started smoking the odd cigarette. I make it funny, but even so, I get post-interview remorse wishing I'd not said it, as it was not only a betrayal of confidence, but also I made it sound like I find it funny, which I don't at all.

John and Jackie Inverdale are visiting when the interview goes out. We get all the inside chat from Wimbledon where for the first time John had gone as a punter, not a commentator – after a thirty-nine-year stint. You remind him of your favourite moment of him commentating there: the famous rainy day, pre the Centre Court roof, when Cliff Richard got hold of a mic and started singing 'Summer Holiday'. The despondent crowd loved it. Cliff, encouraged, went on to sing another. And another. John, you remind him, said sardonically, 'You're listening to Cliff Richard's fifty greatest hits. Only forty-seven more to go.' John is a good guest. Entertaining. Interesting. He used to dep for you on *Drivetime*, including the period between you being taken off the show and Chris Evans starting. There's always a buffer presenter to lessen the shock of the new person starting. In huge loyalty to you, when John signed off his final show on the Friday before Chris started, he ended with the words, 'This is the end of an era. From Monday, the world is orange.' He wasn't booked by Radio 2 again for a long time, but for you and your millions of fans, outraged at the change, it was a fantastic 'up yours' to the controller Lesley Douglas, who had fired you in order to get Chris into the station.

Not only do I enjoy the Inverdales' company, I'm relieved to be missing the Times Radio interview. I'm scared you'll be upset with me for being indiscreet about your smoking. I mean, it doesn't sound good, does it – dying of lung disease and smoking? Personally, I'd feel ashamed. When they leave I say I don't want to hear it back, so you listen on your own when I'm out of earshot. Later you tell me I'm really good. You think I covered a lot of bases, including politics, though that's a subject I try to avoid. I even got in a few statistics about carers. You don't mention the smoking reference. It was my first national radio interview alone about caring. Usually, I can just be your fall guy, letting you do the serious, professional, on-point bits, so your praise means a lot to me.

When I listen back I can hear Fi Glover trying to break in. Dear God – I go on and on. Like it's a therapy session. Carers UK get in touch and are very happy, but even more important is that a woman called Lucasta sends me a private message on Instagram. She thanks me for my honesty and tells me about caring for her dad, who was dying from cancer and living in her sitting room while she juggled her four kids. She ended up putting him in a care home for the time he had left and has felt guilty ever since. She said that listening to me gave her the first modicum of peace since that decision. This blows me away. Bless you, Lucasta. And

I am sure your dad blesses you for caring for him for so long.

Well, *Hello, Dolly!* You've arranged seats for me to see Imelda Staunton in this fabulous musical revival. I return to you as quickly as I can in the morning. When I get back you are laid out on your bed, in pyjamas, unhappy and exhausted. You may have sent me lovely texts while I was gone, but you have had the worst night on the loo and you didn't want me to know. What set you off? You haven't eaten the food I left for you. Or taken your pills. You are weak. You remain in bed, and I feel guilty for my twenty-four hours of stimulation and freedom. You tell me you fall apart when I am not there, and I fear deeply for my week off in France, which starts in ten days.

The next day you are still weak and exhausted. You have gone down a notch. It's the morning that the vicar Helen is coming to give us Communion, and joining her is Simon Everett, the vicar who married us. It's the second time we're having Communion at home, and while you're not a regular church-goer at all, it brings you comfort and allows Helen, who will do your funeral, to get to know you a bit more. You assure me you want to get up for it, but when I return from my exercise class you are fast asleep. I take an executive decision. I tidy your clothes away and arrange chairs around your bed. We will have Communion there. Your chest of drawers becomes an altar, as Helen gets out her doll-sized silver wine goblet and candle. As she starts reading the service I feel tears stinging my eyes because there's such comfort in the words, and something in me lets go like a child. You may be in bed, but your voice is strong as you say the prayers. I love it. No hymns, no sermon, just the words and Sacrament. There's surely a wider market than the infirm for speedy at-home Communions.

On a hot Sunday afternoon I smell smoke. This time you are not the cause. Our neighbour has lit a bonfire just the other side of the fence. I have to close every window and door to protect your lungs. Our main room gets to 26.5 degrees. You call to me, hot and claustrophobic. You need Oramorph. You are panicking. You beg me not to leave you, to hold you. Your oxygen level plummets. I put on your face mask so you can breathe through your nose. When you have calmed you tell me it was the closest to death you have come. Our home still stinks of smoke when I go to bed. If you die tonight, I'm getting our neighbour for manslaughter.

'You are the story that you tell.' These were the wisest, most healing words I was given by a former Buddhist monk when we once holidayed at Kamalaya on Koh Samui. At that time I had been telling a story of deep hurt about your ex. I stopped telling that story and the hurt disappeared. I notice your story has changed in the past week. We have been screening guests to ensure they are not carrying any infection. If you should catch a virus, chest infection or Covid then your story would come to an abrupt end. You would 'drop like a stone' is what Angel Caroline has always said. An awareness of that danger has been in the back of my mind all year. You may slowly and gracefully deteriorate, or you may suddenly go. Needless to say, you have always favoured the former route. However, the story you're telling now is that it is all too much effort. Putting on a shirt, getting into your wheelchair, cleaning your teeth ... these have all been added to the challenge of going to the loo. The only places you are stress-free are your blue chair and bed. All the bits in between are so very tough on you and your lungs. You have almost had enough now, and thus you have started saying, partly in jest yet partly in all seriousness, if someone is sick, bring them in. You're getting ready to drop like a stone, and are starting to think this may be the best way to go.

Bruce Springsteen is playing Wembley on Thursday night. A friend texts that she's sure we could get you accessible tickets. I love her positivity that you could leave the house for this. Bruce was the last gig we went to, in April 2023 in Dublin, with our Irish friends Tommy and Mairead. Mairead is the wild one of their marriage, like you. When we were waiting at the airport I said to her, 'What would happen if you and Johnnie were a couple?' She quickfire replied, 'The first thing we'd do is rob a bank!' My God, how we laughed. It was 11.30 a.m. and you'd already ordered a round of espresso martinis. Dublin was a great place to see Bruce and the band. The RDS Arena is so much smaller than Wembley. It was a beautiful evening, the crowd was brilliant and Bruce was on form. He loves Ireland and that came through. When he ended the show alone on stage with a single spotlight on him and his acoustic guitar, and he sang that 'I'll see you in my dreams', it felt like a farewell. It certainly was yours (and later those lyrics would be spoken at your funeral by and at the suggestion of our friend Jane).

I'm terrified. I have a bad feeling in my chest. You have slept almost all day. Whenever you wake you seem a bit discombobulated. You leave nearly all the food and drink I bring you. You get up for about thirty minutes, but otherwise you're in bed sleeping. This is a first. You're just wiped out. I've been checking on you every half-hour since 5.30 p.m. It is the first evening that I have realised you really will die, that my evenings will always be this quiet. Johnnie, darling, I'm scared. I have to do the next bit without you.

What a night. I wake at 11.45 p.m. and go to check on you. I've left your bedroom door open so I can hear anything. The oxygen machine keeps going whether you're breathing or not, so that drones on all the time. I gingerly walk over to you lying on your side, facing the opposite wall. You're not moving. I can't see you breathing. I move closer and touch your skin. It's cool, clammy. You are breathing but so lightly that your body doesn't appear to move. I return to my room and google signs of near death. I conclude you have a few. I pray for you and fall back into a fitful sleep.

A nightmare wakes me. It's 3.45 a.m. I am certain this means you have passed. I lie there wondering whether I should just leave you as you are because there's no one I can call at this hour, or whether I should check on you. I decide ultimately that I have to go in to see you. And there you lie, like a perfect stone effigy on a tabletop tomb, your arms folded neatly across your chest, your face looking up to heaven. I admire you for your perfect end-of-it-all placement. My Duke. Lying there in peace. I lean in closer. And suddenly you lift one hand to rub your nose! You open your eyes. 'What are you doing in here?' You throw back your duvet and tell me to get in. Together, in your small four-foot divan bed, we settle down, trying to remember where we put our arms and bodies when we sleep together. It has been so long. We sleep for a few blissful hours. When we wake you ask rather critically why I didn't wake you up for supper last night. As if I had cooked. I just finished off scraps and felt sad.

Fear goes straight to your body. I return to my bed and sleep for hours – past the time when I should have left for my weekly Tuesday-morning yoga class. But it doesn't matter. My whole body feels as if it has just been in the boxing ring. I ache. I am weak. There's no way I could do chaturanga today. It will be a very small day, but I must cook some nutritional meals and get them down you.

I have used and abused my friends and my brother Martin and his wife, Kate, quite enough. They have all looked after you in times of my few absences. For the France week I decide that I should pay a carer for the majority of it. Butch (not his real name) used to be in hospitality but has taken up caring. We've known him for years and he is utterly charming. When I brief him in advance I jokingly say, 'No drugs, Butch!' A week later I am telling a friend that I've booked him, and she looks at me askance. 'You do know he had a huge cocaine habit.' We roar with laughter at both my 'No drugs' line to him, and me booking a former coke user to look after a former coke user. I go back home and tell you how funny this is.

'When you say goodbye on Sunday you must say it as if it is the last time you will see Johnnie. Anything could happen while you're away, so you must be prepared for that or you will suffer later on. If he's still here when you return, it will be a bonus.' These are the rather alarming but well-intentioned words from palliative nurse Angel Caroline before I go away.

And when I do look at you as I am about to leave for my respite week in France, your eyes are wide and healthy, sparkling at me. 'I think it will be as good for you to have a break from me as it is for me to go and have a rest,' I say. You don't respond to that, but you do say with confidence, 'I believe I will be here on your return.' I say I believe you will too. There are no tears. Just a hug. You wheel round to the front door to watch me depart. 'I love your arse.' I ask you to say no more. If those are the last words you ever say to me, I can live with it. It would be such a 'you' final comment, as you love that word. 'Arse.'

Driving to the station, I almost turn back. What am I doing? Our days together are numbered. Why am I deliberately spending some of them apart from you? But I remind myself, it is quality, not quantity, that always matters. I am shattered on every level, and I need to replenish so that our final time together can be better. I love you for understanding that, and seeing the profound need in me to rest.

You don't call me once while I'm gone. I always need to know you have woken, though, so you just text me 'Blues Song xx'. ('Well, I woke up this morning ...') You share what you are being served for supper, none of which is a surprise as I either made or bought it all.

My time with my friends Camilla and Amanda in France is beyond precious. I have little to give. We swim, read, go to the village bar, visit markets, eat delicious food at the house. I am removed from the everyday stress. There's nothing I can do for you. Camilla kindly cooks most of the meals, although we all favour suppers of crevettes, salad and fresh baguette. After a week I feel a weight lift off me and a relaxation return to my face.

I return to you renewed. It wasn't just a life saver. It was an 'us' saver. My mindset shifts from you being my heavy burden of a charge who I have to do things for all the time, wondering when this will end, to a remembrance of the fact that I love you and you are my soulmate. I can see your deterioration in the time I was away. I sense that your time is chasing on. So do you. You are sleeping so very much more.

The greatest surprise of my break was your text saying you want a final disco at home. A kitchen wheelchair disco. You send the message when Butch is with you as he stays for dinner and a bottle of wine with you each night. You repay him with a song session, and with that, JohnnieFest is born. I double-check the next morning that it's really what you want. It is, so I will make it happen. Fifty mainly local friends are coming, plus your boss, Helen Thomas. I only quipped with her about it saying, 'Do come' – and she is. So is Mark Goodier, who of all your fellow jocks has always been the kindest and most supportive to us, including delivering us unbelievable food parcels from Ottolenghi, which has given our entertaining a touch of class that would otherwise have been missing.

I'm expecting JohnnieFest to be historic. It will certainly be your final blast on a dance floor. In a way it's your crescendo, but will it be your final act? It's your night. I want it to be everything you hope for, but I also know you want to push the boundaries. You've told me you're going to smoke openly. Fine. And drink a lot. Fine. But there's a further glint in your eye. We have our first spat in months.

'You can't!' I tell you.

'It's my night, you told me.'

'But, Johnnie, if you take drugs you might die. In front of everyone.'

'I won't.'

'You don't know.'

I know what you're doing. You're pushing your boundaries. Your rock 'n' roll heart wants to believe it can be truly naughty again. You want to make believe that you're young and carefree again.

It *is* your night, and I want you to be happy, but I also ask you to remember that we're throwing a party – with guests, so IF you should do something that your weak body cannot tolerate, I ask that you do so past ten o'clock so people will have had a couple of hours of dancing first. And don't, whatever you do, let me realise. And don't do anything to me, like you did at your seventieth-birthday dinner and knees-up when you slipped a tab of MDMA into my unsuspecting mouth. 'It's the Love Drug!' you cheered with drunken glee. I'm not sure about 'love' but I was certainly wired till the early hours and hated it. In fairness, you were utterly repentant later on.

I cannot deny, I am a bit anxious that you are serious about finding some form of non-NHS drugs and that these might finish you off. Equally, a tiny bit of me thinks that if you do, and it does finish you off – what a great way for Johnnie Walker, rebel to the end, to go. It would be so you (even though all the actual rock 'n' rollers these days seem to be as clean as a whistle). It's five days away and I do wonder what lies ahead. In the meantime, I'm ordering festoon lights and wine, and planning what nibbles to serve.

You wanted a kitchen disco and by God you're getting one. I ask you all week if you're up to it. You say you are, but my anxiety grows. I keep saying we can cancel but you don't want to. You want your night. You ask me to email our guests asking for requests. They come in thick and fast. Some great dance tracks, some that you wouldn't even get out of bed for. You compile the best on your iPad and mix them up with your own choices. I check that you have some Stevie Wonder and James Brown, but I don't get involved; the music is the one area I can delegate to you. That and turning on your disco light. I have enough to do with booze, food and lights.

For the few days before I am up at 6 a.m. Really, throwing a party on top of full-time caring is quite an ask, but where you're concerned, I seem to be able to find unexpected reserves of strength, even though I'm running on empty.

The garden is pristine. Festoon lights are up all around the garden. Wine and beers have taken over the fridges. Furniture has been moved and rugs rolled up. Canapés are made, with more being donated by friends. Ice is bought. Helpers are briefed. The fire pit is ready. Outside, chill-out areas have been decorated with blankets and cushions.

You roll down the corridor fifteen minutes before kick-off. You are calm, silent. You speak through music and put on Ryan Adams's 'La Cienega Just Smiled' – possibly to calm me or even lift me, or to say I love you and thank you for this party. You know I love that song – an early memory of our time together.

Our guests arrive on time. By chance my brother Graham is over from Australia and has just this morning landed back from a trip to Kenya. My sister Fiona pops down from Shropshire too. Thank heavens for my siblings leaning in. I go and squeeze into my black cord boiler suit and rock-chick boots. I put on red lipstick to make me feel more energised, and lashings of black mascara. It makes a change from leggings, trainers and a blank visage.

I panic. The room is suddenly very full and loud. There were so many more people I wanted to invite but we had to stay contained. About fifty-five are here. Roddy, ex-army, booms out for the room to be quiet. You wheel yourself out of your disco corner and make a small speech, starting by excusing the cannula but it gives you a constant supply of cocaine for the evening. That goes down well. You talk about it being fifty-eight years since you started DJing at the Bali Hai Bar at the Locarno Ballroom in Birmingham. You thank Helen Thomas, your boss from Radio 2, for coming. You credit yourself for bringing her to the station from Radio 4 to be your *Drivetime* producer (she doesn't argue this point). You also thank Mark Goodier. Then you play your first track, the same one you started with at the Bali Hai: the Four Tops 'Can't Help My Self' … Purple, green and red from the disco light shimmer over the walls and vaulted ceiling. Tacky but suitable.

The dancing starts. It's a slow start, as there's a lot of eating, drinking and talking going on, but soon my girlfriends are giving their legs a great workout. I realise that the main room of our house is made for a party like this. Every bit of its thirty-three-feet length is being used.

Your boss Helen works the room brilliantly. She gets plugged by a songwriter friend about his new single, but mainly she gets lots of praise for hiring Vernon Kay and delights in showing me a video of him tossing the caber in Bute. I ask if she was there. She said she couldn't go there *and* make our party. She chose you, Johnnie. Her devotion and loyalty to you is extraordinary.

Mark Goodier steps in to DJ so you can go and smoke. That's as bad as you get – clearly music and survival are your mindset, in the end; not drugs. But then you have always, since I've known you, been a pro. And you probably only said it to wind me up. You have one G&T and otherwise it's water and popcorn that sustains you. It's sort of odd. You sit in your wheelchair with your iPad next to your valve amp and oxygen machine, and there you stay. You don't want to mingle, though of course you are a sitting duck for people to come and have one-on-one chats. They need that. Many have not seen you all year. This is their goodbye, though I don't think you twig that. I realise as I talk to our guests that you are delighted not to have to make small talk around the room. And then I think back to all our supper parties where you have played music at the end. It dawns on me – this was to get you out of talking! You are a radio man. You have always enjoyed being in a studio alone. A one-way conversation. Because, honestly, you're not very interested in people. It's the music, man! That is your motivation and this is the perfect style of party for you now. It doesn't mean you haven't partied well in the past, because you have. From our wedding party and your book launch after-party at the Union Club, to Bob Harris's unforgettable sixtieth birthday or the balls at Goodwood, you've danced, laughed, drunk and revelled.

There's excitement from anyone who gets their track played. All I asked for was Sister Sledge's 'We Are Family'. I dance with my siblings and think to myself that I never, ever thought that the four of us would dance together while you DJed. And yet here we are – my high point of the evening. I see you smile; you love me dancing. The rock-chick boots soon get replaced by trainers.

Gorgeous Poshie, one of our dear, more ethereal friends who has made you so many cakes, soups and goodies in your periods of ill health that she named herself 'Soup Pest', comes up to me and says how brilliant this is. That we would all be at your funeral, but this way we can all cele-brate you while you're here. And that's it, Johnnie. While you just wanted to see people dancing to the music you play one more time, we are actually providing something far deeper and more profound for our friends.

The music ends at 11 p.m. You announce that this is the final song you will ever live DJ. You *stun* the room by putting on a slow one: 'The Rose' by Bette Midler. 'But,

Johnnie, we need a banger to end on!' I shout across the room. I apologise later for my outburst. The music is your area, and you want to end on a slow dance because in your day that's what you did. We all adjust and grab someone to dance with. Our friend Martyn grabs me, and we sing our hearts out to a song that I got you to love. So in a way I am flattered. There's a huge cheer for you at the end. 'Hip-hip-hooray!' we all chant. And within minutes, like one of the Rolling Stones leaving the stadium quicker than Jumpin' Jack Flash, you're rolling out of there, waving from your wheelchair and heading down the corridor. It is the last time most people in the room will see you. Some leave, though a hardcore stay on. Honestly, no one there will ever forget their farewell evening to you, and while you didn't talk that much, they don't mind because they understand the man you are. A DJ.

You fall on your bed, which makes undressing you hard. Your feet and legs are cold. You are shattered. I tuck you in, forgetting half the things I should do. You are worried. I am worried. Although I don't share that; I just tell you that you were brilliant and that I love you. I return to the party in need of red wine. Gradually guests leave and I clear up till 2 a.m., only to be woken at 4.45 a.m. by the cockerel next door.

Four people stay the night. In the morning, they help me move the furniture back. I leave you in bed. I am too scared that you will have popped off from the strain, so I wait till they have all gone, because if you have I know I want to be alone with you. I am so afraid that I wait to take you a tea until 10.45 a.m. My heart is in my mouth, but there you are, eyes open. And you stay there for the day while I clear up the trash, take down the lights and rearrange everything. I finish around 5 p.m. and slump.

It took four intense, long days of my life to set up the party and then clear it up. There was hardly a piece of furniture that wasn't moved, an area that wasn't lit up. I did food and booze galore and mixed with all our friends. By the end of it I am exhausted, and for me it would have been worth all that energy if you had seemed a little more grateful. You honestly don't seem to have enjoyed yourself. Our guests did – they had a great time – but you can't even thank me with sincerity in your voice or heart. It was too much for you, but specifically people coming to talk to you. You wished you'd been unreachable up on a stage and could have just played music. That was all you wanted – to check you still had the power to make people dance. It wasn't about socialising with people. I don't regret it one bit. It's amazing that we threw a party with you in your state, really amazing, and the thank-yous flood in, but I wonder if you are just too far gone with your health now to actually enjoy yourself.

The next day my body has spoken. I sleep all morning, as do you. The DJing has taken its toll, and so has the hostessing. Never again, Johnnie. I am NOT doing another party for you! But somehow, I don't think you'll be asking me to.

I am smiling to myself here. You obviously forgot that today is *Rock Show* recording day. I've just heard you putting on your voice. And I know you're in your PJs having leapt out of bed when Liz texted you. How can you pull that out of the hat still? If only you could help with the practical stuff too. I am secretly bloody smug that for once I am in bed and you are working.

You have been telling me for months that you only have three weeks left. I've stopped taking it seriously as it has been doing me in. However, a week after the party you are still struggling. There's been a lot of black humour passed among our friends that if the party didn't finish you off, what the hell will? Maybe the after-effects. I give you a bath today (I actually think I'm good at it, and you agree with me). It's an intimate time and you often share more personal thoughts then. You say that you've gone downhill in the past few days. You say that even moving your position in bed can make you out of breath. And you are pretty much on Level 9 of oxygen all the time now – the highest level. I know you are being truthful, as when you swing your legs out of the bath (from the lift), you don't have the strength to stand up for me to put your dressing gown on. For the first time ever you say, 'I hope I die soon.'

I am being given therapy. With my therapist Martine I cry for the first time this year about the fact that I will lose you. Until now I've been in control. What a relief to know I care. She sees that I'm holding on, keeping it all together. She's delighted that I cry. We talk about you a lot. In a way she is preparing me for grief. We talk about your wildness and my lack of it; that I recognised in you an animal I wish I was, and you recognised in me one who could keep you on the straight and narrow. But have I been just too straight with you? I know that behind my back you're a monkey, having a puff and goodness knows what else when you can, trying to break the rules without me knowing. It's my role to be the strict one because if I give you an inch, you take a mile.

I'm in London to check on the flat – which didn't sell, and I am secretly very happy about it. I don't want to lose this connection to the city. I take an early-morning walk through Primrose Hill park up to the classic view of London. I choke up. My heart immediately feels heavy without Darcey Dog at my side, and knowing you will never see this glorious view again – the city in which you lived for most of your life, looking magnificent on this hazy, late-summer morning. I realise I really am already grieving: you, me and Darcey. That was our true inner family, and soon I will be the only one left. Tears start to tumble.

I have two meetings and then I can't wait to return to you. I have your beloved sourdough bread from Little Bread Pedlar on board – possibly your final taste of London.

I lie in bed knowing that I am flying to Rome for two days in the morning. I need to have some meetings with possible heads of department for the film. In February when I went to Sardinia I was overwhelmed with emotion and fear. In

July when I went to France I felt confident you would be there on my return. Now, I am quite calm, because I am OK for you to go. I don't want you suffering any more than you have to. I silently speak to the cells of your body, telling them that I am fine for you to go. I give you permission. You can stop fretting for me. With all my soul I pass that message into your cells.

You get up early to wave me off. You want no one to go in to see you today. The fridge is stacked. You are happy to be on your own. I think about animals and how they like to be alone when they die and wonder if that is what fate has stored up. Much of me thinks you will choose to go when I'm not there, either today or in the future. And I don't mind. In fact, it would be a relief to always remember you alive, with that spark you have.

I return from Rome full of excitement – as ever after a break. The meetings were all a success. I love that feeling of being alive and creative, making bonds with others, and together we will make something special.

You, on the other hand, have taken up smoking like there's no tomorrow. Since we agreed you could smoke at your party, you are now doing so as a matter of course during the day and before bed. You once told me smoking is a socially acceptable form of suicide, and maybe this is what it's about, but I also know that the smell of smoke makes my stomach heave. I am, as I've always told you, allergic to cigarette smoke. That was discovered when I was thirty. So having you wheel down the corridor reeking of it is such a repulsion that I cannot come and help you get into bed or kiss you goodnight. Not for the first time, I think to myself, *It's the fags or me. You choose which you want.* But you know – and so do I – that you will have both. I can hardly demand exclusivity at this point in your life.

I dream that you are driving me to Primrose Hill. You are dressed as you used to be – a shirt, a jacket, good jeans. You don't have any oxygen machine on you. You seem a good ten years younger. You are fit and the Johnnie you used to be, and honestly, when I wake I think you must have died as the dream was so real. To be reminded of how our life was really hurts. It reminds me of how shrunken it has become.

This week we 'celebrated' twenty-three years of meeting. We are both tired and down. It is an awful evening, despite me serving lovely food and wine. You call it a negative night. My fatigue is getting deeper and deeper. I'm aching to return to my power and yet you show no sign of letting me do so.

Self-preservation is becoming my main concern. The words 'care home' are now entering our vocabulary, because I don't know how much more I can take. We discuss you 'releasing me' from caring in November. It sounds cruel, and it's not what I wanted. I want you to die in our home, but I am almost breaking with the effort of it all. As I said on our anniversary … I've really had it with the noisy oxygen machines and long oxygen tubing, pee bottles and commodes, wheelchairs, the constant making of meals, laundry and getting you dressed. The only thing I am not sick of is giving you a bath.

I see your self-destruct button is rearing its head. Your smoking reaches new levels. You are lost in a world of your phone and iPad. I've no idea what you're reading or looking at; you have become too closed to share. It's hard to get through to you. I guess you want to feel alive, and yet the sadness of the smoking is that it's indicative of you giving up.

I have let Helen Thomas at Radio 2 know that you will stop broadcasting at the end of October. She is sad but, like me, she's glad it's your decision and that you can have a proper send-off. You have a chance to play all your favourite tracks one last time, and receive the love. With Helen – and Sharon, the head PR at Radio 2 – we will plan the announcement and press release. There'll be more attention, of course – as if we need that. Do you crave quiet and privacy as much as I do? We still haven't opened all the cards you've been sent. It's like your cancer time all over again. The love that is sent is beautiful, but energy has to be found to deal with it.

The discussion about a care home is firming up. Rather than leaving it as a concept, I'm doing research. You have reached a place where you want me to be free, and while I struggle with the thought of you being incarcerated, I too want me to be free – at least next year. Here's my dilemma: *ANTONIA*, my passion-piece film, has been delayed and delayed because of you. And because I'm not just the writer, and second producer, but also currently attached as the director, it will be all-consuming. It does not mix with caring. Our team have all accepted the delay from this year, but we can't really expect them to go on and on waiting, especially Jayne-Ann who, as lead producer, has been breaking her balls to make this manifest. If by chance you are still around in January, you will be sleeping most of the time, with bedpans your major need. I am not doing that. I wouldn't be strong enough.

Of course, I do wonder if you stopping the show will take away your remaining power. Your life's purpose will be over. But what I am learning is that the human spirit – especially yours – knows no bounds of strength. How are you even alive now, with the dreadful state of your lungs?

I've had the conversation with Helen about your replacements on the shows. It seems Bob Harris was right; he is the natural successor to *Sounds of the 70s*. Shaun Keaveny will do the *Rock Show*. I know you told Helen I should do *Sounds of the 70s*, but that would *never* have happened. I'm sure she laughed as you suggested it, but then you always have been my biggest radio fan. I told her that Liz 'Queen of Rock' Barnes should be considered for the *Rock Show*. Helen knows her mind and she's gone for safe, reliable choices, and thank goodness they are both real radio men and not 'celebs'. I'm not sure if I'll be able to listen to them, though. Having the conversation was hard. To realise that you really are stopping, that it's the end of an era, a career, a lifetime of radio – my heart sinks at the thought. I can't imagine what your heart is doing as you approach your final shows. You will announce it on Sunday, 6 October. How I dread the attention. How many texts and emails will I have to respond to? I'd better leave a day clear to deal with them.

I have great gratitude for your chariot – I know you love pottering around on it. For a man who has always loved vehicles, I give praise for the small joy that (almost) to the end you will enjoy driving something. After it's had a service, I need to drive it back to your room. Holy schmoly, that thing shoots down the corridor with such speed I scream out loud and think I'm going to crash. I swear it could go 30mph. You laugh. The servicing man has left it in fifth gear, while you keep it in first. This begs a question – who needs FIVE gears in a wheelchair?

I see a noticeable change in you. Dark rings have formed around your eyes – it's beyond bags; it's the look of an old person. And without doubt you are spending more time in bed than out. You've also stopped using your beloved blue velvet chair. For the time you spend in the main room 'up', you are staying in the wheelchair. I can't remember when you last got out of pyjamas. Your appetite still exists – but mainly for carbs and comfort food. On Friday evening, which is becoming our date night, you eat almost nothing of the sea trout, samphire, spinach and chickpea dinner that I've lovingly served, but boy, after I've removed the offending healthy food, do you go for some manchego and fruity cheese biscuits, cantucinni biscuits dipped in dessert wine and then an ENTIRE large bag of sweet and salty popcorn!

You have suggested cutting your steroids back from four a day to three, and Rohan Mehta, your consultant, is very much of the opinion that you are the one who knows the right level. Steroids lead to the munchies, and you feel that eating less rubbish may be good for you. Or perhaps you just want to reduce this way of propping up your strength. You take so many pills to keep you going, but more and more I realise that is not what you want. Indeed, I feel quite keenly that while we are not there yet, the dreaded moment may come in November or early December, once you have stopped broadcasting. And let me be quite honest, I hope that is the case. It sounds harsh, but it's nearly the moment to call time.

Your son Sam calls to see how I am. I love that he's concerned about me as well as you. How I wish he lived here and not in Australia. I'm on my early-morning Saturday drive up to Shaftesbury to get your croissant. Somehow this amuses him. He has heard that we're discussing the idea of a care home for you. I hear my voice crack. I cannot hide my emotion of how bloody hard it has been for me this year, how unbelievably challenging you can be to manage. Sam knows you, and he gets it. He laughs when I tell him you are pathologically programmed to be bad. He realises for the first time the incredible toll this is taking on me. I don't mean for him to know this, but it splurges out. I tell him I know no one who has sacrificed as much as I have this year, looking after you. Sam is completely understanding. I thank him for being just one of four people in your family who regularly keep in touch with me to see how I'm doing. Your nieces Michelle and Trudi and cousin Mal are the other three. I love them for recognising how tough this time is and what it is doing to me.

Sam doesn't know if he should come over now or wait for the funeral. I suggest the latter as you two have said your physical goodbye at Heathrow last November. You agree with this completely and even say he shouldn't bother with the funeral. I inwardly disagree on that, as I think Beth will need his brotherly support.

As for care homes, I have suggested that for November you must be here at home. I will need to protect you from your own fallout after stopping work. I think it will hit you hard and that will be one of the most important times for me to support you. To put you into a home just before Christmas feels utterly churlish and wrong, so we have agreed that looking at January onwards would be a good idea. You tell Sam it's what you want because you think it might be fun (really?!), but mainly you want to free me after such an intensive year. I think we both know that it won't happen, though. I'm pretty sure you will call time before that, so possibly it's just an emotional crutch to help keep me going. The thought of light at the end of a long, dark, claustrophobic tunnel.

Insomnia is raising its head again. I'm listening out for you, getting woken by the smallest sound. And in those hours when I toss and turn, any time between 1 a.m. and 6 a.m., I find myself dwelling on the eulogy you want me to do. I've thought of so many openings, so many lines, so many angles. I can only say what I believe, and there will be much that I must not say. I mean, honestly, darling, is it really wise for any man to ask his wife to do this hugely important sign-off? It's just too tempting to complain about all your faults. But of course, you trust me, as you should. You know that despite your multiple flaws, no one has ever fought your corner as hard as I have. Unless you have upset me – and then you feel the full force of my rage, as you should. But how on earth do I sum up someone like you?

I'm out of control. I'm like a spider trying to avoid getting sucked down the plughole but the water is speeding up and I can't hold on. A force is happening beyond my control. I know you are getting worse and suddenly there's not enough time to look after you, get everything done, stay on top of things. I took a sleeping pill last night and still woke four times. I think I hear you ringing a bell, so I get up and find you fast asleep. We keep having power cuts, which make your machine beep constantly and the phone make a weird sound when it comes back on. Thus, I'm oversleeping, not getting enough time to prep everything before I go to an early-morning class. I rush in to your room with your early tea and breakfast on one tray, telling you I can't stop as I'm behind schedule. I fling open your curtains, wheel out the Alien, but I leave the pee bottle full and you gawping, 'Where are you going?' Yoga! Tennis! Fitness class! Back later! Should I be cancelling these classes? I'm starting to feel guilty and yet they keep me going.

My body is out of control too. I am certain the sertraline has filled out my entire stomach area. Or is it comfort eating? Clothes that hung on me last year now fit like a tight girdle. It's so depressing. I know we're all supposed to be body positive, but when my midriff stops certain yoga poses because it's too large, I can't help feeling ashamed. Dare I stop the antidepressants? Will I crumble again as I did in January? Or am I now a hardened carer who has already done so much grieving for our life that I'll be fine? Do I register with a nutritionist? Do I wait till after your final curtain has fallen? I need to be on top of me, my life. Being out of control is my worst state, but to your credit, when I get like this you are supportive, even though you are the cause. You put your own dilemma to one side and focus on mine. When I can get you out of your bubble you are the most wonderful advisor – still.

It doesn't help that I'm filming a short film in two weeks – a directorial debut. I'm paying for it, so I'm asking favours from lots of lovely crew and actors. People are being so kind. They love the script. I feel love all around. I just need more sleep and time.

Helen the vicar has offered to come and give us Communion again on Saturday. She will be our only visitor that day. Two things she prays for strike us: 'That Johnnie will live as long as possible' and 'Forgive us our sins.' When I see Helen out I return to you, and I'm laughing. So are you. 'Bet you didn't pray for me to live as long as possible!' you quip. No, I bloody didn't! Honestly, Johnnie, our humour … Then you add, 'You don't have any sins to forgive, unlike me.' Really, Duke, I'm not perfect. I have sins just like everyone. Just not as many or as large as yours!

I make an enormous social-media mistake afterwards. I am so taken by the prettiness of Helen's travelling Communion kit that I put up an Insta post of it. The floodgates open with friends getting in touch: 'Tiggy! Is Johnnie OK?' It's as if I've said it was your FINAL Communion. We're not there yet.

THEN

TRIP THE LIGHT FANTASTIC

The *Rock Show* got rescheduled to 11 p.m. on a Friday night. This didn't affect you as, since Covid, these were all done as pre-records with your Queen of Rock producer Liz Barnes. While I don't have a great knowledge of or affinity for rock music, I have at times listened alone in my bedroom at 11 p.m. while you already slept in your own room with your oxygen concentrator at your side. It's hard to comprehend that the man I see struggling with breath on a daily basis is pumping out these songs with such energy.

The one band you seem to champion a lot is Greta Van Fleet, and – spoiler alert – I discover it's not a woman, but a band of blokes. I love the title of their song 'Trip the Light Fantastic', so I'm borrowing it, as I believe I tripped the light fantastic myself when I did something with extraordinary foresight in September 2023. I was having my nails painted one Saturday morning and had the most overwhelming sense that I should text Sam in Australia. Sam and I have always got on well. I've never tried to be a stepmother to either of your children. Why would I? For a start my age is directly between yours and theirs, and they were both fully formed adults when we met. In Sam's case, he has been a wonderful addition to my life and I will always be there for him and his family. There was a plan that he would come over the following April, in 2024, for a visit. However, without telling you, I texted him to say that my hunch was that he should come over this autumn. I felt it was too risky to wait till the spring.

He trusted my instinct and booked to come in November for ten days – and what a wonderful ten days it was. We had Sunday lunch at the Grosvenor Arms in Hindon, sitting by the roaring fire. He came with us on a hospital visit for an ultrasound on your heart, and we then went to the Beckford Arms for lunch. And possibly best of all, I booked the two of you into the Pig at Combe as I really wanted you to have a small road trip and some boys' time together. Unlike you, Sam is a foodie, and there he could try the delights of the wood-fired oven in the garden folly and their twenty-five-mile menu for supper. The next day you drove on to the coast to meet up with Beth for fish and chips at the Hive Beach Café at Burton Bradstock. You and your offspring all together. I knew it would be the last time that would happen and suggested you got some great photos of the three of you. I didn't mean a couple of badly taken selfies, but never mind. It's a day that will remain with the three of you forever.

For Sam's final weekend you took him for breakfast at Guy Ritchie's Compton Abbas Airfield so you could eat while you watched small planes take off and land. Sam used to have a flying licence and it's just the boys' sort of thing that excites you. But perhaps the finest afternoon of the stay was when d'Arcy and Gary invited us to Sunday lunch along with our other besties, Jane and Charles. The gang of six plus one. None of them had ever met Sam and they wanted to do this for you. How they loved him. And how surprised they were that he is the absolute antithesis of you. They were thinking, how did such a normal, balanced, intelligent man come from your loins? To quote Sam's best ever line: 'I grew up surrounded by sex, drugs and rock 'n' roll, but I rebelled by getting a degree and going into banking.' I watched you glow with pride at their obvious affection and admiration for him. Somewhere towards the end of lunch, Charles, an imposing man who works in the City, leaned over to Sam and told him not to worry about a thing; they would all be there to help look after his dad.

You drove Sam to the airport the next day. You had it all planned. Your best 007 Seiko watch which you had won at a silent auction for Salisbury District Hospital Stars Appeal, was in your pocket. You knew this would be your physical goodbye. The only thing you inherited from your father was a watch, and so you wanted both Sam and Beth to have a watch from your own collection of wristwear. Handing it over to Sam was a poignant moment for you both and it was the culmination of an amazing ten days. (After you die, I hand Beth the small Seiko and indeed most of your remaining watch collection.)

Sam says he will be indebted to me for the rest of his life for getting him over when I did – when you could still walk, drive and enjoy life. It was a treasured time that really did trip the light fantastic – whatever that actually means.

NOW

THE FINAL SHOW

It's a big build-up to the announcement: press releases, social-media posts – all to be approved by us. The network approaches it all with huge respect. When you record it on your regular Wednesday-afternoon slot I take in a coffee and ask if it's done – the announcement. It is, and yet both you and Liz are so nonchalant about it. No big drama or emotion. You just pop it in at the end of an email about someone else's dad dying of pulmonary fibrosis. Oh, yes – I'll be stopping in a few weeks. Throw-away. So you.

Boom. Sunday, 6 October 2024 at 3.54 p.m., your listeners hear that you are stopping. As your publicist (among many of my jobs), I post an Insta of you waving goodbye in your old Wogan House studio. Beautiful messages are left under this, and what I love is that they all get it. They love you, but they know you're sick and everyone wishes you well. My tweet is a photo of you and Bob Harris at the Eagles concert in Hyde Park in 2022. Robert Plant is singing on the huge screen behind you: 'From one friend to another.' Bob texts me, delighted that I posted a message of such public support of him taking over.

The Radio 2 PR team ask about all the interview requests. We turn them all down, even the *Radio Times* (who, let's face it, have never put you on the cover and so haven't really earned any brownie points from us, despite the radio legend you are supposed to be). I tell them you are doing NO MORE INTERVIEWS. Then Rebecca Hardy from the *Mail* texts me. She has done two articles on us before: after your cancer and after mine. No, I tell her. Then she says how about she comes down and interviews just me? You and I discuss this and agree that would be OK. Then she mentions having ten minutes with you. She's bloody clever!

You're still in bed when she arrives. She and I talk, and it's such a delicate balance, treading the line between the fact that I love you and will miss you, and the fact that I feel bloody tired and trapped, and struggle being your full-time carer. I check on you, and before long you wheel yourself in with your opening gambit to Rebecca: 'She can't wait for me to die!!' It's so funny and magically you set the tone for your interview. We laugh all the way through, which is the very last thing she expected when we were going to be discussing your demise.

Murray, the photographer, arrives – this is the fourth time he's snapped us. Again, like Rebecca, the first time was after your cancer in our Marylebone flat. They have both been the press-media constants of our life, so somehow it feels totally right that they are here in yet another of our homes. Murray is a fan; he's so thrilled to be with us that he can't stop talking. You are fantastically open and friendly. I end up making everyone a sandwich because it's gone 2 p.m. and we haven't even taken a shot yet; it's just banter and laughter, and a bit of hair and make-up. You are talking too much. I remind the room that you're recording your show at 2.30 p.m. and must conserve your energy. I need to conserve mine too. I'm so tired by the time the photos start that I find it hard to muster a smile. You keep delaying the start of your show. You only have three more left. They are so precious and all have to be as good as possible. It's 4.30 p.m. before you get going. Before the recording starts you wheel down the corridor to your den and start listening to tracks. The music drifts up to the kitchen. I walk in to find Murray having a moment; he is not just moved, he's emotional. 'That track …' He excuses himself. I know that it's more than the track. It reminds me of the huge connection there is between you and your listeners. I forget that sometimes; maybe I'm even blind to it. I know it exists because of all the messages, cards and emails that keep arriving, but with Murray I can actually SEE it. He doesn't realise that in that moment he is giving me the understanding of what thousands of people think about you and how very deep their feelings go.

The *Mail* team are with us for well over five hours. I am done for at the end, and worried about you having enough energy for your show, and while your voice sounds croaky at the start, you dig, dig, dig deep and you astound me when I overhear some links. As ever I wonder how you do it. You tell me later that you have to dig down here – you hold your fist to your solar plexus, the seat of strength. You don't do that for me. Just your shows. I get it.

The article is out in the Saturday *Mail*. In the photo you look incredibly happy, spoilt almost. I look pale and tired; I'm hardly smiling. As a result of that article more cards arrive. At least 100 to Johnnie Walker DJ, Dorset. I have to applaud the Post Office; this is a good PR story for them. The reaction to the article is good. It prompts a few more people to get in touch who want to visit (or possibly it's a coincidence). The list is currently Hugh Bonneville (Thursday), which will be hilarious, I know, and just what we need. Then on the wait list is Robert Plant, Michael Eavis, Richard Allinson and your fellow pirate on Radio England Roger 'Twiggy' Day. I need to get through my film shoot and your final show before booking them in.

My shoot is a triumph – I can now legitimately call myself a director. You're thrilled for me and have been incredibly good at keeping your head down and being undemanding. Thank you. I dig as deep as you do for a show, with the result that this weekend I want complete solitude to recoup my energy and do all those things I should, like clean the commode from head to toe and defrost the freezer. Sometimes mundane domesticity is just what the soul needs. I've also caught up on death-facing admin. We've checked your will, done your letter of wishes, contacted the bank, stuck your DNR (do not resuscitate) in an envelope on the front door in the event that paramedics are called out when I'm not here. It all has to be done. The last thing I want is any strife after you've gone.

You sleep and sleep. It's what Nurse Emma said you would do, and she was right. In one week your final show will go out. Friends ask if you're sad, and I tell them relief is all you feel. We both do.

The last song: that's what everyone wants to know about. The *Mail*; Helen your boss. The coolest person about it is Liz, your producer. She knows that you'll find the right thing. You've been toying with the Royal Scots Dragoon Guards playing 'Amazing Grace' – one of those freak Number Ones that happened in the Seventies. 'You can't go out on f***ing bagpipes,' I say in my usual forthright manner. 'I mean, you're not Scottish and you hate the bagpipes …'

I'm at my weekly yoga class, and as I stand in Mountain Pose it comes to me: Judy Collins's 'Amazing Grace'. Back at home I bring my computer, along with your sourdough toast and coffee, into your bedroom. I sit on the lovely wingback chair, as you want to dictate your song list. I throw out the idea of Judy Collins and you tell me that you too had thought that and had just listened to it. It goes on the list as the one to beat. I suggest it will have everyone crying, which is just what you want, and I could use it at your funeral too, so there's a tie-in. Honestly, the things I think about – and voice.

You are itching to dictate your list for the show – the songs spill out of you quicker than I can type. Mink DeVille. The Staple Singers. Johnny Nash. I question why these, and you say simply because you love them – and I never knew. Sister Sledge's 'We Are Family' you want because that's how you look upon your listeners. Elton and Kiki are a given, as is Lou Reed's 'Walk on the Wild Side' because Liz has pulled out that great clip where he realises you are the man that made his career in Europe. You suddenly interject, 'Have you thought that I might pop off after the last show?' I cough, wipe away some tears and say we need to get the list done. (Yes, of course I have thought that, but it's just too close and soon to contemplate that happening.) Songs go in and come out. In the space of twenty minutes there are far too many on the list. You have three punk songs, which I suggest is two too many, and you agree as we have to edit the choices down quite a bit. After a day of reviewing your choices, you go into the show with this list:

HOUR ONE

George Harrison – What is Life

Sister Sledge – We are Family

Roger Daltrey – Giving it All Away

Elton John And Kiki Dee – Don't Go Breaking My Heart

Rod Stewart– Mandolin Wind

Neil Diamond – Holly Holy

Peter Gabriel – Solsbury Hill

The Rolling Stones – Wild Horses/Dead Flowers
Jackson Browne – Fountain of Sorrow
Stevie Wonder – He's Misstra Know-it-All
Mink Deville – Spanish Stroll
Simon & Garfunkel – Song for the Asking

HOUR TWO
Bob Seger – Main Street
Cat Stephens – Father and Son
Nils Lofgren – Shine Silently
Staple Singers – If You're Ready
David Bowie – Drive-in Saturday
Lou Reed – Walk on the Wild Side
Skids – Into the Valley
Van Morrison – Into the Mystic
Paul McCartney & Wings – Band on the Run
Judy Collins – Amazing Grace

Needless to say, it becomes very organic during the show – some songs change and a lot move, often because of trails and timings, and often because you change your mind because a song is too long.

Liz and Paul come down for the final recording. Paul insists it is the right thing to do; he knows you shouldn't end your career by shutting your laptop alone in your den. I get up early to make soda bread, prepare a lunch, clean the floors, get you bathed and dressed. (What? No PJs today?!) Flowers arrive from Helen and Laura at Radio 2 – stunning autumnal colours, and for the first time today I cry. I rush to get a vase and put them in your den for the show. I print out the final song list as Paul and Liz's taxi pulls up in the drive.

It's funny to have their injection of energy in the house, but it's a good thing. They bring flowers, a candle, Bombay Sapphire and a special bottle of Jameson whiskey for you (a new addition to your morning coffee, to go with the first two fags of the day. I learn that Irish whiskey is softer than Scottish so for you it's a delicious addition to your first brew). Plus, an audio surprise: a recording of Sir Rod Stewart making a wonderful impromptu tribute to you, which is to be dropped into the show. My second tears of the day fall.

We prep your den, ring your friend Rodney for an emergency extra microphone for me, and have lunch. I'm already quite tired by the time we start the show at about 3 p.m. You want me on it and to sit opposite you all the way through, until the final half-hour when you want to be alone.

With the four of us in your den it's quite cosy. You don't tell me anything about what you want me to say. That's because you don't know; you don't have a single note in front of you except the list of former producers to thank and the song choices. The rest of it is all off the cuff. Throughout, I am on the backfoot and completely surprised when you suddenly look at me and ask something. 'Do you shine silently?' you ask after Nils Lofgren's song. I have no idea what you're on about. 'I do it noisily,' I respond in a panic, and you laugh, and laugh. It's like that all the way through: I'm a stunned rabbit and come out with garbage. I keep surprising you with the things I say. I find myself talking about my mother, how she hates music and never wanted radios in the car. Why am I talking about her on the radio? She is such a good, kind, Christian woman, and at ninety-three, the most enquiring, fascinated person in the family. I think it's because she is the antithesis of me. Yet I was so influenced by her. I've always fought against that influence. I clearly need therapy about her, but not on-air. (I will later wake in the middle of the night and regret most of the things I said, but I will not share this with you or your production team, as the show is about you, not me. I was only there as a foil to set you off in different directions. But I really do worry that people will think, 'Shut up, Tiggy. It's his last show.' And if they do, I will not blame them. I agree!)

There is one thing I am pleased about: I tell you on-air how proud I am that you have carried on broadcasting these past ten months (which I've not said enough privately). I alone have seen the struggle and the great depths you have had to mine. My voice croaks very slightly. You seem touched and thank me.

For the final half-hour, Liz sets up her computer in our living room and FaceTimes you from the other end of the house, so that you can be completely alone with your listeners, and not distracted by us. She, Paul and I listen to your final links together.

And I cry for the third time today.

There is champagne, photos, and then suddenly Liz and Paul's taxi arrives. Your final show is in the can. You look at me across our dining-room table where we sit, exhausted, and say, 'I think it's just hit me.' And I think it has.

You eat very little supper and are in bed by 8 p.m. I sit on the edge of your bed and tell you how proud I am of you. And I am. You have been an incredible broadcaster for so many years. You are the best, I tell you – unique – and will be so missed.

And now my anxiety starts that you may now stop. Some force has kept you going all year; you have outlasted any doctor's predictions and I believe it is radio that has been your secret weapon. That weapon has now been put down. You have surrendered to your illness. I really do worry that all of a sudden you won't be there, which is probably the reason that I wake at 4 a.m. and start writing.

I continue to wake at 4 a.m. night after night, and every morning I am more aware that I may walk in to find your body rigid. There is no doubt, the exhaustion has hit you, and now, a week after the show went out, I am more worried than ever that you are slowing down. You have pretty much migrated to bed except for supper and an hour of TV most evenings.

Has the force that has kept you alive ended?

Let's talk about that last show, though, because I tell you, my love, it was a masterclass in how to bow out. You were upset that Bob Seger, Van Morrison and Wings were cut, but it was more important to get the talk in. You and Sally, Rod's lovely clip, your stories – it was just perfect. As for your last words: *So thank you for being with me all these years. Take good care of yourself and those you love. And may we walk into the future with our heads held high and happiness in our hearts. God bless you ...* They could not have been better said. You never use a script; the words just come, and they were perfect. Us listening to the show go out with no one else around was the perfect thing. When Judy Collins sang 'Amazing Grace', I sat opposite you and we held both our hands together, tears running down my face, tears in your eyes. It was one of the best moments of eye contact we've ever had. It was a huge, profound moment for you, for me, for your myriad listeners.

The day after the show airs I am euphoric. You have glowing reviews in *The Telegraph* and the *Daily Mail*, and the social-media posts and comments are off the scale. The feedback from the radio world is simply superb. You nailed it. But it's not just pride that I feel, it is that an inordinate weight has lifted from my shoulders. It hits me how, for twenty-three years, we have almost never been off-duty. What if a popstar dies? What if someone wants you for an interview? Are you free for this event? Will you sign this photo? Please listen to my CD! What if you did or said something that got you cancelled? Well, now it's all over. The public life. If Mick Jagger or Paul McCartney should suddenly keel over, you don't need to respond. For the first time ever we can be a private couple. Normal. Just getting through your illness in our own way. The only sense that you were once a public figure is that each day more and more cards find their way to us – on average twenty a day. And the beauty is that because you are in bed all day, you have the time to read them. You cannot believe the things people write, how much you have meant to them. You are the friend they never met, so incredibly important in their lives, and in a way they are grieving you. For many it is the end of their line with Radio 2, and I cannot help but think how very much the BBC undervalued you. There's no point in getting upset, but you always said how they didn't realise just what they had in you. I suspect when they look at the final show's listening figures and see the media coverage, they will realise. I know I am biased, but who else has that special connection that you do with your listeners? You had a God-given communication talent.

It's early November and Quincy Jones has just died. We do not have to react; we can just hear the reactions of others. Meanwhile the cards continue to flow in. There are hundreds and hundreds now, and I've run out of shelf space. Two lovely letters arrive as well. Michael Palin sends such a personal, kind message, telling you that your show was his deceased wife Helen's favourite radio show and how he listened to the final one thinking of her. And TIM DAVIE – only the director general of the BBC! You probably think he's never heard of you, but his letter is so warm, so congrat-ulatory, so appreciative of how you have worked through your illness. He talks of your dedication to music and your listeners. He's even heard our caring podcast – he mentions ME! Fancy us being on his radar. It's humbling. We both say the same thing, as we so often do: it deserves to be framed. It's now in the loo. Because you are touched, you send him a thank-you card. Still a gentleman, Johnnie. (Months later I will meet Tim Davie and he will tell me that while he is sent many cards, yours is one of the only ones he has kept.)

I ask you if you're sure you quit at the right time. You are. Utterly. You didn't have another show in you. And I know you mean it. Timing has always been your forte.

THEN

LA DOLCE VITA

The moment I would like to live again is our first kiss, but the evening I would love to recreate is the best one we ever shared. If ever there was a movie about you, this would be my favourite scene. And I know it would be yours too, for in our whirlwind life, this evening alone stood out as a moment of perfection.

In September 2005 we were driving back from the Italian Formula 1 race at Monza – the one where I ran after Kimi Räikkönen in the paddock (he was my favourite driver; the feeling was clearly not mutual, though, and he got away from me). As we started our meandering drive back home, you behind the wheel of your latest impulse purchase – a burgundy Mercedes sports car (which had 'spoken to you' as you drove past the showroom – honestly!) – and me clutching the map and the *Michelin Guide* the way I loved to do as chief navigator, I suggested a quick detour to the beautiful harbour of Portofino – possibly the only 'fishing' village in Europe where the shops edging it are Prada and Gucci. I don't imagine a single one of the beautiful boats bobbing on the water belong to fishermen. It is picturesque beyond belief, and very hard to negotiate in a car. Driving back out of the village, we passed the sign to the Hotel Splendido. 'That's one of the world's leading hotels,' I informed you in my tour-guide fashion. You immediately turned the wheel and started driving up the steep, curvy, narrow road towards it.

'What are you doing?' I exclaimed.

'Going to have a look.' You always had such a fearless attitude towards life. You pulled up outside the entrance, jumped out and went inside. You strutted out to inform me that they had one room left – and that we were staying in it. I couldn't believe it. Us, at the Splendido!

I'll be honest, though, I found the bedroom pretty unin-spiring. It had unashamedly old-fashioned Italian styling, with plain white walls and furniture that had been there for decades, although at least it had a terrace overlooking the wooded hill between the hotel and the harbour. I made us a cup of Earl Grey tea, as is my habit in the afternoon. You followed it by serving us a Campari and soda from those triangular bottles in the mini-fridge, which have way more Campari than soda. I prepared myself for dinner, thankful that I'd packed my Diane von Furstenberg wrap dress and push-up, deep-plunge bra, and as I stepped out of the bath-room, you let out one of your 'wows'. Having recently started on HRT, I was blossoming out of the low neckline. You told me to stand on the terrace so you could take my photo. It was the best photo ever taken of me. It was also the start of the most magical evening of my life.

We walked through the bar out onto the beautiful terrace, dappled with evening sun. As we were led to our table by the maître d' I could sense that all the men were looking up at me – or certainly at my décolletage. It was the one and only evening of my life when that had happened, when I was the woman who caught people's eye. I felt like I was on fire.

We had a sensational dinner on that terrace looking down to the stunning harbour below. We ate a seafood pasta that blew our minds. I had veal, you had fish, with thin-cut chips (frites Splendido!) and spinach. We drank a bottle of Sicilian Nero d'Avola, which, although it's far from the best Italian wine there is, tasted to us like nectar because the evening was so blessed. The waiters couldn't have been more attentive or polite.

Afterwards, despite me thinking you'd want to hot foot it back to the bedroom, you were taken by the ambience in the bar. In a delightfully *Casablanca* way, there was a pianist in a white dinner jacket tinkling away on the piano. You ordered an espresso and an amaretto on ice (your very naff after-dinner tipple) and another glass of wine for me. We were looking round at the other guests when the pianist nonchalantly threw out a music question. 'Can anyone tell me who recorded this song?' Little did I realise that this was the evening when I would experience the phenomenon of your musical knowledge. You answered instantly. He went on, asking one music question after another. You got them all correct. He momentarily took his hands off the keys and looked across to you. He threw down the gauntlet. 'Sir, if you get this one right, you will be the guest of the week.' You got it in one. He straightened his back. 'Sir, if you get this right, you will be guest of the month.' Bingo. Utterly stunned, he thought for a moment before he said, 'Sir, if you get this next question correct, which I very much doubt you will, you will be guest of the year.' There was a hush in the bar, followed by a respectful nod and a ripple of applause, from not only him but all the other guests, as you instantly gave the correct and utterly obscure answer. From my memory it was the name of a long-gone French singer. How many other people have been guest of the year at the Hotel Splendido? How proud I was. How amazed I was. And how very chuffed you were. The guest of the year at one of the best hotels in the world! The pianist came over to ask quietly just who on earth you were.

Soon afterwards, you knocked back your drink, held out your hand and led me back to our room – you full of swagger, me almost bursting out of my dress with pride. As you shut the door you took my face in your hands to kiss me. I can only say that what followed was the night when I peaked in my womanhood and femininity.

I know that we would have to choose that as the most intoxicatingly magical night of our lives together, as every single romantic star aligned for us. And all thanks to you turning left in your car. It was all truly Splendido.

OUR HIGHLIGHTS ...

Our first kiss.

Getting your MBE from then Prince Charles at
Buckingham Palace ... followed by lunch at Elena's L'Etoile
in Charlotte Street with Sam and Beth.

Our night at the Hotel Splendido in Portofino.

Lockdown 1 – the world left us alone and we loved
five months of doing *Sounds of the 70s* together.

Doing the Silverstone F1 grid walk in 2022 – the power,
the noise, the drivers and the celebs around us ... Woo hoo!

... AND THE LOWLIGHTS

Your cancer diagnosis – the earth collapsed beneath me.

Your emergency operation in the early hours from
peritonitis – I lay awake trying not to plan your funeral
while waiting for the surgeon to call me.

Losing *Drivetime* on Radio 2 – nothing hit you as hard in your career while we were together.

My breast cancer diagnosis – I think you took this harder than me because you were terrified of losing me.

Losing Darcey Dog in 2022 – she was our girl, a dog like no other.

IF I WAS A WRITER (BUT THEN AGAIN, NO)

You are thrilled that I have a book deal. 'This is your time now,' you tell me over and over. I find you reading what I've done so far on my laptop. You ask if I mind, as if it's private. I am so thrilled by your reaction. You love how I write. You love the things I say about you – things that I should have said to your face, but I am better in written words than spoken ones. You say you'd like to write a foreword. Yes, please! Delicately, I ask if you would record it too. More than that, you say you'll interview me. Today is the day we said we would do it, but instead, you sleep all day. You ignore your lunch tray. You don't want anything except my hand, which you grip as I sit next to you on the bed. The recording has to wait. Another corner has been turned. I look at your sleeping face and wonder just how empty it will feel when you're not here, and whether we will actually make that recording.

This week we watch the new Bruce Springsteen documentary *Road Diary*. It covers the build-up to the last tour and tour itself, the one we saw in Dublin. It fills our hearts to see this, to understand why he chose the set list, to meet his band. As it ends you say, 'I do have one sadness … that I will never play Bruce Springsteen on the radio again.' It is a rare moment of self-pity. It reminds me of something Richard Allinson said when we had supper once. He said, 'If any of us DJ's put on Springsteen's "Born to Run" it sounds great. When YOU put it on, Johnnie, it sounds unbelievable. You bastard!' How can it be that a song would sound different when you play it? That one comment shows me how much you have enjoyed sharing your songs. It's been your driving force and now that has gone.

It's hardly surprising you've gone down another level. Mandie, your other favourite district nurse besides Emma, says she expected this, that you will plateau now. I wonder just how many steps down and plateaus there are going to be. I take Mandie to the sitting room to show her your cards and she sheds a tear. She's always been a fan. The one fan who gets to see you in your increasingly vulnerable state.

A few days later and you do interview me. You are sitting up in bed and I am sitting on your wheelchair next to you. You're going to do an interview based on my eight favourite songs. You have my list of songs and that's it. You don't need any notes to say your introduction or ask your questions. And in this half-hour, here is what I learn: that you have taken my life on board; you have listened; you really do know me so well, so much deeper than anyone else. I answer your questions as if we're having supper together. I'm probably a bit too cocky and bold. I know I would have been more circumspect in a studio with someone else, but I feel so safe with you. I am utterly honest. You get the answers from the true me, right down to my core. It is a wonderful final gift from you. I just hope I like my answers when I hear it.

Such is our level of relief and the resultant exhaustion since you stopped Radio 2 that I am pushing visitors away. The very LAST thing I can deal with is giving my very little remaining energy to making small talk. I want to treasure this time with you. It's the first time in our marriage that we've been truly free to be us, and I love it. The vibe at home has changed: it's gentler, more in control. You lie in bed all day and I bring you meals, coffee, your pills. I sit in your wheelchair for catch-ups and to hear what the day's fan mail reveals. Such beautiful sentiments are being sent to you, and I love that you have time to read them all. 'This one's special,' you say and quote the most heartfelt, grateful and beautiful lines. You get up just before supper so you can have it with me at the table, before we then watch an hour of TV – *Rivals*, *The Diplomat* and *MasterChef: The Professionals* are the current selection.

I relent on a guest. For weeks Emily Eavis has been texting to say she wants to bring Michael Eavis over. I push her away while we approach the final show and the week after, but she is gently persistent and suggests this Friday. I cancel my flu jab and agree. I go into guest mode. The house is immaculate; a cake is made; candles are lit. We talk about where we should sit as Michael himself isn't too agile.

What transpires is the funniest visit of them all. Michael cannot get out of the car (it took a huge man to get him in it), so I get an oxygen tank, find a cannula, wrap you up in a jacket, scarf and flat cap, and out you wheel to greet Michael. It's like a reunion of war veterans – two old codgers sharing memories. It seems you are both on your third wife. Michael tells us he's ninety and stresses that he's just a farmer at heart. I bring out mugs of tea and cake. Nick, Emily's lovely husband, grabs a garden table and we have our first outdoor tea party. We share our great moments at Glastonbury, and they all absorb these with delight – Neil Young smashing up his guitar in 2012; I say that we were at the side of the stage and the bass player's wife said, 'Neil is loving this.'

'How can you tell?' I asked.

'He always smashes his guitar when he's happy.' Emily loves this story. Apparently, the great man may return for 2025, though the contract isn't signed yet. To my relief Nick asks if he can take a photo. My phone is in my pocket; I've been hoping for such an opportunity but I'm too polite to ask. We move the table and you precision drive your wheelchair, reversing towards Michael so you're in a photo-ready position. I love it. Two hugely important figures in the British music scene, grandfathers of it almost, together for the final time. It feels like a bit of history. Michael's final words to me, just before they drive off, are, 'It's been incredible really.' I tell him it has been magical, because it has. You have to have a large sprinkling of magic to create a phenomenon like Glastonbury. As they drive away, they all wave with the enthusiasm of young children. And as we come back into the warm and incredibly tidy house, we feel that some of Michael's Glastonbury stardust has been sprinkled on us. It's been one of the best and certainly most original of visits we've had. I will always be grateful that Emily persisted.

We are in such a lovely, stress-free time. We're more secluded. Safe from external forces ... Until I get a call from my brother Martin. He wants to tell me that my mother, *Mutti*, is changing her will. Briefly I wonder if she's leaving me something extra in recognition of my devoted caring for you. However, I joke, as I do, 'Is she taking me out of it?' and as it transpires – she is. She's giving it all to the grandchildren instead of her four children. It's admirable to think about the next generation. And because my siblings all have at least two children each, so their bloodlines will benefit, they are happy. Even the widowed daughters-in-law of my deceased brothers are benefitting. The only one who isn't is me.

I think I'm doing really well at the moment, but with this news I learn that it doesn't take much to floor me. You can't believe it. 'Oh, Tigs. All you do is give. How can she do that to you, and now of all times?'

Why now? The first month when we have no income and I'm wondering how long my little savings pot will manage to keep us going. There's a perception in the family that we're loaded, so I imagine she thinks I don't need any help, but it's not the money – even though it would be helpful – it's the massive symbolism. There is no doubt that within families we slip back into the same roles that we've had since childhood. I suddenly feel like a very hurt youngest child. I cannot sleep when I go to bed as I'm crying too much. I cry on waking.

When I finally pick myself up after two days I call her. 'Hello, darling' – breezy as ever. In my mother's life there is no conflict, no raised voices. Everything is *marvellous*. Her answer to any problem is: 'I'm praying for you Darling' which is wonderful of her, and yet …

It isn't long into our chat that I raise the thorny issue. She is shocked as she honestly doesn't think she's done anything to get upset about. 'It's not my fault I'm childless. It's hard enough, not having kids' I blub. She tells me that I am emotional. Too emotional. And then comes the revelation, the sentence that makes her behaviour towards me make sense. She tells me that when I married you, everything changed, because I was so swept up in your busy life. She was the one who brought me up to be a devoted wife, but it has been at a cost to her and me. She just doesn't understand our world or life. I'm not sure if she disapproves of us, or whether it's her dislike of music and fame, but it is a revelation. Not least because it is an admission of her subconscious distancing from me that began two decades ago.

I have gone from being at the centre of my family to the outside.

So not only have I lost my career, fertility and identity due to our marriage, but I've lost some of my family status too! It's been quite a price. Oh, Johnnie, I should be weeping but I'm not. I don't even have a G&T in my hand, although I could kill for one. I almost feel euphoric that a missing piece of a jigsaw puzzle has been put in place. I have not invented her gentle rejection of me over these years. It's real. I heard Mutti speak her truth. And I am so happy that she did. Indeed, it's incredible.

She agrees to rethink, suggests I should be treated like a grandchild, and thus I would get an eleventh rather than a quarter. Sorry to be so mercenary, but I'm making a point. (For the record, I believe my worth has ended up as equal to two grandchildren. I am happy with this. My existence has been recognised and that's all I wanted. And she'll probably outlive me anyway!)

I'm not sure how I would have coped with this scenario without your love, support and understanding. It makes me realise how alone I will be without you. You may be a bed-ridden Puffing Billy, but you're still my rock. In the words of Bruce, 'If I should fall behind, wait for me.'

I do see the irony. It wouldn't have happened had I not met you, but being with you makes it bearable, and because of it I have learned so much about being a human. I have concluded that families are there to teach us. I wonder how she would have reacted if I'd married a royal, an aristocrat or an actor like Hugh 'Lord Grantham' Bonneville. Is it because you were a motorbike-riding music DJ who once went to rehab that she cannot understand our lives? Oh, I'd love to know, because honestly, she always refers to you as 'Dear Johnnie' so I know she likes you.

Thinking about Lord Grantham, of our many recent guests, he was a particular delight. 'I'd love to come and tell Johnnie what a wonderful actor I am for an hour!' You laugh heartily and are delighted to see him. There's such a difference between seeing people publicly and at home. He's so human with you. So open. Funny. Real. We talk about love and pain. We've all been through it, put others through it. He's going to do *Uncle Vanya* on stage in San Francisco and Washington. That I would love to see. Sadly, you certainly can't. Fortunately, though, you will be able to see *Paddington in Peru*, and you can't wait. Hugh leaves me with beautiful flowers, the warmest hug and a message later: 'You two are an inspiration to the rest of us.' Crikey. Lord Grantham … I wonder what Mutti would think.

'Surely these are the last,' you say. It's almost three weeks since your final show. More than 200 cards have been moved from our overcrowded shelf into a basket – the basket of love and gratitude. Again and again I give thanks that you have the time to reap all these rewards. Your timing has been perfect, but on a day like today, when you are not well, you sleep and sleep deeply. You are lost to me, and when you are like this I wonder whether this is the start of the final decline.

This week is an experiment – a possible-avoidance-of-a-care-home experiment. Vanessa, a well-respected carer, has come to live in and look after you so I can have a week to recover. You stop your two-day-long sleep and perk up just as she arrives and just before I leave. My goodbye is breezy and jokey. I come and say it twice for good measure and then tear off to Careys Manor Hotel & SenSpa in the New Forest to wallow in a hydrotherapy pool for two days.

You text me within an hour of my departure. You miss me. We text and text. You love the contact – we both do. You wish you were sitting opposite me for supper in the Zen Garden restaurant. I order pad Thai because that's what you'd have.

I come to London for the rest of the week. I had visions of seeing so much culture, but it's cold and I'm deeply tired. This morning I don't wake till 10.30 a.m. and I spend the day on the sofa. You report snow in Dorset. Too cold to smoke a fag, you tell me. I am sure I will have lots of texts from you, but there are none so I send you several. You don't reply. You must be asleep. At 6.07 p.m. Vanessa texts me to say you have slept all day. We stay in regular contact. I get takeout black cod from OKA in Primrose Hill village because it's your favourite dish and I'm eating it for you. For the second time this week. It's gone 10 p.m. and you are still sound asleep. This is new behaviour. A resounding dread fills me ... I have always felt you will go when I least expect it. On Monday, when I left you, I certainly did not expect it, and this evening it hits me truly for the first time: at some point soon you will not be there. It's too intolerable to contemplate. You are my soulmate. Yes, I hate being tied to our restrictive life and not being able to go out together, but I have not yet truly thought how it will be without you. I'm scared, Duke. Don't go. Not yet. Not when I'm away from you. Vanessa tells me to get some sleep. She says it's important. She will contact me in the morning if you're still sleeping.

Of course I am fitful. I cannot fall asleep. At 11.15 p.m. my phone buzzes. Dread. But it's you. You have just woken. The relief is … indescribable. I thought you were exiting, but you have revived.

You had guests yesterday – the first ones without me there. Vanessa points out that you perform for guests, but it leaves you depleted. It's now taking at least a day and a half for you to recover from a visit.

I return to you, despite Storm Bert trying to stop me. It takes nearly six hours from London to home as the rail network goes into meltdown. It is so wonderful to be reunited. You can relax again, because I'm here. I know you've missed me, but I am sure the break and seeing a modicum of culture and friends was what I needed. You get that. You're generous in spirit – still.

The 'cuckoo' has been with us most of this year. Next to your bed is a doorbell, and wherever I am is the receiver. We elected on the cuckoo call as the least offensive sound it creates, and it has been invaluable all year. Tonight, the cuckoo calls. I sit bolt upright in bed, a dream violently interrupted, and I am struggling through the black of my bedroom to get to you. You apologise, but also proudly say it's the first time you've had to get me up in the dead of night. We're eleven months into this caper, so you are right to be proud. I hold you, and gently suggest that having an amaretto on ice and a black coffee after two glasses of red wine is probably not a great idea any more. You agree, but watching Knock Out week of *MasterChef*, as we were, can whet the palate. I tuck you back into bed, with fresh PJs on, and lots of blankets as it's the coldest night of the year. I cannot sleep again, not after that rude awakening. I go back to check on you, and you are sleeping like a baby, despite the sound of the new, even louder and more powerful oxygen concentrator.

I am due to go to Shropshire this weekend for my (disinheriting) mother's ninety-fourth birthday. A friend from Dublin, Kara, who asked if she can visit, has bravely agreed to come and stay and look after you, but now, still in the dark of the night, I wonder if it's safe to leave you. I cannot expect anyone other than a paid carer or nurse to deal with what I have dealt with tonight. You are going downhill, and I think my place is here.

Vanessa, experienced and psychic, has a debrief with me. She calls you a fighter, says you are fiercely independent. You wouldn't let her bath you. I am happy that this most intimate part of our caring journey you save for me. She says unless you get an infection you will be with me for Christmas. She thinks you will let go after that. *Maybe* you will get to New Year. We both know you won't make your eightieth in March. It's not even mentioned. For now, I know I must treasure each day. My family accept that by your side is where I should be. Anything else creates too much anxiety for me.

I shop online these days – who doesn't? – and I'm very excited about a pink moleskin suit that has just arrived from Seasalt. I model it for you. 'WOW, WOW, WOW!' you say, clapping your hands together. 'When are you wearing that?'

'Your funeral,' I quip, and you laugh out loud. FANTASTIC! Your laughter reverberates around the room, making me laugh too. I make you laugh quite often at the moment. You are a great audience, and your laugh both on- and off-air is wonderful, genuine, infectious. That is something I will miss hugely. I know radio listeners already are. People keep telling me that Sunday afternoons just aren't the same without you.

If we had a graph of this year, my energetic and emotional line would be at an all-time low. I'm in a perfect storm of exhaustion, domestic chaos, technical issues on the post-production of the short film, concern for you and having to scrub your carpet clean after an accident (while incidentally you happily watch F1 Qualifying sat up in bed above me). I'm too tired for my exercise class. My body aches. I'm a mess. You look at me from your bed when I bring your mid-morning coffee and biscuit and say, 'I'm worried about you, Duch. You're always so full of energy. There must be something wrong with you.' I mean, there, right there, my darling, you show a complete lack of understanding of what this year is doing to me. It's not just that I have to do everything in the house and garden, and run around looking after you, clearing up after your accidents, helping you dress, bathing you and unwinding oxygen tubes that get trapped in your wheelchair wheels. It is the emotion, the stress, the being trapped and the constant sense of anxiety about you. Alone in the kitchen I cry like a little girl who feels sorry for herself.

What I realise I miss, apart from our external life together, is hugs. It's a very real consequence of being in a wheelchair. We're at different levels all day. You can't steal up on me as you used to wrap yourself around me. You'd probably floor me with the footrest and your arms wouldn't reach. It's been such a tough couple of weeks for me, my resilience to knocks is diminishing. I'm not held by anyone and I need to be. I'm not sure how much you see me now, except at night when I kiss you goodnight and you tell me how beautiful, young or lovely I look. But I tell you how hard it is that you can no longer come and hold me when I need it. You push up the wheelchair arms, fold up the footrest and open your arms to me. I lean down and we hold each other for an age. It's beautiful. But my main thought is how thin you are now.

It's the 340th bedtime of the year. That's a lot of wheeling in the commode – renamed Ethel – getting your water and pills, putting your hearing aids in their charging pod, folding down your bedding so you can easily get in, changing your clothing, tucking you in, turning down the oxygen machine once your levels are back up to at least 80 and kissing you goodnight. Tonight, I fall on the bed next to you and say I am going to sleep there. You say that would be lovely, but we both know it won't work. I need decent sleep. I'm hardly drinking now, not eating sugar, exercising more – anything to keep up my strength because I need every ounce I can muster.

You have something very exciting to share – an audio message. As a man who is so cool and nonchalant about praise or adulation, I can only assume that it's from Bruce Springsteen. You get up and wheel into the main room. I am sitting at the dining-room table writing one of our very few Christmas cards, to Mutti. 'I want your complete attention,' you tell me. You ask for the little Bluetooth speaker to make sure it's loud. I'm actually full of excited anticipation – the Boss really would be something. I hope my smile didn't drop too far as I realised it was in fact Brian Aldridge from *The Archers*. I mean, it was hilarious, because the actor who plays him, Charles Collingwood, remained in character, and you were utterly delighted by it. But there was also something about one important radio figure recognising another and that I believe is why you were so chuffed. *The Archers* was one of the things you introduced me to, incredibly.

Now *I* have something to share. My short film, *The Kitchen Garden*, starring Ramon Tikaram and Pippa Haywood, is complete. The editing, grading, titles, music composition and sound mixing are all done. The fact that

I've managed to do this while keeping our show on the road is no small miracle. You wheel yourself to our big table, and I line up the film on my laptop and press play. You cannot believe it – the beauty of it, the lead man being in a wheel-chair (your manual one, which I borrowed. You were of course the inspiration for him being disabled), the honesty of the performances, the hope, the beautiful, searing music at the end. You cry. You can't believe that I wrote, produced and directed this little gem. And I am SO PROUD that finally you get to see something I have written, which has been realised. We both know that my film script for *ANTONIA* has had to be pushed to the back burner, just as it was gaining momentum, but this I squeaked out. Honestly, it means so very much to me that you see it. You will never see *ANTONIA*, which has been with us our entire marriage – me beavering away in dogged belief and hope. This is a teaser for that film and so at least, as a reward for your great patience with me and my dream, you have a sweetener to enjoy. I go to bed tonight thinking if I never direct another thing it won't matter – because I've nailed this one and you love it. It makes my heart swell with pride.

In the spring earlier this year, when they announced that the final delayed episodes of *Yellowstone* would be aired in November, I didn't dare tell you as I knew – yes, knew – that you would miss them, yet we have just finished them – together – along with the final of *Strictly Come Dancing*. Despite you saying that Christmas 2023 was your last, this year's tree is up and tomorrow, on the shortest day, we will celebrate our twenty-second wedding anniversary.

You feel you've gone down another notch. Two really bad panic attacks this week have you as worried as you have been all year. I go into overdrive and get a GP round (the first since January!), speak to our palliative nurse Angel Caroline and the district nurses. Sometimes I think all you need is some reassurance. Who wouldn't be nervous of their moment of demise? Both the doc and Caroline say that you aren't going anywhere yet. Indeed, Caroline and I have a heart to heart. With the greatest compassion, she hopes for your sake that you will suddenly get pneumonia, as then it would be over in days. The alternative is a long, drawn-out decline – as you are already in – going on for months. Dignity will reduce; living will get even harder. You've started saying that you would happily take a pill to end it all. Not before Christmas, obviously, but you say this week you think the end of January will be your time. The not knowing, for both of us, is the biggest challenge there is. If you do get an infection, you will be gone within days and I will be left in shock. Released from caring yes, but facing the unimaginable, which is you not being here.

OUR TOP TWENTY DRAMA SERIES

Breaking Bad

The Bureau

My Brilliant Friend

Chernobyl

Mad Men

Borgen

1883

Yellowstone

The English

The Crown

War and Peace

The Marvellous Mrs Maisel (first two series)

Deutschland 83/86/89

Shōgun

Daisy Jones & the Six

The Bridge

The Queen's Gambit

The White Lotus

Succession

The Morning Show

THEN

MY DUKE (OF EARL)

I have so often wondered why we made a good couple. Indeed, have we made a good couple? People tell us so. We've always been told about our obvious deep love for each other – apparently, it touches and inspires others. Us! Sometimes I think we've conned them all, for I swear we've had as many rows as everyone else.

When I stand back and look at you as objectively as I can, I am amazed by you. You have been such a contradiction: a mixture of huge strengths and weaknesses. But of this I am very proud – the difference in you between our meeting and now is immense. I'd like to think I've helped you to feel better about yourself. A lot better. 'Loving You Makes Me a Better Man' – you have always quoted that song; maybe that's the love that people see.

That September in 2001 when we met, you were financially challenged. Indeed, you were over £40,000 in debt, as you'd spent huge amounts settling your legal bills after your *News of the World* sting. You didn't own anything other than an old second-hand Saab and a Harley-Davidson Fatboy.

You lived in a shitty rented flat. You were still in a period of questioning, having not long left rehab. You were totally clean – no booze, no fags and certainly no cocaine. You were on a spiritual quest; somewhat serious, introverted, quite insecure, with a hugely developed sense of guilt. There was no doubt that you'd been attracted to the sort of women who made you feel bad about yourself, and made you feel guilty. You used to talk with Gordon about the 'Madonna and Whore' syndrome. Using your imagery, you had been excited by 'whores', but your soul said you needed a 'Madonna' to survive. In I walked. No wonder it was a clash of directions for you at the start of our relationship. It was part of your journey. You didn't know what you wanted, which is why I was always understanding about the first cancelled wedding. You were not ready. I don't believe we would have survived if we'd tied the knot then. The Temple of Doom would have been apt. The five-month wait between July and December 2002 was crucial to us succeeding, for in that time you learned more about me, and let yourself go and fall in love with this 'straight' – who wasn't straight at all!

It felt to me as if no one had ever told you 'how wonderful you are', to steal Gordon's lyric. You had been hearing for too long what was bad about you and not what was good. The truth is that you had so much good in you, but you had to see it. I even thought you were paranoid when you said you were convinced your phone was being tapped (and as it happens, it was, but we decided not to act). You seemed at sea. Your shitty rented flat pretty much summed up what you felt you deserved.

I've watched you grow in confidence, relax, embrace the good in life and trust others. In turn, I have become more worldly wise and very much stronger. Possibly trust is the key to love. You could trust me. Whatever you threw at me, you knew that while I might justifiably explode in rage and get upset, I would calm down once I had caught my breath, because we had some unspoken, soul-level connection. I was, and always would be, your greatest supporter and ally. Something in you knew that down to your core.

So often the upset was about smoking, which I fought tooth and nail for you to avoid. I learned that you were probably smoking all the time we've been together, but far behind my back. I thought I was married to a non-smoker. I have thrown my wedding ring at you and left home over fags, and I have to ask myself just why I was so incensed by them. You have been so sick throughout our marriage, and so many people, including me, have sacrificed so much to keep you going. I read smoking as the hugest insult to us all. What a dragon I have been, but really, I was just the person who wanted her soulmate to last as long as possible.

You've always been a profligate spender – money literally burned a hole in your pocket. You have bought masses and masses of completely unnecessary things. If there was money in your account or wallet, you had a deep compulsion to get rid of it – the total opposite of careful me. I tried so many arguments with you – like saving the planet, or thinking about me when you've gone. It didn't touch you. Your attitude was, 'There'll always be a way to survive,' as if survival was the only goal. It does mean, however, that you were hugely generous to many. From *Big Issue* sellers and waiters, through to the charity coffers at Salisbury District Hospital and Carers UK. I've secretly loved that generosity of spirit you've had. I believe it shows your very great goodness of heart. Your financial philosophy (if that isn't too grand a concept for a spending addict) seems to be akin to the one Jesus would hold – not your words, but my take on you. I'm sure this attitude has been a lesson you were here to teach me: not to be worried, to let it flow, to let life carry you. Because it will. As Jean the medium once said to me, there is no money in heaven. It's very much an earthly concern. No wonder you loved all-inclusive resorts. They were heaven on earth for you!

It has been complex, being married to someone who could get so lost in his own shell. A true radio man. Someone who could either be fantastic fun socially or utterly silent. It was always a challenge going out to supper parties. How would you be that evening? Which Johnnie would they see? The ebullient friendly one, or the one who sloped off to the nearest sofa and slept? It was usually the latter, so I had to work hard at supper parties, making excuses or trying to fill the entertainment gap. Close friends accepted and knew this; others could be offended, and we would not be invited back. Oh and when the dreaded question came from a person around the table, 'So Johnnie, how did you get into radio?' AAAAGH! I must confess we would both want to fall head first into our plate of food. Inwardly I'd be screaming, 'Bloody Wiki him!' Honestly, when you started working weekends only, it was fabulous to have the excuse that 'Johnnie needs an early night'.

Your capriciousness certainly kept me on my toes, but equally you'd take a certain amount of shit from me. 'You cannot do that, Johnnie!' or 'Do NOT say that on-air!' (especially if invited onto Radio 4). And you would listen – almost. You seemed to think I was wise.

Your amazing talents on radio gave you a confidence in the studio alone. I sometimes think the best radio people are those with deep questions and insecurities, Kenny Everett being the most brilliant example. Would you have been so good on-air if you were cocksure in the rest of your life?

I saw your strength when you gave me advice. You had the ability to stand back from my situations and give such strong guidance, because you have always been intrinsically stronger than me in spirit. You have survived so many bombs going off in your life; you have been an instinctive fighter, never giving up. You may have surrounded yourself with your petty addictions like smoking, shopping and conspiracy theories, but you would drop all that rubbish when I'd say, 'Duke – I need your help. What should I do?' You could read a situation as well as anyone, and you pushed me to be stronger.

Why do I love you? Apart from knowing your soul … it's because, just as you needed some 'straightness' in your life from me (which I would call 'grounding', because as I keep telling you, I'm really not that straight compared with most), I needed some wildness from you. I love your spirit, your laughter, your courage, your naughtiness, your ability to lead me astray as if it was good for me, your morality, your deep kindness and above all your humility, despite the incredibly successful man you have been. Fame has never gone to your head. Your feet have remained on the ground, and you treat everyone as equals. These are great traits, and you are a fine – if complicated and occasionally flawed – example of a human being. You have taught me so much. You have been the greatest teacher in my life. And that's quite apart from your taste in music. How could I not love you?

NOW

CALLING TIME

Something is going on. Is it the winter solstice? Two years ago you fell out of a helicopter at this time. Last night, in your increasingly independent fashion, you went to turn on your bedroom oxygen machine instead of asking me to do it. The result was that you totally dislodged your bed, pulled the bedding off it and collided with your wingback chair, getting tied up in the tubes from not just one, but two machines. You actually pulled two sections of tubing apart. I was charging round after you, trying to untie your tubes from the wheelchair and put them back together. It was an impossible task. For five minutes our world was in chaos and you had no oxygen. I was furious at you for putting me into that state of panic and yourself in danger, just because you want to be independent.

Tonight, as I put the final touches on our twenty-sec-ond-anniversary dinner, I hear an almighty crash. I run out of the kitchen to find you prostrate across the hall corridor. I throw myself on the floor next to you in my leopard-skin trousers and sexy black top, with tousled hair, bright red lips – and an apron. You're wearing just a T-shirt and pants. I cannot understand how you got to be there, and neither can you. You are metres away from your wheelchair or bed. As the salmon en croute burns in the oven, I am trying to assess you, and then get you up. You have spoken, and you don't appear to have broken anything, but your elbow is cut in two places and there is blood all over the blanket I rest your head on. After fifteen minutes of trying to elevate you, I have to call on my neighbours. Clare comes round and together, very slowly, we get you back up onto the wheelchair. You mutter something about wanting to look nice for our dinner. You've given yourself a hell of a shock – plus a bump on the head. After dinner, when you can't face the gorgeous Chablis, we watch the final episode of *The Day of the Jackal*. You ask if there are two men on the hillside. There is just one. I fret. Do you need the paramedics to check you over? You say you don't. You, like me, are afraid of you being carted off, as you may never return.

We get you to bed; it's slow. 'God bless,' we say to each other. 'Happy anniversary.' And as I come to bed I wonder if your prediction last December that that would be your final Christmas may still prove to be true.

You sleep deeply for over twelve hours. I'm concerned so I call the paramedics, but they won't take you in as you don't want to ever go to hospital again. They are slightly concerned by your double vision last night, your long sleep and your general fogginess. They are great and give me guidance: I need to get a treatment escalation plan sorted with the doctors. The issue of you falling is a new concern, previously unthought of. It's always been an infection that was a threat. You could get a brain bleed if you hit your head again. Clearly, your reducing mobility is now an issue. The lead paramedic speaks to me in the kitchen and gently implies that I should be ready for anything to happen. She also tells me I'm doing a great job of looking after you. It means a lot to me. And after they go, you sleep again.

When you wake at 6.30 p.m. you have no idea if it's day or night, or what day of the week it is. You ask where everyone is – have they all gone to bed? I explain that it's just us who live here and you seem relieved. You ask questions about *The Day of the Jackal*'s final episode. You don't remember a single scene. You ask what I had for supper and I explain it is yet to be cooked, so you come and join me for it. You're a liability in your wheelchair. You crash into furniture, you almost push the kitchen island over and you start loading logs into the lit woodburning stove. I get panicky. You could blow us all up with your oxygen on. I actually start to get worried. You don't speak, you just drive that bloody wheelchair around, creating havoc. You go outside for a fag – you refuse your jacket, although I manage to put your cap and scarf on you. As you sit outside on a cold, wet night in your PJs and a thick cardigan, I have a strong sense that you're having your final smoke. By the time I get you to bed I slump on your bedroom wingback chair with my head in my hands. I can't cope alone anymore. I say out loud, 'I need help now.' I leave your door and mine open, and spend the night fitfully tossing around and listening to your breathing. I go in to check on you four times. I feel you're as close to the end as you have ever been. By 5 a.m. I am too exhausted to keep up the vigilance. I shut the doors and manage three hours of sleep.

When one of the district nurses comes in to check on you in the morning she asks if I need some home care help. It's the first time I've been offered this, and as we have totally dropped the idea of putting you in a home because you are so frail, I answer, 'YES, I absolutely do.' I've carried this on my own for 357 days (a year, minus eight days) so, yes, I need back-up. By the afternoon I am told that as from tomorrow I will have someone coming in for forty-five minutes a day for the next fortnight. I've no idea how it will work out and what the carer will do, but at least it means I can go and get the turkey, as right now I dare not leave you at all. Eating has been hard because your side hurts so much, so now you have your first NHS liquid meal. I don't know if this is a big gear change, or whether you just need to recover from the fall. I realise that I've picked up a chesty cough. I need sleep more than anything.

Despite your declaration that last Christmas would be your final one, we manage a lovely Christmas Day 2024, with my brother Martin and his wife, Kate, coming to cook us a delicious lunch. The stars that they are, and have been all year. You keep going until 6 p.m. and then feel really ill.

Boxing Day, my birthday, is one of my happiest. At supper we are once again the gang of six: d'Arcy, Gary, Jane and Charles arrive with lasagne, cake, profiteroles and a lot of indecently good champagne and wine. Along with cold turkey, baked spuds and salad, we have a right old feast. Even though you start the evening on the edge of proceedings and in tears because you forgot to order a cake (Jane rescued that), you slowly join in and we all have fantastic political banter round the table. Right versus Left: Sir Keir and 'Rachel from Accounts/Complaints' getting plenty of stick from you and Charles; Gary standing up for the environment; d'Arcy saying give Labour time, and me just loving having my besties around our table on my birthday. I couldn't be happier. Jane lights the candles on the cake, while you hold the plate with such pride. Do you believe the candles are burning for you? Or is it your relief that I had a birthday cake after all? I kiss your forehead. Jane, being the talented documentary film director that she is, snaps a photo. It turns out to be your final photo. You look so pleased with yourself.

On Saturday, 28 December I arrange to go to Jane's for a birthday tea with friends so you can have some time alone with one of your relatives. It's all been carefully orchestrated. Just before I leave you tell me the guest is not coming, so on what turns out to be the last day of your life up and about, you sit alone. I cannot cancel as the tea has been arranged for me, and when I return you look forlorn. 'Duke!' I throw my arms around you. You tell me you feel tired and want to go to bed. In the future it breaks my heart that you spent your final afternoon of normality all alone.

So many lasts have happened, and yet at the time we are oblivious to the fact that they would be later labelled with that adjective. Our last intimacy, our last proper hug, our last laugh together, our last supper together at the table, your last afternoon in our sitting room … If we had known they were 'lasts', would we have treasured these precious moments more?

A year ago today we were having an abstemious day as we were preparing to leave early in the morning for your live *Sounds of the 70s* show at Wogan House – your last at that studio, and your last ever live show. This evening I sit on the beautiful wingback chair at the end of your bed and watch you propped up on pillows, trying to eat a crustless egg and cress sandwich, as that has always been one of your go-to sick meals. You haven't eaten or drunk for the past two days and have been so worryingly sick that there have been two doctors and a district nurse (lovely Emma) here, and Cindy, the new carer, has been up five times today. Out of the goodness of her heart. Last night as I bathed you, you said you'd like to go to the local cottage hospital in Shaftesbury for rehydration and some care. Today we learn you are too acutely ill to go there, it being such a small hospital. They will only take you when you are end-of-life, and Emma judges you not to be at that stage. Yet. Though you could easily slip there. It's Salisbury District Hospital or home, and we both know the answer to that. The home care has been increased to twice a day from tomorrow because you are declining. Gorgeous,

272

kind women, Debbie and Cindy, will wash you and change your sheets. It is such a help to me to have them come in that I tell Debbie she is the greatest Christmas present ever.

This evening, as you drop in and out of sleep, having managed just two tiny fingers of egg sandwich, I wonder how much longer you will fight. I ask if I should contact your kids. You flatly reply, 'No.' Shouldn't we ask Beth to come over? 'No.' Either you don't feel as ill as you look and seem, or you're just too weak for visitors. I have realised this about you – if I had to say you were a radio man or a family man, I would definitely say the former.

Tomorrow a hospital bed will arrive for a second time. This time it will have to stay because of the carers. And there is talk of a catheter to make life easier. These are markers – markers that you are slowing down considerably, whether it be in the next two days or the next six weeks. You are so much weaker than you were before the fall eight days ago, and I assume that strength will not return. As I kiss you goodnight we share a little loving joke. I think about saying, 'Enjoy your final night in this bed,' but for once I hold back. You don't need that reminder.

I hear you cry out. It's still dark, being only 6.40 a.m., so I bash into furniture as I run to your room, forgetting we have lights in my panic. You are in distress, half out of bed, your bedding half off it. You have pulled out your oxygen tube. I stick the cannula back up your nostrils and turn you up to MAX. You don't make any sense. You're trying to

communicate with your hands while I try to get the oximeter on your finger. I can't get a reading. I give you a shot of
Oramorph to calm you. I lie on the bed behind you and
hold you, stroking your hair. I know instinctively that this
is it, but your determination to survive is deep. You want
me to call an ambulance, and honestly, this one time, I wish
I'd ignored you, as I wish I had stayed right there in that
loving embrace. However, I do run to get the phone, and I
hold your hand as I speak to the 999 woman. My two-min-
ute-long conversation goes from, 'I think my husband is
dying …' to, 'I think my husband has died.' She asks me to
remove the pillows, straighten your body and tilt back your
head, but I know it's too late. You're not breathing. She asks
me to watch your chest and tell her each time it rises. I am
silent. She says she's sorry for my loss. Your death is recorded
at 6.50 a.m. In the end my final words to you were not, 'I'm
bloody knackered'. Neither were they, 'I love you' or 'thank
you' or 'goodbye my love'. They were me asking incredu-
lously, 'You want me to call an ambulance?!'

I thought you were invincible. You have the spirit of
someone who would never die, and yet here you are before
me, silent. Still. Gone. Elsewhere. My only consolation is
that I was with you, though I honestly cannot say exactly
when you slipped away.

It's New Year's Eve. One year exactly since your last live
show. Day 365 of being so intensely ill. Bless you, my
darling Duke. You are released, my love. I can't quite believe
it. How will my life be without you?

THE TEN MAIN THINGS
I MISS ABOUT YOU

Your infectious laughter.

The warmth of your body holding me.

Watching you broadcasting live in the studio.

Our evenings together – supper and a streamer.

You driving me (your chauffeur name was 'Baines').

Going on holiday together.

Your belief in me.

Complaining about *The Archers*!

The exciting invites.

Your voice on the radio (and in that I am not alone).

WHAT I THINK ARE YOUR MOST
IMPORTANT TRACKS

***

(Guessed by me posthumously)

The Shirelles
WILL YOU STILL LOVE ME TOMORROW
One of your favourites. You would melt when you heard it.

Percy Sledge
WARM AND TENDER LOVE
Your last track on your Radio Caroline shows.

Sam & Dave
SOUL MAN
You loved them and their energy, and particularly this song.

Beatles
ALL YOU NEED IS LOVE
The first song you played when you became a 'criminal' continuing to broadcast on Radio Caroline after the Marine, &c., Broadcasting (Offences) Act became law on 14 August 1967.

Lou Reed
WALK ON THE WILD SIDE

*Your most risqué Record of the Week at Radio 1, which saved
Lou Reed's career. Decades later, when he learned that you were the
'DJ in Europe' who had championed it, he said that you had paid
his rent over all these years.*

Bruce Springsteen
THE RIVER

*I struggle to choose the right track, but you loved his music above
everyone else's. Indeed, I think you recognised his soul, both of you
searching yet sometimes struggling to grasp happiness, and
finding solace from that struggle in music.*

Todd Snider
ALRIGHT GUY

*What you played when you came back from 'gardening leave'
after the News of the World drugs sting in 1999, pre-me.*

Jackson Browne
BEFORE THE DELUGE

*You love the soul and songwriting of JB.
I think this was your favourite.*

Elton John and Kiki Dee
DON'T GO BREAKING MY HEART

*Your last Record of the Week on Radio 1,
which led to Elton's first Number One single. You received a gold
disc, which hung on your den wall.*

Bonnie Raitt
ANGEL FROM MONTGOMERY

*You had a thing about Bonnie – the ultimate rock chick.
The 'Oh, Johnnie' jingle you used was Bonnie after you told her
on-air that you would have married her – or words to that effect.
You were too late!*

NOW

GOODBYE, MY LOVE

Without doubt, your funeral was a triumph. I know we'd discussed a few key things, like the setting for the service and wake – St Peter's Church and the Grosvenor Arms in Shaftesbury – and we'd discussed a few tracks, and who you did not want invited, but mostly you wanted to leave it to me – as you tended to do. And I'm glad you did that, as it became quite an organic production. One thing led to another as it all fell neatly and gloriously into place with ease.

The local Palida Choir who you wanted were brilliant. Yes, live music was the way to go. It's thanks to them that you came in to Joni Mitchell's 'Both Sides Now' – it was already in their repertoire. I think it was a great choice, don't you? And their version of Rani Arbo and Daisy Mayhem's 'Crossing the Bar' – you'd already heard that, and it was completely bang on for a man who started his career on a pirate radio ship. Our spiritual friend Pippa Haywood felt she saw you sat on your coffin, swinging your legs and watching them sing that. Oh, I bet you loved the laughter.

There was a lot. And weren't you touched that your old friend Rick Wakeman played his own funeral composition for you? That was the moment that got everyone, when they truly thought about you.

Getting the guest list right was a challenge. The church has so few seats, and everyone I asked came. Can you believe how many of your radio colleagues turned up? Jeremy Vine, Ken Bruce, Bob Harris, Jo Whiley, Shaun Keaveny, Simon Mayo, Tony Blackburn, Paul Gambaccini, Richard Allinson, Sally Boazman, Helen Thomas and Mark Goodier. Well, Mark had to, as he was doing half your eulogy. I hope you think we did you proud. Robert Plant and his wonderful head of hair certainly turned a few heads in Shaftesbury. As did Michael Eavis with Emily.

One of the people I'd asked to contribute was Paul Venables. He said something that has stayed with me since: 'Twenty-two years ago I was asked to read at Johnnie and Tiggy's wedding. The piece they asked me to read on that day was from a poem called 'The Invitation'. I was looking back over that reading the other day and was really struck by a particular line. It said:

It doesn't interest me who you know – I want to know if you will stand in the centre of the fire with me and not shrink back.

Well Johnnie and Tiggy, you both stood in that fire, with courage and dignity and with love. We all know that Tiggy.' I had never made that connection from our wedding day. But Paul was right. We did stand in the fire, and we never shrunk back.

I wanted more than anything to give you a good send-off, and it went ten times better than I could have imagined. It was the last thing I could do for you. It had to be good, and it was a triumph. The music was amazing, the readings fantastic, but the thing I know you will have loved the most was the seven Harley-Davidsons that waited to follow your hearse out of Shaftesbury with, as you requested, 'Born to Run' blasting out. You had no idea about the bikes. Those were thanks to our ever-loyal Sarah, our right-hand woman for so many years, who made the suggestion and arranged it.

Your funeral was full of love for you, Duke. It was a true reflection of the man you were. It was moving, funny, a bit spiritual, dignified and completely and utterly unforgettable.

P.S. Can I just say I appreciated your little stint at the end of the day. While plenty of people sensed you in church, I was too much in producer mode. But coming to bed later that night and smelling cigarette smoke in my room – bloody hell, you little bugger. Of all the ways to reveal yourself. And yes, I laughed.

TIGGY'S EULOGY

It's a brave man who asks his wife to do his eulogy. It's even braver when that man is Johnnie Walker. But Johnnie was brave. Very brave.

Twenty-two years of marriage to him was a veritable rollercoaster and, honestly, I'm still shaking from the ride. But I will say, I was never bored for one moment – even though occasionally that would have been a relief.

But Johnnie knew, no matter what challenges he put me through, I would always be his most loyal defender and protector, fighting to the hilt for him, be it with the BBC, HMRC or anyone who crossed him.

A lot has been said in the media about him being rebellious, tricky, a maverick, a rule-breaker. But today I want to focus on the brilliant things about Johnnie. And there were a lot.

Of course, we all know he was a superlative broadcaster with fantastic music taste – and his great friend Mark Goodier is going to talk about his career, so I will focus on the less-discussed sides of the man.

Let's start with his name. He was born Peter Dingley in Solihull, the fourth of five children in a family he described as neurotic. He couldn't wait to get away. And out to sea he went, where Radio England gave him a choice of jingle packages: Johnnie Walker or Boom Boom Branigan. The man had taste. But the name Peter never left him. To his family here today he is still Peter or Uncle Peter. UP for short. And it's one of the main reasons he wanted his funeral here at St Peter's – a church he always loved.

His great humour was a joy to all. He had a laugh that reverberated out as if he kept remembering how funny the joke was. On-air it was Sally Traffic who made him laugh. Off-air it was me. Even during his last depleted year, we shared much hilarity together. When a couple of months ago this suit I'm wearing arrived, I styled it for him, as I did all new clothes. 'Wow, wow, wow. That's fantastic. What have you bought it for?' 'Your funeral,' I replied, and he couldn't stop laughing. So naturally I had to wear it today. Our final joke was in the week before he died. There was talk of catheters. When I referred to his Urethra Franklin he was off, almost crying with laughter.

Johnnie was by far the best driver I know. He was fast, confident, dominant and yet safe and remarkably polite. He actually trained at Jim Russell's motor racing school and if he hadn't become a DJ, then he would have aimed for Monaco. His love of F1 continued through his life, and one of his more recent highlights was doing the grid walk at Silverstone in 2022, just before the race started. Johnnie loved energy and power, and you never feel that more than when you're stood among twenty-two F1 cars that are getting ready to race. He had few regrets in his final year, but one of them was that he wouldn't get to see Lewis Hamilton drive a Ferrari.

Johnnie had a naturally generous heart. He wouldn't just give away his last Rolo; he'd go into debt to give you an entire packet. If he saw a *Big Issue* seller he'd call them over, give them £20 and tell them he didn't need the mag because he'd already read it. He donated to many charities – the RNLI, Compassion in World Farming, the Stars Appeal at Salisbury District Hospital and, most notably, Carers UK, the charity supporting unpaid carers, of which we were proud to be co-patrons. Caring for each other through illness proved to be a dominant theme of our time together. He wasn't just generous with his money, but with his time and influence. From walking a wild section of the Great Wall of China with a group of friends, which raised over £65,000, to poetry readings, fundraising events, carers' awards, meeting other unpaid carers at events around the nation, attending tea at Parliament and getting the support of Jeremy Vine and Radio 2 during Carers Week. Johnnie was truly proud of what we achieved together, always happier talking about others in need rather than himself.

Johnnie's strength generally was something quite extraordinary. I've never known a stronger person in will, determination or belief. He almost died in the first year of our marriage during his cancer treatment. He went from a life-support machine back to the Radio 2 *Drivetime* show in four months. Time and again he had health issues – a heart attack, triple heart bypass and double pneumonia to name a few. Again and again, he would return to the studio as soon as he could. His resilience to the pitfalls and challenges of life was remarkable. He lived on 'Planet IS' and not 'Planet SHOULD', never feeling sorry for himself, just driven to keep going. This last year it was truly amazing how long he kept broadcasting. He took it to his very edge, carrying on when most would have stopped, pulling himself out of bed and putting on his performance voice before returning back to bed. It was a shock for me when he died because I didn't think he ever would. He was stoic, brave, never self-pitying. He had wonderful warrior strengths – and probably the strengths you need to be so successful in the public arena.

Despite his success, humility was a key trait of his. I think it's why he was so loved. The first time he shoved me in front of a mic, he was depping on the *Breakfast Show* for Terry Wogan. He would hand me a bunch of text messages to read out. If there was anything complimentary about him, me or the show, he crossed it out. He didn't need the flattery. Indeed, he had no concept of how popular he was. When Steve Wright died last February it was big news. Johnnie almost apologetically warned me that when he went there would hardly be any attention at all. How very wrong he was.

Timing is an art and one he had in spades. He was old school, knowing how to get up to the news without cutting off the track, working out timings fifteen minutes before the top of the hour. But his timing in life was uncannily good too. The night we met we talked about the world being spiritually bereft and how a wake-up call was needed. The next day was 9/11. We got married on the winter solstice – a symbolic day AND the longest night. We also married less than a month before his health started to decline, which on his part was superb timing. His final live show was on New Year's Eve 2023, and his death came exactly one year later, just two months after his final pre-recorded show. When Mandie the nurse came to verify his death that morning she said: 'What timing, Johnnie. New Year's Eve. That's so rock 'n' roll.' Not only was it rock 'n' roll, but Bob Harris was live that afternoon with *Sounds of the 70s* and within ten hours of his death, he had a tribute show unfolding on Radio 2. He died the day the dreaded hospital bed was arriving – so he avoided that, and his Urethra Franklin being 'catheterised'. He was also, selflessly, desperate to release me from the heavy burden of caring, and something in him must have thought Tiggy needs to start 2025 afresh. And I am grateful for that.

Spiritual wisdom was possibly his most profound strength. He had a special moment when he was in rehab on Antigua when he believed God spoke to him. While he wasn't a traditional Anglican man, his belief in God, Jesus and the afterlife was absolute. He believed that on this earth we are spirits on a human journey, here to constantly learn and improve our souls before we pass. He believed we have a preview of our life before we choose it. So whenever he upset me, he'd say, 'But, Tigs, you chose this life.' It was handy.

Well, Johnnie, if I really did choose to be with you, then I obviously wanted to learn a great deal. Through good and bad, you have significantly altered and strengthened the sweet, innocent girl you married twenty-two years ago. You have been the greatest teacher in my life. I just ask that you keep sending me your strength as I continue my journey without you.

As for you, I hope you are now reflecting on the extraordinary life you've lived. You touched so many hearts. And I will always be incredibly proud of you. God bless you, darling Johnnie. And thank you.

MARK GOODIER'S
EULOGY

On the evening of 13 August 1967, aboard a beat-up former fishing boat off the Essex coast, Johnnie was broadcasting to an estimated 22 million listeners across the UK and Europe.

In Johnnie's words, 'I was frightened to death. I was exhilarated, excited. It was just incredible. I knew the moment the second hand swept past the 12 that if I said a word I'd be a criminal, liable for prosecution for the next two years, living in exile in Holland. It was a huge moment.'

Midnight arrived. Johnnie played 'We Shall Overcome', followed by a message to Harold Wilson and then the Beatles' 'All You Need Is Love'. Afterwards, they 'opened the champagne'.

This was Johnnie Walker: a maverick, of immense integrity, a man for whom it was all about the music.

This spirit would see Johnnie continue broadcasting on Radio Caroline long after it was outlawed by Harold Wilson's government, drawing crowds of 'Frinton Flashers' along stretches of the south-east coastline, beaming their headlights out into the dark waters while Johnnie played the likes of the Beatles, Otis Redding and Wilson Pickett and broadcast coded appeals to Dee Dee in London for tea. Within two days an envelope full of spliffs would arrive from Dee Dee, followed by sacksful of PG Tips and Typhoo from the thousands of listeners. Johnnie said: 'I've never seen so many tea bags in my life.' Johnnie was doing one of the things that made him a special broadcaster – talking with, not at, the listener and building his relationship with them.

Johnnie returned to dry land in 1968 and started his longstanding relationship with the BBC with a job at Radio 1 in April '69 – a two-hour show on a Saturday afternoon. Johnnie's rebellious instincts made that relationship at times pretty colourful.

In 1976, frustrated with BBC management's insistence on playing the playlist, and only the playlist, Johnnie suggested listeners who didn't agree with his views on the Bay City Rollers could – I quote – 'take a running jump', and, having been told he was too 'into the music', quit Radio 1 and set sail for the Sunshine State.

But it wasn't plain sailing in the USA – denied a Green Card, Johnnie worked at KSAN in San Francisco for literally the love of radio, spending hours every week crafting documentaries – for no payment whatsoever – and DJing between the bands at concerts and being a promoter on the emerging Punk scene, until it was shut down by the cops.

Johnnie would return to the UK in the early Eighties – to Radio West and to Wiltshire Radio, where he honed speech radio skills that would set him up perfectly for future roles back at the BBC, at Greater London Radio, as a founding presenter on Radio 5, and Radio 1, where he'd present *The Stereo Sequence*.

Saturday afternoons were also where Johnnie landed his own show at what became his forever home, Radio 2. Johnnie was the perfect fit for a radio station that was reinventing itself – and Johnnie stayed for twenty-seven years.

After hosting *Drivetime*, and a late-Sunday-afternoon show, in 2009 Johnnie began hosting *Sounds of the 70s*, the show that would bookend his career and soundtrack many of our lives. It was the perfect show for Johnnie, one he could have done on the hoof, but one he approached with a focus, integrity, tenacity and passion right until the last.

On 27 October 2024 Johnnie presented his final *Sounds of the 70s* from his home in Dorset – my colleagues and I had produced his Sunday shows for eighteen years. We all knew how seriously unwell he was and marvelled at his spirit and strength to keep going for as long as he did.

Johnnie always knew the right songs for the occasion – that last *Sounds of the 70s* was a perfect personal selection.

On that show **Rod Stewart** spoke for many about Johnnie's contribution to radio and music:

'I have to thank you from the bottom of my heart for playing not only my songs, but the Faces and just about every rock band in the world over the years. By doing so you propelled a bunch of unknown layabouts to the top of the charts. Without your support we never may have got there.'

For today, I invited others to express how they feel:

Roger Taylor: 'Johnnie Walker was a true rarity – a powerful radio presence who truly loved the music he presented. He always seemed personally invested in it. As musicians we understood his genuine appreciation, which was rare in our business.'

Ronnie Wood: 'Whenever we sat down for an interview it was more like a chat with a dear old friend, it was never a hassle, never boring and always good fun.'

Mark Knopfler: 'The music always came first with Johnnie. There wasn't a trace of pretension about him: There was passion, humour and a deep love for people and for music, which is why he is missed by so many.'

Joan Armatrading: 'With Johnnie, it was never like doing an interview. He was so warm it was like talking with a friend about music.'

Robert Plant: 'So long, Johnnie Walker, all across the years a defender and gatekeeper of great musical taste ... a cool, kind man who kept the bar high for all of us who loved him ... Time roars and mocks us all ... he gifted a quiet calm, groove and taste that got so many of us through.'

THE MUSIC AT YOUR FUNERAL

Joni Mitchell
BOTH SIDES NOW
Sung by the Palida Choir as your coffin was brought in.

Hymn
DEAR LORD AND FATHER OF MANKIND
... forgive our foolish ways.

GONE BUT NOT FORGOTTEN
Written and played on grand piano by Rick Wakeman.

Rani Arbo and Daisy Mayhem
CROSSING THE BAR
Sung by the Palida Choir.

Hymn
FIGHT THE GOOD FIGHT
Because you always did.

Judy Collins
AMAZING GRACE

Sung by the Palida Choir as your coffin was carried out.

Bruce Springsteen
BORN TO RUN

Blasting out from the hearse as you were driven away.

EPILOGUE

Grief is such an individual journey. I was an empty husk when we waved goodbye to Johnnie on Shaftesbury High Street back in January. I didn't have the strength for grieving then. I was not only tired, but also still in shock, I guess. I almost thought he'd never actually die, because his ability to hold on was so immense. Then, all of a sudden, he just wasn't there. All that intense caring ended in an instant. And while I had a whole year to prepare for that moment, it wasn't at all as I had imagined, and there were still things I'd forgotten to check – and I don't just mean how to turn on the TV. We had a little book that I'd asked him to put all his passcodes in, and most of these were illegible or just plain wrong! Why hadn't I gone over these with him?

At the funeral I was still dealing with the lack of rest, as well as handling the practicalities of life – like the phone call from GT, our accountant, three days after he died: 'Darling, there's no easy time to tell you this, but JW owes £42,000 in tax.' Johnnie had been forced to become PAYE by the BBC for the final twenty months of his career, and we had both assumed the tax deducted was the correct amount. It was not. To say this was a body blow is an understatement. I became like a sleuth trying to access his bank and premium-bond accounts, but they were all empty. Oh, Johnnie! There's only one thing you can do in situations like that, and that's laugh. When I met him he was over £40,000 in debt, and he left me in the same way. That's the circle of life, I guess. The small pot I had saved for us to survive on was all sent to HMRC. I genuinely believe this was one of Johnnie's lessons to me: don't worry about money. You'll always find a way to survive. Survival is currently based on selling his record collection, clothes and innumerable gadgets – thank you to my new friends on Vinted! In a way I feel more financially secure now. I know exactly what I have, and there's no risk of him buying yet more stuff he didn't need. A pair of night-driving glasses arrived exactly one week after he died. He hadn't driven for a year. I actually shouted up to the skies, 'Dear God, please tell me he hasn't got an Amazon account up there.'

I needed sleep and rest, which I got in Jamaica at an adult-only hotel called Couples that we used to go to together on Negril Beach, only now I was set the challenge of being the ONLY single person at a hotel full of romantic duos, facing head on all the fun Johnnie and I had together there in the past. While I admit to sitting at dinner with tears tumbling down my face on occasion, I couldn't have been more warmly embraced by the gorgeous staff. 'Honey

– you look beautiful on the outside this evening. How are you on the inside, baby?'

I honestly felt Johnnie close to me when I arrived. I asked him for a sign – which I quickly got. Our last trip to the Caribbean had been to Grenada. At a fabulously posh hotel there called Calabash, he lay on a sunlounger under a tree listening to music. Suddenly there was an almighty crash. A three-foot-long iguana had fallen out of the tree above him, missing his body by inches. It was shocking and hilarious in equal measure, and became a much-repeated holiday story. On my third morning in Negril, I had just settled on a sunbed under a palm tree when two huge, heavy palm fronds fell loudly from the tree above, narrowly missing me. This caused consternation all around. An American man on a nearby bed said, 'That's gotta be a sign of something.' How right he was.

I met up with friends Pamela and Wayne, who we had met there before, played tennis daily, slept and got invitations to join people for dinner. It's my belief that Johnnie looked down and thought, *She's doing just fine*, and allowed himself to go further upward on his journey. And it's true – I had a fantastic holiday and let my hair down for the first time in a year, relieved to no longer have the stress of caring, and also feeling proud that I could still laugh my head off, be it on a tennis court or at the dinner table. It's honestly been quite a revelation to be able to put myself first again.

I've kept myself busy, possibly to avoid the sadness – I don't mind admitting that. However, on three notable occasions I couldn't hold in the emotion. At a church service for the recently bereaved of the Shaftesbury benefice, I started crying as the first hymn began and didn't stop for the entire service. I was on the verge of howling out loud and had to hold it together as much as I could. Then, visiting my mother at her old folk's home in faraway Ludlow, I sat down, having not seen her for almost a year. 'Darling, such a lot has happened since we last saw each other ...' I dissolved, realising that the mother–daughter bond, no matter the challenges, remains incredibly deep and profound. And finally, on what would have been Johnnie's eightieth birthday on Sunday, 30 March 2025, his executive producer, Paul Thomas, crafted the most incredible tribute show for Radio 2 (it was Pick of the Day/Week in most papers). That and my own solo tribute show later that evening on Boom Radio was all too much for me in one day – so many amazing memories all packed together. The tears that fell when I went to bed that night were so intense that I simply wished I too was in heaven, holding him. The pain was just too great to bear. I ached because I missed him so much.

Tears remain close to the surface. It's easier when people don't ask about him. I'm learning to put on a tough front. At a recent Radio 2 tribute evening for Steve Wright, where I saw many of Johnnie's old colleagues for the first time since he died, I just used the line, 'Please don't be sorry. His body was at its end. He died just when he should.' And that is the truth. Johnnie was absolutely ready to move on.

A particularly spiritual friend, Clare, has seen Johnnie with Jesus. She was so excited to tell me that he looked ten years younger, he was healthy and handsome, and he told her that he had received the answers to all his questions. I wish I knew what those were. He also told her that he recognised how much I had sacrificed to look after him throughout our marriage, and that now he would devote himself to looking after me. And honestly, I'm taking that. I really have had an inner sense of calm and a belief that it will all be OK, because he is with me.

I speak to him every day. Out loud. And I've started channelling him – not his words, but his behaviour. I'm now regularly late for things, and seem pretty unrepentant. I'm speaking my mind when possibly I shouldn't. I'm forgetting to put things in my diary and double-booking myself as a result. I'm saying 'No' when once I would have said 'Yes'. 'Miss Goody Two-Shoes' is starting to walk on the wild side. I'm not stressing about life as once I did. 'No amount of worrying ever changed tomorrow.' Hallelujah, Duke! Not only am I channelling my inner Johnnie, but I am also receiving the love that was once given to him – from his listeners, the radio world, even some musicians – as if I'm his ambassador or substitute. It's been an unexpected, beautiful bonus. I mean, it's quite something when Bonnie Raitt asks if I'd like to come to her gig in London. The woman behind his 'Oh, Johnnie' jingle. Perhaps it's her recognition that I was the wife she could have been! A DJ and a rock star? It would never have worked …

I've thought quite a lot about fame since Johnnie died. Having a public life is a two-edged sword. It brings some sort of power – to be heard, to be invited, to be read … but it also comes with high stakes, certainly today when the culture is to build people up and then smash them down for the slightest mishap, wrong word or misjudgement. I don't think many people are truly cut out for it. You need to have great innate strength, a toughness and self-belief. Johnnie had that. When he slipped up – and he did – he learned from his mistakes, he repented, and he came back stronger, grateful for a second chance. (I think especially of his cocaine bust, which would have broken most people.) His motivation was never fame or money; it was to share the music that he loved. He came from a pure place. I genuinely believe that his fans and listeners know this. That's why they've been so loyal. They have lost a true friend, just as I've lost a loving husband. This book is for them so they can know him a little better. And honestly, they deserve it in return for the support they have given to both of us. Of course, it has also been cathartic for me. It's kept him with me, reliving our best times together (and a few of the bad).

I look at successful politicians, sportspeople, actors, rock stars, presenters, and I have nothing but admiration for how they cope with their public existence. How frightening and stressful it must sometimes be – especially if they are doing it for the wrong reasons … I loved our final two months together when Johnnie had stepped down from radio. It really was our only 'normal' period. And yet by writing this book I've had to question myself about being a public figure. I'm opening both myself and Johnnie up to criticism and judgement. I hold on to the thought that he was delighted I was writing this. 'Write about whatever you want, Duch. It's your time now.' I thank him still for his belief in me and his love. He knew I was starting to struggle at being the support act for so many years. The narrative was always led by him and his career. Now I'm wholly responsible for what happens next, and there is personal reward in that.

There were so many lasts in 2024. And now, as 2025 unfolds, there are firsts. The first roses, swallows, and … film awards. The short film that I made in the autumn has won me the accolade of Best New Director at the New York Film & Cinematography Awards, the Chicago Indie Film Awards and the Tokyo Indie Shorts Awards. I am quite convinced that Johnnie has had a hand in this from on high. That said, I have stood down as the director of my feature film, *ANTONIA*. Not only am I still too knackered after last year, but the budget level is such that we cannot get the final funding in place with me at the helm. I'm OK with this, but I waited for Johnnie to go before making that decision. I am still the writer and second producer – which will be achievement enough for me.

I cannot deny that it's a relief to have de-medicalised the house – to have the rugs back on the floor; to have a home that is calm, stress-free and tidy. But what I would give to see Johnnie's Lexus come down the drive and him strut his way back into the house wearing jeans and a floral shirt, with a bouquet of flowers in his arms. That's why writing the 'Then' sections of this book has been such a joy, remembering those great days when he could walk and drive, giving me my old Johnnie back. I never realised that basic actions like those were such a privilege.

I will be honest and say that I do not miss the caring. At all. It's tough. To the very end, the only part I truly enjoyed was giving Johnnie a bath. It was intimate and gentle, and he had to be present, not in his bubble. Afterwards he was always grateful because he felt so much better. Yes, bathing someone sick is rewarding.

The house feels big and empty without him – watching television alone in a thirty-three-foot-long room feels a bit echoey – but hopefully it will soon sell, and then I can start again somewhere smaller and cosier. I am sure he has it all planned.

It's a sad process, wrapping up someone's life: to look in a wardrobe once full of fabulous clothes and find only wooden hangers; to close down their phone and email accounts; to feel their existence on this earth slowly evaporate. However, in many ways your relationship continues as you discover new things about them – good and bad! One thing I discovered among his piles of stuff was a cassette tape sat in the top left-hand drawer of his desk. It was labelled 'Duchess 2002'. I'd never seen it before. What a beautiful revelation it was to find this time capsule and hear the songs he had selected for me in those first heady months of our courtship. I am sure he led me to the tape. In what better way could he reveal himself to me than in music?

I loved Johnnie from the moment I met him. Nothing has or ever will change that. I feel immensely lucky to have experienced the one thing in life that we all crave, and to know that it lives on. I believe that one day our souls will be reunited, as they were at the Union Club on 10 September 2001. And when the time comes for me to fall back into his arms, I pray that at our feet will be a little black working cocker spaniel, curving her body, wagging her tail furiously, relieved that our little family is finally back together.

THE HIDDEN 'DUCHESS 2002' CASSETTE

Your final gift to me: a selection of tracks recorded onto a cassette, found three months after you passed – at just the time when I needed you most. Thank you, Duke xx

David Bowie
DRIVE-IN SATURDAY

'Tig the Wonderkid' song.

Hootie & the Blowfish
ONLY WANNA BE WITH YOU

'... you and me, we come from different worlds'.

Stevie Wonder
HE'S MISSTRA KNOW-IT-ALL

Which I dedicated to you on Boom Radio for you were a Mr know-it-all when it came to music.

Van Morrison
BRIGHT SIDE OF THE ROAD

Elton John
YOUR SISTER CAN'T TWIST
(BUT SHE CAN ROCK 'N' ROLL)
A surprising, great-energy choice.

David Bowie and Mick Jagger
DANCING IN THE STREET

The Pretenders
STOP YOUR SOBBING

Paul Simon
THE OBVIOUS CHILD
You always did love a great drum beat.

U2
WHERE THE STREETS HAVE NO NAME

The Who
BABA O'RILEY
Yesssss.

Joe Jackson
STEPPIN' OUT

Bruce Springsteen
BORN TO RUN
Naturally.

Prince
DIAMONDS AND PEARLS

Thank you.

Simon & Garfunkel
KEEP THE CUSTOMER SATISFIED

Great choice.

Christopher Cross
SAILING

Very un-you, but I love it, so thank you.

Rolling Stones
SYMPATHY FOR THE DEVIL

World Party
WAY DOWN NOW

Great to hear again.

Michael Jackson
BLACK OR WHITE

Could have chosen better there, for me.
I'd have preferred 'Earth Song'.

Queen and David Bowie
UNDER PRESSURE

Just a classic.

Simply Red
FAIRGROUND

Eagles
THE LAST RESORT

A perfect end to a fabulous tape – 'call someplace paradise,

kiss it goodbye ...'

THANK YOUS

This book would never have been born had it not been for my dear old friend from Bristol University days, the incredibly talented and successful novelist Rachel Joyce. Despite her great stature in literary circles, she has always believed in me and my writing. She contacted me in June 2024, the day after I had been on the Jeremy Vine Radio 2 show, and in the middle of the terrible caring year. 'Are you writing about this time?' she asked. I told her I was not. 'Should I?' 'Yes,' she said firmly. 'I believe you have something to say that hasn't been said before and I know you will do so with the right touch.' High praise indeed. I started writing that night.

Carly Cook has been a friend since she edited Johnnie's autobiography in 2007. She and I went through breast cancer together and she has been down to stay with us several times since. She contacted me after I had been on Times Radio with Fi Glover – about a month after the Jeremy Vine show. She loved that I'd mentioned Johnnie having a crafty fag outside – with lung disease! 'I don't

311

suppose you're writing about this time?' Thanks to Rachel, I was. She asked to be my agent on the spot. Some things are meant to be. Carly has been such a support, not just with the book and securing HarperCollins as the right publishing house for this, but also emotionally. She's incredibly protective. An attack dog who kept the paps at the funeral at a respectful distance, and a passionate fighter who is incredible to have just over your shoulder.

Thank you to Katya Shipster, my editor, who has shown me why everyone always thanks their editor. It has been like the most intense therapy session, and I am indebted to her for her astute questions and fabulous guidance, not least cutting out the parts that were 'TMI' – too much information. All her notes were amazing – the good and the bad ones. To Daisy Ward and Holly Kyte for all their editing and checks – especially spelling! And to the HarperCollins marketing team – Alex Layt and Chris Kwok, who have helped spread the word.

To the island of Tresco, in particular Dean Whillis, who gave me a refuge to run to after the funeral and write. It was the most perfect place to re-find my equilibrium and tap away. I will always be grateful to all the islanders who embraced and supported me – notably Anna Parkes, my dear friend who runs Tresco Gallery in the finest array of clothes ever seen. She is an inspiration. Her story is even more interesting than ours!

To my dear, mainly local, girlfriends who have kept me afloat during the caring year and since – Jane Treays, Susan d'Arcy, Jacquie Glanville, Camilla Royce, Sarah Tanner, Lesley Waters, Lisa Linde, Clare Galtrey and all the fabulous tennis gang. You have kept me sane and loved. Thank you so much. Many of you helped look after Johnnie when I had moments of respite, along with my brother Martin Coldicott and his wife, Kate, Sophie Banisfair, Claire Hooper, Margaret Millward, Lisa Supple, Rodney Wayman, Tommy and Mairead King, Tim McPherson, Beth and Mariana. You gave me much-needed freedom to grab gulps of air. You never questioned giving support and fed Johnnie bloody well!

A thank you to Johnnie's listeners and fans for your love and support. You know who you are. And the thousands of you who send us/me cards, letters and messages on social media – it's like we are friends. I feel blessed to have your strength behind me. I wrote this book for you – so I hope you enjoyed it.

To all who have given me spiritual and emotional healing: Alice Young, Sarah Lownds, Richard Sutton and shaman Anna Hunt.

To Liz 'Queen of Rock' Barnes, Johnnie's producer, for being so patient with his illness, and for reminding me who played at the Peter Green Tribute Show so I could make myself sound like a Princess of Rock in the 'Stardust' chapter. And to executive producer Paul Thomas for knowing that you should be there for the final show, making the amazing tribute shows and keeping a gentle eye on me since. I hope we work together again. You are full of great ideas, music knowledge and compassion.

To Helen Thomas and Radio 2 for the love and support before and after. You have all made me feel like a part of the Radio 2 family. And not just a distant aunt. I have really felt embraced by you all and your love of dear Johnnie.

Mark and Jacqueline Goodier. Oh, you two. So kind, so supportive, so there for us both. Always. Your calmness in our lives has been such a blessing.

To Frank and Rozzi Musker for embracing me into their beautiful Paxos life to recover.

To Johnnie's son Sam, his nieces Trudi and Michelle, and his cousin Mal – thank you for your love and care during and since.

Most of all I have to thank my subject: Johnnie – my Duke – Walker. Without you, darling, I'd have no book. By writing it, I have felt almost as close to you as when you were here. How wonderful to relive our adventure. You gave me one hell of a ride.